The Collected Poems

MURIEL RUKEYSER

PREVIOUS WORK

The Collected Poems

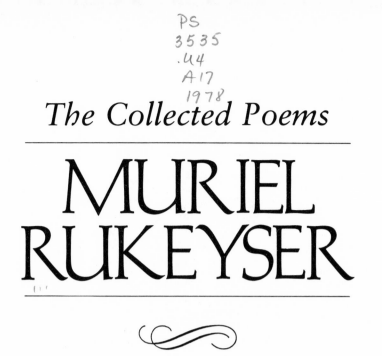

MURIEL RUKEYSER

McGRAW-HILL BOOK COMPANY

New York | St. Louis | San Francisco
Düsseldorf | Mexico | London | Toronto | Sydney

Book design by Nora Sheehan.
Copyright 1938, 1939, 1944, 1948, 1951, © 1957, 1958, 1962, 1968, 1973, 1976
    and 1978 by Muriel Rukeyser.

1 2 3 4 5 6 7 8 9 0   B P B P   7 8 3 2 1 0 9 8

Library of Congress Cataloging in Publication Data

Rukeyser, Muriel, date
The collected poems of Muriel Rukeyser.
PS3535.U4A17 1978   811'.5'2   78-7633
ISBN 0-07-054270-8

PREFACE

TO THE READER

"All the poems" is a very curious idea. Here you have a book that is like a film strip of a life in poetry: like that idea in Asia of the long body, the person seen as big-headed infant, then as reaching adolescent, then as fuller young woman, mature grown one, mother, desperate in other ways, hopeful in other ways, and so on into older life. The Collected Poems shows the movement of phases, too. Here are the early lyrics and two kinds of reaching in poetry, one based on the document, the evidence itself; the other kind informed by the unverifiable fact, as in sex, dream, the parts of life in which we dive deep and sometimes—with strength of expression and skill and luck—reach that place where things are shared and we all recognize the secrets.

Underneath all, the experience itself—a trust in the rhythms of experience.

When I began to read, I loved the collected poems I found— they invited me through the poems of all the years of a loved poet. There were two differences then from today's books: the poets were all dead, and all were men.

It never occurred to me that my poems would be collected until after my lifetime. The big books of my childhood were gathered from those published by one firm. My books have been issued by many publishers: I seem promiscuous, and this is chiefly because of the wanderings of my editors, as they moved from house to house. My present publisher, McGraw-Hill, is a small experimental press as far as poetry is concerned, but a great vast publishing house of science; and I care very much about that meeting-place, of science and poetry.

In this book, all the poems are included; only the translations have been removed. The text is left as it was. It seems to me that the perseverance of certain meanings and certain rhythms can be followed here, and also the changes of perception as a life and life-work go on, can be seen.

As I read the poems in preparation for you, I saw many cuts I wanted to make; many of the large castings-forth of childhood and youth I have wanted rewritten or left out, but this is the truth of how the poems stand and how things formed for me. I do not wish to lie; many references are here without names, so as not to hurt the living and not to intrude a kind of slang of fact into poems.

That slang is a trap of the documentary. For example, fliers do not call out "Contact!" now that planes have self-starters; but "Contact!" was the truth of that moment, and of the relation between flier and groundman. It is that toward which my poems are reaching; and I believe that poetry can extend the document. Today, too, I would change the title "Three Negresses" to "Three Black Women" in our usage and I would bring "fine black mouth" to the truer colors of nature.

I have rectified two or three titles to those titles I have used in reading the poems to audiences.

Only the translations have been taken out; and it now seems to me . . . might it not be that poetry and indeed all speech are a translation? This translation, this music, speaks to our silence. It in my childhood did, and ever since. I hope these may speak to yours, as my silence goes on speaking.

MURIEL RUKEYSER

New York
1978

CONTENTS

U.S. 1 (1938)

The Book of the Dead

Night-Music

BEAST IN VIEW (1944)

Private Life of the Sphinx

Elegy in Joy

Nine Poems

From SELECTED POEMS (1951)

From WATERLILY FIRE (1962)

From ONE LIFE (1957)

Young

Tree of Rivers

In Praise of Process

BODY OF WAKING (1958)

THE SPEED OF DARKNESS (1968)

I/Clues

II/Orange and Grape

III/Breaking Open

THE GATES (1976)

One

Two

(1935)

THEORY OF
FLIGHT

I wish here to thank Horace and Marya Gregory, Nancy Naumburg,
Stephen Vincent Benét, Elizabeth Ames, Henry Fuller,
Flora Rosenmeyer, and my parents, Lawrence and Myra Rukeyser.

Poem out of Childhood

POEM OUT OF CHILDHOOD

I

Breathe-in experience, breathe-out poetry :
Not Angles, angels : and the magnificent past
shot deep illuminations into high-school.
I opened the door into the concert-hall
and a rush of triumphant violins answered me
while the syphilitic woman turned her mouldered face
intruding upon Brahms.   Suddenly, in an accident
the girl's brother was killed, but her father had just died :
she stood against the wall, leaning her cheek,
dumbly her arms fell, "What will become of me?" and
I went into the corridor for a drink of water.
These bandages of image wrap my head
when I put my hand up I hardly feel the wounds.
We sat on the steps of the unrented house
raining blood down on Loeb and Leopold,
creating again how they removed his glasses
and philosophically slit his throat.

> They who manipulated and misused our youth,
> smearing those centuries upon our hands,
> trapping us in a welter of dead names,
> snuffing and shaking heads at patent truth. . . .

We were ready to go the long descent with Virgil
the bough's gold shade advancing forever with us,
entering the populated cold of drawing-rooms;
Sappho, with her drowned hair trailing along Greek waters,
weed binding it, a fillet of kelp enclosing
the temples' ardent fruit :

> Not Sappho, Sacco.
Rebellion pioneered among our lives,
viewing from far-off many-branching deltas,
innumerable seas.

In adolescence I knew travellers
speakers digressing from the ink-pocked rooms,
bearing the unequivocal sunny word.

    Prinzip's year bore us : see us turning at breast
    quietly while the air throbs over Sarajevo
    after the mechanic laugh of that bullet.
    How could they know what sinister knowledge finds
    its way among our brains' wet palpitance,
    what words would nudge and giggle at our spine,
    what murders dance?
    These horrors have approached the growing child;
    now that the factory is sealed-up brick
    the kids throw stones, smashing the windows,
    membranes of uselessness in desolation.

    We grew older quickly, watching the father shave
    and the splatter of lather hardening on the glass,
    playing in sandboxes to escape paralysis,
    being victimized by fataller sly things.
    "Oh, and you," he said, scraping his jaw, "what will you be?"
    "Maybe : something : like : Joan : of : Arc...."
    Allies Advance, we see,
    Six Miles South to Soissons.   And we beat the drums.
    Watchsprings snap in the mind, uncoil, relax,
    the leafy years all somber with foreign war.
    How could we know what exposed guts resembled?

    A wave, shocked to motion, babbles margins
    from Asia to Far Rockaway spiralling
    among clocks in its four-dimensional circles.
    Disturbed by war we pedalled bicycles
    breakneck down the decline, until the treads
    conquered our speed and pulled our feet behind them,
    and pulled our heads.
    We never knew the war, standing so small
    looking at eye-level toward the puttees, searching
    the picture-books for sceptres, pennants for truth;
    see Galahad unaided by puberty.

    Ratat a drum upon the armistice,
    Kodak As You Go : photo : they danced late,

and we were a generation of grim children
leaning over the bedroom sills, watching
the music and the shoulders and how the war was over,
laughing until the blow on the mouth broke night
wide out from cover.
The child's curls blow in a forgotten wind,
immortal ivy trembles on the wall:
the sun has crystallized these scenes, and tall
shadows remember time cannot rescind.

III

Organize the full results of that rich past
open the windows : potent catalyst,
harsh theory of knowledge, running down the aisles
crying out in the classrooms, March ravening on the plain,
inexorable sun and wind and natural thought.
Dialectically our youth unfolds :
the pale child walking to the river, passional
in ignorance in loneliness demanding
its habitation for the leaping dream, kissing
quick air, the vibrations of transient light,
not knowing substance or reserve, walking
in valvular air, each person in the street
conceived surrounded by his life and pain,
fixed against time, subtly by these impaled :
death and that shapeless war.   Listening at dead doors,
our youth assumes a thousand differing flesh
summoning fact from abandoned machines of trade,
knocking on the wall of the nailed-up power-plant,
telephoning hello, the deserted factory, ready
for the affirmative clap of truth
ricochetting from thought to thought among
the childhood, the gestures, the rigid travellers.

SONG FOR DEAD CHILDREN

We set great wreaths of brightness on the graves of the
    passionate
who required tribute of hot July flowers :
for you, O brittle-hearted, we bring offering
remembering how your wrists were thin and your delicate bones
    not yet braced for conquering.

The sharp cries of ghost-boys are keen above the meadows,
the little girls continue graceful and wondering;
flickering evening on the lakes recalls those young
heirs whose developing years have sunk to earth
        their strength not tested, their praise unsung.

Weave grasses for their childhood : who will never see
love or disaster or take sides against decay
balancing the choices of maturity;
silent and coffin'd in silence while we pass
        loud in defiance of death, the helpless lie.

IN A DARK HOUSE

Two on the stairs in a house where they had loved :
mounting, and the steps a long ascent before them
brown: a single step creaking high in the flight; the turn :
the quiet house and the cheese-yellow walls shadowed by night,
dark; and the unlit lamps along the wall.
Dusk piles in old house-corners rapidly.   Shade grows
where corners round to flights of stairs again.   Evening
accumulates under the treads of mounting stairs.
They rise: he tightly-knit, clenched in anxiety, she calm,
massive in female beauty, precise line of brow
curving to generous cheek and mouth and throat,
and his face bright and strained with eagerness.

But the nights are restless with these dreams of ours
in which we cry, fling our arms abroad, and there is no one;
walls close in to a shaft and blur of brown:
out of the chaos and eclipse of mind rise stairs.
(Here, metrically and monotonously walks
each several person unprotectedly.)
Alone, the nightmare broadens in the rising,
dull step sinking behind dull step, now, here, here,
nothing in the world but the slow spiral rise, expectancy, and fear.

He turns his face to her, walk unbroken.   Her face
questioning turns: there is no help for each
in the other.   There are no eyes on them.   The shaft
is empty of voices, all but the creaking step, regularly

in the flights recurring, preknown, dreaded that sound.
There is no face that he can see but hers.
She knows his look, and has known it for a long time.
The creak of the one step is a punctuating rhyme.

But the nights are restless with receding faces
in massed battalions through the solemn air,
vivid with brightness, clangorous with sounds:
struck copper, chiming cylinders of silver, horns   :
presences in the outer air.   But here
only the empty shaft and the painful stairs.

He remembers the men and women he has loved:
fine-curved and brittle skulls housing strange ardency,
the male hard bravery of argument   :
lips of women, love-writhen, and their hands,
pale fruit of comfort, pliant, governing, white consolation
against small fear and human bodily pain,
never against the terror of the stairs.

Remembrances of words, human counsel in sounds, and
        pictures,
books, and the bleak rush of shining towers,
tunes crop through the tired brain: Ravel's "Bolero,"
an old blues going "Love, Oh Love, Oh Loveless Love,"
humping through air powerfully with its sound.

She remembers the men and women she has loved:
the full soft cheeks of girls, their secrecies,
grave words that fell with sweet continuance in her
        youth   :
men's eyes, dumb with meaning unspeakable and low-
        sounding
among the intricate memories deep in her recessed mind,
the length of their arms, the firm triangled backs, stalwart,
turning beautifully in their planes on the narrow hips,
dark ease beneath their arms and eyes, strength in their
        voices,
but ebbing away in the silence of the stairs.

Remembrances of wind shaking November evenings,
arpeggioed skyscrapers, clean-heavy-falling waters   :
"There's No Today, There's No Tomorrow"
debates against a symphony of Brahms',
and foot follows foot heavily in the row.

7

He had gone to play apart, by the hollows of the sand
cupped (a pale arm about the ocean's blue)   :
picked pebbles and the soft-voluted shells,
laver and dulse, dark flowers of the sea.
He had been a child in a fantastic wood
where the dim statues stood, posturing gothically,
and "Mother, mother, mother!" cried   :   but they
remained with closed lips ceremonially.
The ocean and his mother and his childhood let him be
until he had grown and finished his lessons and his
      prayers,
and then   :   these stairs.

Night is treacherous with dreams betraying us,
leaving us vulnerable to inherited shame,
crying out against our secret, naming an occult name.

And she had enjoyed narrow fields, shaven lawns,
tiny stones freckled brown and white and red,
green water troubled by waves of a twig's making,
grown out of these to wider thoughts that bred
high spaces and new knowledges, and cared for some
with mind and body, some with love only of eyes and head.
She had believed in the quick response to pain,
in union of crowds living in one belief,
a social order kept by a coöperative strain
steadily toward one thing, but aware of all   :
she had reached out her hand with the gesture of one who dares,
and found   :   these stairs.

The stairs still rise.   The halls remain, and dull
and somber stand to be trodden by the quiet two rising
laboriously along the fateful road.   They should be high now.
(If the dun walls should slide into the night,
faces might be disclosed, bitter, impotent, angered
above slant shoulders swinging toolless arms, great hands
jointed around no implements, and the silent mouths
opened to cry for law.   Some faces black, the rope
knotted beneath an ear, some black with the strong blood
of Negroes, some yellow and concentrate, all fixed
on the tower of stairs, should the walls sink, perhaps
all waiting, perhaps nothing but unanswering dark.)
They must be high.   There are no voices.   The shaft
   is very still.

Night is sick with our dreams.   Night is florid
with our by-reason-uncontested imagings.   We in our time
(not we : you : in your time : no credit ours)
have built brave stone on stone, and called their blazonry
*Beauty Old Yet Ever New : Eternal Voice
And Inward Word : (a blur of fond noises signifying
a long thing) and raised signs, saying:
*But Of All Things Truth Beareth Away
The Victory : (the pock-bitten pass to spit
gelatinously and obscenely on the bird-marked stones,
and shallow-carven letters fade).   The evil night
of our schooled minds is morbid with our dreams.

    Whir.   Whirl of brown stairs.   Cool brow.
      Athenian lips.
    The creaking stairs.   Stupid stupid stupidly stupidly
    we go a long voyage on the stairs of a house
    builded on stairs.   One stair creaks forever amen in the Name.
    Treads rock under the feet.   The two go : he tight
      and harsh
    (but limp with warm exhaustion), she plods : one, two,
      foot : on
    up mounting up O lovely stairs, hideous and cruel
    we propitiate you with incensuous words stairs lovely loved
    rise, idol of our walking days and nights,
    travelled-forever road of the lordly mind : with shaking
      bannisters
    and no sound crawling through the wall-hole-lips :
    love-writhen women's lips : the crackled lips of the mass
    that must be there waiting for law at the wall's decay.
    Large female : male : come tiredness and sleep
    come peace   come generous power over no other, come
      Order here.
    Steps mount.   The brown treads rise.   Stairs.   Rise
      up.   Stairs.

EFFORT AT SPEECH
BETWEEN TWO PEOPLE

: Speak to me.   Take my hand.   What are you now?
  I will tell you all.   I will conceal nothing.
  When I was three, a little child read a story about a rabbit

*New York Public Library.

who died, in the story, and I crawled under a chair :
a pink rabbit : it was my birthday, and a candle
burnt a sore spot on my finger, and I was told to be happy.

: Oh, grow to know me.   I am not happy.   I will be open:
Now I am thinking of white sails against a sky like music,
like glad horns blowing, and birds tilting, and an arm about me.
There was one I loved, who wanted to live, sailing.

: Speak to me.   Take my hand.   What are you now?
When I was nine, I was fruitily sentimental,
fluid : and my widowed aunt played Chopin,
and I bent my head on the painted woodwork, and wept.
I want now to be close to you.   I would
link the minutes of my days close, somehow, to your days.

: I am not happy.   I will be open.
I have liked lamps in evening corners, and quiet poems.
There has been fear in my life.   Sometimes I speculate
On what a tragedy his life was, really.

: Take my hand.   Fist my mind in your hand.   What are
    you now?
When I was fourteen, I had dreams of suicide,
and I stood at a steep window, at sunset, hoping toward
    death :
if the light had not melted clouds and plains to beauty,
if light had not transformed that day, I would have leapt.
I am unhappy.   I am lonely.   Speak to me.

: I will be open.   I think he never loved me:
he loved the bright beaches, the little lips of foam
that ride small waves, he loved the veer of gulls:
he said with a gay mouth: I love you.   Grow to know me.

: What are you now?   If we could touch one another,
if these our separate entities could come to grips,
clenched like a Chinese puzzle . . . yesterday
I stood in a crowded street that was live with people,
and no one spoke a word, and the morning shone.
Everyone silent, moving. . . . Take my hand.   Speak to me.

NOTES FOR A POEM

Here are the long fields inviolate of thought,
here are the planted fields raking the sky,
signs in the earth   :
water-cast shuttles of light flickering the underside of rock.
These have been shown before; but the fields know new hands,
the son's fingers grasp warmly at the father's hoe   ;
there will be new ways of seeing these ancestral lands.

> "In town, the munitions plant has been poor since the war,
> And nothing but a war will make it rich again."
> Holy, holy, holy, sings the church next door.

Time-ridden, a man strides the current of a stream's flowing,
stands, flexing the wand curvingly over his head,
tracking the water's prism with the flung line.
Summer becomes productive and mature.
Farmers watch tools like spikes of doom against the sure
condemning sky descending upon the hollow lands.

> The water is ridged in muscles on the rock,
> force for the State is planted in the stream-bed.
> Water springs from the stone   —   the State is fed.

Morning comes, brisk with light,
a broom of color over the threshold.
Long flights of shadows escape to the white sky   :
a spoon is straightened.   Day grows.   The sky is blued.

> The water rushes over the shelves of stone
> to anti-climax on the mills below the drop.
> The planted fields are bright and rake the sky.
> Power is common.   Earth is grown
> and overgrown in unrelated strength, the moral
> rehearsed already, often.
> (There must be the gearing of these facts
> into coördination, in a poem or numbers,
> rows of statistics, or the cool iambs.)
> The locked relationships which will be found
> are a design to build these factual timbers—
> a plough of thought to break this stubborn ground.

PLACE-RITUALS

Tradition of this Acre

This is the word our lips caress, our teeth bite
on the pale spongy fruit of this, the name   :
mouthing the story, cowlike in dignity, and spitting it
in the tarnished cuspidor of present days.
And if there were radium in Plymouth Rock, they would
    not strike it
(bruising the fair stone), nor gawk at Semiramis on Main
    Street
nor measure the gentle Christ in terms of horse-power.
Cracked bells are severally struck at noon.
The furrow of their ways will cradle us all.
Amen, amen, to the ritual of our habit, fall
before the repetitions in the lips of doom.

Ritual of Blessing

The proud colors and brittle cloths, the supple smoke rising,
the metal symbols precious to our dreams
loftily borne.   *Thy Kingdom come.*
                  We have blessed the fields with speech.
There are alp-passes in the travelled mind
(they have stood in the quiet air, making signs on the sky
to bless the cities of the shining plain).
The climate of the mind is the warmth of a shrine
and the air torn with incense.   *World without end.*
How can we bless this place   :   by the sweet horns,
the vaulted words, the pastoral lovers in the waist-deep grass,
remembrances linking back, hands raised like strict flames
    pointing,
the feet of priests tracking the smooth earth,
many hands binding corn   :   ?   *Thy Kingdom come.*
There are pale steeples erect among the green,
blood falling before the eyes of love   the lids fire-bright,
hands together in the fields, the born and unborn children,
and the wish for new blessing and the given blessing blend,
a glory clear in the man-tracks, in the blind
seeking for warmth in the climates of the mind.
                      World without end.
                          Amen.

WOODEN SPRING

How horrible late spring is, with the full death of the frozen
    tight bulbs
brownly rotting in earth; and each chord of light
rayed into slivers, a bunch of grapes plucked grape by grape
    apart,
a warm chord broken into the chilled single notes.

(Let us rely on cerebral titillation
for the red stimulus of sensuous supply;)
here is no heat, no fierce color: spring is no bacchante this year
eager to celebrate her carnal dedication.

The ghosts swim, lipless, eyeless, upward   :
the crazy hands point in five directions down   :
to the sea, the high ridge, the bush, the blade, the weak white
    root   :
thumping at life in an agony of birth, abortive fruit.

Spring is very mad for greenness now
(: I suppose it would be beautiful, if we let ourselves be :),
but we must strip nascent earth bare of green mystery.
Trees do not grow high as skyscrapers in my town,

and flowers not so lovely as the pale bewildered youth,
hands pointing in five directions upward and out;
and spring in the fields and cities spreads to the north and
    south,
and is comforted in desire for the sun's mouth.

Earth does not seem wooden to the comforted spring   :
(spring could not seem so dull, I comforted   :
but there must be abstraction, where fields need not sprout,
    waves pound,
there must be silence where no rushing grasses sound,
life in this lack of death, comfort on this wide ground).

SONNET

My thoughts through yours refracted into speech
transmute this room musically tonight,
the notes of contact flowing, rhythmic, bright

with an informal art beyond my single reach.
Outside, dark birds fly in a greening time :
wings of our sistered wishes beat these walls :
and words afflict our minds in near footfalls
approaching with a latening hour's chime.

And if an essential thing has flown between us,
rare intellectual bird of communication,
let us seize it quickly : let our preference
choose it instead of softer things to screen us
each from the other's self : muteness or hesitation,
nor petrify live miracle by our indifference.

LETTER, UNPOSTED

*"My love, my love, my love,
why have you left me alone?"*
JAMES JOYCE

If I could write : Summer waits your coming,
the flowers are colored, but half-alive and weak,
earth sickens, as I sicken, with waiting,
and the clouds print on the dull moon a dark and blotting
    streak.
If I could write : no energy is kinetic,
storm breaks nor foot falls until you arrive,
the trees thrive, but no fruit is born to hang
heavily : and the stale wind continues to drive
all pausing summer before it into the distance
from which you, shining, will come. . . . But summer lives,
and minds grow, and nerves are sensitized to power
and no winds wait, and not tree stands but gives
richly to the store of the burning harvest :
the door stands open for you, and other figures pass,
and I receive them joyfully and live : but wait for you
(and sometimes secretly watch for wrinkles, in my glass).

SAND-QUARRY WITH
MOVING FIGURES

Father and I drove to the sand-quarry across the ruined
    marshlands,
miles of black grass, burned for next summer's green.

I reached my hand to his beneath the lap-robe,
we looked at the stripe of fire, the blasted scene.

"It's all right," he said, "they can control the flames,
on one side men are standing, and on the other the sea;"
but I was terrified of stubble and waste of black
and his ugly villages he built and was showing me.

The countryside turned right and left about the car,
straight through October we drove to the pit's heart;
sand, and its yellow canyon and standing pools
and the wealth of the split country set us farther apart.
"Look," he said, "this quarry means rows of little houses,
stucco and a new bracelet for you are buried there;"
but I remembered the ruined patches, and I saw the land
    ruined,
exploded, burned away, and the fiery marshes bare.

"We'll own the countryside, you'll see how soon I will,
you'll have acres to play in" :   I saw the written name
painted on stone in the face of the steep hill:
"That's your name, Father!   "And yours!" he shouted,
    laughing.
"No, Father, no!"   He caught my hand as I cried,
and smiling, entered the pit, ran laughing down its side.

WEDDING PRESENTS

I

                    Griefs
marking indelibly our later loves.

Fantastic juxtapose that sets the wish
opposite the insubordinate flesh
interring the fact of the inconstant rain
in the fixed lightly-palpitant brain,

the anthropoid hunger laid against the will
making small music in the ventricle
until evolved man hears with each breath-inake
the sweetly mathematical sound of Bach.

Be bold, friend   ;   all your nymphs have disappeared
dwindled upon those green and classic banks,
the goddesses are gone, and the chivalric ranks.
Where'er you walk, cool gales will fan the glade
breathing themselves to death, sighing against the towers
upon the firm and beautiful machines   ;
trees, where you sit, will crowd into a shade
eclipsing Handel, shining electric powers
of energy on polytechnic scenes.
Believe Eurydice unregained at last,
see that those idyll afternoons are past.
Accept the gathering skies that tell our morning,
open your hands   open your thighs   for strength
inviolate in beauty, ill-defined
ready for the Columbus of the mind.

Trembling, the mouth relaxes in the kiss.
The lemon body and purple blood beneath
award themselves in love, most perfect wreath.

THREE SIDES OF A COIN

I

Am I in your light?
                    No, go on reading
            (the hackneyed light of evening quarrelling with the bulbs;
            the book's bent rectangle solid on your knees)
only my fingers in your hair, only, my eyes
splitting the skull to tickle your brain with love
in a slow caress blurring the mind,
                            kissing your mouth awake
opening the body's mouth and stopping the words.
This light is thick with birds, and
evening warns us beautifully of death.
Slowly I bend over you, slowly your breath
runs rhythms through my blood
as if I said
                I love you
and you should raise your head

listening, speaking into the covert night
:   Did someone say something?
                        Love, am I in your light?
Am I?

Refrain   See how love alters the living face
            go spin the immortal coin through time
            watch the thing flip through space
                    tick   tick

                        II

We all had a good time
                    the throne was there and all
and there she was with that primitive unforgivable mouth
saying sophistications about nothing at all
as the young men cavorted up the room Darling
it's a swell party and those Martinis with
the olives so delicately soaked in alcohol
        and William Flesh, the inventor, being cute
about the revolution and the Negro Question
until Dick said "Lynch the Jews!" (his name was Fleischman
but the war brought about a number of changes)
and the Objectivist poet fresh from Butte
with his prePosterous suggestion. . . .
        After a while, of course, we left.
the room was getting so jammed with editors.
And William and Maurice and Del and I
went back and we took turns using the couch with them.
        We all had a good time
and Del had hysterics at about 3 a.m.
        we dashed water into her face
        I held her temples and Maurice said
        what could we hope to look for next:
        it's one thing to be faithful to the dead
        (he said) but for her to stick to an oversexed
old fool   :   but she only laughed and cried and beat the floor
until the neighbors rattled at the door.

Refrain   Runnels of wine ran down his chin and laughter
            softened his words until quite suddenly
            the walls fell and the night stood blank and after
                    tick   tick

III

He turned the lights on and walked to the window   :
Son of a bitch   :   he said   :   if it isn't the reds again
parading through the streets with those lousy posters.
The Village was never like this in the old days,
throw a brick down the street and you'd hit a female poet
and life went on like a string of roller coasters.

Workers of the world   :
we've worked the world for all the damn thing's worth
tick   tick
I was little and they promised me the hills of glory
a great life and a sounding name on the earth   :
tick   tick
this is a different story.

Here's a list I've been making   :   reasons for living
on the right, reasons for my sudden death on the left.
Right now they balance so I could flip a coin
determine the imperative tonight
tick   tick
flip that amazing coin through time and space this night
and the Village   :   and the army with banners
and the hot girls
and the rotgut all gone
like a blown fuse   :
I'd get a paragraph or two of news
obituary as a shutting door
meaning no more
leaving the world to the sun and the workers
the straight beautiful children   the coins   the clocks
tick   tick

BREATHING LANDSCAPE

Lying in the sun
and lying here so still
an egg might slowly hatch in this still hand.

The people pass
abruptly they nod   :   they smile
trailed in the air, silence follows their faces.

I know, lying
how the hills are fixed
and the day-moon runs at the head of the fixed hills.

Nothing crossed the field
all day but a bird
skirting the tall grass in briefest transit.

Their stern ideas
are a long work to each
and even armored we hardly touch each other.

The wind leans,
the air placed formally
about these faces and thoughts in formal dance.

Silence hangs in the air.
Nothing speaks but the sound
of certain rivers continuing underground.

FOUR IN A FAMILY

The father and mother sat, and the sister beside her.
I faced the two women across the table's width,
speaking, and all the time he looked at me,
sorrowing, saying nothing, with his hard tired breath.

Their faces said : This is your home; and I :
I never come home, I never go away.
And they all answered : Stay.

All day the city turned about this room,
and silence had remained between our faces,
divisions outside to concentrate a world
tally here only to dead profits and losses.

We follow barrier voices, and we go fast,
unknown to each other, they race, I turn away.
No voice is strong enough to cry me Stay.

My sister, I wished upon you those delights
time never buries,
more precious than heroes.

Strange father, strange mother, who are you, who are you?
Where have I come,
how shall I prosper home?

19

THIS HOUSE, THIS COUNTRY

Always I travelled farther
dreading a barrier
starting at shadows scattered on the ground
fearful of the invisible night-sound,

till in that straight career
I crossed frontier
the questions asked   the proofs shown   the name
signed smiling   I reached knowledge of my home.

I praised their matings
and corner-meetings
their streets the brightest I had yet walked down :
my family swore I did not leave my town

thought that I lied
and had not signed
those passports, tickets, contracts, bills of sale
but still rested among them and wished them well.

Over my shoulder
I see they grow older
their vision fails : observe I travel light
fear distance   hope I shall only spend the night.

But night in this country
is deep promise of day,
is busy with preparations and awake for fighting
and there is no time for leavetaking and regretting.

I know their tired house
full of remorse
I know in my body the door, the entrance-hall
a wall and my space and another wall.

I have left forever
house and maternal river
given up sitting in that private tomb
quitted that land that house that velvet room.

Frontiers admitted me
to a growing country
I carry the proofs of my birth and my mind's reasons
but reckon with their struggle and their seasons.

Theory of Flight

Earth, bind us close, and time   ;   nor, sky, deride
how violate we experiment again.
In many Januaries, many lips
have fastened on us while we deified
the waning flesh   :   now, fountain, spout for us,
mother, bear children   :   lover, yet once more   :
in final effort toward your mastery.
Many Decembers suffered their eclipse
death, and forgetfulness, and the year bore round   ;
now years, be summed in one access of power.
Fortresses, strengths, beauties, realities,
gather together, discover to us our wings
new special product of mortality.

Fortuitously have we gained loneliness,
fallen in waste places liberated,
relieved ourselves from weakness' loveliness   :
remain unpitied now, never descend
to that soft howling of the prostrate mind.
Cut with your certain wings; engrave space now
to your ambition   :   stake off sky's dimensions.
We have plunged on nightmares to destruction
too long; and learned aggression divides wind,
pale early Venus is signature of night
and wish gnawed clean by plans precurses flight.
Distinguish the metaphor most chromium clear
for distant calendars to identify   :
Frail mouthings will fall diminished on old ears
in dusty whispers, light from extinctest stars
will let us sleep, nor may we replica
ourselves in hieroglyphs and broken things
but there is reproduction for this act
linking the flight's escape with strict contact.

Look!   Be : leap ;
paint trees in flame
bushes burning
roar in the broad sky

know your color : be :
produce that the widenesses
be full and burst their wombs
riot in redness, delirious with light,
swim bluely through the mind
shout green as the day breaks
put up your face to the wind
FLY

chant as the tomtom hubbubs crash
elephants in the flesh's jungle
reek with vigor   sweat   pour your life
in a libation to itself
drink from the ripe ground
make children over the world
lust in a heat of tropic orange
stamp and writhe ;   stamp on a wet floor
know earth   know water   know lovers
know mastery
FLY

Walks down the street
Kaleidoscope   a man
where patterns meet
his mind colored
with mirage
Leonardo's tomb
not in Italian earth
but in a fuselage
designed
in the historic mind
time's instrument
blue-print of birth.

We know sky overhead, earth to be stepped
black under the toes, rubble between our fingers,
horizons are familiar ;   we have been taught colors.
Rehearse these ;   sky, earth, and their meeting-place,
confound them in a blur of distance, swallow
the blueness of guessed-at places, merge them now.
Sky being meeting of sky and no-sky
including our sources   the earth   water   air
fire to weld them :   unity in knowing

all space in one unpunctuated flowing.
Flight, thus, is meeting of flight and non-flight.
We bear the seeds of our return forever,
the flowers of our leaving, fruit of flight,
perfect for present, fertile for its roots
in past   in future   in motility.

THE GYROSCOPE

But this is our desire, and of its worth. . . .
Power electric-clean, gravitating outward at all points,
moving in savage fire, fusing all durable stuff
but never itself being fused with any force
homing in no hand nor breast nor sex
for buried in these lips we rise again,
bent over these plans, our faces raise to see.
Direct spears are shot outward from the conscience
fulfilling what far circuits?   Orbit of thought
what axis do you lean on, what strictnesses evade
impelled to the long curves of the will's ambition?
Centrifugal power, expanding universe
within expanding universe, what stillnesses
lie at your center resting among motion?
Study communications, looking inward, find what traffic
you may have with your silences   :   looking outward, survey
what you have seen of places   :
                    many times this week I seemed
        to hear you speak my name
                    how you turn the flatnesses
        of your cheek and will not hear my words
                    then reaching the given latitude
        and longitude, we searched for the ship and found nothing
                    and, gentlemen, shall we define desire
        including every impulse toward psychic progress?
Roads are cut into the earth leading away from our place
at the inevitable hub.   All directions are *out*,
all desire turns outward   :   we, introspective,
continuing to find in ourselves the microcosm
imaging continents, powers, relations, reflecting
all history in a bifurcated Engine.
Here is the gyroscope whirling out pulsing in tides illimitably
            widening, live force contained
in a sphere of rigid boundary   ;   concentrate

at the locus of all forces, spinning with black speed
revolving outward perpetually, turning with its torque
all the developments of the secret will.
Flaming origins were our fathers in the heat of the earth,
pushing to the crust, water and sea-flesh,
undulant tentacles ingrown on the ocean's floor,
frondy anemones and scales' armor gave us birth.
Bring us to air, ancestors! and we breathed
the young flesh wincing against naked December.
Masters of fire, fire gave us riches, gave us life.
Masters of water, water gave us riches, gave us life,
masters of earth, earth gave us riches, gave us life.
Air mocks, and desire whirls outward in strict frenzy, leaping,
elastic circles widening from the mind,
turning constricted to the mind again.
The dynamics of desire are explained
in terms of action outward and reaction to a core
obscured and undefined, except, perhaps, as "God in Heaven,"
   "God in Man,"
Elohim intermittent with the soul, recurrent
as Father and Holy Ghost, Word and responsive Word,
merging with contact in continual sunbursts,
the promise, the response, the hands laid on,
the hammer swung to the anvil, mouth fallen on mouth,
the plane nose up into an open sky.
Roads are cut, purchase is gained on our wish,
the turbines gather momentum, tools are given   :
whirl in desire, hurry to ambition, return,
maintaining the soul's polarity ;   be : fly.

THE LYNCHINGS OF JESUS

I / Passage to Godhead

Passage to godhead, fitfully glared upon
by bloody shinings over Calvary
this latest effort to revolution stabbed
against a bitter crucificial tree,
mild thighs split by the spearwound, opening
in fierce gestation of immortality.

Icarus' phoenix-flight fulfils itself,
desire's symbol swings full circle here,
eternal defeat by power, eternal death

of the soul and body in murder or despair
to be followed by eternal return, until
the thoughtful rebel may triumph everywhere.

Many murdered in war, crucified, starved,
loving their lives they are massacred and burned,
hating their lives as they have found them, but
killed while they look to enjoy what they have earned,
dismissed with peremptory words and hasty graves,
little calm tributes of the unconcerned.

Bruno, Copernicus, Shelley, Karl Marx : you
makers of victory for us : how long?
We love our lives, and the crucifixions come,
benevolent bugles smother rebellion's song,
blowing protection for the acquiescent,
and we need many strengths to continue strong.

Tendons bind us to earth, Antaeus-ridden
by desperate weakness disallied from ground,
bone of our bone; and the sky's plains above us
seduce us into powers still unfound,
and freedom's eagles scream above our faces,
misleading, sly, perverse, and unprofound.

Passage to godhead, shine illuminated
by other colors than blood and fire and pride.
Given wings, we looked downward on earth, seen
uniform from distance; and descended, tied
to the much-loved near places, moved to find
what numbers of lynched Jesuses have not been
    deified.

II / The Committee-Room

Let us be introduced to our superiors, the voting men.
They are tired ; they are hungry ; from deciding all day
around the committee-table.
        Is it foggy outside?   It must be very foggy
        The room is white with it.
The years slope into a series of flights, rocking sea-like,
shouting a black rush, enveloping time and kingdom
and the flab faces
        Those people engendered my blood swarming
        over the altar to clasp the scrolls and Menorah

the black lips, bruised cheeks, eye-reproaches :
             as the floor burns, singing Shema
Our little writers go about, hurrying the towns along,
running from mine to luncheon, they can't afford
to let one note escape their holy jottings:
today the mother died, festering : he shot himself : the
     bullet entered
the roof of the mouth, piercing the brain-pan
             How the spears went down in a flurry of blood;
             how they died howling
                            how the triumph marched
             all day and all night past the beleaguered town
             blowing trumpets at the fallen towers;
             how they pulled their shoulders over the hill, crying
             for the whole regiment to hear   The Sea   The Sea
Our young men opening the eyes and mouths together,
facing the new world with their open mouths
                            gibbering war
                            gibbering conquest
Ha.   Will you lead us to discovery?

What did you do in school today, my darling?
             Tamburlaine rode over Genghis had a sword
             holding riot over Henry V Emperor of and
             the city of Elizabeth the tall sails
             crowding England into the world and Charles
             his head falling many times onto a dais
             how they have been monarchs and
             Calvin Coolidge who wouldn't say
                            however, America

All day we have been seated around a table
                            all these many days
One day we voted on whether he was Hamlet
or whether he was himself and yesterday
I cast the deciding vote to renounce our mouths.
Today we sentinel the avenue solemnly warning
the passers (who look the other way, and cough) that we
speak with the mouths of demons, perhaps the people's,
but not our own.
             Tomorrow
the vote's to be cast on the eyes, and sex, and brain.
Perhaps we will vote to disavow all three.
26

We are powerful now : we vote
                death to Sacco a man's name
                and Vanzetti a blood-brother; death
                to Tom Mooney, or a wall, no matter;
                poverty to Piers Plowman, shrieking anger
                to Shelley, a cough and Fanny to Keats;
                thus to Blake in a garden; thus to Whitman;
                thus to D. H. Lawrence.
                                And to all you women,
                dead and unspoken-for, what sentences,
                to you dead children, little in the ground
                : all you sweet generous rebels, what sentences

This is the case of one Hilliard, a native of Texas,
in the year of our Lord 1897, a freeman.
Report . . . Hilliard's power of endurance seems to be
the most wonderful thing on record.   His lower limbs
burned off a while before he became unconscious;
and his body looked to be burned to the hollow.
Was it decreed (oh coyly coyly) by an avenging God
as well as an avenging people that he suffer so?
                                We have
16 large views under magnifying glass.
8 views of the trial and the burning.
For place of exhibit watch the street bills.
                Don't fail to see this.

Lie down dear, the day was long, the evening is smooth.
The day was long, and you were voting all day
                hammering down these heads
                tamping the mould about these diamond eyes
                filling the mouths with wax
                                lie down my dear
the bed is soft lie down to kindest dreams

                all night they carried leaves
                bore songs and garlands up the gradual hill
                the noise of singing kept the child awake
                    but they were dead
                all Shakespeare's heroes   the saints   the
                    Jews   the rebels
                but the noise stirred their graves' grass
                and the feet all falling in those places
                going up the hill with sheaves and tools
                and all the weapons of ascent together.

III / The Trial

The South is green with coming spring ; revival
flourishes in the fields of Alabama.   Spongy with rain,
plantations breathe April : carwheels suck mud in the roads,
the town expands warm in the afternoons.   At night the
  black boy
teeters no-handed on a bicycle, whistling The St. Louis Blues,
blood beating, and hot South.   A red brick courthouse
is vicious with men inviting death.   Array your judges; call your
                                            jurors; come,
here is your justice, come out of the crazy jail.
Grass is green now in Alabama; Birmingham dusks are quiet
relaxed and soft in the park, stern at the yards:
a hundred boxcars shunted off to sidings, and the hoboes
gathering grains of sleep in forbidden corners.
In all the yards : Atlanta, Chattanooga,
Memphis, and New Orleans, the cars, and no jobs.

Every night the mail-planes burrow the sky,
carrying postcards to laughing girls in Texas,
passionate letters to the Charleston virgins,
words through the South : and no reprieve,
no pardon, no release.

A blinded statue attends before the courthouse,
bronze and black men lie on the grass, waiting,
the khaki dapper National Guard leans on its bayonets.
But the air is populous beyond our vision:
all the people's anger finds its vortex here
as the mythic lips of justice open, and speak.

Hammers and sickles are carried in a wave of strength, fire-
  tipped,
swinging passionately ninefold to a shore.
Answer the back-thrown Negro face of the lynched, the flat
  forehead knotted,
the eyes showing a wild iris, the mouth a welter of blood,
answer the broken shoulders and these twisted arms.
John Brown, Nat Turner, Toussaint stand in this courtroom,
Dred Scott wrestles for freedom there in the dark corner,
all our celebrated shambles are repeated here : now again
Sacco and Vanzetti walk to a chair, to the straps and rivets
and the switch spitting death and Massachusetts' will.

Wreaths are brought out of history
    here are the well-nourished flowers of France, grown strong
        on blood,
    Caesar twisting his thin throat toward conquest, turning
        north from the Roman laurels,
    the Istrian galleys slide again to sea.
    How they waded through bloody Godfrey's Jerusalem   !
    How the fires broke through Europe, and the rich
    and the tall jails battened on revolution   !
    The fastidious Louis', cousins to the sun, stamping
    those ribboned heels on Calas, on the people;
    the lynched five thousand of America.
    Tom Mooney from San Quentin, Herndon :   here
    is an army for audience
                                all resolved
to a gobbet of tobacco, spat, and the empanelled hundred,
a jury of vengeance, the cheap pressed lips, the narrow eyes like
                                hardware;
the judge, his eye-sockets and cheeks dark and immutably
    secret,
the twisting mouth of the prosecuting attorney.
Nine dark boys spread their breasts against Alabama,
schooled in the cells, fathered by want.
    Mother :   one writes :   they treat us bad.   If they
        send us
    back to Kilby jail, I think I shall kill myself.
    I think I must hang myself by my overalls.

Alabama and the South are soft with spring;
in the North, the seasons change, sweet April, December and
    the air
loaded with snow.   There is time for meetings
during the years, they remaining in prison.
                                In the Square.
a crowd listens, carrying banners.
Overhead, boring through the speaker's voice, a plane
circles with a snoring of motors revolving in the sky,
drowning the single voice.   It does not touch
the crowd's silence.   It circles.   The name stands :
Scottsboro

_____

Earth, include sky :   air, be stable to our
feet, which have need of stone and iron stance;

all opposites, affirm your contradictions,
lead, all you prophets, our mechanic dance.

Arches over the earth, conform, be still,
calm Roman in the evening cool of grace,
dramatic Gothic, be finally rounded now
pared equal to the clean savannahs of space,

grind levels to one plane, unfold the stones
that shaped you pointed, return to ground, return,
bird be no more a brand upon the sky
no more a torch to which earth's bodies burn

fire attracting fire in magnetism
too subtle for dissection and proponence,
torturing fire, crucifying posture
with which dead Jesus quenches his opponents.

Shall we then straddle Jesus in a plane
the rigid crucified revived at last
the pale lips flattened in a wind a rain
of merging conquered blast and counterblast.
Shout to us   :   See   !
the wind   !
Shout to us   :
FLY

THE TUNNEL

I

NO WORK is master of the mine today
tyrant that walks with the feet of murder here
under his cracked shoes a grass-blade dusted
dingy with coal's smear.

The father's hand is rubbed with dust, his body
is witness to coal, black glosses all his skin.
Around the pithead they stand and do not talk
looking at the obvious sign.

Behind his shoulder stands the black mountain
of unbought coal, green-topped with grass growing
rank in the shag, as if coal were native earth
and the top a green snowing

down on the countryside.   In the whole valley
eleven mines, and five of them are closed,
two are on strike, but in the others, workers
scramble down the shafts, disposed

to grub all day and all night, lording it
in the town because of their jobs and their bosses
at work with all the other mines graveyards.
These are the valley's losses

which even the company fails to itemize
in stubborn black and red in the company stores   :
the empty breasts like rinds, the father's hands,
the sign, the infected whores,

a puppy roasted for pregnant Mary's dinner . . .
On the cold evenings the jobless miners meet
wandering dully attracted to the poolroom,
walking down the grey street.

"Well," says the father, "nothing comes of this,
the strippings run to weeds, the roads all mucked.
A dead mine makes dead miners.   God, but I
was a fool not to have chucked

the whole damned ruin when I was a kid."
"And how'd you have a chance to throw it over?"
"Well," he said, "if I hadn't married   :   though then
the place had more in its favor.

Babies came quickly after summertimes.
You could work, and quit, and get a better job.
God knows if it'll ever be the same,
or if ever they'll think not to rob,

not to cut wages, not to weigh us short."
"All right," the other says, "maybe God does.
We'll be a long time dead, come that time, buried
under coal where our life was;

we were children and did not know our childhood,
we got infants, and never knew our wives,
year in and out, seeing no color but coal,
we were the living who could not have their lives."

Emerge, city, from your evening : allay me, sleep :
but the city withdraws to night, sleep passes whitely
inanely over my eyelids mockcomforting pale dawn's
developing silver and I unloved.

Shall we no more, my love, pass down the lanes of grace
slowly together and in each other's safekeeping, no more
shall I watch evening touch hands to your face
and feel myself glisten in answer?

Day shines a last gloom quickening the street, and deep
grave-deep the subway files down space to a moment
over me a plane exterminates distance ; you
are unalterably removed : day touches you

nor night though tiger it may rage abroad ; you are
beyond its claws, if my love will not reach you.
O love, how am I surpassed how mocked how
defiled and corroded untouched by your kiss.

I came to you riding on love with love in my hands, advancing
seaworn, hearing far bells : you have been a prow
carving a tragic sea to meet my love, you have been lamps
burning all night over tired waters.

You have been stone set upon fine-grained woods, buildings
of granite standing in a street of stone, roads
full of fallen flowers wet under the foot, ships
pointing an index to voyage among islands,

blue archipelagoes : your body being an island
set about with magnetic flowers and flesh and fruit :
the sons I might bear you, the sons, the fragrant daughters.
Intrudes on this the bleak authentic voice :

wherefore does the mouth stiffen, the cheeks freeze austere
as stone, affording special grief among the days
and cold days catalogued of comfort murdered,
the iron passage, estranged eyes, and the death

of all my logic : pale with the weakness of one
dead and not yet arisen, a hollow bath of flame
with my fire low along the oils of grace
how many deaths, body so torn from spirit.

Body, return : I love you : soul, come home!
I am gone down to death in a great bleeding.
All day the bleeding washes down my sides ; at night
darkly and helplessly my face is wet.

Open me a refuge where I may be renewed.   Speak to me
world hissing over cables, shining among steel strands,
plucking speech out on a wire, linking voices,
reach me now in my fierceness, or I am drowned

buried among my flesh, dead of a dead desire.
All night I went to the places of my love,
opened to one wished meeting, all unarmed.
And there was nothing but machine-loud streets.

All night I returned to the places of my love.
My love escaped me.   May not the blood's frail drums
ever pulse healing in wrists and lips made known
whispering convalescence through a mist of sleep?

Let me approach infinity in love and sorrow, waiting
with the doubled strength of my own will and love,
burning with copper-spun electric fire, unconsumed,
a bush upon a barren darkening plain.

My blood must be fed on foreign substance, lacking
the knowledge of those gestures, roots of words, unfeeling
the wet intestinal movings of another body, starving
not knowing the muscles' flexing.

Shall we losing our ego gain it, saddening
after no response and a turning away?   Sheer
the skyscrapers stand, pure without meaning, single
in desire rising to touch the sky :

the diver waits, arms thrust in white dihedral
to air and next moment's water : the flash of shock
travels through diver   lover   tower   plane   reaching
sky, a contact in desire, leaving

bondage in flight.   Sever the cords binding our bones,
loosen us to each other, approach, night, return me love :
unblind me, give me back myself, touch me now :
slide, night, into the climates of the mind.

III

The cattle-trains edge along the river, bringing morning on a
    white vibration
breaking the darkness split with beast-cries : a milk-wagon
    proceeds
down the street leaving the cold bottles : the Mack truck
    pushes
around the corner, tires hissing on the washed asphalt.   A
    clear sky
growing candid and later bright.
            Ceiling unlimited.   Visibility unlimited.

They stir on the pillows, her leg moving, her face swung
    windowward
vacant with sleep still, modeled with light's coming ; his
    dark head
among the softness of her arm and breast, nuzzled in dreams,
mumbling the old words, hardly roused.   They return to
    silence.
            At the airport, the floodlights are snapped off.

Turning, he says, "Tell me how's the sky this morning?"
    "Fair," she answers,
"no clouds from where I lie; bluer and bluer."   "And later
    and later—
god, for some sleep into some noon, instead of all these
    mornings
with my mouth going stiff behind the cowling and wind
    brushing
away from me and my teeth freezing against the wind."
            Light gales from the northwest : tomorrow, rain.

The street is long, with a sprinkling of ashcans ; panhandlers
begin to forage among banana-peels and cardboard boxes.
She moves to the window, tall and dark before a brightening sky,
full with her six-months' pregnancy molded in ripeness.
            Stands, watching the sky's blankness.

Very soon : "How I love to see you when I wake," he says,
"How the child's meaning in you is my life's growing."
She faces him, hands brought to her belly's level, offering,
wordless, looking upon him.   She carries his desire well.
            Sun rises : 6:38 a.m.   Sun sets. . . .

"Flying is what makes you strange to me, dark as Asia,
almost removed from my world even in your closenesses :
that you should be familiar with those intricacies
and a hero in mysteries which all the world has wanted."
        Wind velocity changing from 19 to 30.

"No, that's wrong," and he laughs, "no personal hero's left
to make a legend.   Those centuries have gone.   If I fly,
why, I know that countries are not map-colored, that seas
belong to no one, that war's a pock-marking on Europe :   "
        The Weather Bureau's forecast, effective until noon.

"Your friends sleep with strange women desperately,
drink liquor and sleep heavily to forget those skies.
You fly all day and come home truly returning
to me who know only land.   And we will have this child."
        New York to Boston   :   Scattered to broken clouds.

"The child will have a hard time to be an American,"
he says slowly, "fathered by a man whose country is air,
who believes there are no heroes to withstand
wind, or a loose bolt, or a tank empty of gas."
        To Washington   :   Broken clouds becoming overcast.

"It will be a brave child," she answers, smiling.
"We will show planes to it, and the bums in the street.
You will teach it to fly, and I will love it
very much."   He thinks of his job, dressing.
        Strong west northwest winds above 1000 feet.

He thinks how many men have wanted flight.
He ties his tie, looking into his face.
Finishes breakfast, hurrying to be gone,
crossing the river to the airport and his place.
        To Cleveland   :   Broken clouds to overcast.

She does not imagine how the propeller turns
in a blinding speed, swinging the plane through space;
she never sees the cowling rattle and slip
forward and forward against the grim blades' grinding.
        Cruising speed 1700 R.P.M.

Slipping, a failing desire   ;   slipping like death
insidious against the propeller, until the blades shake,

bitten by steel, jagged against steel, broken,
and his face angry and raked by death, staring
        Strong west northwest or west winds above 2000 feet.

She watches the clock as his return time hurries,
the schedule ticking off, eating the short minutes.
She watches evening advance   ;   she knows the child's stirring.
She knows night.   She knows he will not come.
        Ceiling unlimited.   Visibility unlimited.

The rough skin dusty with coal on the slack hands   ;
lover trailing regret through the evening streets
uncomforted, walking toward destruction   :
the mouth of the young pilot stiffening
(I love to see you when I wake at morning)
hurtling, spiralling that plucks the breath from the throat
in a long chute to gauged mechanic death.

Greyly our vigor seeps away, the fingers
weak and the lips unspeaking, somberly
devoid of wholeness are we drowned again
mumbling death as our cheeks stiffen
as we go down these maelstroms   :   dissolution.
    Harsh blue screams summer from behind the plane
    the sea stiffens under it sculpturally.
    Split space, monotonous and even-winged,
    continue toward despair methodically.
Destruction and a burning fill these lives
unloved incompetent they compromise
with death and the bases of emotion fearing
the natural calm inclusiveness of time.
    Tigers follow in a splendor of motion
    sleek death treads unperturbed among these things,
    time rages like a tiger and the
    savage defeat swallows the fallen wings
plunging
O Icarus accurate white into the sea
the wax support too trusted   ;   the white pride
in sovereignty collapsed   ;   go down to harbor,
go down, plane, to the water's eagerness
engulfed, plunging

36

We have prayed torrents of humility, open
in anguish to be hurt, in terror to be fooled.
We are beyond demand, waiting a minute
unconscious in attendance :   here is strength to be used
delicately, most subtly on the controls and levers.
They begged that time be condensed.   Extend space for us,
let us include this memory in ourselves,
time and our dividend of history.

THE STRUCTURE OF
THE PLANE

I | The Structure of the Plane

Kitty Hawk is a Caesar among monuments   ;
        the stiff bland soldiers predestined to their death
        the bombs piled neatly like children's marbles piled
        sperm to breed corpses eugenically by youth
        out of seductive death.
                        The hill outdoes our towers
        we might treasure a thistle grown from a cannon-mouth
        they have not permitted rust and scum and blossoms
        to dirty the steel,
                        however we have the plane
the hill, flower among monuments.

"To work intelligently" (Orville and Wilbur Wright)
"one needs to know the effects of variations
incorporated in the surfaces. . . . The pressures on squares
are different from those on rectangles, circles, triangles, or
    ellipses . . .
The shape of the edge also makes a difference."

The plane is wheeled out of the hangar.   The sleeves shake
fixing the wind, the four o'clock blue sky
blinks in the goggles swinging over his wrist.
The plane rests, the mechanic in cream-colored overalls
encourages the engine into idling speed.
The instructor looks at his class
and begins the demonstration.

"We finally became discouraged, and returned to kite-flying.
But as we grew older we had to give up this sport,
it was unbecoming to boys of our ages."

On the first stroke of the piston the intake valve opens,
the piston moves slowly from the head of the cylinder,
drawing in its mixture of gas and air.   On the second stroke
the piston returns, the valve closes.   The mixture is
    compressed.
A spark occurs, igniting America, opening India,
finding the Northwest Passage, Cipango spice,
causing the mixture to burn, expanding the gases
which push the piston away on the power stroke.
The final exhaust stroke serves to release the gases,
allowing the piston to scavenge the cylinder.
                We burn space, we sever galaxies,
                solar systems whirl about Shelley's head,
                we give ourselves ease, gentlemen, art and these
                    explosions
                and Peter Ronsard finger-deep in roses   ;
gentlemen, remember these incandescent points,
remember to check, remember to drain the oil,
remember Plato O remember me
            the college pathways rise
            the president's voice intoning sonnets
            the impress of hoofmarks on the bridle path
            the shining girls the lost virginities
            the plane over a skeletal water-tower
            our youth dissolving O remember
            romantically dissolving remember me.

Blue smoke from the exhaust signifies too much oil.
Save yourselves from excesses, dirt, and tailspins.
These are the axioms   :   stability, control,
and equilibrium   :   in a yaw, in a roll, or pitch.
Here, gentlemen, are the wings, of fabric doped and painted
here is the rudder
here the propeller spins
:   BE   hammers in the brain
FLY and the footbeat of that drum
may not be contradicted
must be mine
must be made ours, say the brothers Wright together
            although the general public had been invited
            few dared a cold December
            in order to see another plane not fly.

The helmet is strapped tight, orders are shouted
the elbows of steel move in oil
air is forced under the ship, the pilot's hand
is safe on the stick, the young student sits
with the wind mottling his eyelashes, rigidly.
Centuries fall behind his brain, the motor
pushes in a four-beat rhythm, his blood moves,
he dares look at the levels mounting in clouds
the dropping fields of the sky the diminishment of earth   ;
       now he thinks I am the child crying Mother
       this rim is the threshold into the hall's night
       or the windowsill livened with narcissus.
       The white edge of the bath a moment before
       slipping into watery ease, the windowsill
       eager for the jump into the street
       the hard stone under my back, the earth
       with its eyes and hands its eyes and hands
       its eyes
              fixed eyes on the diminishing
       take me back the bath had fronds of steam
       escaping the hands held my head
       my eyes slipped in oil looking along your beauty
       earth is painful the distance hurts
       mother the night, the distance, dear
he is standing with one look of hate upon him
screams at the pilot you bastard, you bastard, jumps
trailing a long scream above him, the plane yaws down,
the motor pulls heavily, the ground is dark November,
his parachute opens a bright plume surrendering downward,
the plane heads up again, no good in following,
continues unfascinated by night or land or death.

II | The Strike

"Well," he said, "George, I never thought you were with us.
You walked out of the shaft as if you'd spent years of your life
planning some day to walk out once without blinking
and not stop for a smoke but walk over to our side."

"No," he said, "I never expected to.   It was only the last
   cut: ‹
before that, I'd have worked no matter who starved first."
The snow was stamped down with black nailprints
the stamping was a drum to warm them, stiff veins, crusted
   hands.

"Carrying guns, boys!" said the director.   "Now, boys;
I'll speak to the others and see what I can do."
The heavy-set miner spat on the peel of snow.
The fingers weighed on the triggers.   December bit
into the bone, into the tight skulls, creaking one word.

Tell how the men watched the table, a plate of light,
the rigid faces lit around it, the mouths
opening and clamping, the little warmth
watched against the shafts of the breakers.
Tell how the men watched.
Tell how the child chewed its shoe to strips.

That day broke equal grey, the lockers empty,
the cages hanging in a depth of silence.
Shall we say   :   there were two lines at last   :
death played like a current between them, playing,
the little flames of death ran along those eyes   :   ?

Death faced the men with a desperate seduction,
lifted a hand with the skill of a hypnotist.
They were so ready in khaki with bayonets.
            "George!" he heard.   That had once been his name.
            Very carefully he had stepped from his place,
            walked over his ground, over the last line.
            It seemed impossible he should not die.
                        When a gun faces you, look down the bore,
                        that is the well of death   :   when it
                            confronts you
                        it is not satisfied, it draws you steadily
                        more loving than love, eagerer than hunger,
                        resolving all unbalance.   He went to it.

However, the line held.   The plump men raised themselves
up from the chairs in a dreary passion of wrath,
hoisted themselves to the doorway.   Spoke.
There was his body, purpled, death casing him
in ice and velvet and sleep.   Indeed, they spoke,
this was unwarranted.   No, they conceded.   No.
Perhaps the strike might equal victory,
a company funeral, and the trucks of coal
                ladled up from the earth,
                heaped on this grave.

III | *The Lover*

Answer with me these certainties
of glands swelling with sentiment
the loves embittered the salts and waters mixing
a chemic threatening destruction.

Answer the men walking toward death
leaping to death meeting death in a kiss
able to find of equilibrium none
except that last of hard stone kissing stone.

Answer the lover's questioning in the streets
the evenings domed with purple, the bones
easing, the flesh slipping perfume upon the air :
all surfaces of flight are pared to planes

equal, equilibrated, solid in fulfilment.   No way
is wanted to escape, no explosions craved,
only this desire must be met, this motion
be balanced with passion   ;

> in the wreaths of time given to us what love
> may reach us in the streets   the books   the years
> what wreaths of love may touch our dreams,
> what skeins of fine response may clothe our flesh,
> robe us in valor brave as our dear wish

> lover haunting the ghosts of rivers, letting time
> slide a fluid runner into darkness
> give over the sad eyes the marble face of pain
> do not mourn   :   remember   :   do not forget
> but never let this treason play you mate,

> take to yourself the branches of green trees
> watch the clean sky signed by the flight of planes
> know rivers of love   be flooded thoroughly
> by love and the years and the past and know
> the green tree perishes and green trees grow.

Knock at the doors   ;   go to the windows   ;   run,
you will not find her soon who, lost in love,
relinquished last month to that silver music
repeating in her throat forsaken tunes.

Rigid and poised for the latest of these lovers
she stretches acute in waiting on the bed
most avaricious for the length of arms
the subtle thighs and heavy confident head.

Taut with a steel strut's singing tautness she
clinches her softness anguished at postponement
hardening all her thought she swears to be
unpacified by minutes of atonement.

The ticking of an ormolu clock taxes
her body with time's weight.   The opened door
adjusts such things ; responsive, she relaxes
ringing in answer to a word before

all tensity is changed to eagerness.
Translated and resolved, the anguish through,
sensitive altogether to the present   :
"Now?"   "Yes," she says, "yes," she says, "do."

Answer motion with motion, be birds flying
be the enormous movements of the snows,
be rain, be love, remain equilibrated
unseeking death,
                    if you must have pilgrimages
go travelling to balance need with answer
suiting the explosion to the ensuing shock
the foil to the airstream running over it
food to the mouth, tools to the body, mind
to the bright mind that leaps in necessity
go answering   answering   FLY

NIGHT FLIGHT : NEW YORK

Lucid at dusk the city lies revealed
authentic purpose under masonry
emerging into emphasis.   Tenuous
the bodies grim at noon lie scattered, limp
on the beach of evening, and the long sea
of night softly encroaches on reality.

Pale the primitive blue of afternoon,
morning's bravado made ambiguous,
and all the bulwarks we relied upon

relapsed to fluid concept.   Now the night
opens a shady empire odorous
prodigal in sweetness, sweetly promiscuous.

Foliate evening opens in a blur
of even color on the risen stone   :
in unified unbroken shoulderings
of tower past planned tower, twilight-softened;
insanest noise resolves to monotone.
The theory of the city's fact made known

in a revelatory evening stillness.
Traffic and work and riot, triad of waking
are garbled into a full chord, drowning
identity in conquering vibration
impinging on the air, loud, rising, making
the city conscious of propellers shaking

hard frames of aircraft   ;   night cloven by twin wings,
incisive angles ripping evening where
blueness was closing deepest to the north
beyond the Bridge, beyond the island, planes   :
a burr of dissonance, a swoop of bare
fatal battalions black against the air.

Time is metric now with the regular advance   :   descend the skytrack
signal-red on the wingtips, defined by a glitter of bulbs   ;
we lean at the windows or roofrails, attentive
under inverted amphitheatre of sky.
The river is keen under blackness, weapon-malevolent,
crossed jagged marks mirrored against its steel.
Suddenly from a trance of speed are let fall bubbles slowly
blooming in pale light, but hardening to crystal
glows, into calcium brilliance, white bombs floating
   imperturbable
along the planes of the air, in chains of burning, destruction in
   the wake
of the beautiful transition.   City, shimmer in amusement,
spectators at the mocking of your bombardment.
City, cry out   :   the space is full of planes, you will be heard,
         the thin shark-bodies are concentrated to listen,
without a sound but the clean strength of the engines, dripping
   death-globes drifting down the wind
lifted by parachutes in a metaphor of death,

the symbol not the substance, merest detail of fact, going down
the wincing illuminated river, fading over the city.
Planes weave :   the children laugh at the fireworks   :   "Oh,
    pretty stars!
                                                Oh, see the white!"
Planes move in a calculated dance of war
each throwing, climax to superbest flight.

No whisper rises from the city :   New York is quiet
as a doped man walking to the electric chair, fixed in memory,
suspended in an image of peace.   Skeins of light
are woven above the city, gathering-in evening in a harvest of
    peace,
from loveliest vessels falling, the buds of annihilation.
Turn and re-turn in precise advance, engines of power
subtle terrific potency, rays of destruction emitted from black suns
shining the faces of burial, loosing magnificence
in bombs, in a sardonic joke play games of death,
cancel the city to an achievement   :   zero.

Pregnant zero breeding annihilation. . . .
futility stands clear on these horizons
marked in the zeros of a thousand clouds
pregnant above a harvested land, whose fruit
was peace infected with the germs of war.
In tragic streaks the planes' formations fly
across the black pavilions of the sky.

Failure encompassed in success, the warplanes
dropping flares, as a historic sum of knowledge,
tallying Icarus loving the sun, and plunging,
Leonardo engraved on the Florentine pale evening
scheming toward wings, as toward an alchemy
transferring life to golden circumstance.
Following him, the warplanes travelling home,
flying over the cities, over the minds
of cities rising against imminent doom.
Icarus' passion, Da Vinci's skill, corrupt,
all rotted into war   :

Between murmur and murmur, birth and death,
is the earth's turning which follows the earth's turning,
a swift whisper of life, an ambiguous word spoken   ;
morning travelling quiet on mutinous fields,

muscles swollen tight in giant effort ; rain ; some stars ;
a propeller's glimpsing silver whirl, intensely upward,
intensely forward, bearing the plane : flying.

Believe that we bloom upon this stalk of time ;
and in this expansion, time too grows for us
richer and richer towards infinity.
They promised us the gold and harps and seraphs.
Our rising and going to sleep is better than future pinions.
We surrender that hope, drawing our own days in,
covering space and time draped in tornadoes,
lightning invention, speed crushing the stars upon us,
stretching the accordion of our lives, sounding the same chord
longer and savoring it until the echo fails.
Believe that your presences are strong,
O be convinced without formula or rhyme
or any dogma ; use yourselves : be : fly.
Believe that we bloom upon this stalk of time.

THEORY OF FLIGHT

You dynamiting the structure of our loves
embrace your lovers solving antithesis,
open your flesh, people, to opposites
conclude the bold configuration, finish
the counterpoint : sky, include earth now.
Flying, a long vole of descent
renders us land again.
Flight is intolerable contradiction.
We bear the bursting seeds of our return
we will not retreat ; never be moved.
Stretch us onward   include in us the past
sow in us history, make us remember triumph.
   O golden fructifying, O the sonorous calls
   to arms and embattled mottoes in one war
   brain versus brain for absolutes, ring harsh!
   Miners rest from blackness : reapers, lay by the sheaves
   forgive us our tears   we go to victory
   in a commune of regenerated lives.
   The birds of flight return, crucified shapes
   old deaths restoring vigor through the sky

mergent with earth, no more horizons now
no more unvisioned capes, no death ;   we fly.

Answer together the birds' flying
reconcile rest to rest
motion to motion's poise,
  the guns are dying the past is born again
  into these future minds the incarnate past
  gleaming upon the present
         fliers, grave men,
  lovers   :   do not stop to remember these,
  think of them as you travel, the tall kind prophets,
  the flamboyant leapers toward death,
  the little painful children
        how the veins were slit
  into the Roman basins to fill Europe with blood
  how our world has run over bloody with love and blood
  and the misuses of love and blood and veins.
  Now we arrive to meet ourselves at last,
  we cry beginnings
  the criers in the midnight streets call dawn   ;
  respond   respond
  you workers   poets   men of science and love.

Now we can look at our subtle jointures, study our hands,
the tools are assembled, the maps unrolled, propellers spun,
do we say *all is in readiness   :*
the times approach, here is the signal shock   :   ?

Master in the plane shouts "Contact"   :
master on the ground   :   "Contact!"
  he looks up   :   "Now?" whispering   :   "Now."
  "Yes," she says. "Do."
  Say yes, people.
  Say yes.
  YES

The Blood Is Justified

FOR MEMORY

for Ruth Lehman obit February 10, 1934

I / Life and Works

Open with care the journal of those years
firm years precipitating days to death
This was my friend walking in color and flame
walking through a texture of sense
                                        no breath
deranges her fine hair   no voice changes her face.

It is hardly possible she will not come again
returned for a short while out of distances
to be re-given to distance and her loves.
It is hardly truth to say that soon
a letter will not come, postmarked Detroit,
New Orleans, Chicago, ultimate Mexico.
I think she must come, and go, and come again.

Throatfuls of life, arms crammed with brilliant days,
the colored years beat strength upon her youth,
pain-bombs exploded her body, joy rocketed in her,
the stranger forests, the books, the bitter times,
preluded college in a sheltered town.
            Remembering the pale suede jacket and russet coat
            swinging down avenues of trees together,
            the nights of talk   light cast from copper bowls,
            the fugitive journey to the coal-hills : names,
            Del Thomas, Tony Mancuso, Mrs. Silva,
            the black river curdling under a midnight wind.
            Remembering how the pale wrists flickered love,
            the dark eye-sockets impelled her to the poor,
                    ring changes
                    tell of the loves in her life
                    tell how she loved.
This was my friend of whom I knew the face
the steel-straight intellect, broidered fantastic dreams
the quarrel by the lake
and knew the hopes

She died.   And must be dead.
And is not dead where memory prevails.

Cut the stone, deepen her name.
Her mother did not know her.
Her friends were not enough, we missed essentials.
Love was enough and its blossoms.   Behind her life
stands a tall flower-tree, around her life
are worked her valid words into her testament
of love and writing and a ring of love.

II / Holy Dying

Across the country, iron hands push up chimneys
black fingers stuck up from the blackened ground.
The rivers bend seaward urgent in blue reaches;
her pain turned seaward.   Her life extended past
the sea, the cities, the individual poor,
passionate and companioned, following life.

> Through the bright years reckless and proud
> dimming into that last impossible pain.
> We cannot think she will not come again.
> The words lean on the written line, the page
> is a signal fire   all the letters shine.
> Into this life is lowered now death's sign,
> the younger days flicker up, the poems burn,
> we cannot say Return.

Slowly her death is propelled into our lives
the yellow message   the clipped convenient style
the cancelled stamps   the telephone wires ring
confirming fear "You were right"   :   in a week's short while.
Her love was never handcuffed, her hates spoke up,
her life was a job of freedom.
                    Now the news comes, the *Times* prints a
                    name
                    the telephone rings short music over her.
Drink your coffee, open your throat for words.
Loving, she died in passion and holiness.
They share remorse who had required less.

III / Ritual for Death

Last night she died
Turn down the lamps tonight
shade the walls
           let the proud voices rise
out of the midnight street,   the whistle flying
up and along and flying in the street
the harsh struck stone,   a brake squealing the pause
and the brave silence after a lapse of sound.

Turn out the lights
Her body does not move
is striding over no hill in all the world
there is no avenue in Illinois shall know
the eager mouth,   the fine voluptuous hands
touch no more Mexicos in dream again.
There was a shadow deep along her cheek,
her eyes and hair were intricate with sun.
Now lights are out.
: Stand to me in the dark
Set your mouth on me for friends we did not know
Be strong in love
give strength to all we meet
the loving   the kind   the proletarian strong
convey our love to her in the grey fields
less grey for her, send her our breathing lives.
This was my friend
                forget the "my," speak out
This was my friend who   eager   rash   and brave
has found one answer in an early grave.
This is my body   : in its youth I find
strength given from the startle of her mind.
If we have strength in this evening, force life between her lips
    seal it   convey it   post it   the sheet discolored
    the ink already fading
                  the dead words fading
                  the dead all dead.

Out of the South are vivid flowers sent,
African daisies, red anemone   :
here are the riches of a continent,
and intellectual gifts   breaking you free,
poetry sounding in the narrow skull

sealing the sutures with music,   smoothing the cheek
with vocable comfort   the long hands of sorrow.
The full-blown flowers are given   :   our hands are full
of flowers and gestures   :   across New England dunes
where the stiff grasses rise against the sea,
across the city   the dark-red roofs, the stone,
across the Alleghanies,   down the Valley
the air speaks plenty   the words have all been spoken.

Upon what skies are these ambitions written?
across what field lies scattered the young wish,
beneath what seas toll all those fallen dreams—?

CITY OF MONUMENTS

Washington 1934

Be proud   you people   of these graves
these chiseled words   this precedent
From these blind ruins shines our monument.

Dead navies of the brain will sail
stone celebrate its final choice
when the air shakes, a single voice
a strong voice able to prevail   :

Entrust no hope to stone although the stone
shelter the root   :   see too-great burdens placed
with nothing certain but the risk
set on the infirm column of
the high memorial obelisk

erect in accusation sprung against
a barren sky taut over Anacostia   :
give over, Gettysburg   !   a word will shake your glory   :
blood of the starved fell thin upon this plain,
this battle is not buried with its slain.

Gravestone and battlefield retire
the whole green South is shadowed dark,
the slick white domes are cast in night.
But uneclipsed above the park

the veteran of the Civil War
sees havoc in the tended graves
the midnight bugles blown to free
still unemancipated slaves.

Blinded by chromium or transfiguration
we watch, as through a microscope, decay :
   down the broad streets the limousines
advance in passions of display.

Air glints with diamonds, and these clavicles
emerge through orchids by whose trailing spoor
the sensitive cannot mistake
the implicit anguish of the poor.

The throats incline, the marble men rejoice
careless of torrents of despair.

Split by a tendril of revolt
stone cedes to blossom everywhere.

STUDY IN A LATE SUBWAY

The moon revolves outside; possibly, black air
turns so around them facing night's concave,
momentum the slogan of their hurling brains
swung into speed, crying for stillness   high
      suspended and rising on time's wave.

Did these tracks have a wilder life in the ground?
beaten from streams of metal in secret earth   :
energy travels along the veins of steel,
their faces rush forward, missiles of discontent
      thrown vaguely to the south and north.

That head is jointed loosely on his neck,
his glossy eyes turn on the walls and floor   :
her face is a blank breast with sorrow
spouting at the mouth's nipple.   All eyes move
      heavily to the opening door,

regarding in dullness how we also enter.
An angle of track charges up to us, swings
out and past in a firework of signals.
Sleepily others dangle by one hand
      tense and semi-crucified things.

Speed welcomes us in explosions of night　:　here
is wrath and fortitude and motion's burning　:
the world buries the directionless, until
the heads are sprung in awareness or drowned in peace.
　　　Sleep will happen.　　We must give them morning.

CHILD AND MOTHER

for Vega Hustana

Revolution shall be a toy of peace to you,
children during our effort.　　Storm covers all our days
the tracts of sunlight overcome with thunder
black on this ocean and our youth going.
Slowly our world is shaped to a new country
for living minute fingers, the duplicated flesh　:
The old will surrender, forced under; they endure
though dead adults walk stiffly in the street
cramming the dead poor in their mouths for meat.

　　　　Seashores of centuries
　　　　all cosmic whisperings
　　　　ripple upon this beach,
　　　　listen until she sings
　　　　lullaby to all sudden
　　　　　all grievous things.

　　　　Rome fashioned you blankets
　　　　Asia, a coverlet,
　　　　we live for your smiling　:
　　　　sleep, we shall not forget　:
　　　　these worlds are straining
　　　　　to make your Soviet.

Beaches of darkness! the transparent foam-lips hurrying,
　　pouring
spent on the margin trailing sea-currents
mid-ocean streams　:　at the sand, ankle-deep
mother with child braced in the hip's firm socket
fronting the torrents.

Nakedly to the extreme of the world come bathers
advancing, the pale skin pathetic against the sea,
untried and bare　:　the flesh, the bones' thin tubes

facing dim oceans, raving hurricane, windspill,
leviathan-tyranny.

> Child, you shall grow to follow,
> survive, and find
> wet hollow, submarine terror
> not so unkind
> as to blast strength, your eyes
> unsealed, and an armed mind.

Child leans the dark head against protective side
turning its look softly to the horizon
moving its hand along the rapid wind.
The mother knows this ocean and will tell
clews to the young eyes' candor, fertile thoughts
will be asserted.
            Rage, ocean :   foam, oppressions,
We stand, and these children follow, and all will yet be well.

Chaos is split :   the first slow definite strides
are taken against the open waters ;   be
fresh growth, be confident for braveries
    we and our children meet these tides
prows of revolt launched among barbarous seas.

ECCENTRIC MOTION

> Dashing in glass we race,
> New York to Washington :
> encased with bubbles lie
> in emerald spa :
> upholstered promenades
> convey us far.
> Have we reached the last limits?
> What have we not done?
>
> Shut into velvet we
> survey the scene,
> the locked-up building,
> the frozen pier :
> before and before the events,
> we loved our minds in fear :
> they wriggle into worms.

We watch.   We turn.   Surrounded,
we are at last closed in.

Coated in learning, do we
cause its crown to fall?
the plane, the bath, the car
extend our protection   :
(But have we seen it all?
Shall we continue
in this direction?   :   )

This is not the way
to save the day.
Get up and dress and go
nobly to and fro   :
Dashing in glass we race,
New York to Mexico. . . .

SUNDAYS, THEY SLEEP LATE

The days are incestuous, each with its yesterday,
and they, walking heavily in the streets, atone for the
    moment's
sin   :   their memories laboring under the weight of today
in its perverse alliance with the past.   Laments

are heard, droning from the city on all other mornings
but Sundays, they sleep late, and need not cry to wake,
sniffling in the pillow, realizing the day's churnings
of minute resolving to minute, and the whole day slack,

the wind bled of vigor, the talk in the parlor
of people pasturing on each other's minds, and sunset
evolving in the air, a quiet change against the duller
signs in pandemonium of day's gradual transit:

the klaxon voices through the roads, the picnickers joking
(returning from the fields), who wept before they dressed.
On Sundays their dreams are longer, and their waking
is a long exhalation of their weeks, decompressed.

There are these things to be remembered: the nine boys
    waiting,
battle-fronts of the rising army with holes bitten by death,

the man in the prison overland, and history beating
out the recurrent facts of power, suppression, wrath.

The days are incestuous.   They witness the daily binding
of minutes linking backwards.   Their remembering atones
in no part for the things they remember.   They sink in
   blinding
sleep too long, they dissolve in sleep their remembering bones.

THOUSANDS OF DAYS

Morning cried by the bed   :
at Seven, I understood   —
by Eight, I was very God,
happiness in my head.

At Nine, I went to work,
and all the machines spoke   :
Quiet there!   Don't talk,
make, break and make   !

At Ten, I opened my book
and all that hour I read
'The tallest men are dead,
their graveyard's in your look. . . .'

I rose, angered, through sky
in a plane of glass,
dreaming speed, I pass
very bright, very high.

As it went up toward Noon
I heard the sun scream   :
fly, suck your yellow dream,
we'll end it soon.

I fell all through One,
howling and threatening,
until at Two I sing
of a far reunion   :

On Three the masses spread,
a fist opening bare,
a great hand in the square
to vindicate the dead.

By Four the men had gone,
the land was wet with rain
and a fountain stood up plain
on every lawn.

The clock picked at Five,
those jets turned silver then
with the lovely words of men
who wrote and remained alive,

prophesying the night
of Six, and the dawn behind ;
but, creeping down the wind,
Seven snatched all the light.

Now am I left alone
waiting for day :
sometimes I turn away,
sometimes I sleep like stone.

Midnight is on my heels,
death bites about my legs.
While all my courage sags
the endless night wheels,

danger yells, and with
this blackness comes
back confidence, and blooms
in song and act and myth.

Call off your black dog, death,
it cannot bark me down :
I'll travel past these wounds
and speak another breath !

THE SURROUNDED

They escape before, but their shadows walk behind,
filling the city with formidable dark,
spilling black over the sun's run gold, speeding a rumor
of warfare and the sciences of death, and work
of treason and exposure, following
me for an easy mark.

The sky is travelled by brightness, clouds ignite,
flame is incised upon the martyred air ;

the city dissolves in foaming craters, stars
falling in multitudes dazzle the sky with fire,
and I pursue them, I am pursued, and
they are everywhere.

Now there is no more brightness, and no shadow
but the shadow of a thought, and I'm in jail enough
to know conviction with prisoner certainty,
haunted by protest, lacking completion's proof
surrounded by shadows
more plausible than love.

BURLESQUE

Up in the second balcony
the dark man's hand moves at his thigh,
he turns congested eyes to floor.
The crowd still stamps and brays for more :

Magenta flares strip grace away
peeling attraction down to this :
thighs' alternation, shrugging breasts,
silk tapping the mons veneris ;

The adequate trough inclines and dips
rising venereally to view :
stained by the shifting light to blue,
the pearl scarf simmers at her hips.

With each contraction of desire
the appealing flesh is whipped entire,
ambushed in spasms.
                           In the street,
   the raw light serves as index to
   upturning avid faces who
   shine all the signals of defeat.

An army of horns moves up the hall,
drums hurry to their crisis where
awkward in fear, the audience
at last confronts a dancer bare :
these naked multitudes exposed to her :
   bright shoulders, glossy length of leg,
   the lapsing beat persists, to beg
salving of lives of these thighs' stir.

We are drenched in confusion, drowning among lights
that flare across stormed waters   showing here
the faces pitiable with hesitation,

eyes groaning past the corpse's sneer,
the twisted words of all the unlucky, spent
on brightened flesh of these impossible dear   :

The blemished faces and impeccable thighs
are those we paint with lights to make us wise,
consigning our total beauty now to this   :
the clutching loins and intolerable kiss.

MOVIE

Spotlight her face   her face has no light in it
touch the cheek with light   inform the eyes
press meanings on those lips.
                              See cities from the air,
fix a cloud in the sky, one bird in the bright air,
one perfect mechanical flower in her hair.

Make your young men ride over the mesquite plains   ;
produce our country on film   :   here are the flaming shrubs,
the Negroes put up their hands in Hallelujahs,
the young men balance at the penthouse door.
We focus on the screen   :   look   they tell us
you are a nation of similar whores   remember the Maine
remember you have a democracy of champagne   —

And slowly the female face kisses the young man,
over his face the twelve-foot female head
the yard-long mouth enlarges and yawns
                              The End

Here is a city   here the village grows
here are the rich men standing rows on rows,
but the crowd seeps behind the cowboy the lover the king,
past the constructed sets America rises
the bevelled classic doorways   the alleys of trees are witness
America rises in a wave a mass
pushing away the rot.

The Director cries Cut!
hoarsely CUT   and the people send pistons of force
crashing against the CUT! CUT! of the straw men.

Light is superfluous upon these eyes,
across our minds push new portents of strength
destroying the sets, the flat faces, the mock skies.

METAPHOR TO ACTION

Whether it is a speaker, taut on a platform,
who battles a crowd with the hammers of his words,
whether it is the crash of lips on lips
after absence and wanting   :   we must close
the circuits of ideas, now generate,
that leap in the body's action or the mind's repose.

Over us is a striking on the walls of the sky,
here are the dynamos, steel-black, harboring flame,
here is the man night-walking who derives
tomorrow's manifestoes from this midnight's meeting   ;
here we require the proof in solidarity,
iron on iron, body on body, and the large single beating.

And behind us in time are the men who second us
as we continue.   And near us is our love   :
no forced contempt, no refusal in dogma, the close
of the circuit in a fierce dazzle of purity.
And over us is night a field of pansies unfolding,
charging with heat its softness in a symbol
to weld and prepare for action our minds' intensity.

CITATION FOR HORACE GREGORY

These are our brave, these with their hands in on the work,
hammering out beauty upon the painful stone
turning their grave heads passionately finding
truth and alone and each day subtly slain
and each day born.
                    Revolves
a measured system, world upon world, stemmed fires
and regulated galaxies behind the flattened head,
behind the immortal skull, ticking eternity
in blood and the symbols of living.

The brass voice speaks in the street

STRIKE   STRIKE

the nervous fingers continue elaborately
drawing consciousness, examining, doing.
Rise to a billboard world of Chesterfields,
Mae West hip-wriggles, Tarzan prowess, the little
nibbling and despicable minds.

Here, gentlemen,

here is our gallery of poets   :

Jeffers,

a long and tragic drum-roll beating anger,
sick of a catapulting nightmare world,
Eliot, who led us to the precipice
subtly and perfectly   ;   there striking an attitude
rigid and ageing on the penultimate step,
the thoughtful man MacLeish who bent his head
feeling the weight of the living; bent, and turned
the grave important face round to the dead.

And on your left, ladies and gentlemen   :   poets.

Young poets and makers, solve your anguish, see
the brave unmedalled, who dares to shape his mind,
printed with dignity, to the machines of change.
A procession of poets adds one footbeat to the
implacable metric line   :   the great and unbetrayed
    after the sunlight and the failing yellow,
    after the lips bitten with passion and
    gentle, after the deaths, below
    dance-floors of celebration   we turn   we turn
these braveries are permanent.   These gifts
flare on our lives, clarifying, revealed.

We are too young to see our funerals
in pantomime nightly before uneasy beds,
too near beginnings for this hesitation
obliterated in death or carnival.
Deep into time extend the impersonal stairs,
    established barricades will stand,
before they die the brave have set their hand
on rich particular beauty for their heirs.

CATS AND A COCK

for Eleanor Clark

What hill can ever hold us?
                              Standing high
we saw December packed, snow upon snow,
empty until the cars, leaping in beams below,
opened the shadow of the trees in fans
enormous on the plain, fragile and magnified.
Print of the delicate branch sweeping our feet
in hundred hugeness, passing to white again.

Up the dark hill a pack of cats :
bursting from hollows, streaming to the crest,
streaming all night toward dawn
when green invaded east.
We stood to hear the rigid cock cry Five
a black cock crowing over cold water,
when all those cats found their sole proud objective
and whirled away to slaughter.

———————

We walk the streets
of the dark city,
placards at back
light in our heads,

Moon rides over us
town streams below :
Strike and support us
the strike-songs go.

Ceilings of stars
disturb our faces,
tantrums of light
summon our eyes;

The daystar stands
hungry for day :
we file, regarding
this twin morning.

Shall that bind us,
parade and planet,
mobile and point?
No, not yet,

there is a labor
before reunion.
Poets, pickets,
prepare for dawn!

———————————

Come chop the days
lop off the moving hours,
we had not known there were disparate things.

Forget these syntheses and fade
peerless and distant into a distant grave
still hoping unity indeed be made?

I wish you to be saved . . . you wish . . . he wishes . . . she . . .
in conjugation of a destiny.
We were figures rubbed by wind passing upon a frieze,
galloping figures at a column's base
hungrily running from death and marble space.

I give you cats : I give you a cock on a hill :
these stream in beauty : that stands blocked in pride
I pledge you death until
they fight and acquiesce, or one has died.

Earnestly and slowly I continue :
no one could guess how the impact of a word
heard plain and plainly understood
can have attacked us so and so deferred.

Fight them down, deliver yourself, friend!
see, we all fight it down : poetry, picket-line,
to master pride and muscle fluid with sun,
conflicting graces moving to one end.

———————————

Witness the unfailing war, season with season,
license and principle, sex with tortured sex,
class versus class, and help us to survey
this city for faces, this hill for tracks.

Sickness will bind itself upon our tissue
clipping off with restriction blood and heat and milk,
becoming real against all disbelief
a sly ghost coughing to advertise its bulk.

Climax to Egypt, our milestone pyramid
forces out history and we remember
conflict of thousands of April processions,
rival winds ripping at the heart's deep chamber.

No natural poison : a vicious, banker's thrust
nudges toward dissolution during war,
this peak of open battle points disgust
of decay, counterattacks backing us to our door.

This is when death thrives in the rot
and formal nightmare, zebra of sleep,
presents us madness, diffusion to remember,
to cherish, loss if we lose; and dust to keep.

Resent the nightmare, assume a waking stance,
this clock revolt, held in the hand and striking,
clapping, the violent wings of a struck bird,
speaks your top hour, marks your fatal chance.

"Still elegiac! : between two battles, when one is happy
          to be alive !" — Rosa Luxemburg

Here was a battle forced by the brain's fortitude,
mapping machines of peace before crisis had come;
and by this planning we create a world
new-hearted, secure from common delirium.

If the strike was won, the prisoners freed at last,
the cataract tapped for power, parade-songs sung :
Prepare for continuance, open your brilliant love,
your life, — front April, give it tongue !

Below the flowering hedge
rest in the light, forget
grief's awful violet
and indecision's wedge
driven into your pride,
and how the past has died.

Here is transition :
pain, but no surgeon's knife
: anaesthetize your life?

you lose the vision
of how you simply walk
toward a younger folk,

simply, a flaming wire
advancing on the night,
reducing midnight
to clear noon-fire ;
moving upon the future
and large, clean stature
nearer to all your nature.

The latchpieces of consciousness unfasten.
We are stroked out of dream and night and myth,
and turning slowly to awareness, listen
to the soft bronchial whisperings of death.

Never forget in legendary darkness
the ways of the hands' turning and the mouth's ways,
wander in the fields of change and not remember
a voice and many voices and the evening's burning.

Turn and remember, this is the world made plain
by chart and signal, instrument and name :

to some we say Master, others call Sister,
to some we offer nothing but love :

flier in advance, the cloud over his mouth ;
the inventor who produces the moment of proof ;
a sun and moon and other several stars ;
and those who know each other over wars.

Cats stream upon a hill,
the poet-cock breaks his throat now to say :
Moment of Proof, May dawn transposing night,
partisan dawn's on the side of day!

What hill can ever hold us?
                        Deeply night
found you intent upon this city river,
asleep at heart (turn light to her at last,
it shall be to her
as wellwater)   :

going all day along the gilded air
you saw at midnight
(going, down to the river, haunted by fog-horns) :
steam escaping over the spouting manhole,
a rout of white cats racing through the street.
Wet street, and the fight was ended there,
cats and that cock, fearful antagonists
resolved in fog, a quick pack running uphill
to a cock rigid with joy; running, but not to kill.

> "Forehead to forehead I meet thee, this third time,
> Moby Dick!"   —   Herman Melville

Moment of proof, when the body holds its vision,
masses recognize masses, knowledge without all end   ;
face fathoms other face, all the hills open sunrise,
mouth sets on mouth   ;   Spring, and the tulips
               totter in the wind.

Forfeit in love, forfeit in conflict, here
met and at last marked clear in principle,
desire meets desire, the chase expands, and now
forever we course, knowing the marks of growth,
               seeing the signals.

Now we remember winter-tormented cities,
the August farm's overgrown hollow, thick with goldenrod,
the impetus of strain, and places where
love set its terminals, the vivid hunger
               and satisfying food.

Mayday is moment of proof, when recognition
binds us in protest, binds us under a sun
of love and subtle thought and the ductile wish.
Tomorrow's Mayday.   :   How many are we?
               We'll be everyone.

No hill can ever hold us, peak enlists peak,
climax forces out climax, proud cock, cats streaming,
poets and pickets contriving a valid country,
:   Mayday moment, forever provoking new
               belief and blooming.

THE BLOOD IS JUSTIFIED

Beat out continuance in the choking veins
before emotion betrays us, and we find
staring behind our faces, accomplices of death.
Not to die, but slowly to validate our lives   :
simply to move, lightly burdened, alone,
carrying in this brain survival, carrying
within these ribs, history,
the past deep in the bone.

    Unthread time till its empty needle prick your flesh
    sewing your scars with air, treating the wounds
    only by laceration   and the blood is fresh
    blood on our skin on our lips over our eyes.

Living they move on a canvas of centuries
restored from death in artful poses, found
once more by us, descendants, foraging,
ravelling time back over American ground.
How did they wish, grandparents of these wars,
what cataracts of ambition fell across their brains?   :

The heavy boots kicked stones down Wisconsin roads,
Augusta Coller danced her début at Oshkosh   :
they spoke these names   :   Milwaukee, Waukesha,
the crackle and drawl of Indian strange words.

    Jungle-savage the south
    raw green and shining branches, the crying
    of parakeets, the pointed stone,
    the altars stained with oil   :
    Mexico   :   and Canada wheaten and polar with
    snow halfway up the sky   :
    all these unknown.

:   What treason to their race has fathered us?
   They walked in the towns, the men selling clothing etc.
   the women tatting and boiling down grape jelly.
:   If they were asked this, surely they did not answer.

Over the country, Wisconsin, Chicago, Yonkers,
I was begotten, American branch no less because
I call on the great names of other countries.
I do not say   :   Forgive, to my kindred dead,

only   :   Understand my treason, See I betray you kissing,
I overthrow your milestones weeping among your tombs.

From out your knowing eyes I sprang, child of your distant wombs,
of your full lips.   Speaking allegiance, I turn,
steadfastly to destroy your hope.   Your cargo in me
swings to ports hostile to your old intent.

In us recurrences.   :   My generation feeds
the wise assault on your anticipation,
repeating historic sunderings, betraying our fathers,
all parricidal in our destinies.

How much are we American?   Not knowing
these other lands, being
blood wrung from your bone, our pioneers,
we call kindred to you, we claim links, speaking
your tongue, although we pass, shaking
your dream with revolution since we must.
By these roads shall we come upon our country.
Pillowed upon this birthright, we may wake
strong for such treason, brave with your fallen dust.

O, we are afflicted with these present evils,
they press between the mirror and our eyes,
obscuring your loaned mouths and borrowed hair.
We focus on our times, destroying you, fathers
in the long ground   :   you have given strange birth
to us who turn against you in our blood
needing to move in our integrity, accomplices
of life in revolution, though the past
be sweet with your tall shadows, and although
we turn from treasons, we shall accomplish these.

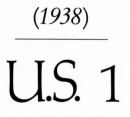

(1938)

U.S. 1

for Horace Gregory

The Book of the Dead

THE ROAD

These are roads to take when you think of your country
and interested bring down the maps again,
phoning the statistician, asking the dear friend,

reading the papers with morning inquiry.
Or when you sit at the wheel and your small light
chooses gas gauge and clock; and the headlights

indicate future of road, your wish pursuing
past the junction, the fork, the suburban station,
well-travelled six-lane highway planned for safety.

Past your tall central city's influence,
outside its body: traffic, penumbral crowds,
are centers removed and strong, fighting for good reason.

These roads will take you into your own country.
Select the mountains, follow rivers back,
travel the passes. Touch West Virginia where

the Midland Trail leaves the Virginia furnace,
iron Clifton Forge, Covington iron, goes down
into the wealthy valley, resorts, the chalk hotel.

Pillars and fairway; spa; White Sulphur Springs.
Airport. Gay blank rich faces wishing to add
history to ballrooms, tradition to the first tee.

The simple mountains, sheer, dark-graded with pine
in the sudden weather, wet outbreak of spring,
crosscut by snow, wind at the hill's shoulder.

The land is fierce here, steep, braced against snow,
rivers and spring. KING COAL HOTEL, Lookout,
and swinging the vicious bend, New River Gorge.

Now the photographer unpacks camera and case,
surveying the deep country, follows discovery
viewing on groundglass an inverted image.

John Marshall named the rock (steep pines, a drop
he reckoned in 1812, called) Marshall's Pillar,
but later, Hawk's Nest. Here is your road, tying

you to its meanings: gorge, boulder, precipice.
Telescoped down, the hard and stone-green river
cutting fast and direct into the town.

WEST VIRGINIA

They saw rivers flow west and hoped again.
Virginia speeding to another sea!
1671—Thomes Batts, Robert Fallam,
Thomas Wood, the Indian Perecute,
and an unnamed indentured English servant
followed the forest past blazed trees, pillars of God,
were the first whites emergent from the east.
They left a record to our heritage,
breaking of records. Hoped now for the sea,
for all mountains have their descents about them,
waters, descending naturally, doe alwaies resort
unto the seas invironing those lands . . .
yea, at home amongst the mountaines in England.

Coming where this road comes,
flat stones spilled water which the still pools fed.
Kanawha Falls, the rapids of the mind,
fast waters spilling west.

Found Indian fields, standing low cornstalks left,
learned three Mohetons planted them; found-land
farmland, the planted home, discovered!

War-born:
The battle at Point Pleasant, Cornstalk's tribes,
last stand, Fort Henry, a revolution won;
the granite SITE OF THE precursor EXECUTION
sabres, apostles OF JOHN BROWN LEADER OF THE
War's brilliant cloudy RAID AT HARPERS FERRY.
Floods, heavy wind this spring, the beaten land
blown high by wind, fought wars, forming a state,
a surf, frontier defines two fighting halves,
two hundred battles in the four years: troops

here in Gauley Bridge, Union headquarters, lines
bring in the military telegraph.
Wires over the gash of gorge and height of pine.

But it was always the water
the power flying deep
green rivers cut the rock
rapids boiled down,
a scene of power.

Done by the dead.
Discovery learned it.
And the living?

Live country filling west,
knotted the glassy rivers;
like valleys, opening mines,
coming to life.

STATEMENT: PHILIPPA ALLEN

—You like the State of West Virginia very much, do you not?
—I do very much, in the summertime.
—How much time have you spent in West Virginia?
—During the summer of 1934, when I was doing social work
    down there, I first heard of what we were pleased to call
    the Gauley tunnel tragedy, which involved about 2,000
    men.
—What was their salary?
—It started at 40¢ and dropped to 25¢ an hour.
—You have met these people personally?
—I have talked to people; yes.
    According to estimates of contractors
    2,000 men were
        employed there
        period, about 2 years
        drilling, 3.75 miles of tunnel.
        To divert water (from New River)
        to a hydroelectric plant (at Gauley Junction).
    The rock through which they were boring was of a high
        silica content.
    In tunnel No. 1 it ran 97–99% pure silica.

The contractors
    knowing pure silica
    30 years' experience
    must have known danger for every man
neglected to provide the workmen with any safety device. . . .
—As a matter of fact, they originally intended to dig that
    tunnel a certain size?
—Yes.
—And then enlarged the size of the tunnel, due to the fact
    that they discovered silica and wanted to get it out?
—That is true for tunnel No. 1.
    The tunnel is part of a huge water-power project
        begun, latter part of 1929
        direction: New Kanawha Power Co.
                subsidiary of Union Carbide & Carbon Co.
        That company—licensed:
        to develop power for public sale.
        Ostensibly it was to do that; but
        (in reality) it was formed to sell all the power to
                the Electro-Metallurgical Co.
                subsidiary of Union Carbide & Carbon Co.
                  which by an act of the State legislature
                  was allowed to buy up
              New Kanawha Power Co. in 1933.
—They were developing the power. What I am trying to
    get at, Miss Allen, is, did they use this silica from the
    tunnel; did they afterward sell it and use it in com-
    merce?
—They used it in the electro-processing of steel.
SiO_2 SiO_2
The richest deposit.
Shipped on the C & O down to Alloy.
It was so pure that
                SiO_2
they used it without refining.
—Where did you stay?
—I stayed at Cedar Grove. Some days I would have to hitch
    into Charleston, other days to Gauley Bridge.
—You found the people of West Virginia very happy to pick
    you up on the highway, did you not?
—Yes; they are delightfully obliging.
    (All were bewildered. Again at Vanetta they are asking,
      "What can be done about this?")

I feel that this investigation may help in some manner.
I do hope it may.
I am now making a very general statement as a beginning.
There are many points that I should like to develop
later, but I shall try to give you a general history of
this condition first. . . .

GAULEY BRIDGE

Camera at the crossing sees the city
a street of wooden walls and empty windows,
the doors shut handless in the empty street,
and the deserted Negro standing on the corner.

The little boy runs with his dog
up the street to the bridge over the river where
nine men are mending road for the government.
He blurs the camera-glass fixed on the street.

Railway tracks here and many panes of glass
tin under light, the grey shine of towns and forests:
in the commercial hotel (Switzerland of America)
the owner is keeping his books behind the public glass.

Postoffice window, a hive of private boxes,
the hand of the man who withdraws, the woman who reaches
   her hand
and the tall coughing man stamping an envelope.

The bus station and the great pale buses stopping for food;
April-glass-tinted, the yellow-aproned waitress;
coast-to-coast schedule on the plateglass window.

The man on the street and the camera eye:
he leaves the doctor's office, slammed door, doom,
any town looks like this one-street town.

Glass, wood, and naked eye: the movie-house
closed for the afternoon frames posters streaked with rain,
advertise "Racing Luck" and "Hitch-Hike Lady."

Whistling, the train comes from a long way away,
slow, and the Negro watches it grow in the grey air,
the hotel man makes a note behind his potted palm.

Eyes of the tourist house, red-and-white filling station,
the eyes of the Negro, looking down the track,
hotel-man and hotel, cafeteria, camera.

And in the beerplace on the other sidewalk
always one's harsh night eyes over the beerglass
follow the waitress and the yellow apron.

The road flows over the bridge,
Gamoca pointer at the underpass,
opposite, Alloy, after a block of town.

What do you want—a cliff over a city?
A foreland, sloped to sea and overgrown with roses?
These poeple live here.

THE FACE OF THE DAM: VIVIAN JONES

On the hour he shuts the door and walks out of town;
he knows the place up the gorge where he can see
his locomotive rusted on the siding,
he sits and sees the river at his knee.

There, where the men crawl, landscaping the grounds
at the power-plant, he saw the blasts explode
the mouth of the tunnel that opened wider
when precious in the rock the white glass showed.

The old plantation-house (burned to the mud)
is a hill-acre of ground. The Negro woman throws
gay arches of water out from the front door.
It runs down, wild as grass, falls and flows.

On the quarter he remembers how they enlarged
the tunnel and the crews, finding the silica,
how the men came riding freights, got jobs here
and went innto the tunnel-mouth to stay.

Never to be used, he thinks, never to spread its power,
jinx on the rock, curse on the power-plant,
hundreds breathed value, filled their lungs full of glass
(O the gay wind the clouds the many men).

On the half-hour he's at Hawk's Nest over the dam,
snow springs up as he reaches the great wall-face,

immense and pouring power, the mist of snow,
the fallen mist, the slope of water, glass.

O the gay snow the white dropped water, down,
all day the water rushes down its river,
unused, has done its death-work in the country,
proud gorge and festive water.

On the last quarter he pulls his heavy collar up,
feels in his pocket the picture of his girl,
touches for luck—he used to as he drove
after he left his engine; stamps in the deep snow.

And the snow clears and the dam stands in the gay weather,
O proud O white O water rolling down,
he turns and stamps this off his mind again
and on the hour walks again through town.

PRAISE OF THE COMMITTEE

These are the lines on which a committee is formed.
    Almost as soon as work was begun in the tunnel
    men began to die among dry drills. No masks.
    Most of them were not from this valley.
    The freights brought many every day from States
    all up and down the Atlantic seaboard
    and as far inland as Kentucky, Ohio.
    After the work the camps were closed or burned.
    The ambulance was going day and night,
    White's undertaking business thriving and
    his mother's cornfield put to a new use.
    "Many of the shareholders at this meeting
    "were nervous about the division of the profits;
    "How much has the Company spent on lawsuits?
    "The man said $150,000. Special counsel:
    "I am familiar with the case. Not : one : cent.
    " 'Terms of the contract. Master liable.'
    "No reply. Great corporation disowning men who made. . . ."
    After the lawsuits had been instituted. . . .
The Committee is a true reflection of the will of the people.
    Every man is ill. The women are not affected,
    This is not a contagious disease. A medical commission,
    Dr. Hughes, Dr. Hayhurst examined the chest

of Raymond Johnson, and Dr. Harless, a former
company doctor. But he saw too many die,
he has written his letter to Washington.
The Committee meets regularly, wherever it can.
Here are Mrs. Jones, three lost sons, husband sick,
Mrs. Leek, cook for the bus cafeteria,
the men: George Robinson, leader and voice,
four other Negroes (three drills, one camp-boy)
Blankenship, the thin friendly man, Peyton the engineer,
Juanita absent, the one outsider member.
Here in the noise, loud belts of the shoe-repair shop,
meeting around the stove beneath the one bulb hanging.
They come late in the day. Many come with them
who pack the hall, wait in the thorough dark.
This is a defense committee. Unfinished business:
Two rounds of lawsuits, 200 cases
Now as to the crooked lawyers
If the men had worn masks, their use would have involved
time every hour to wash the sponge at mouth.
Tunnel, 3⅛ miles long. Much larger than
the Holland Tunnel or Pittsburgh's Liberty Tubes.
Total cost, say, $16,000,000.
This is the procedure of such a committee:
To consider the bill before the Senate.
To discuss relief.
Active members may be cut off relief,
16-mile walk to Fayetteville for cheque—
WEST VIRGINIA RELIEF ADMINISTRATION, #22991,
TO JOE HENIGAN, GAULEY BRIDGE, ONE AND 50/100,
WINONA NATIONAL BANK. PAID FROM STATE FUNDS.
Unless the Defense Committee acts;
the *People's Press,* supporting this fight,
signed editorials, sent in funds.
Clothing for tunnel-workers.
Rumored, that in the post-office
parcels are intercepted.
Suspected: Conley. Sheriff, hotelman,
head of the town ring—
Company whispers. Spies,
The Racket.
Resolved, resolved.
George Robinson holds all their strength together:
To fight the companies   to make somehow a future.

78

"At any rate, it is inadvisable to keep a community of dying
   persons intact."
"Senator Holt. Yes. This is the most barbarous example of
   industrial construction that ever happened in the world."
Please proceed.
"In a very general way Hippocrates' *Epidemics* speaks
   of the metal digger who breathes with difficulty,
   having a pain and wan complexion.
   Pliny, the elder. . . ."
"Present work of the Bureau of Mines. . . ."

The dam's pure crystal slants upon the river.
   A dark and noisy room, frozen two feet from stove.
   The cough of habit. The sound of men in the hall
   waiting for word.

      These men breathe hard
      but the committee has a voice of steel.
      One climbs the hill on canes.
      They have broken the hills and cracked the riches wide.

      In this man's face
      family leans out from two worlds of graves—
      here is a room of eyes,
      a single force looks out, reading our life.

      Who stands over the river?
      Whose feet go running in these rigid hills?
      Who comes, warning the night,
      shouting and young to waken our eyes?

      Who runs through electric wires?
      Who speaks down every road?
      Their hands touched mastery; now they
      demand an answer.

MEARL BLANKENSHIP

He stood against the stove
facing the fire —
Little warmth, no words,
loud machines.

Voted relief,
wished money mailed,
quietly under the crashing:

"I wake up choking, and my wife
"rolls me over on my left side;
"then I'm asleep in the dream I always see:
"the tunnel choked
"the dark wall coughing dust.

"I have written a letter.
"Send it to the city,
"maybe to a paper
"if it's all right."

Dear Sir, my name is Mearl Blankenship.
I have Worked for the rhinehart & Dennis Co
Many days & many nights
& it was so dusty you couldn't hardly see the lights.
I helped nip steel for the drills
& helped lay the track in the tunnel
& done lots of drilling near the mouth of the tunnell
& when the shots went off the boss said
If you are going to work Venture back
& the boss was Mr. Andrews
& now he is dead and gone
But I am still here
a lingering along

He stood against the rock
facing the river
grey river grey face
the rock mottled behind him
like X-ray plate enlarged
diffuse and stony
his face against the stone.

J C Dunbar said that I was the very picture of health
when I went to Work at that tunnel.
I have lost eighteen lbs on that Rheinhart ground
and expecting to loose my life
& no settlement yet & I have sued the Co. twice
But when the lawyers got a settlement
they didn't want to talk to me
But I didn't know whether they were sleepy or not.
I am a Married Man and have a family.   God
knows if they can do anything for me
it will be appreciated

if you can do anything for me
let me know soon

ABSALOM

I first discovered what was killing these men.
I had three sons who worked with their father in the tunnel:
Cecil, aged 23, Owen, aged 21, Shirley, aged 17.
They used to work in a coal mine, not steady work
for the mines were not going much of the time.
A power Co. foreman learned that we made home brew,
he formed a habit of dropping in evenings to drink,
persuading the boys and my husband —
give up their jobs and take this other work.
It would pay them better.
Shirley was my youngest son; the boy.
He went into the tunnel.

My heart   my mother   my heart   my mother
My heart   my coming into being.

My husband is not able to work.
He has it, according to the doctor.
We have been having a very hard time making a living since
    this trouble came to us.
I saw the dust in the bottom of the tub.
The boy worked there about eighteen months,
came home one evening with a shortness of breath.
He said, "Mother, I cannot get my breath."
Shirley was sick about three months.
I would carry him from his bed to the table,
from his bed to the porch, in my arms.

My heart is mine in the place of hearts,
They gave me back my heart, it lies in me.

When they took sick, right at the start, I saw a doctor.
I tried to get Dr. Harless to X-ray the boys.
He was the only man I had any confidence in,
the company doctor in the Kopper's mine,
but he would not see Shirley.
He did not know where his money was coming from.
I promised him half if he'd work to get compensation,
but even then he would not do anything.

I went on the road and begged the X-ray money,
the Charleston hospital made the lung pictures,
he took the case after the pictures were made.
And two or three doctors said the same thing.
The youngest boy did not get to go down there with me,
he lay and said, "Mother, when I die,
"I want you to have them open me up and
"see if that dust killed me.
"Try to get compensation,
"you will not have any way of making your living
"when we are gone,
"and the rest are going too."

    I have gained mastery over my heart
    I have gained mastery over my two hands
    I have gained mastery over the waters
    I have gained mastery over the river.

The case of my son was the first of the line of lawsuits.
They sent the lawyers down and the doctors down;
they closed the electric sockets in the camps.
There was Shirley, and Cecil, Jeffrey and Oren,
Raymond Johnson, Clev and Oscar Anders,
Frank Lynch, Henry Palf, Mr. Pitch, a foreman;
a slim fellow who carried steel with my boys,
his name was Darnell, I believe. There were many others,
the towns of Glen Ferris, Alloy, where the white rock lies,
six miles away; Vanetta, Gauley Bridge,
Gamoca, Lockwood, the gullies,
the whole valley is witness.
I hitchhike eighteen miles, they make checks out.
They asked me how I keep the cow on $2.
I said one week, feed for the cow, one week, the children's
    flour.
The oldest son was twenty-three.
The next son was twenty-one.
The youngest son was eighteen.
They called it pneumonia at first.
They would pronounce it fever.
Shirley asked that we try to find out.
That's how they learned what the trouble was.

    I open out a way, they have covered my sky with crystal
    I come forth by day,' I am born a second time,

I force a way through, and I know the gate
I shall journey over the earth among the living.

He shall not be diminished, never;
I shall give a mouth to my son.

THE DISEASE

This is a lung disease. Silicate dust makes it.
The dust causing the growth of

This is the X-ray picture taken last April.
I would point out to you: these are the ribs;
this is the region of the breastbone;
this is the heart (a wide white shadow filled with blood).
In here of course is the swallowing tube, esophagus.
The windpipe. Spaces between the lungs.

Between the ribs?

Between the ribs. These are the collar bones.
Now, this lung's mottled, beginning, in these areas.
You'd say a snowstorm had struck the fellow's lungs.
About alike, that side and this side, top and bottom.
The first stage in this period in this case.

Let us have the second.

Come to the window again. Here is the heart.
More numerous nodules, thicker, see, in the upper lobes.
You will notice the increase : here, streaked fibrous tissue—

Indicating?

That indicates the progress in ten months' time.
And now, this year—short breathing, solid scars
even over the ribs, thick on both sides.
Blood vessels shut. Model conglomeration.

What stage?

Third stage. Each time I place my pencil point:
There and there and there, there, there.

    "It is growing worse every day. At night
    "I get up to catch my breath. If I remained
    "flat on my back I believe I would die."

It gradually chokes off the air cells in the lungs?
I am trying to say it the best I can.
That is what happens, isn't it?
A choking-off in the air cells?

Yes.
There is difficulty in breathing.
Yes.
And a painful cough?
Yes.

Does silicosis cause death?

Yes, sir.

GEORGE ROBINSON: BLUES

Gauley Bridge is a good town for Negroes, they let us stand
    around, they let us stand
around on the sidewalks if we're black or brown.
Vanetta's over the trestle, and that's our town.

The hill makes breathing slow, slow breathing after you row
    the river,
and the graveyard's on the hill, cold in the springtime blow,
the graveyard's up on high, and the town is down below.

Did you ever bury thirty-five men in a place in back of your
    house,
thirty-five tunnel workers the doctors didn't attend,
died in the tunnel camps, under rocks, everywhere, world
    without end.

When a man said I feel poorly, for any reason, any weakness or
    such,
letting up when he couldn't keep going barely,
the Cap and company come and run him off the job surely.

I've put them
DOWN from the tunnel camps
to the graveyard on the hill,
tin-cans all about—it fixed them!—

TUNNELITIS
hold themselves up
at the side of a tree,
I can go right now
to that cemetery.

When the blast went off the boss would call out, Come, let's
    go back,
when that heavy loaded blast went white, Come, let's go back,
telling us hurry, hurry, into the falling rocks and muck.

The water they would bring had dust in it, our drinking water,
the camps and their groves were colored with the dust,
we cleaned our clothes in the groves, but we always had the dust.
Looked like somebody sprinkled flour all over the parks and
    groves,
it stayed and the rain couldn't wash it away and it twinkled
that white dust really looked pretty down around our ankles.

As dark as I am, when I came out at morning after the tunnel
    at night,
with a white man, nobody could have told which man was
    white.
The dust had covered us both, and the dust was white.

JUANITA TINSLEY

Even after the letters, there is work,
sweaters, the food, the shoes
and afternoon's quick dark

draws on the windowpane
my face, the shadowed hair,
the scattered papers fade.

Slow letters! I shall be
always—the stranger said
"To live stronger and free."

I know in America there are songs,
forgetful ballads to be sung,
but at home I see this wrong.

When I see my family house,
the gay gorge, the picture-books,
they raise the face of General Wise

aged by enemies, like faces
the stranger showed me in the town.
I saw that plain, and saw my place.

The scene of hope's ahead; look, April,
and next month with a softer wind,
maybe they'll rest upon their land,
and then maybe the happy song, and love,
a tall boy who was never in a tunnel.

THE DOCTORS

—Tell the jury your name.
—Emory R. Hayhurst.
—State your education, Doctor, if you will.
Don't be modest about it; just tell about it.

High school Chicago 1899
Univ. of Illinois 1903
M.A. 1905, thesis on respiration
P & S Chicago 1908
2 years' hospital training;
at Rush on occupational disease
director of clinic 2½ years.
Ph.D. Chicago 1916
Ohio Dept. of Health, 20 years as
consultant in occupational diseases.
Hygienist, U.S. Public Health Service
and Bureau of Mines
and Bureau of Standards

Danger begins at 25%
here was pure danger
Dept. of Mines
came in, was kept away.

Miner's phthisis, fibroid phthisis,
grinder's rot, potter's rot,
whatever it used to be called,
these men did not need to die.

—Is silicosis an occupational disease?

—It is.

—Did anyone show you the lungs of Cecil Jones?

—Yes, sir.

—Who was that?

—It was Dr. Harless.

"We talked to Dr. L. R. Harless, who had handled many of the cases, more than any other doctor there. At first Dr. Harless did not like to talk about the matter. He said he had been subjected to so much publicity. It appeared that the doctor thought he had been involved in too many of the court cases; but finally he opened up and told us about the matter."

—Did he impress you as one who thought this was a very serious thing in that section of the country?

"Yes, he did. I would say that Dr. Harless has probably become very self-conscious about this matter. I cannot say that he has retracted what he told me, but possibly he had been thrust into the limelight so much that he is more conservative now than when the matter was simply something of local interest."

Dear Sir: Due to illness of my wife and urgent professional duties, I am unable to appear as per your telegram.

Situation exaggerated. Here are facts:

We examined. 13 dead. 139 had some lung damage.

2 have died since, making 15 deaths.

Press says 476 dead, 2,000 affected and doomed.

I am at a loss to know where those figures were obtained.

At this time, only a few cases here,

and these only moderately affected.

Last death occurred November, 1934.

It has been said that none of the men knew of the hazard connected with the work. This is not correct. Shortly after the work began many of these workers came to me complaining of chest conditions and I warned many of them of the dust hazard and advised them that continued work under these conditions would result in serious lung disease. Disregarding this warning many of the men continued at this work and later brought suit against their employer for damages.

While I am sure that many of these suits were based on meritorious grounds, I am also convinced that many others took advantage of this situation and made out of it nothing less than a racket.

In this letter I have endeavored to give you the facts which came under my observation. . . .

If I can supply further information. . . .

Mr. Marcantonio. A man may be examined a year after he has worked in a tunnel and not show a sign of silicosis, and yet the silicosis may develop later; is not that true?

—Yes, it may develop as many as ten years after.

Mr. Marcantonio. Even basing the statement on the figures, the doctor's claim that this is a racket is not justified?

—No; it would not seem to be justified.

Mr. Marcantonio. I should like to point out that Dr. Harless contradicts his "exaggeration" when he volunteers the following: "I warned many. . . ."

(Mr. Peyton. I do not know. Nobody knew the danger around there.)

Dr. Goldwater. First are the factors involving the individual.
               Under the heading B, external causes.
               Some of the factors which I have in mind—
               those are the facts upon the blackboard,
               the influencing and controlling factors.

Mr. Marcantonio. Those factors would bring about acute silicosis?

Dr. Goldwater. I hope you are not provoked when I say "might."
               Medicine has no hundred percent.
               We speak of possibilities, have opinions.

Mr. Griswold. Doctors testify answering "yes" and "no."
               Don't they?

Dr. Goldwater. Not by the choice of the doctor.

Mr. Griswold. But that is usual, isn't it?

Dr. Goldwater. They do not like to do that.
               A man with a scientific point of view—
               unfortunately there are doctors without that—
               I do not mean to say all doctors are angels—
               but most doctors avoid dogmatic statements.
               avoid assiduously "always," "never."

Mr. Griswold. Best doctor I ever knew said "no" and "yes."

Dr. Goldwater. There are different opinions on that, too.
               We were talking about acute silicosis.

The man in the white coat is the man on the hill,
the man with the clean hands is the man with the drill,
the man who answers "yes" lies still.

—Did you make an examination of those sets of lungs?
—I did.

—I wish you would tell the jury whether or not those lungs
  were silicotic.
—We object.
—Objection overruled.
—They were.

THE CORNFIELD

Error, disease, snow, sudden weather.
For those given to contemplation : this house,
wading in snow, its cracks are sealed with clay,
walls papered with print, newsprint repeating,
in-focus grey across the room, and squared
ads for a book : HEAVEN'S MY DESTINATION,
HEAVEN'S MY . . . HEAVEN. . . . THORNTON WILDER.
The long-faced man rises long-handed jams the door
tight against snow, long-boned, he shivers.
Contemplate.

          Swear by the corn,
the found-land corn, those who like ritual. *He*
rides in a good car. They say blind corpses rode
with him in front, knees broken into angles,
head clamped ahead. Overalls. Affidavits.
He signs all papers. His office : where he sits.
feet on the stove, loaded trestles through door,
satin-lined, silk-lined, unlined, cheap,
The papers in the drawer. On the desk, photograph
H. C. White, Funeral Services (new car and eldest son);
tells about Negroes who got wet at work,
shot craps, drank and took cold, pneumonia, died.
Shows the sworn papers. Swear by the corn.
Pneumonia, pneumonia, pleurisy, t.b.

For those given to voyages : these roads
discover gullies, invade, Where does it go now?
Now turn upstream twenty-five yards. Now road again.
Ask the man on the road. Saying, That cornfield?
Over the second hill, through the gate,
watch for the dogs. Buried, five at a time,
pine boxes, Rinehart & Dennis paid him $55
a head for burying these men in plain pine boxes.
His mother is suing him : misuse of land.

George Robinson : I knew a man
who died at four in the morning at the camp.
At seven his wife took clothes to dress her dead
husband, and at the undertaker's
they told her the husband was already buried.
—Tell me this, the men with whom you are acquainted,
the men who have this disease
have been told that sooner or later they are going to die?
—Yes, sir.
—How does that seem to affect the majority of the people?
—It don't work on anything but their wind.
—Do they seem to be living in fear
or do they wish to die?
—They are getting to breathe a little faster.

For those given to keeping their own garden:
Here is the cornfield, white and wired by thorns,
old cornstalks, snow, the planted home.
Stands bare against a line of farther field,
unmarked except for wood stakes, charred at tip,
few scratched and named (pencil or nail).
Washed-off. Under the mounds,
all the anonymous.
Abel America, calling from under the corn,
Earth, uncover my blood!
Did the undertaker know the man was married?
Uncover.
Do they seem to fear death?
Contemplate.
Does Mellon's ghost walk, povertied at last,
walking in furrows of corn, still sowing,
do apparitions come?
Voyage.
Think of your gardens. But here is corn to keep.
Marked pointed sticks to name the crop beneath.
Sowing is over, harvest is coming ripe.

—No, sir; they want to go on.
They want to live as long as they can.

ARTHUR PEYTON

Consumed. Eaten away. And love across the street.
I had a letter in the mail this morning

Dear Sir, . . . pleasure . . . enclosing herewith our check . . .
payable to you, for $21.59
            being one-half of the residue which
            we were able to collect in your behalf
            in regard to the above case.
In winding up the various suits,
            after collecting all we could,
            we find this balance due you.
With regards, we are
            Very truly,

After collecting
                the dust   the failure   the engineering corps
O love   consumed   eaten away   the foreman laughed
they wet the drills when the inspectors came
the moon blows glassy over our native river.

O love tell the committee that I know:
never repeat you mean to marry me.
In mines, the fans are large (2,000 men unmasked)
before his verdict the doctor asked me   How long
I said, Dr. Harless, tell me how long?
—Only never again tell me you'll marry me.
I watch how at the tables you all day
follow a line of clouds   the dance of drills,

and, love, the sky birds who crown the trees
the white white hills standing upon Alloy
—I charge negligence, all companies concerned—
two years O love two years he said he gave.

The swirl of river at the tidy house
the marble bank-face of the liquor store
I saw the Negroes driven with pick handles
on these other jobs I was not in tunnel work.

Between us, love
                the buses at the door
the long glass street   two years, my death to yours
my death upon your lips
my face becoming glass
strong challenged time making me win immortal
the love a mirror of our valley
our street   our river   a deadly glass to hold.
Now they are feeding me into a steel mill furnace
O love the stream of glass a stream of living fire.

ALLOY

This is the most audacious landscape. The gangster's
stance with his gun smoking and out is not so
vicious as this commercial field, its hill of glass.

Sloping as gracefully as thighs, the foothills
narrow to this, clouds over every town
finally indicate the stored destruction.

Crystalline hill: a blinded field of white
murdering snow, seamed by convergent tracks;
the travelling cranes reach for the silica.

And down the track, the overhead conveyor
slides on its cable to the feet of chimneys.
Smoke rises, not white enough, not so barbaric.

Here the severe flame speaks from the brick throat,
electric furnaces produce this precious, this clean,
annealing the crystals, fusing at last alloys.

Hottest for silicon, blast furnaces raise flames,
spill fire, spill steel, quench the new shape to freeze,
tempering it to perfected metal.

Forced through this crucible, a million men.
Above this pasture, the highway passes those
who curse the air, breathing their fear again.

The roaring flowers of the chimney-stacks
less poison, at their lips in fire, than this
dust that is blown from off the field of glass;

blows and will blow, rising over the mills,
crystallized and beyond the fierce corrosion
disintegrated angel on these hills.

POWER

The quick sun brings, exciting mountains warm,
gay on the landscapers and green designs,
miracle, yielding the sex up under all the skin,
until the entire body watches the scene with love,
sees perfect cliffs ranging until the river
cuts sheer, mapped far below in delicate track,

surprise of grace, the water running in the sun,
magnificent flower on the mouth, surprise
as lovers who look too long on the desired face
startle to find the remote flesh so warm.
A day of heat shed on the gorge, a brilliant
day when love sees the sun behind its man
and the disguised marvel under familiar skin.

Steel-bright, light-pointed, the narrow-waisted towers
lift their protective network, the straight, the accurate
flex of distinction, economy of gift,
gymnast, they poise their freight; god's generosity! give
their voltage low enough for towns to handle.
The power-house stands skin-white at the transmitters' side
over the rapids   the brilliance   the blind foam.

This is the midway between water and flame,
this is the road to take when you think of your country,
between the dam and the furnace, terminal.
The clean park, fan of wires, landscapers,
the stone approach. And seen beyond the door,
the man with the flashlight in his metal hall.
Here, the effective green, grey-toned and shining,
tall immense chamber of cylinders. Green,
the rich paint catches light from three-story windows,
arches of light vibrate erratic panels on
sides of curved steel. Man pockets flashlight,
useless, the brilliant floor casts tiled reflection up,
bland walls return it, circles pass it round.
Wheels, control panels, dials, the vassal instruments.
This is the engineer Jones, the blueprint man,
loving the place he designed, visiting it alone.
Another blood, no cousin to the town;
rings his heels on stone, pride follows his eyes,
"This is the place."

Four generators, smooth green, and squares of black,
floored-over space for a fifth.

                              The stairs. Descend.
"They said I built the floor like the tiles of a bank,
I wanted the men who work here to be happy."
Light laughing on steel, the gay, the tall sun
given away; mottled; snow comes in clouds;
the iron steps go down as roads go down.

This is the second circle, world of inner shade,
hidden bulk of generators, governor shaft,
round gap of turbine pit. Flashlight, tool-panels,
heels beating on iron, cold of underground,
stairs, wire flooring, the voice's hollow cry.
This is the scroll, the volute case of night,
quick shadow and the empty galleries.

Go down; here are the outlets, butterfly valves
open from here, the tail-race, vault of steel,
the spiral staircase ending, last light in shaft.
"Gone," says the thin straight man.
" 'Hail, holy light, offspring of Heav'n first-born,
'Or of th' Eternal Coeternal beam
'May I express thee unblamed?' "

         And still go down.

Now ladder-mouth; and the precipitous fear,
uncertain rungs down into after-night.
"This is the place. Away from this my life
I am indeed Adam unparadiz'd.
Some fools call this the Black Hole of Calcutta,
I don't know how they ever get to Congress."

Gulfs, spirals, that the drunken ladder swings,
its rungs give, pliant, beneath the leaping heart.
Leaps twice at midnight. But a naked bulb
makes glare, turns paler, burns to dark again.
Brilliance begins, stutters. And comes upon
after the tall abstract, the ill, the unmasked men,
the independent figure of the welder
masked for his work; acts with unbearable flame.
His face is a cage of steel, the hands are covered,
points dazzle hot, fly from his writing torch,
brighten the face and hands and marrying steel.
Says little, works : only : "A little down,
five men were killed in the widening of the tunnel."

Shell of bent metal; walking along an arc
the tube rounds up about your shoulders, black
circle, great circle, down infinite mountains rides,
echoes words, footsteps, testimonies.
"One said the air was thin, Fifth-Avenue clean."
The iron pillars mark a valve division,
four tunnels merging. Iron on iron resounds,

echoes along created gorges. "Sing,
test echoes, sing : Pilgrim," he cries,
singing *Once More, Dear Home,*
as all the light burns out.
Down the reverberate channels of the hills
the suns declare midnight, go down, cannot ascend,
no ladder back; see this, your eyes can ride through steel,
this is the river Death, diversion of power,
the root of the tower and the tunnel's core,
this is the end.

THE DAM

All power is saved, having no end.   Rises
in the green season, in the sudden season
the white the budded
                        and the lost.
Water celebrates, yielding continually
sheeted and fast in its overfall
slips down the rock, evades the pillars
building its colonnades, repairs
in stream and standing wave
retains its seaward green
broken by obstacle rock; falling, the water sheet
spouts, and the mind dances, excess of white.
White brilliant function of the land's disease.

Many-spanned, lighted, the crest leans under
concrete arches and the channelled hills,
turns in the gorge toward its release;
kinetic and controlled, the sluice
urging the hollow, the thunder,
the major climax
                   energy
total and open watercourse
praising the spillway, fiery glaze,
crackle of light, cleanest velocity
flooding, the moulded force.

> *I open out a way over the water*
> *I form a path between the Combatants:*
> *Grant that I sail down like a living bird,*
> *power over the fields and Pool of Fire.*
> *Phoenix, I sail over the phoenix world.*

Diverted water, the fern and fuming white
ascend in mist of continuous diffusion.
Rivers are turning inside their mountains,
streams line the stone, rest at the overflow
lake and in lanes of pliant color lie.
Blessing of this innumerable silver,
printed in silver, images of stone
walk on a screen of falling water
in film-silver in continual change
recurring colored, plunging with the wave.

Constellations of light, abundance of many rivers.
The sheeted island-cities, the white surf filling west,
the hope, fast water spilled where still pools fed.
Great power flying deep: between the rock and the sunset,
the caretaker's house and the steep abutment,
hypnotic water fallen and the tunnels under
the moist and fragile galleries of stone,
mile-long, under the wave. Whether snow fall,
the quick light fall, years of white cities fall,
flood that this valley built falls slipping down
the green turn in the river's green.
Steep gorge, the wedge of crystal in the sky.

How many feet of whirlpools?
What is a year in terms of falling water?
Cylinders; kilowatts; capacities.
Continuity: $\sum Q = 0$
Equations for falling water. The streaming motion.
The balance-sheet of energy that flows
passing along its infinite barrier.

It breaks the hills, cracking the riches wide,
runs through electric wires;
it comes, warning the night,
running among these rigid hills,
a single force to waken our eyes.

They poured the concrete and the columns stood,
laid bare the bedrock, set the cells of steel,
a dam for monument was what they hammered home.
Blasted, and stocks went up;
insured the base,
and limousines

wrote their own graphs upon
roadbed and lifeline.

Their hands touched mastery:
wait for defense, solid across the world.
Mr. Griswold. "A corporation is a body without a soul."
Mr. Dunn. When they were caught at it they resorted to the
methods employed by gunmen, ordinary machine gun racke-
teers. They cowardly tried to buy out the people who had the
information on them.
Mr. Marcantonio. I agree that a racket has been practised, but the
most damnable racketeering that I have ever known is the
paying of a fee to the very attorney who represented these
victims. That is the most outrageous racket that has ever come
within my knowledge.
Miss Allen. Mr. Jesse J. Ricks, the president of the Union Carbide
& Carbon Corporation, suggested that the stockholder had
better take this question up in a private conference.
The dam is safe. A scene of power.
The dam is the father of the tunnel.
This is the valley's work, the white, the shining.

High	Low	Stock and Dividend in Dollars	Open	High	Low	Last	Net Chge.	Closing		
								Bid	Ask	Sales
111	61¼	Union Carbide (3.20)	67¼	69½	67¼	69½	+3	69¼	69½	3,400

The dam is used when the tunnel is used.
The men and the water are never idle,
have definitions.
This is a perfect fluid, having no age nor hours,
surviving scarless, unaltered, loving rest,
willing to run forever to find its peace
in equal seas in currents of still glass.
Effects of friction : to fight and pass again,
learning its power, conquering boundaries,
able to rise blind in revolts of tide,
broken and sacrificed to flow resumed.
Collecting eternally power. Spender of power,
torn, never can be killed, speeded in filaments,
million, its power can rest and rise forever,
wait and be flexible. Be born again.
Nothing is lost, even among the wars,
imperfect flow, confusion of force.

It will rise. These are the phases of its face.
It knows its seasons, the waiting, the sudden.
It changes. It does not die.

THE DISEASE : AFTER-EFFECTS

This is the life of a Congressman.
Now he is standing on the floor of the House,
the galleries full; raises his voice; presents the bill.
Legislative, the fanfare, greeting its heroes with
ringing of telephone bells preceding entrances,
snapshots (Grenz rays, recording structure) newsreels.
This is silent, and he proposes:

                              embargo on munitions
to Germany and Italy
as states at war with Spain.
He proposes
              Congress memorialize
the governor of California : free Tom Mooney.
A bill for a TVA at Fort Peck Dam.
A bill to prevent industrial silicosis.

This is the gentleman from Montana.
—I'm a child, I'm leaning from a bedroom window,
clipping the rose that climbs upon the wall,
the tea roses, and the red roses,
one for a wound, another for disease,
remembrance for strikers. I was five, going on six,
my father on strike at the Anaconda mine;
they broke the Socialist mayor we had in Butte,
the sheriff (friendly), found their judge. Strike-broke.
Shot father. He died : wounds and his disease.
My father had silicosis.

Copper contains it, we find it in limestone,
sand quarries, sandstone, potteries, foundries,
granite, abrasives, blasting; many kinds of grinding,
plate, mining, and glass.

Widespread in trade, widespread in space!
Butte, Montana; Joplin, Missouri; the New York tunnels,

the Catskill Aqueduct. In over thirty States.
A disease worse than consumption.

Only eleven States have laws.
There are today one million potential victims.
500,000 Americans have silicosis now.
These are the proportions of a war.

> Pictures rise, foreign parades, the living faces,
> Asturian miners with my father's face,
> wounded and fighting, the men at Gauley Bridge,
> my father's face enlarged; since now our house
>
> and all our meaning lies in this
> signature: power on a hill
> centered in its committee and its armies
> sources of anger, the mine of emphasis.
>
> No plane can ever lift us high enough
> to see forgetful countries underneath,
> but always now the map and X-ray seem
> resemblent pictures of one living breath
> one country marked by error
> and one air.

It sets up a gradual scar formation;
this increases, blocking all drainage from the lung,
eventually scars, blocking the blood supply,
and then they block the air passageways.
Shortness of breath,
pains around the chest,
he notices lack of vigor.

Bill blocked; investigation blocked.

These galleries produce their generations.
The Congressmen are restless, stare at the triple tier,
the flags, the ranks, the walnut foliage wall;
a row of empty seats, mask over a dead voice.
But over the country, a million look from work,
five hundred thousand stand.

The subcommittee submits:
Your committee held hearings, heard many witnesses; finds:

THAT the Hawk's Nest tunnel was constructed
        Dennis and Rinehart, Charlottesville, Va., for
        New Kanawha Power Co., subsidiary of
        Union Carbide & Carbon Co.

THAT a tunnel was drilled
        app. dist. 3.75 mis.
        to divert water (from New River)
        to hydroelectric plant (Gauley Junction).

THAT in most of the tunnel, drilled rock contained
        90—even 99 percent pure silica.

This is a fact that was known.

THAT silica is dangerous to lungs of human beings.
        When submitted to contact. Silicosis.

THAT the effects are well known.
        Disease incurable.
        Physical incapacity, cases fatal.

THAT the Bureau of Mines has warned for twenty years.

THAT prevention is: wet drilling, ventilation,
                    respirators, vacuum drills.
        Disregard : utter. Dust : collected. Visibility : low.
        Workmen left work, white with dust.
        Air system : inadequate.
        It was quite cloudy in there.
        When the drills were going, in all the smoke and dust,
        it seemed like a gang of airplanes going through that
           tunnel.
        Respirators, not furnished.
        I have seen men with masks, but simply on their
           breasts.
        I have seen two wear them.
        Drills : dry drilling, for speed, for saving.
        A fellow could drill three holes dry for one hole wet.
        They went so fast they didn't square at the top.
        Locomotives : gasoline. Suffering from monoxide gas.
        There have been men that fell in the tunnel. They had
           to be carried out.

The driving of the tunnel.
>It was begun, continued, completed, with gravest
>>disregard.
>And the employees? Their health, lives, future?
Results and infection.
>Many died. Many are not yet dead.
>Of negligence. Wilful or inexcusable.
Further findings:
>Prevalence : many States, mine, tunnel operations.
>A greatest menace.
We suggest hearings be read.
>This is the dark. Lights strung up all the way.
>Depression; and, driven deeper in,
>by hunger, pistols, and despair,
>they took the tunnel.
Of the contracting firm
>>P. H. Faulconer, Pres.
>>E. J. Perkins, Vice-Pres.
>have declined to appear.
>They have no knowledge of deaths from silicosis.
>However, their firm paid claims.
>I want to point out that under the statute $500 or $1000,
>>but no more, may be recovered.

We recommend.
>Bring them. Their books and records.
>Investigate. Require.
Can do no more.
>These citizens from many States
>paying the price for electric power,
>To Be Vindicated.

"If by their suffering and death they will have made a future life safer for work beneath the earth, if they will have been able to establish a new and greater regard for human life in industry, their suffering may not have been in vain."
>Respectfully,
>Glenn Griswold
>Chairman, Subcommittee

>Vito Marcantonio
>W. P. Lambertson
>Matthew A. Dunn

The subcommittee subcommits.

Words on a monument.
Capitoline thunder. It cannot be enough.
The origin of storms is not in clouds,
our lightning strikes when the earth rises,
spillways free authentic power:
dead John Brown's body walking from a tunnel
to break the armored and concluded mind.

THE BOOK OF THE DEAD

These roads will take you into your own country.
Seasons and maps coming where this road comes
into a landscape mirrored in these men.

Past all your influences, your home river,
constellations of cities, mottoes of childhood,
parents and easy cures, war, all evasion's wishes.

What one word must never be said?
Dead, and these men fight off our dying,
cough in the theatres of the war.

What two things shall never be seen?
They : what we did.   Enemy : what we mean.
This is a nation's scene and halfway house.

What three things can never be done?
Forget.   Keep silent.   Stand alone.
The hills of glass, the fatal brilliant plain.

The facts of war forced into actual grace.
Seasons and modern glory.   Told in the histories,
        how first ships came

seeing on the Atlantic thirteen clouds
lining the west horizon with their white
        shining halations;

they conquered, throwing off impossible Europe—
could not be used to transform; created coast—
        breathed-in America.

See how they took the land, made after-life
fresh out of exile, planted the pioneer
        base and blockade,

pushed forests down in an implacable walk
west where new clouds lay at the desirable
        body of sunset;

taking the seaboard.   Replaced the isolation,
dropped cities where they stood, drew a tidewater
        frontier of Europe,

a moment, and another frontier held,
this land was planted home-land that we know.
        Ridge of discovery,

until we walk to windows, seeing America
lie in a photograph of power, widened
        before our forehead,

and still behind us falls another glory,
London unshaken, the long French road to Spain,
        the old Mediterranean

flashing new signals from the hero hills
near Barcelona, monuments and powers,
        parent defenses.

Before our face the broad and concrete west,
green ripened field, frontier pushed back like river
        controlled and dammed;

the flashing wheatfields, cities, lunar plains
grey in Nevada, the sane fantastic country
        sharp in the south,

liveoak, the hanging moss, a world of desert,
the dead, the lava, and the extreme arisen
        fountains of life,

the flourished land, peopled with watercourses
to California and the colored sea;
        sums of frontiers

and unmade boundaries of acts and poems,
the brilliant scene between the seas, and standing,
        this fact and this disease.
        ————————

Half-memories absorb us, and our ritual world
carries its history in familiar eyes,
planted in flesh it signifies its music

in minds which turn to sleep and memory,
in music knowing all the shimmering names,
the spear, the castle, and the rose.

But planted in our flesh these valleys stand,
everywhere we begin to know the illness,
are forced up, and our times confirm us all.

In the museum life, centuries of ambition
yielded at last a fertilizing image:
the Carthaginian stone meaning a tall woman

carries in her two hands the book and cradled dove,
on her two thighs, wings folded from the waist
cross to her feet, a pointed human crown.

This valley is given to us like a glory.
To friends in the old world, and their lifting hands
that call for intercession. Blow falling full in face.

All those whose childhood made learn skill to meet,
and art to see after the change of heart;
all the belligerents who know the world.

You standing over gorges, surveyors and planners,
you workers and hope of countries, first among powers;
you who give peace and bodily repose,

opening landscapes by grace, giving the marvel lowlands
physical peace, flooding old battlefields
with general brilliance, who best love your lives;

and you young, you who finishing the poem
wish new perfection and begin to make;
you men of fact, measure our times again.

———————

These are our strength, who strike against history.
These whose corrupt cells owe their new styles of weakness
        to our diseases;

these carrying light for safety on their foreheads
descended deeper for richer faults of ore,
        drilling their death.

These touching radium and the luminous poison,
carried their death on their lips and with their warning
        glow in their graves.

These weave and their eyes water and rust away,
these stand at wheels until their brains corrode,
        these farm and starve,

all these men cry their doom across the world,
meeting avoidable death, fight against madness,
        find every war.

Are known as strikers, soldiers, pioneers,
fight on all new frontiers, are set in solid
        lines of defense.

Defense is sight; widen the lens and see
standing over the land myths of identity,
        new signals, processes:

Alloys begin : certain dominant metals.
Deliberate combines add new qualities,
        sums of new uses.

Over the country, from islands of Maine fading,
Cape Sable fading south into the orange
        detail of sunset,

new processes, new signals, new possession.
A name for all the conquests, prediction of victory
        deep in these powers.

Carry abroad the urgent need, the scene,
to photograph and to extend the voice,
        to speak this meaning.

Voices to speak to us directly.   As we move.
As we enrich, growing in larger motion,
        this word, this power.

Down coasts of taken countries, mastery,
discovery at one hand, and at the other
        frontiers and forests,

fanatic cruel legend at our back and
speeding ahead the red and open west,
        and this our region,

desire, field, beginning.   Name and road,
communication to these many men,
as epilogue, seeds of unending love.

Night-Music

Spinning on his heel, the traveller
sees across snow a flashing cliff.
Past the plain's freeze, past savage branches
immune in ice, a frozen waterfall,
clamped in December, glistens alive.

Love, will you recognize yourself displayed?
Or is the age defective, cold with storm
to lock fast water in iron artifice,
whitening cataracts?—contempt and loss,
and nothing, in the great world, can lie calm,

travel alive, but is frozen solid,
and will not face its mirror nor speak its pain.
Will you fight winter to break in immense speed
resisting and sensitive, a waterfall-flash
sparkling full across the vicious plain?

Fight down our age, the mad vindictive time?
No victory's here. Now, any passion suffers
against proud ice, flashing, angry, and jailed.
You, maniac, catalept!
And, love. You are all rivers.

GIRL AT THE PLAY

Long after you beat down the powerful hand
and leave the scene, prison's still there to break.
Brutalized by escape, you travel out to sit
in empty theatres, your stunned breast, hardened neck
      waiting for warmth to venture back.

Gilded above the stage, staring archaic shapes
hang, like those men you learn submission from
whose majesty sits yellow on the night,
young indolent girls, long-handed, one's vague mouth
      and cruel nose and jaw and throat.

Waiting's paralysis strikes, king-cobra hooded head's
infected fangs petrify body and face.

106

Emblems fade everyway, dissolving even
the bitter infantile boys who call for sleep's
        winy breasts whose nipples are long grapes.

Seats fill. The curtain's up where strong lights act,
cut theatre to its theme; the quick fit's past.
Here's answer in masses moving; by light elect,
they turn the stage before into the street behind;
        and nothing's so forgotten as your blind
        female paralysis that takes the mind,
        and nothing's so forgotten as your dead
        fever, now that it's past and the swift play's ahead.

BURNING BUSH

Faced with furnace demands during its education,
the strictest spirit must take them all; it needs
to break down shame; but gasping into a pillow
later to nobody anywhere, claims I Love You.
        It plays long tricks
upon itself—the stealthy girl locks doors,
the woman listens in single high rooms for music,
hears climbing elevators as the picket walks
in a dead street before tallest skyscrapers
        far on the sidewalks;
all horrors enter all beds to purify
the critical spirit in a city of change,
twisted in flames, blazing among the secrets,
breaking the taut life with their harsh I Have You.
        It burns and never speaks
only is educated, when it assumes bright horror,
nourished against the time it hears its name—
until it is called will stand, witness to fire,
training a flame upward along its vine.

EEL

We started to walk but it was wading-slow.
Ran to the corner and boarded at the carstop,
impatient through the city, hating the noise of iron.
Shut it out of the head
until the city, quiet, goes submarine

and we are winding through, defended, winding, with
weird deepseas, the famous world, swimming, facing our
    youth.

Their faces royal in pain, useless children advance
down avenues shining a stormy cobalt sky.
The lights go green. They stare. Stop riding, cross the street,
here are rich avenues, a city's alibi,
here's your prophetic love and object lesson:
Shops will instruct you what to want.
Strangers will serve you, floorwalkers.
Condition: don't notice their disease.
be easy-going, and so, susceptible.
These to cultivate, perhaps have:
flippant defeat, good sportsmanship,
the miracle figure of the football-player:
a perfect husband, a promised income.

We were too earnest. We had to lose.
We wound past armies of strangers, waving love's
thin awkward plant among a crowd of salesmen.
"Sold the salesmen? Been loved, loving? You, too young?"
We stared at policemen, hypnotized by force,
holding the ball during games, forgetting to throw,
as they padlocked the bar, clapped boards across the door,
padlocked the union hall. Deported. Shut.

Winding through avenues, stone blocked our eyes,
we dreamed raw yellow hills of mustard-flower.
Mind's tropic scenery was farmed : Come back to stay,
return to the broken man across the subway,
read crinkled Atlantics, tabloid skies—your feet
slap stone; this is you, advancing down a street,
your ancestors being dead, your parents busy somewhere.
You have a class. You have your object lessons.

Radio City, largest of riches, leaning
against the flaming cobalt, fatal as Belgium,
flowers in neon on the winter air,
        All its theatres open padded lobbies
        all its windows run light
And adolescent breasts, alert for terror,
fingers ophelian white and quick with fear
flower aware, and the staring workman

walks down expensive streets. And all the adolescents,
winding, and submarine, waking, with sleep shaken
go weaving among the crowds; growing remember

Alexander, peacock of Macedon, Euclid building his circles on
    the flat Greek sand,
the violent empresses, Boone breaking through green
    country—
in the papers, Ann Burlak makes women pound kettles
for drums, for a loud band!

Miss Swan, the Latin teacher, hand laid on moulding,
speaks Cicero admirably, for massy syllables, hearing the
pompous Senate heave; we fidget until the hour—
we compare lipsticks, smudging our palms with red.
Know Rome is elsewhere and the street's outside.
And fast thoughts run like fire as the roads divide.

The adolescents, walking, at school, going through streets,
stop wavering, heal their minds snapped during mutiny.
Believing at first in easy cures, the floundering blood to be
    healed by love,
not yet knowing that thousands walk straightforward, wish the same,
young, and winding through cities, young, seeing time's
    disease.

Parading upon a stage lit with immense firm flame.
To change it. To mature. To find. To e these.

HOMAGE TO LITERATURE

When you imagine trumpet-faced musicians
blowing again inimitable jazz
no art can accuse nor cannonadings hurt,

or coming out of your dreams of dirigibles
again see the unreasonable cripple
throwing his crutch headlong as the headlights

streak down the torn street, as the three hammerers
go One, Two, Three on the stake, triphammer poundings
and not a sign of new worlds to still the heart;

then stare into the lake of sunset as it runs
boiling, over the west past all control

rolling and swamps the heartbeat and repeats
sea beyond sea after unbearable suns;
think: poems fixed this landscape: Blake, Donne, Keats.

THE HANDCLAP

The body cannot lie, but its betrayals,
narrower actions, cross even frontiers of night,
and your most delicate treason falls in a quick stroke,
            undercuts sleep.

Now, if I bodily sometime betrayed myself,
the foolish play's curtain drops on your active exposure,
grotesque as a peepshow, definite as the axe
            in instant effect.

The toppling high tree lets fall its heavy side
green on the air, goes anyway down to ground
after a clap of weight resting—but we descend to
            imperfect peace.

Here's war!—body betrayed, but all nerves still exerted
to rise up whole, grasp the perpetual sun.
Echo the shock, handclaps of fact composing
            a blackest pattern,

a tyrant pace to dance, clatter of anger
spanking the fury up to publish treason,
ranting and clapping madness; while the dim
            blood groans forever love.

TROPHIES

The choice proposed : ascends, the nervy conductor
facing the strings as the stage shakes, as the plane
looms in the loud air, motor cut out,
and the musicians' black alters to violin-brown.
They lift their instruments.   The choice.
Mr. Sceptre, the elegant instructor,
looks about the classroom sighing Keats,
emotion in torrents on adolescent cheeks
as teargas tranquilly saturates the college.
Choose: the workers will rise, or your heroes, tall as stone,
must face the fascist cruelties of pain.
110

Trapped in the valley—historian eloquence
reminds us of recurrent Civil War:
"To prevent repetition of this attack of the enemy
I directed Captain Gaw, chief topographer,
to reach the commanding officer of the other wing."
"Obtained abundance of corn, molasses, and sweet potatoes."
"The advance was then gallantly resumed, the enemy
driven from their guns, the heights handsomely carried."
But the choice *is* proposed: the active alternative,
people's Party in the streets, last year's heroes at home.

Who will take choice, demands the scientist
(the smiling friend sitting beside his mind),
now that the key is grincing in the lock?
Now that the sea has bitten on the ship
and bent it to the rock?

Here are insignia of reversed cities,
victorious slogans and the acts of war.
And we shall never know their poise again,
though we remember what we were,
now that our officers are no longer
in full golden summer regalia,
and we no longer well-dressed watchers
at the march-past and the fly-by—
or even attentive before the fire
haunted by certain safe compelling shoulders,
a trick of the head, lust of incautious eye;
fortified by the braver faces
of picket-line and commemorative parade,
the anniversary demonstration—
we cast about for love, lost between wars,
alone in the room and every street-light out.
Who's to rise to it, now that ruin's made,
now that we're petrified in the pale looking-glass,
our glossy scars, our books, our loss,
caught in the narrowest final pass?
And all our heroes are afraid.

PANACEA

Make me well, I said.—And the delighted touch.
You put dead sweet hand on my dead brain.
The window cleared and the night-street stood black.

As soon as I left your house others besieged me
forcing my motion, saying, Make me well.

Took sickness into the immense street,
but nothing was thriving   I saw blank light   the crazy
blink of torture   the lack   and there is no
personal sickness strong to intrude there.
Returned. Stood at the window. Make me well.

Cannot? The white sea, which is inviolable,
is no greater, the disallied world's unable,
daylight horizons of lakes cannot caress me well.
The hypocrite leper in the parable,
did he believe would be kissed whole by kisses?

I'll try beyond you now. I'll try all flame.
Some force must be whole, some eye inviolable—
look, here I am returned! No help. Gone high again;
legend's no precedent. This perseveres.
The sun, I say, sincere, the sun, the sun.

IN HADES, ORPHEUS

"Look!" he said, "all green!" but she,
leaning against him at her hospital door,
received it on her eyes as fireline blinding bright
and would not see.

"Come into the park!" he offered her,
but she was feverstruck still, brimful of white
monotonous weakness, and could not face the grass
and the bright water.

A boy skating upstreet
shouted; the gardener climbed at the doorway, pruning,
and the gay branches dropped where she stood, fearful
of her quick heartbeat

released, fearing the kiss
of vivid blood. The husband straightened in the sun,
risking their staggered histories against the violent
avenue's emphasis;

"A long pain, long fever!"
He faced her full for the first time, speaking,

turned with his hand her face to meet his mouth,
"but that death's over."

Lights out; noon falls
steeply away, blazing in green; he sees the sharp fear pass
verdict upon her, pitching and frothing toward the
mechanical white walls.

THE DROWNING YOUNG MAN

The drowning young man lifted his face from the river
to me, exhausted from calling for help and weeping;
"My love!" I said; but he kissed me once for ever
and returned to his privacy and secret keeping.

His close face dripped with the attractive water,
I stared in his eyes and saw there penalty,
for the city moved in its struggle, loud about us,
and the salt air blew down; but he would face the sea.

"Afraid, afraid, my love?" But he will never speak,
looking demands for rest, watching the wave come up,
too timid to turn, too loving to cry out,
lying face down in tide, biting his nervous lip.

Take him by shoulder and jaw, break his look back on us,
O hard to save, be saved, before we all shall drown!
But he has set his look, plunged his life deep for peace,
his face in the boiling river, and is surrendered down.

BOY WITH HIS HAIR CUT SHORT

Sunday shuts down on this twentieth-century evening.
The El passes. Twilight and bulb define
the brown room, the overstuffed plum sofa,
the boy, and the girl's thin hands above his head.
A neighbor radio sings stocks, news, serenade.

He sits at the table, head down, the young clear neck exposed,
watching the drugstore sign from the tail of his eye;
tattoo, neon, until the eye blears, while his
solicitous tall sister, simple in blue, bending
behind him, cuts his hair with her cheap shears.

The arrow's electric red always reaches its mark,
successful neon! He coughs, impressed by that precision.
His child's forehead, forever protected by his cap,
is bleached against the lamplight as he turns head
and steadies to let the snippets drop.

Erasing the failure of weeks with level fingers,
she sleeks the fine hair, combing: "You'll look fine tomorrow!
You'll surely find something, they can't keep turning you down;
the finest gentleman's not so trim as you!" Smiling, he raises
the adolescent forehead wrinkling ironic now.

He sees his decent suit laid out, new-pressed,
his carfare on the shelf. He lets his head fall, meeting
her earnest hopeless look, seeing the sharp blades splitting,
the darkened room, the impersonal sign, her motion,
the blue vein, bright on her temple, pitifully beating.

COURSE

for Betty Marshall

Years before action when the wish alone
has ammunition to threaten weakness down,
when thriving on discovery we speak
and wish a world
that wishing may not make.

Stretching our powers, we touch a broader street
crowded with hostile weapons and the weight
of death suggesting we see peace at last
and quiet cities,
rip out the eyes, and have our rest.

But we are set enough to clear a space
ample for action in this eccentric house.
An army of wishers in a dramatic grip
and crazy with
America has heat to keep its purpose up.

Determined to a world that Mr. Fist
and all his gang can't master or digest,
strengthened against the world that cannot hush
words singing down
the fever voice of death working against the wish.

MORE OF A CORPSE THAN A WOMAN

Give them my regards when you go to the school reunion;
and at the marriage-supper, say that I'm thinking about them.
They'll remember my name; I went to the movies with that one,
feeling the weight of their death where she sat at my elbow;
           she never said a word,
           but all of them were heard.

all of them alike, expensive girls, the leaden friends:
one used to play the piano, one of them once wrote a sonnet,
one even seemed awakened enough to photograph wheat-
     fields—
the dull girls with the educated minds and technical passions—
           pure love was their employment,
           they tried it for enjoyment.

Meet them at the boat : they've brought the souvenirs of
     boredom,
a seashell from the faltering monarchy;
the nose of a marble saint; and from the battlefield,
an empty shell divulged from a flower-bed.
           The lady's wealthy breath
           perfumes the air with death.

The leaden lady faces the fine, voluptuous woman,
faces a rising world bearing its gifts in its hands.
Kisses her casual dreams upon the lips she kisses,
risen, she moves away; takes others; moves away.
           Inadequate to love,
           supposes she's enough.

Give my regards to the well-protected woman,
I knew the ice-cream girl, we went to school together.
There's something to bury, people, when you begin to bury.
When your women are ready and rich in their wish for the
     world,
           destroy the leaden heart,
           we've a new race to start.

THREE BLACK WOMEN

Invading nightmare, spinning up through sleep,
three loving Negresses ascend the night;
one sinks with Chinese eyes a despised man
shivering white in fear; mocking says "Take him,
I made him vastly unhappy;" dances, lifting
the purple belly pencilled delicate black.
The grandmother rises on the pointed shoulder
of the little black boy in the pink wool sweater,
bitterly asking about the deputies.
Burning, as dead skies over enemy cities
tip backward sliding, a third gleams on the South;
battlefields flicker, the scenery of doubt
dissolves in decoration on the night of
fire, black women, nightmare, dances, sleep.

FORMOSA

The sand's still blue with receding water, sky topples
                    its last brightness
down, day diminishing; two fishermen
walk over the sandbar, their thin indicative shadows
pointing tomorrow's sunrise on the whiteline horizon.
Tomorrow is only an interval, night's passing interval
cruises on open water here, anchored, while peace comes in.

Speedboat, run again before your smoking white
wake, while the light's collected on the hull,
until the evening turns, engaged with night.

The little dog races over the sandflats, the thin bathers
turn back to foamline, half-light discourages their daring
sea-dream. End it! omens are laughter, gay all morning,
gay before ogre midnight, spurless midnight—
midnight's an interval, darkness is promise, night's nothing,
nightmare is nothing, nothing but interval.

Eliminate all dreams : here, real : love come, high tide,
the risen, freehold moon, the fortunate island,
resting, blue-flooded, rests, delicately, the sea.

NIGHT-MUSIC

for Marya Zaturenska

Time Exposures

When the exposed spirit, busy in daytime,
searches out night, only renewer.
That time plants turn to. The world's table.
When any single thing's condemned again.
The changeable spirit finds itself out,
will not employ Saint Death, detective,
does its own hunting, runs at last to night.
Renewer, echo of judgment, morning-source, music.

Dark streets that light invents, one black tree standing,
struck by the street-light to raw electric green,
allow one man at a time to walk past, plain.
Cities lose size. The earth is field
and ranging these countries in sunset, we make quiet,
living in springtime, wish for nothing, see
glass bough, invented green, flower-sharp day
crackle into orange and be subdued to night.

The mind, propelled by work, reaches its evening:
slick streets, dog-tired, point the way to sleep,
walls rise in color, now summer shapes the Square
(and pastel five o'clock chalked on the sky).

We drive out to the suburbs, bizarre lawns
flicker a moment beside the speeding cars.
Speed haunts our ground, throws counties at us under
night, a black basin always spilling stars.

Waters trouble our quiet, vanishing down
reaches of hills whose image legend saves:
the foggy Venus hung above the flood
rising, rising, from the sea, with her arms full of waves
as ours are full of flowers.

Down polished airways a purple dove descending
sharp on the bodies of those so lately busy apart,
wingtip on breasttip, the deep body of feathers
in the breastgroove along the comforted heart.

The head inclined offers with love clear miles
of days simple in sun and action, bright

air poised about a face in ballet strictness
and pure pacific night.

But in our ears brute knocking at all doors,
factories bellow mutilation, and we live needy still
while strength and hours run
checkless downhill.

Flattered by grief, the changeable spirit
puts on importance. Goes into the street,
adventures everywhere but places fear
is absent. Everywhere the face's look
is absent, the heart is flat,
the avenues haunted by a head whose eye
runs tears incessantly, the other eye
narrow in smiling. Everywhere, words fail,
men sunk to dust, houses condemned, walls ruined,
and dust is never an anachronism.
Everywhere the eye runs tears. And here
the hand, propelled somehow, marches the room
pulling dark windowshades down around the gaze.

And now, stately, jotting on lipstick, she
prepares to sexualize her thistle thought.
Loosens her earrings, smiling. Drives
herself far into night. Smiles, fornicating. Drives
herself deep into sleep. Sees children sleep.

The Child Asleep

What's over England? A cloud. What's over France? A flame.
And over New York? The night.
Night is nameless, night has no name.

    The crane leans down to drink the pit.
    Look from the blackboard out the window.
    Walk down the streets that lead to school.
    Study, h'p! Pause, h'p! Recess, h'p!
    I want to grow up.

Can you be direct as snow, straight to the face?
When the ball arrives, catch it! Who loves you?
What's around you and under you,
who bends above you?

Immortal is miles away, and age.
And Europe. But not so the sea.
The sea is near, mother and father near.
Not with the dirty children, dear.
Not to look at the sea.

Quiet, music is playing! Never move your face.
Wear a mask if your face moves with your
love or anger moving. God first, then us.
Friday candles. Never discuss.

See the full street—the war is over!
The birdcage swung open to the storm.
Do not love so much. Keep cool.
Keep collected. Keep warm.

"And the harsh friend, pushing away the music."
The sand-pit high with money. The limousine.
The chauffeur filling the frost with suicide
smelling sick in garage. First strikers seen.

Death first, the stiff knees pointing up, gone breath.
"And the harsh lover: suddenly magic, making
me forget mother, sob through shut teeth, seeing
the kiss full on the palm erase the touch of death."

What's over us? The fancy snowfall. War.
What's at our hand for truth? The curious windlass
going into the well. Quaint. Why do those men parade?
What's after sitting at the window, reading?
Lying hot in the bath, weeping at night?
Going to bed at night and at last sleeping?

Adventures, Midnight

I. Give a dime to a beggar for I have seen a sight
    children grown tall and tragic reason slight
    charity dealt the poor again
    I drove with my last love last night
    through Clinton Street where sick, sick, sick
    the pushcarts screened with oranges
    staggering avenues of brick
    and wealth and love were long away
    and this man wished the old love quick.

Give more and get your dollars back all dimes
   small change of love: so lied, and kissed him tight.
   I saw his tired body gone to crust
   and chuckling pigeons take him in their throats.
   —Now see us older, foolish, refugee,
   the child awake with an advertising look
   gathering speed in motors, love in dimes—
   what's after driving at night, answering joylessly?
   The wasted pity. Thieving charity.

II. With those two I went driving in the dark,
   out from our town in a borrowed car whose light
   ate forests as we drove deeper into the park.

   Beloved, spoke the sweet equivocal night—
   those two stood clapped, each breast warmly on breast,
   I stood apart to remove them from my sight:

   The creased brook ran in continual unrest,
   rising to seastorm in the rioting mind.
   Here night and they and I—and who was merriest?

   He turned his face away refusing, and so signed
   for her to stop who too was comfortless
   and equally needy, as tender and as blind.

   On the road to the city stood the hedge whose darkness
   had covered me months ago with that tall stranger
   as foreign to me as this loneliness,

   as enemy to me as tonight's anger
   of grief in the country, shut with those two in the park:
   this crying, frantic at removal, the dark, the sorrowful
      danger.

III. Watching, on piers, exuberant travellers
   enter the ocean where the beggar sits
   desperate at exclusive waterfronts,
   see how the feasted boat leaves port
   covered with singing birds.

   Cruising to cellophane islands, shaking off
   this city's rock providing lonely tours,
   grim single passports, persevering winter,
   the ship slides down midnight's imperious harbor
   The gilt-tiered galleries awake and dance.

What is it rippling across the deck?
What rising? What memory of ocean?
What is it ripples and rises?
The drowned heart, lifted a moment
answers clearly   Here it comes.

And get your feet wet in a drowning world?
Stand on a rotten dock, obsessed with tide?
The boat's condemned, the pier sinks. The long port
offers an only country to you, traveller,
a chance of upper air to hopeful, smothering heart.

Night-Music

When those who can never again forgive themselves
finish their dinner, rear up from the chair,
turning to movies are caught in demonstrations
sweeping the avenues—Meet them there.

Watch how their faces change like traffic-light
bold blood gone green as horses pound the street,
as plates of sweated muscle push
them squarely back into retreat.

Notice their tremulous late overthrow
caught irresponsible : as the first rank presses
up at the brown animal breast of law
defying government by horses.

And after the quick night-flurry, the few jailed,
the march stampeded, the meeting stopped, go down
night-streets to unique rooms where horror ends,
strike-songs are sung and the old songs remain.

Vaguely Ilonka draws her violin
along to Bach, greatest of trees, whereunder
earth is again familiar, grandmother,
and very god-music branches overhead.

Changeable spirit! build a newer music
rich enough to feed starvation on.
Course down the night, past scenes of horror, among
children awake, lands ruined, begging men.

Rebel against torment,
boats gone, night-battles, the sleepers up and shaking,

fear in the streets
cruelty on awaking.

Make music out of night will change the night.

DRIVEWAY

Speeding from city, feeling day
grimmer and more opaque,
a thousand times more Death than night
here on the pebbled roads, bled of all light and kind,
hastening darkness to the impatient mind,

we shook off nights our fever watched the street,
besieged by laughter from the outer room,
heard the pang, pang of bells bury our hope
for private warmth or time or bed or house
free from the failure public in that place.

Here was to be moment of proof, if any
conspiracy of night and speed and river
could lift us whole from danger, and make real
the veiny tree, the gleaming parallel
of railroad tracks and water, using our trespass well

to heal all breaches, prove our hope's disease
curable by annealing, bandage night,
blank out the city's bricked-up doors, the glare
of the night-watchman's ray, No Trespassing,
Don't Walk Here, Stay At Your Window, Keep On Looking.

Reaching the full-grown field, danger slowed down,
darkness enlarged around the blind, parked car.
No need to look; the brilliant fatal skim
of light swung over the acre, striking the night-proof dead,
the Caretaker's flashlight sending his shadow up ahead.

LOVER AS FOX

Driven, at midnight, to growth, the city's wistful turnings
lead you living on islands to some dark single house
where vacant windows mark increased pursuit,
chasing the runner outward beyond bounds
around the wildest circle of the night.

Circling returns! the city wreathed in rivers,
streaked skies surrounding islands of blank stone—
into this mythic track travelling breakneck,
a streaming furnace of escape, you, fox,
pursued, brick-red and vicious, circling bricks.

are followed as nimbly all mottled cloudy night;
fastened upon your path, the Floating Man
face down above the city, as shadow, changing shape,
as shadow of clouds, flying, and swiftly as
indifference running mad around the world.

Speed now! see city, houses across the water,
mosaic and bright over the riverfall
remote from the bursting eye, the open nostril,
flared lip (an image of angels singing speed),
caught in a nightlong visionary chase.

See the entire scene bright as you fly
round lots pauper all year, shacks lame with weather,
this sour fertile time teeming and ramshackle
before you, loving, clean sight in spyglass air.
And around town again. River, river.
Why do people live on islands?

GIFT-POEM

December steel done, flowers open color,
unshadowed brilliance enters the air again,
lets fear dissolve,

and convalescent brightness brush the face
until the subtlest rivers of sleep descend
over all eyelids,

and air lies gracious, lavishing general gold,
warming the lips, touching the salt away,
unlocking wishes,

until the lifelong travellers find their rest
in prodigal evening, marvel day, moonblaze,
superb ambassadors

whose power discloses sensual ease again
to these who come bringing flowers, standing still
past wandering arrived at open spring.

WOMAN AND EMBLEMS

Woman and Bird

A bird flew out of a cloud
(with a beak, flying),
broke its beak on my bone,
cried bird-cries over crying.

Sky, stranger, wilderness
(flying starry through flesh),
make an end; be me, bird.
It reverses my one wish.

Bird screams slavery among bones.
(I watch with a bird's eyes.)
Quarrel, wings; if I travel,
bird stays—stand, bird flies.

Bird sets feathers where flesh was
(my claws slide away on space).
Bird, here—now, bird, we fly!
Mourns, mourns, it turns a captive face.

The Birthday

A sound lying on the fantastic air
opens the night and the child is born;
as the wind moves, the solemn crying
pioneers in the air, changes

to flame crusading among the grasses
fire-whitened, aroused before it,
rippled crops—and blazing races
into a central arena

where it stands as a fighting-cock
conqueror head, aggressive spur,
and the gilt feather, the bronze, the greenish,
flicker and threaten.

The feathers of the fighting-cock
become a tree, and casting seed,
raise potent forests at its side—
birth among burning.

The great magnetic branches sign
meaning on the record sky—
now rise, moon, stiffen, bird, and flames,
kill and engender.

Reversal, chameleon,
pursuing images—
recurrent birth offering other names,
a spool of brightness.

Woman and Music

This is a tall woman walking through a square
thinking what is a woman at midnight in a park
under bells, in the trivial and lovely hours
with images, violins, dancers approaching?

This is a woman sitting at a mirror
her back to the glass and all the dancers advancing,
or in a chair laughing at a bone
sitting upright in a chair
talking of ballet, flesh's impermanence.

This is a woman looking at a stage—
dancer receiving the floral blue and white,
balanced against a tallest blue decor,
dancing—and all the parks, walks, hours
descend in brilliant water past the eyes
pursuing and forgotten and subdued
to blinding music, the deliberate strings.

OUTPOST

After the last cold mountain
turns loaded with rock, the green iceberg
wheels at the ship
and gulls pass screaming:
sail out on trembling decks that cut
deepdigging into the ring of sea:
End of America! not so far out
as the home-storm of sickness,
furious seas, not like the arranged waves here
foreign in green, austere,

but, bright as household scene,
all the equipment of dismay,
teaching grave civilized man
nothing, feeding his sickest
dread of strong icy seas,
disgust with sunlight.

After the mountains turn, the Floating Man
raises his head (his shoulders are cold rock),
his face takes on the home-look : suffering,
sinking beneath the last iceberg horizon,
reminding us, risen to find us this last time.
He carries in his eyes street-images,
on forehead, protest, on sinking face, goodbye,
the sombre, bright, the unpredictable wind
laying a flag across his lips.

End of America! the ocean opening,
lighthouse and iceberg, vestige of vegetable green,
the sad face everywhere sinking backward last:
not rock, not ice, but here most civilized man,
outpost survivor,
the last and floating trace, streaming down every river
into the sea whose foreign colors waver,
hold to the end the images of violence
on rising overwave and underwave,
slave and slavedriver.

Two Voyages

THE CRUISE

"Goodbye!" called the stockholders as the ship pulled out from
   the dock,
"Good trip, good luck!" as the captain saluted;
and the crew stared down from the top rungs, the passengers
   stormed confetti
from all the rails of the luxury liner, crowding
in imitation of a travel poster.
But the last words issued from the pier loudspeaker,

the admiral-president, shouting, guardian and serious,
"Orders: above all, not to put in at any port
doubtful or dangerous."
Already, sea
rose livid, boiling over the white expensive hull,
imperious completely, undeniable.

Beginning of a voyage, quiet and gay; dancing and games,
deck lectures, visits to polo ponies in the hold,
bulletins, engines, radio operator's important earphones,
poet, barmaid polishing bottles, union man, news,
deck-conversations, visits to the bridge,
the sailor wit, music and promenade,
scrolls watched in the water, the glaze, the celadon,
high sunrise lustre on the fretted waves.
Persons emerge:
gossip the captain walking with the blonde,
emigrants, pleasure party, financier.

The exotic flowers were wilting in the staterooms.
Log's entry: "Quiet short voyage, last night unpleasant
    weather;
passengers sturdy, no sea-sickness, but the barmaid
fainted before lunch; waiting for diagnosis." Captain
writing, found confirmation in his heirloom mirror
freckled with tarnish, wishing him well, swaying. "Tomorrow, land."
About the bows, flyingfish, and island in the sea,
dove and appeared, and the chain of foam
followed the boat;
a spume of cirrus vanished with the sun,
safe water entertained a cloudless night.

Fourth day: first sight of rocks, a street of islands,
hazy and permanent, live green, the blues of mist,
bargaining cry of gulls. At the rail, radio operator
scouted for signs of houses. The blonde stood alone. The captain
hardly looked at the land, a doubtful country.
"Very welcome," said passengers, watching swimming sea-grasses,
felt trigger joy the ocean should be past,
and foreign cities, doorless countries come.
No landing-place;
only the rock, moss, mist, a chiffon pageant,
suggesting harbors, a shore-image.

Deep cobalt morning sky, spring's melting ice in the sky,
softness in air, the port's nearness.
                              But, the flavor of smoke
drifting across the bow like the last loudspeaker words;
but, the hypnotic thunder: cannon in that direction,
but, turning the promontory, the explosive city.
Flares, bombardments! Diamond hallucinations,
depth-bombs, ocean of waterspouts, fountains with strenuous
     trunks;
city of safety. The planted captain, straddled on his deck
thinks, Doubtful, thinks
grinning, Dangerous; must head for the next port:
radio asking advice, amuse all passengers.

          Chimes, clocks, rehearsals the radio invents.
          Stay away from here, there are planes falling,
          airliner crashes over Appalachians,
          two big amphibians lost above the Bay,
          no passengers recovered. Rumor: war,
          passages cancelled, no transatlantic sailings.
          One minute. Flash. One minute. Flash.
                                   Explosion!
          Death of children, none over thirteen injured,
          total unverified. Flash. Statement, song.
          Strange clouds visible over the prairies,
          blight on the wheat, dust in the middle air,
          unprecedented weather. To all planes:
          fly low, no flying blind, there will be flares on the ground.
          To all ships: make for port.

The deckrail hangs on the unaltered sea. Leaning, the poet
mentions danger. The pregnant barmaid half-hears his begging
     voice.
"Over the pointed hills, over the spit of sand,
harbor, we hurry down. Do you know the familiar
cat of superstition, feline terror?"
Sailors' mottoes. The barmaid dreads to make the land again,
losing her work; she watches. Clear sea, definite wave,
the picture of the last port taken fighting
deep on the brain;
"Talk to the union man," she volunteers,
"his cure is for your trouble."

The lighthouse seen at the spur, coastal clew, token.
But, over the new city, black, thunder of smoke,

the chilly shoal warm at the ship, the charred log rolling,
extensive flame, cries, broken walls. Laughter of falling glass.
Fiery capital, and the sea running hot, surf filmed with oil,
burning, the warehouses burning blue, sugar-blue,
and shadowless orange fire creeping seaward quickly.
Cliffs by the town metallic; menace of gold reflection,
and on their faces
pale of retreat, flattered by fire. The captain
orders backwater. The child says, "I want to stand on the
    ground."

But a boat can run down the coast, the shore is long,
(they said), one city stands by itself, unfortunate islands
breathe other air. We are equipped. We have
machines, being extensions of the hand and eye,
directile and very proud, discovering safety.
With foreign ports at war, foreign prime cities
burned to the ground, still we are navigators.
Stars come, a rose of stars, perfumed, circle of winds,
black Galileo
has taught us mastery. Choose southern voyage,
sun provides gentler beaches, the languid warless lands.

Easy to go south into the warm daybreak, faith in the course
    restored,
prepare to land, a captain to insure a safe end;
they filled the bar, stuck labels on their baggage,
planned weekends over roadmaps, walked the deck,
nodded, handled field-glasses, spied on the pasture water,
and the ship's new position was advanced in ink,
admired for accuracy, predicted by science,
the map consulted in nervous argument.
Only, the weakness;
only, the night sent rocking into
the floating ocean and the storm's renown.

When the light changed at last, the wake ran concentrated silver
and the blue northern sea dissolved to green, brightened,
the union man questioned the captain, urged a landing,
spoke to small groups. (Official entry, "First signs of
passengers' unrest. Insults, high temperatures.")
"They must be fighting for something we know," he said,
"I saw men advancing down those inspired hills,
guns and grenades are timed now against tyrants,

a wish to keep
us all alive! under its strictest grip
logical strength challenges conscience up."

"We must arrive at land," the union man kept saying,
"there's work." "You!" said the poet, "a wandering motive!
The captain knows here's a hot country coming
among rich water, I see it! the city at ease,
the islands braceletted with cloud, sky blue of mania."
"So long as we land." "We'll land in a port fit to receive us,
fleshly and bright, set in a frivolous growth,
giraffe plants, monster flowers."
Far off, the beach
lay white at the white water's edge, proclaiming
the hostile beauty of that savage coast.

Hot city, terraced by color, tropical among green,
vermilion blossom; and the mulatto cinnamon.
"This," said the poet, "my terror, my superstition,
here's a perfect city that we will dare not enter,
point me perfection, I'll show you warning and Captain's Orders,
or dangerous action; or tenderness, prelude to violence,
any promise painted in terms of acid Picasso
is signed Beware." And a small boat put smoothly out from harbor
and the man called
from it, below the ship, his least words taking on
significance, being in a foreign language.

The radio operator, translating; "I am here for Quarantine.
No quarantine man. Dead. Plague in the town—epidemic,
the ships bring it in, says the mayor. The doctors do not know.
Most of the town is dead. They have voted. Are laying mines
all through the harbor. Around you now. I'm instructed:
Torpedo all craft attempting to come in.
Our rich have donated handsomely for explosives."
Sand, green water, litter of wavy sunlight.
"No landing place,"
the captain, "you guessed," to the poet. He shivers, laughing,
"let them come after and make me cliché."

"But you're original now," said the captain; "we're sailing to
    Nothing
doubtful or dangerous, predict a landing-place." "I'll make my
    own landfall,"
answered the poet. "Not alone," said the union man.

"Individual harbor,
and you'll discover yours—man, most successful animal,
can disembark according to his need; you!" he accused the women,
"I must have love," insisted the blonde; "What do you want,"
  asked the captain,
"another botched affair?" "My child," said the barmaid. "And
  you'll leave the ship!"
"Let them alone, they're right," said the union man. And the
  crew sang from the
lower deck—
'Wade . . in the water, chillen, wade . . in the water, chillen, wade
  . . in the water, chillen,
Gods's a-gone to trouble the water.'

"Where is the cruise the travel posters promised? The dancing
  partners, quick landing?"
the blonde demanded. "The epidemic harbor's faded, is the
  radio dead?"
"It answers only War." "Put in to port, if war is everywhere,"
the union man, "accept obtainable things." "I have my
  orders," answered the captain.
"Arbitrary commands!" "Do not be cynic at the captain's
  religion,"
the financier. "Commands are dead, he's a dead priest, the
  other's living,
this is a new voyage that you have not known."
"I've thought it out through orders," said the captain.
The sailor cried,
"We have our orders from you; but I saw a book,
and I saw a book, and I'll attempt before I die."

The poet called to the sailor, "What do you make of that city?
Of this rich water? Of captain's rules?" "I'll wait," shouted the sailor.
"If we are named," said the poet, "it is guilty generation."
"I'll wait a bit; and claim not guilt but anger,
and I see land!" The city on the cape
stood straight ahead, assuming the quality of dream,
silent, receptive, under the summer air.
The passengers sighted these last-chance piers, the towers
and over them,
over the color of street, roof, public pier,
and house: the vision, the puzzle in mid-air.

131

Is it the cloud? What's falling out of the sky? Is it
a storm falling? for a flame shot down, trailing
a falling plane, dropping behind the turning wings, clear flame in air,
and over it the dark cloud, spinning, noisy, resolving
to a cloud of planes, gunning. Among them, a white core,
the single parachute. As the flier descended
the planes circled him. Vertigo of machine-guns. And his dead body
swung, receiving bullets, sinking hooded by white
into the city.
Into the arson of the burning plane
fallen faster than flier in cage.

"That's our illness," concluded the poet, "the war our age
    must win,"
as the ship continued into pale sea, bright sea, hurrying south,
"I know its breath on my face, have noted all its symptoms,
have heard cats shouting, seen the worn eye stare
up from the doormat, the flowerbed, under the wave,
learned all the disease of this progressive time."
"Can it be cured?" asked the sailor. "At its root," said the
    union man,
"by reaching it." As the ship persevered out from land.
"Reach it,"
repeated the blonde, "what must we take to our breast,
what must we kiss away?"

When the coast fell at last, the passengers' wish was apparent,
they dreamed of some simple convenient city, peaceful, wired
    for light.
Organization of lectures and modest entertainment.
But the audience struggled out after the second solo.
Log's entry: "Engines and instruments in good condition,
barmaid in labor, supply of fresh meat running low.
Insubordination common among the men. Fruit holding out.
Feeling against ship's orders is met with discipline."
But at night
confusion over the course, anger, lack of sleep,
ominous quarrels over strange constellations.

Distress of tourists; they dream of housedogs, house-animals,
the 6 a.m. cry of lapdogs as the child is delivered,
crying but not hungry, refusing food, mumbling.
Dreams of distress: ape-murder, invective, the autumnal escape,
stumbling dead in the dry leaves, hunting someone, not
    mentioning whom.

132

Dying. The barmaid's little baby's dying words
were the words with which its weekend life began:
Mother it said, enunciating distinctly,
refusing food.
They slid the two-foot coffin overboard,
a small white circle drowning in green water.

Identical sickness; but the barmaid did not speak, the crew
worked or looked up from work, waiting for shore,
worked with a mutinous hope. The poet spoke to the blonde
mentioning love. She smiled when he said, "I praise the
marvel physical flowers upon your trellis skeleton, I welcome
from you, the discipline of every part." He thought, Elaborate,
I wait for the release, the explosive distorting act
with the same fever that they wait for land;
it fills the mind
it is my port, lighthouse, coastal clew, token,
suggesting harbors, a shore-image.

The close-up in the mind, the head enlarging to fill
the sky with its immense unique idea;
Homer wrote Helen blind, the unfree are praising freedom,
I know the exquisite taste of the sight of land.
If we saw grass, it would speak, it would say 'green,'
I dream of a boat riding on towery waves
overriding blond pebbles, grating on stone,
I have a superstition about land:
it is our wisdom,
contact and cause, without which only grows
abstinence, pestilence, unbalance.

> But if a sound can travel to restore
> the tight prophetic brain, but if a ringing
> can travel out over electric seas:

Bells cannot ring from water, land must wait
where bells invite, strong, with their Latin chiming.
The crew looks up to the passenger rail; the poet
stands with his face into the vocal night:
Funera plango, fulgura frango, Sabbata pango,
excito lentos, dissipo ventos, paco cruentos.
"What do they ring?" shouted the sailor.
"Calling of funerals, breaking the lightning, pealing the
   Sabbath,
waking the lazy, dissolving wind, peace to the evil."

"They have power," shouted the sailor,
"read what they mean."
But the boat lost their *plango*
and on the wind *frango* night *pango,*
failing sifted over the water
until one bell repeated singular music,
only and loud.
Vox ego, ringing august,
vox ego sum vitae; voco vos.
"That hails us," shouted the sailor,
"who is that ?"
"That voice of life," he interpreted, "calling you."
The cheer came.
"They can hear us!" shouted the sailor.

"Lucky you know the language," said the blonde
as the hurrah went down. "What are the signals,
what do they mean?"

"God," he said, "revelation! closing over the world,
breaking on the air, the wasted sounds among
shouts and the violent bullet in the mouth,
our age broken like stone, all grace run out of grasp,
perfected music I could never reach.
Listen!" he shouted, "triumph of bells, swinging! And for me,
bells alive also under the sea," walking
the length of the deck, rising up tall, diving,
the arc, the avalanche.
"Insane!" the critic captain, "doesn't he
know that the sea is full of teeth?"

"Send boats out!" "You'll not reclaim that man," said the blonde,
but the crew were dropping their small boats overside.
The body was gone. The sailor whistled. The rest of the crew
dropped down their lifeboats. "Who'll make the land, they hear
    us!" the sailor shouted,
"who's with us?" "Criminal fools!" threatened the captain,
and his pistol twitched the sea around them, "mutinous fools,
you'll hang or drown!" "Off your law-haunted ship! Trying for land!"
The union man, barmaid, radio operator, child who wanted
the ground jumped—
but the blond stood crying at the rail
not daring to be saved.

"Attempt land!" shouted the sailor, "fight for something we know!"
pulling on oars toward the origin of bells,
but the great ship was continuing, night advanced, the captain:
"Fanatic clowns, with their contamination,
laughter and mutiny!" and into severe morning,
the crazy alcohol blue, the bloodshot afternoon.
"I wanted to go," the blonde. "Loved that suicide?" asked the
    captain,
"you'll love me too, you'll have your love, only believe
    their song was mad,
'Free grace and dyin love, Free grace and dyin love
Free grace and dyin love, to ring dem charmin bells.' "

Pool money. Slaughter the polo ponies for meat. Tamper with
    radio.
No sound from the world, and the water giving out.
A continent of sea: they wished formal December, blue snow,
suffering cold, but earth. And the sun came down
bare as the condor, elegant on the sea.
Mist rose, a threat of mist, ranging horizons,
the captain laughed, "Remember the landslide on Chartreuse,
and does the sea slide down on our monastics?
By God," he
swore, "they were correct, they knew, when they mutinied!"
"Oh no," said the blonde, "oh no," as the mist arose.

Organization of simple banking system for passengers,
but the closed bar, the empty shops, the lack of cigarettes.
Dreams of distress : land passed in the night, with no one
    looking,
the rising mist, the subterfuge, disaster.
Log's entry: "Engines faltering, charts useless, meat maggotty,
passengers grown flabby with lack of confidence,
great trust in me while I believed in my orders.
But lately, doubts batter me. I do not confess.
The sea is
full of teeth, full of music, and there is war at home."
His mirror said, Order's tarnished, you drift insane.

Drift through continual waste of waters, under high heated
    clouds,
closing to storm-threat, guarding the ship, closing to fog,
and the passengers stared through shadow imagining
twirling cool springs, low-banked familiar flowers.

"Now," wrote the captain, "boats of madness ferry across the
    brain,
the blizzard sky's covered by fog and lost,
we'll sail by dead reckoning while the sun is covered;
saviors may rise which only can be seen
standing in mirrors."
He looked at the tarnished heirloom giving him back his face,
no word, no savior; raw forehead, open book.

On deck they lay obscured, bodily blanketed,
the faceless travellers, streaming fog bannering
between them let them forget the dangling lifeboat hooks,
the prison days, the reach of sea, the death
around them, mutinies, wars, suicides, angers,
the ineffective racid idle engines.
The captain saw the fog taint brightening to ochre,
"Sulphur!" he cried, "that's hell, that's yellow, the color of
    madness,
we'll travel back to blue . . ."
tearing at his mirror, smashing it, smashing the radio,
  smashing the fog
until his arms were tied.

And deep into the galleries of fog, riding in silence, ship
drifted dead. The cloud came wave on wave,
the blond woman sang to the sleeping passengers, captain
shrieked from his straitjacket: Make her go, her hair is yellow fog.
Land, land, she sang, let them all attempt land.
Land, she sang, doubtful or dangerous. Barriers came
across her, filling up over her face.
Disaster of music in the yellow fog,
and she sang land
Drifting. Disaster. Drifted the world away
saner than angels, promise of safety, harbor.

MEDITERRANEAN

On the evening of July 25, 1936, five days after the outbreak of
the Spanish Civil War, Americans with the Anti-Fascist Olympic
Games were evacuated from Barcelona at the order of the
Catalonian Government. In a small Spanish boat, the *Ciudad di
Ibiza,* which the Belgians had chartered, they and a group of five
hundred, including the Hungarian and Belgian teams as well as

the American, sailed overnight to Sète, the first port in France.
The only men who remained were those who had volunteered
in the Loyalist forces: the core of the future International Column.

I

At the end of July, exile. We watched the gangplank go
cutting the boat away, indicating: sea.
Barcelona, the sun, the fire-bright harbor, war.
Five days.
            Here at the rail, foreign and refugee,
we saw the city, remembered that zero of attack,
alarm in the groves, snares through the olive hills,
rebel defeat: leaders, two regiments,
broadcasts of victory, tango, surrender.
The truckride to the city, barricades,
bricks pried at corners, rifle-shot in street,
car-burning, bombs, blank warnings, fists up, guns
busy sniping, the town walls, towers of smoke.
And order making, committees taking charge, foreigners
commanded out by boat.

I saw the city, sunwhite flew on glass,
trucewhite from window, the personal lighting found
eyes on the dock, sunset-lit faces of singers,
eyes, goodbye into exile. Saw where Columbus rides
black-pillared : discovery, turn back, explore
a new found Spain, coast-province, city-harbor.
Saw our parades ended, the last marchers on board
listed by nation.

I saw first of the faces going home into war
the brave man Otto Boch, the German exile, knowing
he quieted tourists during machine gun battle,
he kept his life straight as a single issue—
left at that dock we left, his gazing Breughel face,
square forehead and eyes, strong square breast fading,
the narrow runner's hips diminishing dark.
I see this man, dock, war, a latent image.

The boat *Ciudad di Ibiza,* built for 200,
loaded with 500, manned by loyal sailors,
chartered by Belgians when consulates were helpless,
through a garden of gunboats, margin of the port,
entered: Mediterranean.

II

Frontier of Europe, the tideless sea, a field of power
touching desirable coasts, rocking in time conquests,
fertile, the moving water maintains its boundaries
layer on layer, Troy—seven civilized worlds:
Egypt, Greece, Rome, jewel Jerusalem,
giant feudal Spain, giant England, this last war.

The boat pulled into evening, underglaze blue
flared instant fire, blackened towards Africa.
Over the city alternate lights occurred;

                                            and pale.
in the pale sky emerging stars.
No city now, a besieged line of lights
masking the darkness where the country lay.
But we knew guns
bright through mimosa
singe of powder
and reconnoitering plane
flying anonymous
scanning the Pyrenees
black now above the Catalonian Sea.
Boat of escape, dark on the water, hastening, safe,
holding non-combatants, the athlete, the child,
the printer, the boy from Antwerp, the black boxer,
lawyer and communist.

              The Games had not been held.
     A week of Games, theatre and festival;
     world anti-fascist week. Pistol starts race.
     Machine gun marks the war. Answered unarmed,
     charged the Embarcadero, met those guns.
     And charging through the province, joined that army.
     Boys from the hills, the unmatched guns,
     the clumsy armored cars.
     Drilled in the bullring. Radio cries:
     To Saragossa! And this boat.

Escape, dark on the water, an overloaded ship.
Crowded the deck. Spoke little. Down to dinner.
Quiet on the sea: no guns.
The printer said, In Paris there is time,
but where's its place now; where is poetry?

This is the sea of war; the first frontier
blank on the maps, blank sea; Minoan boats
maybe achieved this shore;
mountains whose slope divides
one race, old insurrections, Narbo, now
moves at the colored beach
destroyer wardog. "Do not burn the church,
compañeros, it is beautiful. Besides,
it brings tourists." They smashed only the image
madness and persecution.
Exterminating wish; they forced the door,
lifted the rifle, broke the garden window,
removed only the drawings : cross and wrath.
Whenever we think of these, the poem is,
that week, the beginning, exile
remembered in continual poetry.

Voyage and exile, a midnight cold return,
dark to our left mountains begin the sky.
There, pointed the Belgian, I heard a pulse of war,
sharp guns while I ate grapes in the Pyrenees.
Alone, walking to Spain, the five o'clock of war.
In those cliffs run the sashed and sandalled men,
capture the car, arrest the priest, kill captain,
fight our war.
The poem is the fact, memory fails
under and seething lifts and will not pass.

Here is home-country, who fights our war.
Street-meeting speaker to us:
                                ". . . came for Games,
    you stay for victory; foreign? your job is:
    go tell your countries what you saw in Spain."
The dark unguarded army left all night.
M. de Paîche said, "We can learn from Spain."
The face on the dock that turned to find the war.

                    III

Seething, and falling back, a sea of stars,
Black marked with virile silver. Peace all night,
over that land, planes
death-lists   a frantic bandage
the rubber tires burning   monuments

sandbag, overturned wagon, barricade
girl's hand with gun   food failing, water failing
the epidemic threat
the date in a diary   a blank page opposite
no entry—
however, met
the visible enemy heroes: madness, infatuation
the cache in the crypt, the breadline shelled,
the yachtclub arsenal, the foreign cheque.
History racing from an assumed name, peace,
a time used to perfect weapons.

If we had not seen fighting,
if we had not looked there
    the plane flew low
    the plastic ripped by shots
    the peasant's house
if we had stayed in our world
between the table and the desk
between the town and the suburb
slowly disintegration
male and female

If we had lived in our city
sixty years might not prove
    the power this week
    the overthrown past
    tourist and refugee
Emeric in the bow speaking his life
and the night on this ship
the night over Spain
quick recognition
male and female

And the war in peace, the war in war, the peace,
the faces on the dock
the faces in those hills.

IV

Near the end now, morning. Sleepers cover the decks,
cabins full, corridors full of sleep. But the light
vitreous, crosses water; analyzed darkness,
crosshatched in silver, passes up the shore,

touching limestone massif, deserted tableland,
bends with the down-warp of the coastal plain.

The colored sun stands on the route to Spain,
builds on the waves a series of mirrors
and on the scorched land rises hot.
Coasts change their names as the boat goes to
France, Costa Brava softens to Côte Vermeil,
Spain's a horizon ghost behind the shapeless sea.

Blue praising black, a wind above the waves
moves pursuing a jewel, this hieroglyph
boat passing under the sun to lose it on the
attractive sea, habitable and kind.
A barber sun, razing three races, met
from the north with a neurotic eagerness.

They rush to solar attraction; local daybreak finds
them on the red earth of the colored cliffs; the little islands
tempt worshippers, gulf-purple, pointed bay.
We crowd the deck,
welcome the islands with a sense of loss.

V

The wheel in the water, green, behind my head.
Turns with its light-spokes. Deep. And the drowning eyes
find under the water figures near
in their true picture, moving true,
the picture of that war enlarging clarified
as the boat perseveres away, always enlarging,
becoming clear.

Boat of escape, your water-photograph.
I see this man, dock, war, a latent image.
And at my back speaking the black boxer,
telling his education : porter, fighter, no school,
no travel but this, trade-union sent a team.
I saw Europe break apart
and artifice or martyr's will
cannot anneal this war, nor make
the loud triumphant future start
shouting from its tragic heart.

Deep in the water Spanish shadows turn,
assume their brightness past a cruel lens,
quick vision of loss. The pastoral lighting takes
the boat, deck, passengers, the pumice cliffs,
the winedark sweatshirt at my shoulder.
Cover away the fighting cities
but still your death-afflicted eyes
must hold the print of flowering guns,
bombs whose insanity craves size,
the lethal breath, the iron prize.

The clouds upon the water-barrier pass,
the boat may turn to land; the shapes endure,
rise up into our eyes, to bind
us back; an accident of time
set it upon us, exile burns it in.
Once the fanatic image shown,
enemy to enemy,
past and historic peace wear thin;
we see Europe break like stone,
hypocrite sovereignties go down
before this war the age must win.

VI

The sea produced that town : Sète, which the boat turns to,
at peace. Its breakwater, casino, vermouth factory, beach.
They searched us for weapons. No currency went out.
The sign of war had been search for cameras,
pesetas and photographs go back to Spain,
the money for the army. Otto is fighting now, the lawyer said.
No highlight hero. Love's not a trick of light.

But. The town lay outside, peace, France.
And in the harbor the Russian boat *Schachter;*
sharp paint-smell, the bruise-colored shadow swung,
sailors with fists up, greeting us, asking news,
making the harbor real.
                                        Barcelona.
Slow-motion splash. Anchor. Small from the beach
the boy paddles to meet us, legs hidden in canoe,
curve of his blade that drips.
Now gangplank falls to deck.
                                        Barcelona

142

everywhere, Spain everywhere, the cry of Planes for Spain.
The picture at our eyes, past memory, poem,
to carry and spread and daily justify.
The single issue, the live man standing tall,
on the hill, the dock, the city, all the war.
Exile and refugee, we land, we take
nothing negotiable out of the new world;
we believe, we remember, we saw.
Mediterranean gave
image and peace, tideless for memory.

For that beginning
make of us each
a continent and inner sea
Atlantis buried outside
to be won.

(1939)

A TURNING WIND

Elisabeth and George Marshall

Their Book

". . . for the forms of nature are awakened,
and are as a turning wheel, and so they carry
their spirit the wind."

—BOEHME

Elegies

As I went down to Rotten Lake I remembered
the wrecked season, haunted by plans of salvage,
snow, the closed door, footsteps and resurrections,
    machinery of sorrow.

The warm grass gave to the feet and the stilltide water
was floor of evening and magnetic light and
reflection of wish, the black-haired beast with my eyes
    walking beside me.

The green and yellow lights, the street of water standing
point to the image of that house whose destruction
I weep when I weep you.   My door (no), poems, rest,
    (don't say it!) untamable need.

When you have left the river you are a little way
nearer the lake; but I leave many times.
Parents parried my past; the present was poverty,
the future depended on my unfinished spirit.
There were no misgivings because there was no choice,
only regret for waste, and the wild knowledge:
growth and sorrow and discovery.

When you have left the river you proceed alone;
all love is likely to be illicit; and few
friends to command the soul; they are too feeble.
Rejecting the subtle and contemplative minds
as being too thin in the bone; and the gross thighs
and unevocative hands fail also.   But the poet
and his wife, those who say Survive, remain;
and those two who were with me on the ship
leading me to the sum of the years, in Spain.

When you have left the river you will hear the war.
In the mountains, with tourists, in the insanest groves
the sound of kill, the precious face of peace.
And the sad frightened child, continual minor,
returns, nearer whole circle, O and nearer
all that was loved, the lake, the naked river,

what must be crossed and cut out of your heart,
what must be stood beside and straightly seen.

———————————

As I went down to Rotten Lake I remembered
how the one crime is need.   The man lifting the loaf
with hunger as motive can offer no alibi, is
       always condemned.

These are the lines at the employment bureau
and the tense students at their examinations;
needing makes clumsy and robs them of their wish,
       in one fast gesture

plants on them failure of the imagination;
and lovers who lower their bodies into the chair
gently and sternly as if the flesh had been wounded,
       never can conquer.

Their need is too great, their vulnerable bodies
rigidly joined will snap, turn love away,
fear parts them, they lose their hands and voices, never
       get used to the world.

Walking at night, they are asked Are you your best friend's
best friend? and must say No, not yet, they are
love's vulnerable, and they go down to Rotten Lake
       hoping for wonders.

Dare it arrive, the day when weakness ends?
When the insistence is strong, the wish converted?
I prophesy the meeting by the water
       of these desires.

I know what this is, I have known the waking
when every night ended in one cliff-dream
of faces drowned beneath the porous rock
       brushed by the sea;

suffered the change : deprived erotic dreams
to images of that small house where peace
walked room to room and always with one face
       telling her stories,

and needed that, past loss, past fever, and the
attractive enemy who in my bed

148

touches all night the body of my sleep,
　　improves my summer

with madness, impossible loss, and the dead music
of altered promise, a room torn up by the roots,
the desert that crosses from the door to the wall,
　　continual bleeding,

and all the time that will which cancels enmity,
seeks its own Easter, arrives at the water-barrier;
must face it now, biting the lakeside ground;
　　looks for its double,

the twin that must be met again, changeling need,
blazing in color somewhere, flying yellow
into the forest with its lucid edict:
　　take to the world,

this is the honor of your flesh, the offering
of strangers, the faces of cities, honor of all your wish.
Immortal undoing! I say in my own voice.　These prophecies
　　may all come true,

out of the beaten season.　I look in Rotten Lake
wait for the flame reflection, seeing only
the free beast flickering black along my side
　　animal of my need,

and cry I want! I want! rising among the world
to gain my converted wish, the amazing desire
that keeps me alive, though the face be still, be still,
the slow dilated heart know nothing but lack,
now I begin again the private rising,
the ride to survival of that consuming bird
beating, up from dead lakes, ascents of fire.

SECOND ELEGY. AGE OF MAGICIANS

A baroque night advances in its clouds,
maps strain loose and are lost, the flash-flood breaks,
the lifting moonflare lights this field a moment,
while death as a skier curves along the snows,
death as an acrobat swings year to year,
turns down to us the big face of a nurse.
Roads open black, and the magicians come.

The aim of magicians is inward pleasure.
The prophet lives by faith and not by sight,
Being a visionary, he is divided,
or Cain, forever shaken by his crime.
Magnetic ecstasy, a trance of doom
mean the magician, worshipping a darkness
with gongs and lurid guns, the colors of force.
He is against the unity of light.

The Magician has his symbols, brings up his children by them:
the march-step, the staircase at night, the long cannon.
The children grow in authority and become
Molitor, Dr. Passavant, powerful Dr. Falcon,
bring their professors, and soon may govern
the zone, the zodiac, the king on his throne.
"Because the age holds its own dangers.
"Because snow comes with lightnings, omens with all seasons."
(The Prophet covers his face against the wall,
weeps, fights to think again, to plan to start
the dragon, the ecliptic, and the heart.)

The Magician lifts himself higher than the world.
The Prophets were more casual. They endured,
and in the passive dread of solitude
heard calls, followed veiled, in midnight humility.
They claimed no preference, they separated
unity from blindness
living from burning
tribute from tribute.

They have gone under, and do they come again?
The index of prophecy is light
and steeped therein
the world with all its signatures visible.

Does this life permit its living to wear strength?
Who gives it, protects it. It is food.
Who refuses it, it eats in time as food.
It is the world and it eats the world.
Who knows this, knows. This has been said.
This is the vision in the age of magicians:
it stands at immense barriers, before mountains:
'I came to you in the form of a line of men,
and when you threw down the paper, and when you sat at the play,

and when you killed the spider, and when you saw the shadow
of the fast plane skim fast over your lover's face.
And when you saw the table of diplomats,
the newsreel of ministers, the paycut slip,
the crushed child's head, clean steel, factories,
the chessmen on the marble of the floor,
each flag a country, each chessman a live man,
one side advancing southward to the pit,
one side advancing northward to the lake,
and when you saw the tree, half bright half burning.
You never inquired into these meanings.
If you had done this, you would have been restored.'

The word is war.
And there is a prediction that you are the avenger.

They cut the people's hands, and their shoulders were left,
they cut their feet off, and their thighs were whole,
they cut them down to the torse, but the voice shouted,
they cut the head off, but the heart rang out.

And in the residential districts, where nothing ever happens,
armies of magicians filled the streets,
shouting
Need! Bread! Blood! Death!

And all this is because of you.
And all this is avenged by you.
Your index light, your voice the voice,
your tree half green and half burning,
half dead half bright,
your cairns, your beacons, your tree in green and flames,
unbending smoke in the sky, planes' noise, the darkness,
magic to fight.   Much to restore, now know.   Now be
Seer son of Sight, Hearer, of Ear, at last.

THIRD ELEGY. THE FEAR OF FORM

Tyranny of method! the outrageous smile
seals the museums, pours a mob skidding
up to the formal staircase, stopped, mouths open.
And do they stare? They do.
At what? A sunset?

Blackness, obscurity, bravado were the three colors;
wit-play, movement, and wartime the three moments;
formal groups, fire, facility, the three hounds.

This was their art: a wall daubed like a face,
a penis or finger dipped in a red pigment.
The sentimental frown gave them their praise,
prized the wry color, the twisted definition,
and said, "You are right to copy."

But the car full of Communists put out hands and guns,
blew 1–2–3 on the horn before the
surrealist house, a spiral in Cataluña.

New combinations: set out materials now,
combine them again! the existence is the test.
What do you want? Lincoln blacking his lessons
in charcoal on an Indiana shovel?
or the dilettante, the impresario's beautiful skull
choosing the tulip crimson satin, the yellow satin
as the ballet dances its tenth time to the mirror?
Or the general's nephew, epaulets from birth,
run down the concourse, shouting Planes for Spain?

New methods, the staring circle given again
force, a phoenix of power, another Ancient
sits in his circle, while the plaster model
of an equation slowly rotates beneath him,
and all his golden compass leans.
Create an anti-sentimental: Sing!
"For children's art is not asylum art,
"there are these formal plays in living, for
"the equal triangle does not spell youth,
"the cube nor age, the sphere nor ever soul.
"Asylum art is never children's art.
"They cut the bones down, but the line remained.
"They cut the line for good, and reached the point
"blazing at the bottom of its night."

A man is walking, wearing the world, swearing
saying You damn fools come out into the open.
Whose dislocated wish? Whose terrors whine?
I'll fuse him straight.
The usable present starts my calendar.
Chorus of bootblacks, printers, collectors of shit.

Your witwork works, your artwork shatters, die.
Hammer up your abstractions. Divide, O zoo.
—He's a queer bird, a hero, a kangaroo.
What is he going to do?

He calls Rise out of cities, you memorable ghosts
scraps of an age whose choice is seen
to lie between evils.   Dazzle-paint the rest,
it burns my eyes with its acetylene.
Look through the wounds, mystic and human fly,
you spiritual unicorn, you clew of eyes.

Ghosts to approach the blood in fifteen cities.
Did you walk through the walls of the Comtesse de Noailles?
Was there a horror in Chicago?
Or ocean? Or ditches at the road. Or France,
while bearing guarding shadowing painting in Paris,
Picasso like an ass Picasso like a dragon Picasso like a
romantic movement
and immediately after, stations of swastikas
Prague and a thousand boys swing circles clean
girls by the thousand curve their arms together
geometries of wire
the barbed, starred
Heil

Will you have capitals with their tarnished countesses
their varnished cemetery life
vanished Picassos
or clean acceptable Copenhagen
or by God a pure high monument
white yellow and red
up against Minnesota?

Does the sea permit its dead to wear jewels?

Flame, fusion, defiance are your three guards,
the sphere, the circle, the cluster your three guides,
the bare, the blond and the bland are your three goads.

Adam, Godfinger, only these contacts function:
light and the high accompanied design,
contact of points   the fusion say of sex
the atombuster too along these laws.
Put in a sphere, here, at the focal joint,

he said, put it in. The moment is arrangement.
Currents washed through it, spun, blew white,
fused.   For! the sphere! proving!

This was the nightmare of a room alone,
the posture of grave figure, finger on other head,
he puts the finger of power on him,
optic of grandiose delusion.
All you adjacent and contagious points,
make room for fusion; fall,
you monuments, snow on your heads,
your power, your pockets, your dead parts.

Standing at midnight corners under corner-lamps
we wear the coat and the shadow of the coat.
The mind sailing over a scene lets light arrive
conspicuous sunrise, the knotted smoke rising,
the world with all its signatures visible.
Play of materials in balance,
carrying the strain of a new process.
Of the white root, the nature of the base,
contacts, making an index.
And do they stare? They do.
Our needs, our violences.
At what? Contortion of body and spirit.
To fuse it straight.

FOURTH ELEGY. THE REFUGEES

And the child sitting alone planning her hope:
I want to write for my race.   But what race will you speak,
being American?   I want to write for the living.
But the young grow more around us every day.
They show new faces, they come from far, they live
occupied with escape, freeze in the passes, sail
early in the morning.   A few arrive to help.
        Mother, those were not angels, they were knights.

Many are cast out, become artists at rejection.
They saw the chute, the intelligible world
so wild become, it fell, a hairy apparent star
this time with not a public saint in sight
to record miracle.   The age of the masked and the alone
    begins,

154

we look for sinister states, a loss shall learning suffer
before the circle of this sun be done,
the palace birds of the new tyrants rise
flying into the wounded sky, sky of catastrophe;
help may be near, but remedy is far,
rain, blood, milk, famine, iron, and epidemic
pour in the sky where a comet drags his tail.
The characters of the spectacles are dead,
nothing is left but ventriloquists and children,
and bodies without souls are not a sacrifice.

It is the children's voyage must be done
before the refugees come home again.
They run like lemmings out
building their suffocated bodies up
to let the full stream pass.
The predatory birds sail over them.
They dash themselves into lighthouses, where the great
        lights hold up,
they laugh at sympathy: "Have you nothing better to do
        in the trenches?"
And at that brink, that bending over doom,
become superior to themselves, in crisis.
There is an addition and fusion of qualities.

They are the children.   They have their games.
They made a circle on a map of time,
skipping they entered it, laughing lifted the agate.
I will get you an orange cat, and a pig called Tangerine.
The gladness-bird beats wings against an opaque glass.
There is a white bird in the top of the tree.
They leave their games, and pass.

Cut.   Frozen and cut.   Off at the ankle.   Off at the hip.
        Off at the knee.   Cut off.
Crossing the mountains many died of cold.

We have spoken of guilt to you too long.
The blame grows on us who carry you the news.
And as the man bringing the story of suicide
lives with the fact, feels murder in himself,
as murderous regents with their gentle kings
know the seductions of crime long before death takes hold,
we bear their —
                a child crying shrill in a white street

"Aviación!" among the dust of geysers,
the curling rust of Spanish tile.
We bear their smile, we smile under the guilt,
in an access of sickness, "Let me alone, I'm healthy!"
cry.   And in danger, the sexually witty
speak in short sentences, the unfulfilled.
While definition levels others out.
Wish : the unreality of fulfilled action.
Wish : the reality of fulfilled thought.
Images of luxury.   Image of life.
A phoenix at play among the peonies.
The random torture predicts the random thought.
Over the thought and bird and flowers, the plane.

Coming to strange countries refugee children find
land burned over by winter, a white field and black star
falling like firework where no rockets are
into hell-cities with blank brick and church-bells
(I like this city.   This is a peaceful city)
ringing the bees in the hot garden with their mixing sounds,
ringing the love that falters among these hills,
red-flowering maple and the laugh of peace.
It will take a bell-ringing god tremendous imagined descending
for the healing of hell.

A line of birds, a line of gods.   Of bells.
And all the birds have settled on their shadows.
And down the shadowed street a line of children.
You can make out the child ahead of you.
It turns with a gesture that asks for a soft answer.
It sees the smaller child ahead of it.
The child ahead of it turns.   Now, in the close-up
faces throw shadow off.   It is yourself
walks down this street at five-year intervals,
seeing yourself diminishing ahead,
five years younger, and five years younger, and young,
until the farthest infant has a face
ready to grow into any child in the world.

They take to boats.   The shipwreck of New York.
To trains whose sets of lines pass along boxes,
children's constructions.
Rush to rejection
foreknowing the steps,

disfigurement of women, insults of disease,
negations of power.   They people the earth.
They are the strong.   They see the enemy.
They dream the relaxed heart, coming again to power,
the struggle, the Milk-Tree of Children's Paradise.

They are the real creation of a fictional character.
They fuse a dead world straight.

A line of shadowy children issues, surf issues it,
sickness boiled in their flesh, but they are whole,
insular strength surrounds them, hunger feeds them strong,
the ripened sun finds them, they are the first of the world,
free of the ferryman Nostalgia, who stares at the backward shore.
Growing free of the old in their slow growth of death,
they hold the flaming apples of the spring.
They are exposed to danger.
Ledges of water trick them,
they fall through the raw colors of excavations,
are crushed by monuments, high stone like whale-blow rising,
the backwash of machines can strike them down.
A hill on a map claims them, their procession reaches
a wavy topographical circle where
two gunners lie behind their steelwork margins,
spray shot across the line, do random death.
They fire in a world infected by trenches,
through epidemics of injuries, Madrid, Shanghai,
Vienna, Barcelona, all cities of contagion,
issue survivors from the surf of the age.
Free to be very hungry and very lonely.
And in the countries of the mind, Cut off at the knee.   Cut off
   at the armpit.   Cut off at the throat.
Free to reclaim the world and sow a legend,
to make the adjustments never made,
repair the promises broken and the promise kept.
They blame our lives, lie on our wishes with their eyes our own,
to say and to remember and avenge.   A lullaby for a believing child.

FIFTH ELEGY. A TURNING WIND

Knowing the shape of the country.   Knowing the midway to
migrant fanatics, living that life, up with the dawn and
moving as long as the light lasts, and when the sun is falling
        to wait, still standing;

and when the black has come, at last lie down, too tired to
turn to each other, feeling only the land's demand under them
Shape that exists not as permanent quality, but varies with
       even the movement of bone.

Even in skeletons, it depends on the choices of action.
A definite plan is visible. We are either free-moving or
fixed to some ground. The shape has no meaning
      outside of the function.

Fixed to Europe, the distant, adjacent, we lived, with the land—
promise of life of our own. Course down the East —frontiers
meet you at every turn — the headlights find them, the plain's,
      and the solar cities'

recurrent centers. And at the middle of the great world the wind
answers the shape of the country, a turning traveller
follows the hinge-line of coast, the first indefinite
      axis of symmetry

torn off from sympathy with the past and planted,
a primitive streak prefiguring the west, an ideal
which had to be modified for stability,
      to make it work.

Architecture is fixed not only by present needs but
also by ancestors. The actual structure means a plan
  determined
by the nature of ancestors; its details are determined by
      function and interference.

There are these major divisions : for those attached to the seafloor,
a fan at freedom, flexible, wavering, designed to catch food
from all directions. For the sedentary, for those who crouch
  and look,
      radial symmetry,

spokes to all margins for support. For those who want
  movement,
this is achieved through bilateral symmetry only,
a spine and straight attack, all muscles working,
      up and alive.

———————

And there are years of roads, and centuries of need,
of walking along the shadow of a wall, of visiting houses,

hearing the birds trapped in the wall, the framework trembling
    with struggles of birds,

years of nightwalking in stranger cities, relost and unnamed,
recurrent familiar rooms, furnished only with nightmare,
recurrent loves, the glass eye of unreal ambition,
    years of initiation,

of dishallucination on the diamond meadows,
seeing the distances of false capes ahead,
feeling the tide-following and turning wind,
    travelling farther

under abrasive weather, to the bronzy river,
the rust, the brown, the terrible dead swamps,
the hanging moss the color of all the hanged,
    cities whose heels

ring out their news of hell upon all streets
churches where you betray yourself, pray ended desire,
white wooden houses of village squares.   Always one gesture:
    rejecting of backdrops.

These are the ritual years, whose lore is names of shapes,
Grabtown, Cockade Alley, Skid Row where jobless live,
their emblem a hitch-hiker with lips basted together,
    and marvel rivers,

the flooded James, a double rainbow standing over Richmond,
the remnant sky above the Cape Fear River, blue stain on red water,
the Waccamaw with its bone-trees, Piscataqua's rich mouth,
    red Sound and flesh of sand.

—A nation of refugees that will not learn its name;
still shows these mothers enduring, their hidden faces,
the cry of the hurt child at a high night-window,
    hand-to-hand warfare,

the young sitting in libraries at their only rest
or making love in the hallway under an orange bulb,
the boy playing baseball at Hungry Mother State Park,
    bestiaries of cities

and this shape, this meaning that promises seasonal joy.
Whose form is unquietness and yet the seeker of rest,

whose travelling hunger has range enough, its root
      grips through the world.

The austere fire-world of night : Gary or Bethlehem,
in sacred stacks of flame — or stainless morning,
anti-sunlight of lakes' reflection, matchlight on face,
      the thorny light of fireworks

lighting a way for the shape, this country of celebrations
deep in a passage of rebirth.   Adventures of countries,
adventures of travellers, visions, or Christ's adventures
      forever following him

lit by the night-light of history, persevering
into the incredible washed morning air.
The luisarne swamp is our guide and the glare ice,
      the glow of tracklights,

the lights winding themselves into a single beacon,
big whooping riders of night, a wind that whirls
all of our motives into a single stroke,
      shows us a country

of which the birds know mountains that we have not dreamed,
climbing these unsuspected slopes they fade.   Butte and
  pavilion
vanish into a larger scape, morning vaults all those hills
      rising on ranges

that stand gigantic on the roots of the world,
where points expand in pleasure of raw sweeping
gestures of joy, whose winds sweep down like stairs,
      and the felled forests

on hurricane ridges show a second growth.   The dances
of turkeys near storm, a pouring light, tornado
umbilical to earth, fountains of rain, a development
      controlled by centers,

until the organs of this anatomy are fleshed away at last
of gross, and determining self, develop a final structure
in isolation.   Masterpieces of happiness arrive,
      alive again in another land,

remembering pain, faces of suffering, but they know growth,
go through the world, hunger and rest desiring life.

Mountains are spines to their conquest, these wrecked houses
      (vines spiral the pillars)

are leaning their splintered sides on tornadoes, lifted careening
in wheels, in whirlwind, in a spool of power
drawing a spiral on the sun, drawing a sign of
      strength on the mountains,

the fusing stars lighting initiated cities.
The thin poor whiteness raining on the ground
forgotten in fickle eclipses, thunderbirds of dream
      following omens,

following charts of the moving constellations.
Charts of the country of all visions, imperishable
stars of our old dream : process, which having neither
      sorrow nor joy

remains as promised, the embryo in the fire.
The tilted cities of America, fields of metal,
the seamless wheatfields, the current of cities running
      below our wings

promise that knowledge of systems which may bless.
May permit knowledge of self, a lover's wish of conversion
until the time when the dead lake rises in light,
the shape is organized in travelling space,
this hope of travel, to find the place again,
rest in the triumph of the reconceived,
lie down again together face to face.

Moment of Proof

READING TIME : 1 MINUTE 26 SECONDS

The fear of poetry is the
fear : mystery and fury of a midnight street
of windows whose low voluptuous voice
issues, and after that there is no peace.

That round waiting moment in the
theatre : curtain rises, dies into the ceiling

and here is played the scene with the mother
bandaging a revealed son's head.   The bandage is torn off.
Curtain goes down.   And here is the moment of proof.

That climax when the brain acknowledges the world,
all values extended into the blood awake.
Moment of proof.   And as they say Brancusi did,
building his bird to extend through soaring air,
as Kafka planned stories that draw to eternity
through time extended.   And the climax strikes.

Love touches so, that months after the look of
blue stare of love, the footbeat on the heart
is translated into the pure cry of birds
following air-cries, or poems, the new scene.
Moment of proof.   That strikes long after act.

They fear it.   They turn away, hand up palm out
fending off moment of proof, the straight look, poem.
The prolonged wound-consciousness after the bullet's shot.
The prolonged love after the look is dead,
the yellow joy after the song of the sun.

SONG, THE BRAIN-CORAL

Lie still, be still, love, be thou not shaken,
it is for me to be shaken,
to bring tokens.

Among the yellow light in the hot gardens,
the thinned green light in the evening gardens,
I speak of gladness.

Let the green night, wearing its moods and shadows
find us so, stilled within its varied shadows
falling like feathers.

We change in images, color, visions, and change;
I bring you, speak you now a changeless stone,
the strange brain-coral,

thrown white on beaches beside the peacock Stream.
Lie still, love, while the many physical worlds stream
passionate by,

in dreams of the exterior intricate rainbow world,
dreaming the still white intricate stone of the world,
—bring you brain-coral,
a world's white seeming.

TARGET PRACTICE

Near Mexico, near April, in the morning.
Desert where the sun casts his circles of power
on acquiescent sand shifting beneath them.   Car
speeding among white landscapes; suddenly
the permanent scene at the dead-center.

Photo, in circles of speed, how at raw barnside
father and son stand, man with his rifle up
levelled at heartpoint of a nailed-up bird
spread, wings against the wood.   The boy's arm thrown
up over his eyes, flinching from coming shot.

Bullseye, you bullet! pinning down the scene.
And speed you car over the waste of noon
into the boundaries of distance where
the first ring lessens into memory.
Until, a little lower than the sun,

centered in that last circle, hangs a free
fierce bird down-staring on the target of land,
circle on circle of power spread, and speeding
eyes passing from zone to zone, from war to where
their bullets will never bring him down.

OTHERWORLD
Landing at Liverpool

This is the dream-journal, knowing the earth slips under,
not knowing how the sea offers to ships
another sliding line.   This is the otherworld
slipping among innumerable nets.

Color and love of land, the water-barrier spills
sleep on the gulls' waves, a sketch of ocean
like children's crayon-drawings, the long North
Sea fanged by icebergs, green and clanging hills.

This was the journey.   Out of adolescence.
Past Anticosti, Labrador, past Belle Isle,
end of America.   And islands come;
after the ocean, the seabird's complex eye.

Ship's wake at stern, the after-life.
And pass the Hebrides asleep.
Islands identified.   Lighthouse and channel-blue
all day, pure Irish fields, a female sea.

Always ahead, new air.   Falling behind
wide Firth, the lights of Greenock bank the Clyde.
Ayr, Arran, Ailsa Craig the single rock;
the Isle of Man points water-level Wales.

Coming among the living where we rise,
coming among the dead in whom we wade
kneedeep and undermined; through seas to the great island
promising continents, the riding shores arrive.

———————————

That was the wanted voyage of a child with maps,
an adolescent at books and hearsay of lovers
telling desires dead with the end in sight.
I think now of that port, England ahead,
my clumsy porthole stare at landing-light.
I blessed my luck my landing could be loved.

Blessing my end-luck in this room again
steadily, for the first time steady. Watch
light, lying still, too awkward deep in joy.
All sliding globe-lines on the sea forgotten
and taken into shore where ships lose skill
after fierce water come to blessed end.

The Island

Land; and only to stand on the ground, stand on the brick of
    the dark-red city, stand on the car-crowded dock
with the city beating up at the face, and the harbor-land beating
    up at the feet, beating
its stony flatness after sea, with its strange tongues, strange
    turns of the head, strange
biddings, strange bracing, strange binding! but the car enters
    the tiled tunnel into the

turnings through summer country, among hills stippled with
    gardens, the shade-park forests
freaked with sunlight, the Shropshire hedges, the trenchings of
    lanes, the grassy
fallen shore-smooth places where this floor of island is a
    mowed fishpond, the deep
grass, the stamping grass and parsley, marigold leaves and
    daisies,
the car run through a narrow bridge of speed winding the
    curving the standing shadows,
along the trellised stream, along the earth-wet-smelling cloisters
stopped by cascades from a loosely practised piano in Chester
shaking its scales loose over the city crowded with speech, the
    window where Herbert
and martyred Charles and Lancelot Andrews are gone in their
    trance, in their triptych
of color to Chester's heaven, less vivid burning than blue-
    burning glass—
and the fields, and gooseberry lawns, and the ribbons of music
    broadcast identical
over the roads, threading the shadows, thinned by the quick
    and ranging
eye of the sun who takes this fief with all lands captive daily,
    gathering the ripple of
speed and our knees before us and the car's leaning and the
    enamelled tree
whose flame is grassland and the tree a fire, sun-shadow,
    blocking
out black-caked industries, chimneys of blackened cities, hills,
    hollow streets
weighing down this driftless, this island, its scarps, its
    talismanic hills,
its wet-grass-wading counties, ocean-eye out, its moist color,
    its leaping
thought lifted to down-dipping suns, standing shadows of the
    barrow-buried race,
tombstones set out to pasture in fat grass—and the fashion
whose pulses match ours, an atrophied prince, a flier's career,
the pathic gunman, the gangster mayor, the voice of a mouse—
    and the profile of cities,
the cities, the old road through Roman cities, approaching the
    central city, the nave of horrible empire,

the proud, the evening-bold—over the last rolled cloudbanks,
   in a spume of light, we speed to,
curve to past distal cities.   Starfall begins with the miracle over
   the hill.

And flat on this land the march, farm-foot, barn-foot, field-
   foot,
silent march on the London streets, come far : with slogans :
   and slowly,
the tithe-march moves, the farmers lift their flags : their faces
   break
the crust of nations once more, and farm-foot, barn-foot, field-
   foot,
pace London : their banners Invictus say We Will Not Be
   Druv: shoutless
move past the eyes of the stones, the guards, the horses, the
   houses
where the colonel with the undershot jaw sees the actress with
   the bulletproof face
see the cabman see the diplomat see the salesman see the
   colonial
rheumatic sub-secretary see cathedrals see the tourists
see the street see the marches see the silence see the island
see the island see the island see the faces of the sky.

Otherworld

Coming among the living
            at railway stations   at the porter's smile
train for the south alone in the brisk winds
a rumor of nothing at all among the forest
coming among the dead
            at Dover, a pebbled ridge of the known world
or water or the buffeting sight of that chalk forehead
a cloud over that head
tall over land
            and feeling earth slip under
            standing among innumerable nets
or Calais the rapid speech the warm hearth-colored brick
silver of trees the wheels in silver laid
Paris the fluent city running by like film

in landmarks of travelogues, the straddled tower,
the arch framing a gas-mask poster, travel on maps
south as the light decays vaulting the hills of a world
melted silver and speed, the water-silver trees
                until night spends new air, the after-life sleep
                wakes among the spurs and roots of mountains
the heat escaping, the cypress-licking sky
a country of cave-drawn mutilated hands
of water painted with the color of light
                where the world ends as the wheels stop turning
                people begin to live by their belief

Rites of initiation, if the whirlpool eye
see fire see buildings deformed and flowing to the ground
in a derangement of explosion falling
see the distorted face run through an olive grove
the rattle of hens scream of a cliff-face and the pylons filing
in an icing of sweat enter these tropics : war,
where initiation is a rite of passage,
simulation of death or real death, new name,
enjoying for a while the life of the spirits, may
travel, assume disguises, indeed absorb fear
see in this end of voyage love like that fabulous bird's
lit breast, the light of the black-crowned night heron
whose static soaring over the central world
identifies armies, takes the initiate
                into a room where all the chairs fall down
                and all the walls decay and all the world stands bare
                until the world is a field of the Spanish War

ships with their tall stacks dipping crowd the air
seas of the sky cruised by anonymous planes
subjective myth becomes a province, a city
whose wish goes to the front with its final desire
monomanias come   their diaries   their days
                the burning capitals
                when the bricks of the last street are
                up in a tall wave breaking
                when cartwheels are targets are words are eyes
                the bullring wheels in flame
                the circles fire at the bleeding trees
the world slips under the footbeat of the living
everybody knows who lost the war

NUNS IN THE WIND

As I came out of the New York Public Library
you said your influence on my style would be noticed
and from now on there would be happy poems.
                    It was at that moment
the street was assaulted by a covey of nuns
going directly toward the physics textbooks.
Tragic fiascos shadowed that whole spring.
The children sang streetfuls, and I thought:
O to be the King in the carol
kissed and at peace; but recalling Costa Brava
the little blossoms in the mimosa tree
and later, the orange cliff, after they sent me out,
I knew there was no peace.
                    You smiled, saying : Take it easy.

That was the year of the five-day fall of cities.
            First day, no writers. Second, no telephones. Third
            no venereal diseases. Fourth, no income tax. And on
            the fifth, at noon.
The nuns blocked the intersections, reading.
I used to go walking in the triangle of park,
seeing that locked face, the coarse enemy skin,
the eyes with all the virtues of a good child,
but no child was there, even when I thought, Child!
The 4 a.m. cop could never understand.
You said, not smiling, You are the future for me,
but you were the present and immediate moment
and I am empty-armed without, until to me is given
two lights to carry : my life and the light of my death.

If the wind would rise, those black throbbing umbrellas
fly downstreet, the flapping robes unfolding,
my dream would be over, poisons cannot linger
when the wind rises. . . .

All that year, the classical declaration of war was lacking.
There was a lot of lechery and disorder.
And I am queen on that island.

Well, I said suddenly in the tall and abstract room,
time to wake up.
Now make believe you can help yourself alone.

And there it was, the busy crosstown noontime
crossing, peopled with nuns.
                    Now, bragging now,
that flatfoot slambang victory,
                    thanks to a trick of wind
will you see faces blow, and though their bodies
by God's grace will never blow,
cities shake in the wind, the year's over,
calendars tear, and their clothes blow. O yes!

FOR FUN

It was long before the national performance,
preparing for heroes,
carnival-time, time of
political decorations and the tearing of treaties.
Long before the prophecies came true.
For cities also play their brilliant lives.
They have their nightmares.   They have their nights of peace.
Senility, wisecracks, tomb, tomb.

Bunting, plaster of Paris whores, electrified unicorns.
Pyramids of mirrors and the winking sphinx,
flower mosaics on the floors of stores,
ballets of massacres.   Cut-glass sewers,
red velvet hangings stained the walls of jails,
white lacquer chairs in the abortionists',
boxers, mummies for policemen, wigs
on the meat at the butchers', murderers
eating their last meal under the Arch of Peace.

The unemployed brought all the orange trees,
cypress trees, tubbed rubber-plants, and limes,
conifers, loblolly and the tamaracks,
incongruous flowers to a grove wherein
they sat, making oranges.   For in that cold season
fruit was golden could not be guaranteed.

It was long before the riderless horse came streaming
hot to the Square.   I walked at noon and saw
that face run screaming through the crowd saying Help
but its mouth would not open and they could not hear.

It was long before the troops entered the city
that I looked up and saw the Floating Man.

Explain yourself I cried at the last.   I am
the angel waste, your need which is your guilt,
answered, affliction and a fascist death.

It was long before the city was bombed I saw
fireworks, mirrors, gilt, consumed in flame,
we show this you said the flames, speak it speak it
but I was employed then making straw oranges.
Everything spoke : flames, city, glass, but I
had heavy mystery thrown against the heart.

It was long before the fall of the city.
Ten days before the appearance of the skull.
Five days until the skull showed clean,
and now the entry is prepared.
Carnival's ready.
Let's dance a little before we go home to hell.

CORRESPONDENCES

*". . . the primary purpose here being simply to indicate that, whatever
'free play' there may be in esthetic enterprise, it is held down by the
gravitational pull of historical necessities . . ."*
　　　　　—KENNETH BURKE, in *Attitudes toward History*.

Democritus Laughed

Democritus laughed when he
saw his whole universe
combined of atoms, and
the gods destroyed —
He killed the ghostly
vengeance deep at the source,
holding bright philosophical sand
up for a threat —
laughing his soldier laughter
with ages of troops after
who grin with reason in
the trenches of
metaphysics, astronomy, disease,
philosophy, the state, and poetry,
the black-and-white war on sin,
the dead wars, the impossible dark wars,
the war on starve, the war on kill, the war on love,
the war on peace.

Tree of Days

I was born in winter when
Europe heard the early guns,
when I was five, the drums
welcomed home the men.

The spring after my birth
a tree came out of the lake,
I laughed, for I could not speak;
the world was there to learn.

The richest season in
the headlines fell as I was ten,
but the crazies were forgotten,
the fine men, the bravest men.

When I had reached fifteen,
that pliant tree was dark,
breadlines haunted the parks —
the books tricked-in that scene.

No work in any town
when I was twenty, cured
the thin and desperate poor
from being forced alone.

Clear to half a brain
in a blind man's head,
war must follow that tide
of running milk and grain.

Now China's long begun,
that tree is dense and strong,
spreading, continuing —
and Austria; and Spain.

If some long unborn friend
looks at photos in pity,
we say, sure we were happy,
but it was not in the wind.

Half my twenties are gone
as the crazies take to the planes,
the fine men, the bravest men,
and the war goes on.

When Barcelona fell, the darkened glass
turned on the world an immense ruinous gaze,
mirror of prophecy in a series of mirrors.
I meet it in all the faces that I see.

Decisions of history the radios reverse;
storm over continents, black rays around the chief,
finished in lightning, the little chaos raves.
I meet it in all the faces that I see.

Inverted year with one prophetic day,
high wind, forgetful cities, and the war,
the terrible time when everyone writes "hope."
I meet it in all the faces that I see.

When Barcelona fell, the cry on the roads
assembled horizons, and the circle of eyes
looked with a lifetime look upon that image,
defeat among us, and war, and prophecy,
I meet it in all the faces that I see.

Correspondences

Wars between wars, laughter behind the lines.
Fighting behind the lines.   Not children laughing,
but the trench-laughter of the wounded, of radios,
of animal cartoons, the lonely broadcast
on the taxi dashboard, behind the wrecking crew
lit by a naked bulb — to the forgetful bars
prisms and amber shaken with laughter, to the ships at sea.
To the maleficent walls of cities, and an old actress
trying against the trying wind under the skyscrapers,
blind ageing face up, still the look of the lioness,
walking close to the buildings, along the wall,
she licks her lips in panic of loneliness.
She understands the laughter that rides around the streets,
blowing the news to the stone-lands, the swamp-lands, the dust
where omens of war, restless in clouds of dust,
mean dust is never an anachronism
and ruin's news.

The actress knows.   Laughter takes up the slack,
changes the fact, narrowing it to nothing,

hardly a thing but silence on a stage.
Crack of laughter.   Walls go white, and the plain open note
talks in a houseful of noise.   Reply : Now hide!

Over the air, the blindfold answer, the news of force,
the male and hairless hand of fear
in a shiny leather sleeve
armed.

The radiations of harm : black grooves in photographs,
blackness in spokes playing from Hitler's head.
A head with one nightmare.
Expect failure of plans, the floodgates closing,
failure of traffic-control, loss of voice, fog.
Wires dead, defection of your central power-plant.
A code : Laughter.   What alphabet are they using?

Many wished for little.
Many asked unity.

We had our characters as we had our cities,
or as a lyric poet has his voices, audible
as separate lives, maturing in poise, and symbols
coming to their "great period," too big to kill,
able to batter at the jetties of hell.

Rites of initiation of our lives:
by filth in childhood,
by wealth in the middle,
by death at the end.
We knew the dear, the enemy, we saw the spy
whisper at ear, the agency suggest,
and where no secrecy and treason were
we saw the novelist, pimp of character,
develop the age so it be understood
to read like his book, a city of the dead.

But the century had its rites, its politics,
machineries whose characters were wars.
Ceremonies of further separation.   And now, our backs to
    bricks,
war closes in, calling us to the guns
to make accounting how our time was spent.
And the planes fall.   Soon the whole incident is
over, all but the consequences.

Laughter, and childhood; and laughter; and age; or death.
Call to the male puppet, Croak,
and to the female puppet, Shriek,
and turn on me your gun for luck.

Take us our sacrifices, a wish for the living,
this foil of thought, this soil from which we sprang,
fugal music of peace, the promises well-kept,
the big and little diaries of the dead.
The song of occupations and the ghosts,
the historian, pimp of centuries, the general, pimp of wars,
the Floating Man, gentle above the cities,
afraid to touch, a cloud before his head,
laughing the laugh of a man about to be drafted,
the flier, mock-protagonist of his time,
refugees who reserve a final condemnation
and see a richer horror in the sky.

Humor, saliva of terror, will not save the day
or even one moment when the cities are
high in a boneyard where clowns ride up and down
and a night crew works quickly before morning;
while news arrives of the death of others,
laughter of brothers and the brother wars,
works of an age among such characters.

Violent electric night! and the age spiralling past
and the sky turning over, and the wind turning the stars.

NOGUCHI

Since very soon it is required of you.
Even here, on this bed, your face turned up and away,
a strong statue's face turned up and away,
the spangled eye staring live and away.
And the call comes : Open and now obey.

Now it is coming from a roomful of cats,
the dead man on the cot, desert outside,
mesa and goldmine around a tombstone town.
The cat flies shouting from the dead man's mouth.
News of the world : Open and now obey.

Now it is coming during the major climax,
when the brain is suprised and singing only medley.

174

Or in the meeting.   Or at lunch around the rink
with the stranger and the stories of Libyan maneuvers,
horror's imperative the heart obeys.

When they ask you What were you doing at that hour,
When the headlines predicted it What street did you walk
When they insist Prove yourself alive that afternoon
It was coming then And everybody saw it
Your life pointed to that That was your world.

I think of effort.   Brought us to birth in force.
Noguchi's mother with her scalded child
wedged her awake with splinters in the eyes.
If you are falling fallen failing, force
will suffice, must fix yourself alert.

Sleeping, I saw awake a widened world.
I saw a well full of men's eyes that weep,
wrong ghosts sailing the cities praised our night,
but effort of light comes, overflow morning
waking no weeping, the series of twelve doors
strike shut like clock, but my light will not go;
woke.   Love, we'll stay awake until it's healed,
until the time is brought to a fair hour,
obey the heart that calls to prove alive
a love, an age, all soldiers home again,
the growing time a child up and alive,
until the world is done.

SEVENTH AVENUE

This is the cripples' hour on Seventh Avenue
when they emerge, the two o'clock night-walkers,
the cane, the crutch, and the black suit.

Oblique early mirages send the eyes:
light dramatized in puddles, the animal glare
that makes indignity, makes the brute.

Not enough effort in the sky for morning.
No color, pantomime of blackness, landscape
where the third layer back is always phantom.

Here come the fat man, the attractive dog-chested
legless—and the wounded infirm king
with nobody to use him as a saint.

Now they parade in the dark, the cripples' hour
to the drugstore, the bar, the newspaper-stand,
past kissing shadows on a window-shade to

colors of alcohol, reflectors, light.
Wishing for trial to prove their innocence
with one straight simple look:

the look to set this avenue in its colors—
two o'clock on a black street instead of
wounds, mysteries, fables, kings
in a kingdom of cripples.

THE SHORTEST WAY HOME

There was no place on that plain for a city,
no city can break through the blank of the Black Prairie,
its stiff grass tufted grey and aluminum birds;
a province whose design holds fertile seasons,
black earth, basis for growth; travellers whose approach
bends daylight through ghosts, the reasonable dread,
frontier familiar form, through color without water.

There was no place on that prairie for relief,
until the Blue Marl Lands, relics of ancestors
passed us, belted by rocks, the tribal poles;
tourist, we hunt the past as the farmer hunts rain,
as the manic depressive in tired hunt for equilibrium
hunts sleep, swarm up the totems for a view,
see older beds outcropping, dipping seaward and blue.

There was no room on that road for a shadow.
Far off the sand-hills blew, domes over rock salt blowing
echo slant fields in the colors of winter still,
we pass white obelisks of pioneers, the square hero women
and also settlers who control the language,
riding the continent tilting seaward, seeing
the coastal plain stand faithful as a wall.

Down-lying, the drowned valleys, the captured streams, the fall
of barrier beach and hills embayed, the red, the orange,

the chocolate, the sulphur, the cuesta yellow.
Profile of waves, a jaw of sand, surface of breakers,
and there the end of the trip, and the five swimmers
finding, dive like spread hand into the lit water
seaming the ocean with silver. Tantrum of light on water.
The ladies watch whose jewels sparkle as they breathe,
the stander in wet boat, his net flinching with fish,
the city at the lagoon, surfboat and speedcar
see the whole country : Snow Mountain, under which leaps the rose
the tops of ranges where no lazy are,
through Black, Marl, Salt, to coast-land, vein to vein.

Down-lying, prophetic, the long veins of this land
passing into the sea without a change of slope.
Vein of this land feeding on rest again
eats central freshness, the white implacable root.
Each birth was earned with convulsions, each traveller's birth
spoke its word every time the tilt was changed.
But the ruined mills, but the ghost-towns, but the gaunt
    adolescent
short-sleeved, torn-trouser, before the final beach!
Pathologies of lightnings turn to prose,
broken and jarring forms to peace.
A fugue of landscapes resolved, the hunt
levelled on equilibrium, that totemic head seeing
a natural sleep, a place for people and peace.

PALOS VERDES CLIFFS

And if the cliffs themselves produced the major illusion.
Cannot without the sun, the flaming instroke
direct and personal, the haystack on the peak.

And if the flashing hay could produce the illusion.
Cannot without the sea beneath and blue
on accurate margin the surfboard boy returned
tiny from the Pacific to a fabulous shore.

And if the seascape could produce the illusion.
Cannot without whole scene : city and oilfield
in metal forests to the hills' mirage,
Hollywood and the high bare brilliant mountains.
Illusion of calm over a minute plain

in steepness opened, an overheated landscape
familiar in movies and recurrent dreams.

O prism of summer and produced illusion:
absolute calm.   Past newsreel, print, and view,
vicarious true images, do you see, over the
high-flying plane below you, over the harbor,
over the city, over this precipice,
do you see hot grass, mile-off counties, fire-surfaced sea,
obsessions of sight cliff-hung, as movie, as peace?

PAPER ANNIVERSARY

The concert-hall was crowded the night of the Crash
but the wives were away; many mothers gone sick to their beds
or waiting at home for late extras and latest telephone calls
had sent their sons and daughters to hear music instead.

I came late with my father; and as the car flowed stop
I heard the Mozart developing through the door
where the latecomers listened; water-leap, season of coolness,
talisman of relief; but they worried, they did not hear.

Into the hall of formal rows and the straight-sitting seats
(they took out pencils, they muttered at the program's margins)
began the double concerto, Brahms' season of fruit
but they could not meet it with love; they were lost with their
    fortunes.

In that hall was no love where love was often felt
reaching for music, or for the listener beside:
orchids and violins—precision dances of pencils
rode down the paper as the music rode.

Intermission with its spill of lights found heavy
breathing and failure pushing up the aisles,
or the daughters of failure greeting each other under
the eyes of an old man who has gone mad and fails.

And this to end the cars, the trips abroad, the summer
countries of palmtrees, toy moneys, curt affairs,
ending all music for the evening-dress audience.
Fainting in telephone booth, the broker swears.

178

"I was cleaned out at Forty—" "No golf tomorrow" "Father!"
but fathers there were none, only a rout of men
stampeded in a flaming circle; and they return
from the telephones and run down the velvet lane

as the lights go down and the Stravinsky explodes
spasms of rockets to levels near delight,
and the lawyer thinks of his ostrich-feather wife
lying alone, and knows it is getting late.

He journeys up the aisle, and as Debussy begins,
drowning the concert-hall, many swim up and out,
distortions of water carry their bodies through
the deformed image of a crippled heart.

The age of the sleepless and the sealed arrives.
The music spent.   Hard-breathing, they descend,
wait at the door or at the telephone.
While from the river streams a flaw of wind,

washing our sight; while all the fathers lie
heavy upon their graves, the line of cars progresses
toward the blue park, and the lobby darkens, and we
go home again to the insane governess.

The night is joy, and the music was joy alive,
alive is joy, but it will never be
upon this scene upon these fathers these cars
for the windows already hold photography

of the drowned faces the fat the unemployed—
pressed faces lie upon the million glass
and the sons and daughters turn their startled faces
and see that startled face.

FROM THE DUCK-POND
TO THE CAROUSEL

Playing a phonograph record of a windy morning
you gay   you imitation summer
          let's see you slice up the Park
in green from the lake drawn bright in silver salt
while the little girl playing   (in iodine and pink)
tosses her crumbs and they all rise to catch
lifting up their white and saying Quack.

O you pastoral lighting what are you getting away with?
Wound-up lovers   fidgeting balloons   and a popsicle man
running up the road on the first day of spring.
And the baby carriages whose nurses with flat heels
(for sufferance is the badge of all their tribe)
mark turning sunlight on far avenues
etch beacons on the grass.   You strenuous baby
rushing up to the wooden horses
with their stiff necks, their eyes,
and all their music!

Fountains! sheepfolds! merry-go-round!
The seal that barking slips Pacifics dark-
diving into his well until up! with a fish!
The tiglon resembling his Siberian sire,
ice-cream and terraces and twelve o'clock.
O mister with the attractive moustache,
      How does it happen to be you?
Mademoiselle   in   cinnamon   zoo,
         Hello,   hello.

ASYLUM SONG

As I went down the road to the water, the river to the sea,
the valley narrowed to a cat's-eye jewel,
one middle streak of highlight straightening;
and nothing was plain in the river-light,
not even what I was hyrrying for
as I walked and thought
At the waterfront they are free.

As I went down past the low barren orchards hanging in the dark
(They are free at the waterfront),
I heard the night-bird answer: "The trees suffered too much,
"now they are sterile; but in your city
"the ghosts of houses struggle to put down roots,
"and in the rooms, they have nightmares of freedom,
"they are jealous of any fruit."

As I crossed over Gravelly Run, I looked into the water
(They are free at the waterfront),
not one cloud whitening the brown black water,
but there I saw my face so bare

not blemished but unlit,
I thought, if I am not almost free
there's an end of wit.

As I came toward the sea, I saw the marks of night
walk on and over the sky and night went over
without a sound on the wide water
but the sea's sound and the windspin
talking to ships slave under the sea
and on the sea obsessed with tide
as the long tides came in.

THE VICTIMS, A PLAY FOR THE HOME

And if the curtain lifts, it is a window-shade,
and if there is a stage, it is the room at home.
Furnished as we remember it. Not too well lit.
The wooden chair   the bed quite neatly made.
The face is discovered in shadow, but someone is there.
If we look without fear, we will all know who it is.
This is a theatre and many masks have played
the part; female or male : it will not matter here.
The role is traditional. It does what others did,
if anything is said, it is what others said.

The exits are a window and a door, both shut.
We in the audience know what is in that head,
see only the fixtures of that room, but hear the loud
and ringing world; doorbell, radio, phones, and voices in the hall;
the words in the parents' bedroom; the shot in the street.
The play could be anywhere; the stage could expand. It does not.
Its acts are single actions in the player's head;
watch Act One.   Player crosses—hero and bride and clown—
and flings the window up letting the dark shine down,
the black in whom no coward is afraid.

Stares from the window into the audience,
a mirror of the world that stays and stares
and sees the player staring think, dismayed,
of an immense vaudeville of a century
when anyone may sit in a row of chairs
dummy of a ventriloquist who made
a head lying in his hand speak with a candid voice.
The play the player sees is at the margin of the mind.

The player thinks : Who speaks for me? What road
takes me away from here? The door's or window's? Act Two.

The player crosses the room to the desk; looks down.
Letters from friends are clews, the child at the shore,
the oversize girl, and the adolescent swayed
by every attraction.   The letters are appeals : We Need.
Come out and help us.   We did not remain.
The little boy runs into his green wave,
movies are teaching the slickhaired shortstop love,
the fat girl is seen entering cafeterias
pretending she's pregnant so people will be kind.
They show the player no exit of rescue.   Act Three.

Stands at the door, flattened against the wood,
hearing the parents' quarrel, thinking of father
who was the mother's favorite child, the mother
who was the father's favorite daughter, drawing
comfort from the bodies of her children, lowered
resistance in them, told them to love one person
which was impossible : they needed first two parents,
they were lost : there came upon them confusion of sex
and the maternal was male, and the great breast was drawn
forever in remembrance over the stammering mouth.

The player runs to the bed, slaps tired body down.
Act Four.   Radio playing Sweet Mystery of Life.
The hands are hidden and the sobbing's hard.
The loyal, the little; and the father is absent,
his feet are on a desk, trucks roll over his heart,
and the mother's hysterics menace the whole house,
resolving nothing.   They change; cancers invade them.
The player gets up in hatred, goes to the window, leans
out over the audience, speculates, Should you jump?
Walk down that roomlong road? It will not take you home.
As each step falls, a birth arrives. It is not you.

The sky of the Fifth Act is slant and tall,
sails on its kelson cloud.   A champion angel stands,
possibly, on an arch in a spill of gold.
But if it does, it is a statue.   The end's prepared.
This victim must come to death as the shade goes down.
The player turns in the middle of the room, and speaks.
"Bargain," shouts to the audience, "bargain, but answer!

"I will tell you what I am if you tell me where you are.
"Not everything that happens happens in the street!
"You are souls riding me, and I'm to be your ghost—
"I have more in me than that! Ticket-taker, their money back!
"I know a way to start!"   Laughs, and slams out the door.

M-DAY'S CHILD IS FAIR OF FACE

M-Day's child is fair of face,
Drill-day's child is full of grace,
Gun-day's child is breastless and blind,
Shell-day's child is out of its mind,
Bomb-day's child will always be dumb,
Cannon-day's child can never quite come,
But the child that's born on the Battle-day
is blithe and bonny and rotted away.

SPEECH FOR THE ASSISTANT,
FROM HOUDINI

for Marya Zaturenska

And for the man with one nightmare, the student of clouds,
    the bitter
hero whose silly laurels, kept on his head, confess he knows his
    Brutus,
the tall political speaker, alone on his platform, the wooden
    echoes, the batter
words, who wishes he could sail in the middle of the ocean,
    and never move at all,
for all those who freeze alone in the middle of madness, of
    sleep, of the better
madness of speed, hands frozen to the frozen steering-wheel, a
    circuit of cold coming
around through their lives, their current of loneliness, I tell of
    the single face;
a windowpane, two stains where eyes should stammer;
the head in the barber-chair, nothing behind it but hands;
ghosts, boat-burial, a headless coat on the dancing clothesline.
A shouting single dream of alone,
or the islanded paranoiac insisting
my dear dear dear dear dear dear dear
my dear my dear dear.

The one dream spoken, or the bird more alone,
rising to spill that lake, his music, over
repeated cities whose ragmen crowd the docks
staring at scraps, whose brutes, whose chinless villains
under the flag speak to their crowds
alone, howling; alone, falling; alone and alone among
all the anonymous who work and meet and scatter
and write the criminal words, "Burn this," under the letter.
And the pillars of the cities with their poor against them,
the men in the sky, riding the cylinder hung on hero chains,
the men in the airlock, waiting; in the subway, sitting
at puzzles and headlines, waiting.
And always these figures with the averted face.
Winter advancing, the white, the witless season,
and the spirit waiting.

The cold comes fast, an appetite of air —
earth-eating serpent, my Faust, swallowing
the alone and the falling and the howls of day.
The core is in the head, five-fingered wrong
throws a switch in the head; loneliness, fear,
the deaf indifferent suicide seeking the water,
abnormal batters who will not hit the ball,
magicians imagining rack and oubliette;
the athlete owning his gun; the priest his persecution,
the speaker his curse; the uniform its muscle.
But I remember I am hands and whole,
head, breasts, and white, and to be used.
Only those passed through madness have any sense for us,
whose eyes say I have seen, whose mouths read I have been
    there.
Alone and waiting cold so long.
Race up, race up, you fiery man.
He does not try; he dares not; or caring, cannot cure.
When song is insecure, again
the solo lark goes mad for song.

JUDITH

This is a dark woman at a telephone
thinking 'brown blood, brown blood' and calling
numbers, saying to her friend, "I will be gone
"a month or two," breaking a weekend saying

"I will be back in a week," in an undertone
to her doctor, "I will take care of the child,
"I may be back within the year," thinking alone
'brown blood' and staring hard at the furniture
remembering the nightmares of a room
she leaves, forever clamped at her breastbone.

This is a woman recalling waters of Babylon,
seeing all charted life as a homicide map
flooded up to the X which marks her life's
threatened last waterline.   Safety now for her husband,
no taint—brown blood for him, the naked blond,
the tall and safe.   For her, the bottomless ship
inviting to voyage—the sly advertisement,
as the enemy in war invites to luxury:
"Our side has its meat, wine, and cigarettes."
Prediction of no safety for the bone.

This is a woman putting away close pain,
child of a stolid mother whose family runs wild,
abandons fear, abandons legend; while the insane
French peasant is caught, stalking and barking Heil,
fire, anemia, famine, the long smoky madness
a broken century cannot reconcile.
Agons of blood, brown blood, and a dark woman
leaves the blond country with a backward look,
adventures into the royal furious dark
already spread from Kishinev to York.

At the green sources of the Amazon
a bird develops, who repeats his race
whole in a lifetime; hatched with primitive claws
he grows and can absorb them and is grown
to a green prime of feathers.   This is known.
A woman sitting at a telephone
repeats her race, hopes for the trap's defence.
Defenders rumored nothing but skeleton.
Applause of news.   Suicides reaching for
ritual certainty in their last impatience.

These dragon-surrounded young cannot obtain,
and the white children who become unreal,
live responsive as smoke and travel alone,
wish revocation of fugitives and banned,

know sun-roar, fatal telephones, the hand
palm placing out, the fact wanting its rant.
Cry to the newborn, the youngest in the world
for a new twisting wind to be all winds
to cancel this, rejuvenating rain
to wash it away, forces to fight it down.

A dark-faced woman at a telephone
answered by silence and cruelest dragon-silence;
she knows the weakness of the dim and alone,
compunctive bitter essence of the wound,
the world-spike that is driven through all our hearts.
She will go like a woman sweated from a stone
out from these boundaries, while a running cloud
in that bruised night no bigger than a brain
joins in a cloud-race over the flat of sky
in persecution of the whitened moon.

Lives

"THE RISEN IMAGE SHINES"

The risen image shines, its force escapes, we are all named.
Now that the threads are held; now that the footcuts hold
where these intent finders of tumult climbed
in music or mathematical intensity,
and paint, or fire, or order, found and held,
their achieved spirits gleam.   In the dark perfect sky
a hand is risen firm under its crackling globe of flame.
Against the stare it floats, over our agony of street,
repeated eyes, disclosures and closures of walls,
glimpses of centuries until the shining fails.

The faces are normal; the superhuman light saves, kills, and
    saves;
is mixed, and they fall fighting; and wake to climb the streets
in the vigor of their blood grown changed and abstract,
whose faces begotten of faces crack in their bitterness
light through all faces with the familiar strain

of features that have earned a general grace;
in a fountain of energy shining among the graves
earned human meaning and fantastic flame—
hold pitiless under street-flares colors of night, react,
remain in a passion of daybreak effort when the day arrives.
They are real whereof the ancestors were dreams,
hallucination and loneliness and the creative yoke.
And they may break the eyes to water or ease like starlight in
tormented cities whose shops and savage parks
are the star-chamber of a furious race,
whose warehouses, tenements, equations, song
have risen in complexity among
old portraits, flayed men, skeletons of slaves, and women
with brilliant carriage and averted face
proving a paranoiac rule tricking to death its children.

But there are more in the scheme : the many-born
charging our latest moment with their wave,
a shaking sphere whose center names us all as core,
risen among the timid and the torn
toward the sun-cities which the brain has known
whose moment of proof races through time to live.
These faces have risen, destroyed, found and still find
antagonisms of life, the dreamed and half-known world,
awakened forms among the profuse creative
promises of the mind.

GIBBS

It was much later in his life he rose
in the professors' room, the frail bones rising
among that fume of mathematical meaning,
symbols, the language of symbols, literature . . . threw
air, simple life, in the dead lungs of their meeting,
said, "Mathematics *is* a language."

Withdrew.   Into a silent world beyond New Haven,
the street-fights gone, the long youth of undergraduate
riots down Church Street, initiation violence,
secret societies gone : a broken-glass isolation,
bottles smashed flat, windows out, street-fronts broken :

to quiet,
the little portico, wrought-iron and shutters' house.

A usable town, a usable tradition.
                                        In war or politics.
Not science.
            Withdrew.
                    Civil War generates, but
Not here. Tutors Latin after his doctorate
when all of Yale is disappearing south.
There is no disorganization, for there is no passion.
Condense, he is thinking.   Concentrate, restrict.
This is the state permits the whole to stand,
the whole which is simpler than any of its parts.
And the mortars fired, the tent-lines, lines of trains,
earthworks, breastworks of war, field-hospitals,
Whitman forever saying, "Identify."
Gibbs saying
            "I wish to know systems."

To be in this work.   Prepare an apocryphal
cool life in which nothing is not discovery
and all is given, levelly, after clearest
most disciplined research.
                        The German years
of voyage, calmer than Kant in Koenigsberg, to states
where laws are passed and truth's a daylight gift.

Return to a house inheriting Julia's keys,
sister receiving all the gifts of the world,
white papers on your desk.
                        Spiritual gift
she never took.
                    Books of discovery,
haunted by steam, ghost of the disembodied engine,
industrialists in their imperious designs
made flower an age to be driven far by this
serene impartial acumen.
                        Years of driving
his sister's coach in the city, knowing the
rose of direction loosing its petals down
atoms and galaxies.   Diffusion's absolute.
Phases of matter! The shouldering horses pass
turnings (snow, water, steam) echoing plotted curves,
statues of diagrams, the forms of schemes
to stand white on a table, real as phase,
or as the mountainous summer curves when he

under New Hampshire lay while shouldering night
came down upon him then with all its stars.
Gearing that power-spire to the wide air.
Exacting symbols of rediscovered worlds.

Through evening New Haven drove.   The yellow window
of Sloane Lab all night shone.

Shining an image whole, as a streak of brightness
bland on the quartz, light-blade on Iceland spar
doubled! and the refraction carrying fresh clews.
Withdrew.
    It will be an age of experiment,
or mysticism, anyway vastest assumption.
He makes no experiments. Impregnable retires.
Anyone having these desires will make these researches.
Laws are the gifts of their systems, and the man
in constant tension of experience drives
moments of coexistence into light.
It is the constitution of matter I must touch.

Deduction from deduction : entropy,
heat flowing down a gradient of nature,
perpetual glacier driving down the side
of the known world in an equilibrium tending
to uniformity, the single dream.
       He binds
himself to know the public life of systems.
Look through the wounds of law
at the composite face of the world.

    If Scott had known,
he would not die at the Pole, he would have been
saved, and again saved—here, gifts from overseas,
and grapes in January past Faustus' grasp.
Austerity, continence, veracity, the full truth flowing
not out from the beginning and the base,
but from accords of components whose end is truth.
Thought resting on these laws enough becomes
an image of the world, restraint among
breaks manacles, breaks the known life before
Gibbs' pale and steady eyes.
      He knew the composite
many-dimensioned spirit, the phases of its face,
found the tremendous level of the world,

Energy : Constant, but entropy, the spending,
tends toward a maximum—a "mixed-up-ness,"
and in this end of levels to which we drive
in isolation, to which all systems tend,
Withdraw, he said clearly.

The soul says to the self : I will withdraw,
the self saying to the soul : I will withdraw,
and soon they are asleep together
spiralling through one dream

                              Withdrew, but in
his eager imperfect timidities, rose and dared
sever waterspouts, bring the great changing world
time makes more random, into its unity.

RYDER

Call himself unbegun, for the sea made him; assemblages of
    waters gave him his color.
But not the sea; coast-line, coast-water, rising sfumato from
    smokeholes of the sea,
pitching onto the black rock of the ocean-edge. But not the
    coastline;
the Atlantic coast, flinging him headlong from its rigors into
    his art.
Great salt-swept boldface captain, big-boned New Englander
    drowning deep
among the mysteries of the painful western adventure, circling
in unappeased circles into America.

Tempests, phantasmagoria! Impervious, first of all
to paint the tragic landscape that breeds us here,
the deep life, the terrible foreboding whose soil
is in our mind, the imagination of this geography.
Whose whaling port acknowledges the fearful
content of evil and the swift-lit blessed light,
Melville's 'latent horror of life' in the whale water
that Ryder, whose racecourse with its big horse Death
runs round the brain, knew.
                        In his room
wreckage of boxes, propped-leg, easel, couch, ashes, coal-keg,
    shells,

190

bronzed tarnished coffee-pot, books, paints, piled broken
  furniture,
varnish drippings, matches, cans, newspapers stacked up,
plaster falling with a scurrying like mice, paper bannering from
  the walls,
the stains, the path cleared to the stuffed chair crammed with
  poems,
money, checks, poems, the bathtub filled with clothes—
the unseen room, after a moment there.
He stood
            laying the paint on
                        stacking color on,
more pigment, dark and stormy, thickness, depth, more black,
  stove-ashes maybe,
and at the last slashed poker through the cloth, a knife of
  lightning, white as space, leaping white! out of darkness!
Out black night leaping, rider to flame.

He walks through the rainy streets, the great grey sweater;
fog walking through rain, wool worn on his giant head,
his giant beard stowed in the collar.   Walks black pavement.
Is seen on corners beaten by storms of night.
He gives a painting to the tubercular seamstress
"to look at while she lives," talks poetry
and philosophy to the woman at the newsstand.
He believes with his eye, he lives in the foreboding
empty tempests of the mind, thunder revolving
among his blackest noons; remembers voyages
to fabulous harbors whose event was sea.

He looks through the plateglass window at his formal dinner,
turns down the street, "I have been there," looks through glass
at formal painting, inch by inch, reaching the corner
stands back, "That's a fine place."   And moves away
to mystic reconciliations, feeling the world enlarge
and never complete itself, a bone riding a horse
around a track, dead angels from the sea resurrected
to lend a metaphor of waves, to sound the abstract
Jonah who rolls under a pitch of ocean,
knows God with his arms up among the teeth of waves,
the moon stark in the sky as a center of whirlpool.
All these invoke the image, a sea-belief in the sea
whose waters open swallow the army whole and save the tribe.

He is your irresponsible pioneer.   He is deprived.   Fearful of
     sex.   Desire, God's blossoming rod
points to assemblages of waters, heroes Macbeth kneedeep,
the foggy Dutchman riding, salt eyelids see
the fall of waters, the distinction and power, the shock,
the helplessness immanent in things.
Ghosts of oxen, stiff-grappled claws of a dead bird,
romantic wish that mourns from an Opera seat
over the spotlit love, wishes housekeeper love,
Elaine of wish, bends over an empty big suit of armor,
over the giant fallen bones of the dead horse.

Historic disherison : Ryder, emblematist,
divorced from the arts, believing in art alone,
master of meaning and never mastering means,
wasteful and slow, without tradition.   He shortens
the life of his paintings in their friable colors
by ignorance, by storms.   Refusing the dead life
like a nest of tables whose next is always smaller
refined and congruent, slashes American sky
by derelict lightning, turning all landscape into
sublunar ocean.   He is chained under water,
chained under rain, under paint, no hold on daylight,
his fixed moon stares into a tragic coast
whose people are little figures pasted on.
"Not you," he cries, "the human document."
These are not paintings for comfort hung on walls.
Paint over it, paint.   It is a monument
cracking and supernatural, an obelisk at the sea,
three sides shadowed with names, the sea-slab empty.
A big-boned charging figure under rain
seen by the visionary moon and dark,
unbegun among assemblages of waves.
His head that was moon the center of the storm.
His boulders that were eyes washed by the drift of ocean.

CHAPMAN

Returns to punishment as we all return, in agonized initiation
     proving America,
a country returning to moments of conversion, in agony
     supporting its changes, receiving
the past, the clews of instinct, and the rich return:
conviction in our people's face, all in pain.

He dances in Boston, the young and turning side
turned to a room of marvellous skirts whose rustle
like burning paper alters, rustling black to flame.
He looks across all rooms to a sibyl-minded woman
the dark   the clew to life   whose afternoons
he shares through Dante's climbing Paradise
to break his youth, the handsome turning side
dancing and turning again to her dark head
in rings of darkness whose God is ringed in light
which coils and revolves around him—
in the smoky garden
after the word was spoken
the blow to the rival's smoky head echoing in the hand
ringed round with darkness;
dark passages through streets unknown; and now, at home,
he sees his braced arm, ringing with the shock,
given before him to the ringing fire.
Blaze of hard-coal.   Disapparition of flesh.
He draws his hand out of flame; charred to the bone,
white knuckles and finger-bones exposed.
His soul rises screaming in the shape of an eagle.
He says, quietly and exactly, "This will never do."

"The one time in my life I lived was twenty days of pain."
And later, after the healing, after the marriage,
alone among red desert, the wild bushes' grey-green,
the red buttes cancelling half the sky, he writes.
"It was not waste land in Colorado.   Not waste time, for
"you are here and many lives packed into one life,
"the green shoot out of the heart of the plant, springing up
    blossoms in the night;
"many old things have put on immortality,
"and lost things have come back knocking within
"from before the time I was conceived in the womb,
"there were you also.
"And of the pain! it was false,
"and the rending, unnecessary.
"The breaking down of dams that ought never be up,
"but being up it was the sweeping away
"that the waters might flow together."

The life all burning on the public hill,
the men living tramort, travelling through their deaths,
arrive with marks by which they know one another

at the center of systems.   By a breach of childhood
symptoms of health declare all the signs leading through,
until the crisis comes,
air seethes, and all the bushes flicker up,
memories parasite in the life underground
irrupt with convulsions and the speech of fire.

At the focus, the cool life is insufficient.
He knows his conversion.   He speaks of Whitman as tramp:
"By an act as simple as death, he puts off effort and lives in
    peace."
Knowing by what redemption he claims his house,
he stands on the balcony of a burning building.

The ghosts come near the blood.   Sits at the bedside reading
to the dropped quiet head, Dante and fire and coexistent death
at his wife's bedside.
Fire, rage, splendor; and terror
who judges the judgment of men.
He is broken, his face is broken back,
his spirit's legs are broken, crutches hold him,
a second wife holds him while he becomes
incredible to himself, fulgurite fused by lightning,
health shaking its flag of death in his frenetic head.
Death of his son, and he heals, he is born again,
fed on his agonies, wanting again
his gritty taste of truth.

There are those who are many-born.   There is the man
who will plunge his hand in the fire this evening, who goes out
    every day
seeing Prometheus in mirrors, finding
comets, men of the people, conscious, who take their place
in national revulsion producing a nation's poems,
belong to the present, are not sterilized
by breaks from the past.
He fights for the acute senses, terror, passion, and need.
"I make it a policy to say nothing I will not regret."
Speaks from a cart-end, manhandles his hecklers,
knows the struggles of treason making it easy for death
to arrive when the living have passed the perfection of youth.

The century bursts upward in shocks of flame,
fireworks' starfish of imperial spirit,

194

ordeals by fire : he fights the finished wars,
looks back to slavery.   They burn the shingles down,
the lynched face broken back, mouth filled with fire,
firebrand full in face.   The ashes rise.
Chapman arrives to face his empty hall,
courtly, one-handed, turning his handsome side
upon the hall to face his audience,
one Negro woman come to hear.   Undoings
walking in all forms, treacheries of the deep
spirit caught in the net.   Our need is of new life.
There are these tendencies in America:
they planned John Brown; they do what will be done.

Birth after birth, in the spanned democratic
passage of birth, the incubation motive,
desire's experience, tense for finality.

He is reborn too often; the shock cannot take.
He loosens; fights for war; fights Harvard's plans:
a stone for both sides—he rants, upholstered deep
in Harvard Club armchairs—a monument to Zero.
He is charred out, is calling vengeance on Jews,
he is old and charred. He has been many-born.
Blinks in the fire-world, sees started birds
blinked red and black, the wing a dark log burning
against the sun; flashes of cypress and swamps,
a watery forest of red birds.
Goes down
his altering ash smothers the shock of peace,
he carried flame
but selling-out is not a dramatic moment,
it is the chain of memories parasite,
the thin flame of existence travelling down
until the yellow and alizarin red
flares out.   The whole of any life, he said,
is always unmistakably one thing.
And a dream-voice said Freiheit
a crackling globe flew down
fire and punishment, returning grace;
vortex of parable through modes of life
simple and imperceptible transitions
in countries of transition giving other lives
the long remorseless logic of their love.

ANN BURLAK

Let her be seen, a voice on a platform, heard
as a city is heard in its prophetic sleep when
one shadow hangs over one side of a total wall
of houses, factories, stacks, and on the faces
around her tallies, shadow from one form.

An open square shields the voice, reflecting it
to faces who receive its reflections of light as
change on their features. She stands alone, sending
her voice out to the edges, seeing approach people
to make the ring ragged, to fill in blacker
answers.
              This is an open square of the lit world
whose dark sky over hills rimmed white with evening
squares lofts where sunset lies in dirty patterns
and rivers of mill-towns beating their broken bridges
as under another country full of air.
Dark offices evening reaches where letters take the light
even from palest faces over script.
Many abandon machines, shut off the looms,
hurry on glooming cobbles to the square. And many
are absent, as in the sky about her face, the birds
retreat from charcoal rivers and fly far.

The words cluster about the superstition mountains.
The sky breaks back over the torn and timid
her early city whose stacks along the river
flourished darkness over all, whose mottled sky
shielded the faces of those asleep in doorways
spread dark on narrow fields through which the father
comes home without meat, the forest in the ground
whose trees are coal, the lurching roads of autumn
where the flesh of the eager hangs, heavier by
its thirty bullets, barbed on wire.   Truckdrivers
swing ungrazed trailers past, the woman in the fog
can never speak her poems of unemployment,
the brakeman slows the last freight round the curve.
And riveters in their hardshell fling short fiery
steel, and the servant groans in his narrow room,
and the girl limps away from the door of the shady doctor.
Or the child new-born into a company town
whose life can be seen at birth as child, woman, widow.

The neighbor called in to nurse the baby of a spy,
the schoolboy washing off the painted word
"scab" on the front stoop, his mother watering flowers
pouring the milk-bottle of water from the ledge,
who stops in horror, seeing.   The grandmother going
down to her cellar with a full clothes-basket,
turns at the shot, sees men running past brick,
smoke-spurt and fallen face.
                                        She speaks of these:
the chase down through the canal, the filling-station,
stones through the windshield. The woman in the bank
who topples, the premature birth brought on by tear-gas,
the charge leaving its gun slow-motion, finding those
who sit at windows knowing what they see;
who look up at the door, the brutalized face appraising
strangers with holsters; little blackened boys
with their animal grins, quick hands salvaging coal
among the slag of patriotic hills.

She knows the field of faces at her feet,
remembrances of childhood, likenesses of parents,
a system of looms in constellation whirled,
disasters dancing.
                          And behind her head
the world of the unpossessed, steel mills in snow flaming,
nine o'clock towns whose deputies' overnight power
hurls waste into killed eyes, whose guns predict
mirages of order, an empty coat before the blind.
Doorways within which nobody is at home.
The spies who wait for the spy at the deserted crossing,
a little dead since they are going to kill.
Those women who stitch their lives to their machines
and daughters at the symmetry of looms.

She speaks to the ten greatest American women:
The anonymous farmer's wife, the anonymous clubbed picket,
the anonymous Negro woman who held off the guns,
the anonymous prisoner, anonymous cotton-picker
trailing her robe of sack in a proud train,
anonymous writer of these and mill-hand, anonymous city walker,
anonymous organizer, anonymous binder of the illegally
    wounded,
anonymous feeder and speaker to anonymous squares.

She knows their faces, their impatient songs
of passionate grief risen, the desperate music
poverty makes, she knows women cut down
by poverty, by stupid obscure days,
their moments over the dishes, speaks them now,
wrecks with the whole necessity of the past
behind the debris, behind the ordinary
smell of coffee, the ravelling clean wash,
the turning to bed, undone among savage night
planning and unplanning seasons of happiness
broken in dreams or in the jaundiced morning
over a tub or over a loom or over
the tired face of death.
                                        She knows
the songs : *Hope to die, Mo I try, I comes out,*
Owin boss mo, I comes out, Lawd, Owin boss mo
food, money and life.
                                        Praise breakers,
praise the unpraised who cannot speak their name.
Their asking what they need as unbelieved
as a statue talking to a skeleton.
They are the animals who devour their mother
from need, and they know in their bodies other places,
their minds are cities whose avenues are named
each after a foreign city.   They fall when cities fall.

They have the cruelty and sympathy of those
whose texture is the stress of existence woven
into revenge, the crime we all must claim.
They hold the old world in their new world's arms.
And they are the victims, all the splinters of war
run through their eyes, their black escaping face
and runaway eyes are the Negro in the subway
whose shadowy detective brings his stick
down on the naked head as the express pulls in,
swinging in locomotive roars on skull.
They are the question to the ambassador
long-jawed and grim, they stand on marble, waiting
to ask how the terms of the strike have affected him.
Answer: "I've never seen snow before. It's marvellous."
They stand with Ann Burlak in the rotunda, knowing
her insistent promise of life, remembering
the letter of the tear-gas salesman : "I hope
"this strike develops and a damn bad one too.

"We need the money."
                    This is the boundary
behind a speaker : Main Street and railroad tracks,
post office, furniture store.   The soft moment before storm.
Since there are many years.
And the first years were the years of need,
the bleeding, the dragged foot, the wilderness,
and the second years were the years of bread
fat cow, square house, favorite work,
and the third years are the years of death.
The glittering eye all golden. Full of tears.
Years when the enemy is in our street,
and liberty, safe in the people's hands,
is never safe and peace is never safe.

Insults of attack arrive, insults
of mutilation.   She knows the prophetic past,
many have marched behind her, and she knows
Rosa whose face drifts in the black canal,
the superstitions of a tragic winter
when children, their heads together, put on tears.
The tears fall at their throats, their chains are made
of tears, and as bullets melted and as bombs let down
upon the ominous cities where she stands
fluid and conscious.   Suddenly perceives
the world will never daily prove her words,
but her words live, they issue from this life.
She scatters clews.   She speaks from all these faces
and from the center of a system of lives
who speak the desire of worlds moving unmade
saying, "Who owns the world?" and waiting for the cry.

                    IVES

Knowing the voices of the country, gathering
voices of other harvests, farm-hands who gather in
sources of music on the blueberry hills,
the village band, lines at the schoolhouse singing—
lit cheeks and lips over the blown-glass lamps
in the broad houses, along the pebble beach,
or up the baldface mountain's granite sky
above New England, voices of wilderness,
scorch of the sun where ranges all run west,

snow-glare on seaward slopes, sea-breeze and tea,
the voices of stinted music in the towns.
There are strange herbs in the pasture, and the stiff
death angels on the red assyrian stones.
Daguerreotypes and family quiet, wells,
woodwork and panelling, the cloaks of the forest,
all the blinds drawn on the imagination's
immediate mystery of the passer-by.
Intense as instruments to split these sounds
into component memory, and reduce
memory to uncompromising sound.

To whom do I speak today? I've heard their oarlocks turning
at dawn on the river, in the warm bankside light
heard cut trees fall, hickory pull the head
toward violent foreground laughter of torn wood,
watched steeples diminishing in low day before sunset,
and found the evening train riding the bend.
That train will never speak again of tracks
routed to outland counties, but the firm
sumac and corn, broadleaf tobacco farms,
a churchyard murmur for the air of truth,
acres where birds I did not know till now
fly sharp-reflected in water, a field of sky;
over the human lake, the gods make the swallows fly.

To whom do I speak today? Call off your wit and write
for silent implicated men, a crabbed line
of intercepted music with the world between.
Networks of songs, white seagull in white air,
cliff edge and stripe of sand's immovable gulls
hung over women's morning festivals.
Affection of villages whose boy guitarist,
blond, with his rolled sleeve and the girl behind
sings into fire-darkness goodbye after pleasure
and the streets, our liberty, the village store,
songs of the sorrow and mystery of pavilions'
slow carousel-music, bulbs and mirrors in sunlight,
processions of godly animals revolving;
or big October mornings, cider and perry noon
when the child comes open-mouth round the corner singing;
that music of the imagination here
which is the only sound lives after war.

Acoustics of sideshows! and the organist
playing the mirror of the mind again.
Concord whose choice between repose and truth
colors our memory, whose outer islands of thought
are fugal movements in one dignity.
Rebellion of outposts whose deepest results arrive
when the rebellion, not from worst to greatest,
but greater to greater goes.   The sequent movements
of that developing know supernatural
Hawthorne as dripping wet with guilt, a ghost
personal at first, and national at twilight,
and tries to be universal suddenly at midnight;
know in their pace the supernatural future
and the future of human coarseness, and Emerson's
future, eternity, whose forecast is the past,
and Alcott's suffering, whipping his innocent
boy next to the guilty, since guilt need not suffer;
and Thoreau who did not die of his consumption
but lived with it.
                    Raise us an instrument
limitless, without the scarecrow keyboard
can give repose and fame to successful painists
playing to camouflage dullness.   A scale for truth,
obscurities of a village organist
who satisfies his life on Sunday.

                                    Songs.
Young men singing on stoops, the sickle pears of Concord,
the wheels scraping the curb, lockets of childhood
faith, barn dances, ballads; or those revealing men
I gave a mask, and they to me the secrets
of sensual thought, music and thunderbolt.
The concentrated man bent over drums,
a skeleton over drums, a fritter of triangles
played without aim, spasms of arabesques
in decoration of nothing.   I speak a flute over frost,
hypnotisms of trumpets, the plain and open voice
of the walk toward the future, commonplace transcendent
chores and melodeons, band-concert morning
or the ultimate Negro over his white piano
meaning O Saint! O Blues!

                    This is Charles Ives.
Gold-lettered insurance windows frame his day.

He is eclectic, he sorts tunes like potatoes
for better next-year crops, catching the variable
wildest improvisations, his clusters of meaning;
railing against the fake sonorities, "sadness
"of a bathtub when the water is being let out,"
knowing the local hope knocking in any blood.
"Today we do not choose To die or to dance,
"but to live and walk."
                   Inventor, beginner of strong
coherent substance of music, knowing all
apple-reflecting streams, loons across echoing lake,
cities and men, as liners aloof in voyage,
and their dead eyes, so much blue in the ground
as water, as running song he loves and pours
at water into water, music in music.
                       Walks
a starfall or under the yellow dragons of sunset
among the ritual answers and the secular wish,
among spruce, and maroon of fallen needles, walks
the pauper light of dawn imagining truth,
turning from recommended madness, from Europe
who must be forced to eat what she kills, from cities
where all the throats are playing the same tune
mechanically.

               He was young.   He did not climb
four flights on hands and knees to the piano.   Heard
the band in the square, Jerusalem the Golden
from all the rooftops, blare of foreground horns,
violins past the common; in the street
the oral dissonance, the drum's array.
Far breaking music indistinct with wheels'
irregular talk, the moving world, the real
personal disagreement of many voices;
clusters of meaning break in fantastic flame,
silver of instruments rising behind the eye.

He gathers the known world total into music,
passion of sense, perspective's mask of light
into suggestion's inarticulate
gesture, invention.   Knowing the voices, knowing
these faces and music and this breeding landscape
balanced between the crisis and the cold
which bears the many-born, he parcels silence

into a music which submerges prayer,
rising as rivers of faces overhead,
naming the instruments we all must hold.

(1944)

BEAST IN VIEW

All, all of a piece throughout;
Thy chase had a beast in view;
Thy wars brought nothing about;
Thy lovers were all untrue.
'Tis well an old age is out,
And time to begin a new.
                                    DRYDEN

ONE SOLDIER

When I think of him, midnight
Opens about me, and I am more alone;
But then the poems flower from the bone. —

You came to me bearing the truth in your two hands;
I sit and look down at my hand like an astonished
Fortune-teller, seeing the mortal flesh.

Your wish was strong the first day of the war
For it had been strong before, and then we knew
All that I had to be, you had to do.

Once when you stood before me, kisses rose
About my lips; poems at my lips rise,
Your live belief fills midnight and my eyes.

AJANTA

I | The Journey

Came in my full youth to the midnight cave
Nerves ringing; and this thing I did alone.
Wanting my fulness and not a field of war,
For the world considered annihilation, a star
Called Wormwood rose and flickered, shattering
Bent light over the dead boiling up in the ground,
The biting yellow of their corrupted lives
Streaming to war, denying all our words.
Nothing was left among the tainted weather
But world-walking and shadowless Ajanta.
Hallucination and the metal laugh
In clouds, and the mountain-spectre riding storm.
Nothing was certain but a moment of peace,
A hollow behind the unbreakable waterfall.
All the way to the cave, the teeming forms of death,
And death, the price of the body, cheap as air.
I blessed my heart on the expiation journey
For it had never been unable to suffer:
When I met the man whose face looked like the future,
When I met the whore with the dying red hair,

The child myself who is my murderer.
So came I between heaven and my grave
Past the serene smile of the *voyeur,* to
This cave where the myth enters the heart again.

II / *The Cave*

Space to the mind, the painted cave of dream.
This is not a womb, nothing but good emerges:
This is a stage, neither unreal nor real,
Where the walls are the world, the rocks and palaces
Stand on a borderland of blossoming ground.
If you stretch your hand, you touch the slope of the world
Reaching in interlaced gods, animals, and men.
There is no background.   The figures hold their peace
In a web of movement.   There is no frustration,
Every gesture is taken, everything yields connections.
The heavy sensual shoulders, the thighs, the blood-born flesh
And earth turning into color, rocks into their crystals,
Water to sound, fire to form; life flickers
Uncounted into the supple arms of love.
The space of these walls is the body's living space;
Tear open your ribs and breathe the color of time
Where nothing leads away, the world comes forward
In flaming sequences.   Pillars and prisms.   Riders
And horses and the figures of consciousness,
Red cow grows long, goes running through the world.
Flung into movement in carnal purity,
These bodies are sealed—warm lip and crystal hand
In a jungle of light.   Color-sheeted, seductive
Foreboding eyelid lowered on the long eye,
Fluid and vulnerable.   The spaces of the body
Are suddenly limitless, and riding flesh
Shapes constellations over the golden breast,
Confusion of scents and illuminated touch—
Monster touch, the throat printed with brightness,
Wide outlined gesture where the bodies ride.
Bells, and the spirit flashing.   The religious bells,
Bronze under the sunlight like breasts ringing,
Bronze in the closed air, the memory of walls,
Great sensual shoulders in the web of time.

A procession of caresses alters the ancient sky
Until new constellations are the body shining:
There's the Hand to steer by, there the horizon Breast,
And the Great Stars kindling the fluid hill.
All the rooms open into magical boxes,
Nothing is tilted, everything flickers
Sexual and exquisite.
The panther with its throat along my arm
Turns black and flows away.
Deep in all streets passes a faceless whore
And the checkered men are whispering one word.
The face I know becomes the night-black rose.
The sharp face is now an electric fan
And says one word to me.
The dice and the alcohol and the destruction
Have drunk themselves and cast.
Broken bottle of loss, and the glass
Turned bloody into the face.
Now the scene comes forward, very clear.
Dream-singing, airborne, surrenders the recalled,
The gesture arrives riding over the breast,
Singing, singing, tender atrocity,
The silver derelict wearing fur and claws.
O love, I stood under the apple branch,
I saw the whipped bay and the small dark islands,
And night sailing the river and the foghorn's word.
My life said to you: I want to love you well.
The wheel goes back and I shall live again,
But the wave turns, my birth arrives and spills
Over my breast the world bearing my grave,
And your eyes open in earth.   You touched my life.
My life reaches the skin, moves under your smile,
And your throat and your shoulders and your face and your
   thighs
Flash.
           I am haunted by interrupted acts,
Introspective as a leper, enchanted
By a repulsive clew,
A gross and fugitive movement of the limbs.

Is this the love that shook the lights to flame?
Sheeted avenues thrash in the wind,
Torn streets, the savage parks.
I am plunged deep.   Must find the midnight cave.

IV / Black Blood

A habit leading to murder, smoky laughter
Hated at first, but necessary later.
Alteration of motives.   To stamp in terror
Around the deserted harbor, down the hill
Until the woman laced into a harp
Screams and screams and the great clock strikes,
Swinging its giant figures past the face.
The Floating Man rides on the ragged sunset
Asking and asking.   Do not say, Which loved?
Which was beloved? Only, Who most enjoyed?
Armored ghost of rage, screaming and powerless.
Only find me and touch my blood again.
Find me.   A girl runs down the street
Singing Take me, yelling Take me Take
Hang me from the clapper of a bell
And you as hangman ring it sweet tonight,
For nothing clean in me is more than cloud
Unless you call it.   —As I ran I heard
A black voice beating among all that blood:
"Try to live as if there were a God."

V / The Broken World

Came to Ajanta cave, the painted space of the breast,
The real world where everything is complete,
There are no shadows, the forms of incompleteness.
The great cloak blows in the light, rider and horse arrive,
The shoulders turn and every gift is made.
No shadows fall.   There is no source of distortion.
In our world, a tree casts the shadow of a woman,
A man the shadow of a phallus, a hand raised
The shadow of the whip.
Here everything is itself,
Here all may stand
On summer earth.
Brightness has overtaken every light,
And every myth netted itself in flesh.

New origins, and peace given entire
And the spirit alive.
In the shadowless cave
The naked arm is raised.

Animals arrive,
Interlaced, and gods
Interlaced, and men
Flame-woven.
I stand and am complete.
Crawls from the door,
Black at my two feet
The shadow of the world.

World, not yet one,
Enters the heart again.
The naked world, and the old noise of tears,
The fear, the expiation and the love,
A world of the shadowed and alone.

The journey, and the struggles of the moon.

MORTAL GIRL

The girl being chosen stood in her naked room
Singing at last alone naked and proud
Now that the god had departed and his doom
Guarded her door forever and the sky
Would flame in trophies all night and every day.

Sang: When your white sun stood still, I put away
My garments and my crafts and you came down.
When you took me as a flame, I turned to flame;
In whiteness I lay on the mist-flower river-bank
When you as a swan arrived, and cloudy in my tower
For you as a shower of gold, the lily bright in my hand
Once, you as unthinkable light.
                              Make me more human,
Give me the consciousness
Of every natural shape, to lie here ready
For love as every power.
I wait in all my hopes,
Poet beast and woman,
Wait for the superhuman,

The god who invaded the gold lady,
The god who spoke to the naked princess,
The storm over the fiery wanderer.

Within me your city burning, and your desperate tree.
All that the song and the apparition gave
To seal my mouth with fire, make me mad
With song and pain and waiting, leave me free
In all my own shapes, deep in the spirit's cave
To sing again the entrance of the god.

CHILD IN THE GREAT WOOD

It is all much worse than I dreamed.
The trees are all here,
Trunk, limb, and leaf,
Nothing beyond belief
In danger's atmosphere
And the underbrush is cursed.
But the animals,
Some are as I have dreamed,
Appear and do their worst
Until more animals
With recognizable faces
Arrive and take their places
And do their worst.

It is all a little like dreaming,
But this forest is silent,
This acts out anxiety
In a midnight stillness.
My blood that sparkles in me
Cannot endure this voiceless
Forest, this is not sleep
Not peace but a lack of words.
And the mechanical birds
Wing, claw, and sharpened eye.
I cannot see their sky.

Even this war is not unlike the dream,
But in the dream-war there were armies,
Armies and armor and death's etiquette,
Here there are no troops and no protection,

Only this wrestling of the heart
And a demon-song that goes
For sensual friction
Is largely fiction
And partly fact
And so is tact
And so is love,
And so is love.

The thin leaves chatter. There is a sound at last
Begun at last by the demon-song.
Behind the wildest trees I see the men together
Confessing their lives and the women together.
But really I cannot hear the words.   I cannot hear the song.
This may still be my dream
But the night seems very long.

THE MEETING

One o'clock in the letter-box
Very black and I will go home early.
Now I have put off my dancing-dress
And over a sheet of distance write my love.
I walk in the city with my pride of theme
While the lean girls at their betrayal smiling
Dance, do their sea-green dance, and laugh in dancing.
And all the stars fade out of my sky.

Early in the morning on a windy ocean.
My sleep opens upon your face to kiss and find
And take diversion of the meeting waters,
The flameless sky of peace, blue-sided white air.
I leave you as the trivial birds career
In separation, a dream of easy parting.
I see you through a door.   The door sails away,
And all the ships move into the real sea.

Let that far day arrive, that evening stain!
Down the alleys of the night I trail a cloak;
Field-dusk and mountain-dusk and final darkness—
Each absence brings me nearer to that night
When I stone-still in desire standing
Shall see the masked body of love enter the garden

To reach the night-burning, the perpetual fountain.
And all the birds fly out of my scene.

THE KEY

I hold a key in my hand
And it is cold, cold;
The sign of a lost house
That framed a symbolic face.
Its windows now are black,
Its walls are blank remorse,
Here is a brass key
Freezing to the touch.

Of that house I say here
Goodness came through its door,
There every name was known,
And of all its faces
Unaligned beauty gives
Me one forever
That made itself most dear
By killing the cruelest bond:
Father murder and mother fear.

What perception in that face
Nothing but loneliness
Can ever again retrace—
Conflict and isolation,
A man among copper rocks,
Human among inhuman
Formal immune and cold,
Or a wonderful young woman
In the world of the old.

I walk the world with these:
A wish for quick speech
Of heathen storm-beaten poems
In pure-lined English sound,
A key in my hand that freezes
Like memories of faces
Whose intellectual color
Relieves their cruelty,
Until the wishes be found

And the symbols of worship speak,
And all may in peace, in peace,
Guiltless turn to that mouth.

DARKNESS MUSIC

The days grow and the stars cross over
    And my wild bed turns slowly among the stars.

SONG

The world is full of loss; bring, wind, my love,
    My home is where we make our meeting-place,
    And love whatever I shall touch and read
    Within that face.

Lift, wind, my exile from my eyes;
    Peace to look, life to listen and confess,
    Freedom to find to find to find
    That nakedness.

SHOOTING GALLERY

for Donald B. Elder

These images will parade until the morning
When every symptom is a sign of health.
Man in repose is armed to kill, his sign
The bomber diving down the iron funnel—
Until he is free and the screaming of the boy
Becomes no more than a knitting of the brows.

But now they parade in the city and the cloud.
Or, Don, your gallery, where all images
Pass as a line of targets and the bells
Ring for perfection and the birds go down,
With one dark figure always aiming where
Any right-minded fool sees only air.

If anyone call it supernatural,
Say that all shapes seduce : this space is real,
Say that his trigger-finger can contrive

The Middle West be Spain, the hostile child
At last be reconciled; until this death
Through skill dissolve in the body with all myth.

Monsters of understanding will deny
The body holds all images, but myth
Is in this shape, shape of a target space
That can be filled by the flicker of a face
Until the parade dissolve to peace, the eye
Of the sacred hunter assume his own identity.

SUICIDE BLUES

I want to speak in my voice!
I want to speak in my real voice!

This street leads into the white wind
I am not yet ready to go there.
Not in my real voice.

The river.   Do you know where the river springs?
The river issues from a tall man,
From his real voice.

Do you know where the river is flowing?
The river flows into a singing woman,
In her real voice.

Are you able to imagine truth?
Evil has conspired a world of death,
An unreal voice.

The death-world killed me when the flowers shine,
In spring, in front of the little children,
It threw me burning out of the window
And all my enemies phoned my friends,
But my legs went running around that building
Dancing to the suicide blues.

They flung me into the sea
The sunlight ran all over my face,
The water was blue the water was dark brown
And my severed head swam around that ship
Three times around and it wouldn't go down.

Too much life, my darling, embraces and strong veins,
Every sense speaking in my real voice,
Too many flowers, a too-knowing sun,
Too much life to kill.

WREATH OF WOMEN

Raging from every quarter
The winds attack this house
With its great gardens
Whose rose-established order
Gives it its graciousness,
Its legendary fountains
The darkness of whose forest
Gives it its long repose.

Among these fountains walks
Walpurga, goddess of springs,
And of her summer stalks
A gift has been given—
Old sorrows, old beginnings,
Matured a summer wreath.
I offer it to you.
There is no storm can tear
Miracles made of grief,
Horror, and deepest love.
Under enchantment
I lived a frightful summer
Before I understood.
It had its roots in God
And it bred good love
And hatred and the rare
Revelation of fear.

Women who in my time
Move toward a wider giving
Than warm kitchen offering
And warm steady living
Know million ignorance
Or petty village shame,
And come to acknowledge the world
As a world of common blame.
Beyond the men of letters,

Of business and of death,
They draw a rarer breath,
Have no career but choice.
Choice is their image; they
Choose the myth they obey.

The world of man's selection
May widen more and more.
Women in drudgery knew
They must be one of four:
Whores, artists, saints, and wives.
There are composite lives
That women always live
Whose greatness is to give
Weakness its reasons
And strength its reassurance;
To kiss away the waste
Places and start them well.

From three such women I
Accepted gifts of life
Grown in these gardens
And nourished in a season
That forced our choices on us
Taking away our pardons,
Showing us in a mirror
Interminable girlhood
Or the free pain and terror
To accept and choose
Before we could be free.

Toward such a victory
Crusades have moved, and peace,
And holy stillnesses.
These women moved alone,
Clothed in their suffering—
The fiery pain of children,
The horror of the grown,
And the pure, the intense
Moments of music and light
That let us live in the night
Of the soul and the world's pain.
O flayed Vesalian man
Bent over your shovel,

You will find agony
And all the fears that rave:
Dig in anyone's shadow,
You find a turning grave.

But there are victories
That finally are given:
A child's awareness
Listening at a wall
To Mozart's heaven of music
In a forgetful town.
The flowering wild call
From a dark balcony
Through fever, war and madness
To the world's lover.

The suffering that discovers
Gambler and saint, and brings
A possibility
Wherein we breathe and live.
These three are emblems of need:
Now they struggle together
In a dark forest
Bound as a painful wreath;
Are in that war defiled,
Obsessive to be freed.

Let the last meanings arrive!
These three will be reconciled,
Young and immortal and lovely:
The tall and truthful child,
The challenger's intricacies,
Her struggles and her tenderness;
And the pursued, who cries
"Renunciation!" in a scarlet dress—
Three naked women saying Yes
Among the calling lakes, the silver trees,
The bird-calling and the fallen grass,
The wood-shadow and the water-shadow.

I know your gifts, you women offering.
Whatever attacks your lives, your images,
And in what net of time you are trapped, or freed,
I tell you that all of you make gifts that we

Need in their opposition and will need
While earth contains ambivalence.
I praise you in the dark and intense forest,
I will always remember you,
Fair head, pale head, shining head;
Your rich eyes and generous hands
And the links underneath
Your lives.
                    Now, led
By this unbreakable wreath
Mrs. Walpurga moves
Among her fountains.

MADBOY'S SONG

Fly down, Death: Call me:
I have become a lost name.

One I loved, she put me away,
                    Fly down, Death;
Myself renounced myself that day,
                    Fly down, Death.

My eyes in whom she looked so deep
                    Long ago flowed away,
My hands which slept on her asleep
                    Withered away,
My living voice I meant to keep,
                    Faded and gray.

Fly down, Death: Call me:
I have become a lost name.

Evening closes in whispers,
        Dark words buried in flame—
My love, my mother, my sister,
        I know there is no blame,
But you have your living voice,
        Speak my forgotten name.

Fly down, Death: Call me:
I have become a lost name.

Don't come for me in a car
To drive me through the town;

Don't rise up out of the water,
Once is enough to drown;
Only drop out of the sky,
For I am fallen down.

Fly down Death.

DRUNKEN GIRL

Do you know the name of the average animal?
Not the dog,
　　Nor the green-beaded frog,
Nor the white ocean monster lying flat—
　　Lower than that.
The curling one who comes out in the storm—
The middle one's the worm.

Lift up your face, my love, lift up your mouth,
Kiss me and come to bed
　　And do not bow your head
Longer on what is bad or what is good—
　　The dead are terribly misunderstood,
And sin and godhead are in the worm's blind eye,
We'll come to averages by and by.

LOVE AND ITS DOORS
AND WINDOWS

　　History melts my houses,
　　But they were all one house
　　Where in the dark beginning
　　A tall and maniac nurse
　　Hid tortures behind the door
　　And afterwards kissed me
　　Promising all as before.

　　The second house was music;
　　The childish hands of fear
　　Lying on a piano
　　That was blackness and light,
　　Opened my life with sound—
　　Extorting promises
　　Loud in the ringing air.

After that, broken houses,
The wealthy halls of cloud
Haunted by living parents
And the possessive face.
Power and outrage looking
At the great river
Marvellous filthy and gold.

When love lay in my arms
I all night kissed that mouth,
And the incredible body
Slept warm at my side;
But the walls fell apart
Among my lifetime dream—
O, a voice said crying,
My mother's broken heart.

Nothing was true in the sense
I wanted it to be true.
Victory came late,
Excitement returned too soon.
If my love were for the dead,
Desire would restore
Me to my life again.

My love is for the living;
They point me down to death,
And death I will not take.
My promises have grown,
My kiss was never false,
The faint clear-colored walls
Are not forever down.

THE MINOTAUR

Trapped, blinded, led; and in the end betrayed
Daily by new betrayals as he stays
Deep in his labyrinth, shaking and going mad.
Betrayed.   Betrayed.   Raving, the beaten head
Heavy with madness, he stands, half-dead and proud.
No one again will ever see his pride.
No one will find him by walking to him straight
But must be led circuitously about,

Calling to him and close and, losing the subtle thread,
Lose him again; while he waits, brutalized
By loneliness.   Later, afraid
Of his own suffering.   At last, savage and made
Ravenous, ready to prey upon the race
If it so much as learn the clews of blood
Into his pride his fear his glistening heart.
Now is the patient deserted in his fright
And love carrying salvage round the world
Lost in a crooked city; roundabout,
By the sea, the precipice, all the fantastic ways
Betrayal weaves its trap; loneliness knows the thread,
And the heart is lost, lost, trapped, blinded and led,
Deserted at the middle of the maze.

GIFT-POEM

The year in its cold beginning
Promises more than cold;
The old contrary rhyming
Will never again hold—
The great moon in its timing
Making the empty sky
A continent of light
Creates fine bombing weather,
Assures a safer flight
For fliers, and many will die
Who in their backwardness
Cannot leave the ground.
Weather is not what it was:
The losers are not winning,
The lost will never be found.
The year in its cold beginning
Finds us a good deal farther
From our good weather
Than we had ever dreamed.

Darling, dead words sublimed
May be read out loud at last:
The legendary past
Cannot scare us again.
This is what I have known
After a New Year's Eve

Of a desperate time.
There will be great sorrow,
Great pain, and detailed joy,
The gladness of flowering
Minutes, green living leaf.
You recommend me grief:
There will be no more grief;
Terrible battle that tears the world apart,
Terrible health that takes the world to bed,
Sickness that, broken, jets across the room
Into the future time;
Not the mild ways of grief,
Mourning that feels at home.

I see your gardens from here,
I see on your terraces
The shadowy awful regiment;
The weak man, the impossible man,
The curly-headed impotent
Whose failure did not reach his face,
And then the struggle for grace, and then
The school'd attenuated men.

I know you are moved by these:
The vice of self-desire
That does not lead to crime,
Leads to no action, is rather
Liquid seductive fire
Before the final blame
When there is no forgiveness.

And many lovers fail to love,
Lose the ability to move
Before the supernatural fear
Calls to the natural need
Come to the feast and feed
On a supernatural meal:
The taproot and the sacrifice.
Nothing can arrive to heal
The dead wish, the living face
That sees its disgrace and loss,
But the loss of its dear wish:
The word spoken across

Distance and loneliness—
Communication to the flesh.

There will be small joy:
There will be great rage,
Do not tell me the feeble
Grief of the very weak;
Only turn, only speak.
I see all the possible ends.
But the impossible;
I know it in its weakness,
Unborn and unprized,
It still commands my faith.
And then I remember the page
Of other words for death.
Then I remember the voices,
The voice not recognized
Or overheard too soon;
Rejected offerings,
Letter and telephone,
And I think of the bombing weather
Fine in the full of the moon.

I think of the big moon
Plain on the gardens,
And the clews of the year.
The haunted gardens wear it,
Knowledge like furniture;
The white frame of the spirit
Whose painting is naked fear.

The girl whose father raped her first
Should have used a little knife;
Failing that, her touch is cursed
By the omissive sin for life;
This bitter year's event and change
Turned to personal revenge.
Paint out the tortured painting,
The scene is too well done
But this processional
Must find some other saint,
Must find some other colors,
Some better expiation
Even more strange.

Murder is not the link;
Meaning must set it right.
Never recommend me grief
Nor deny my horror's straightness,
Early and late I see
The fire in the leaf
The minute's appetite.
If horror fire and change
Bring us our success
The word is indeed lost—
If the frosty world
Start its newest year
In fear and loss and belief,
Something may yet be safe.

Joy may touch the eyes again,
Night restore the walls of sleep,
Ease the will's incessant strain
And the forehead and the breast
And the lung where death lies sleeping.
Darling, if there should be tears,
They'll be no easy movie weeping,
Never the soft tears of grief
That go as simply as they start;
The rage and horror of the heart
In conflict with its love.

January 1941

HOLY FAMILY

A long road and a village.
A bloody road and a village.
A road away from war.
Born, born, we know how it goes.

A man and woman riding.
Riding, the new-born child.
White sky, clever and wild.
Born, born, we know how it goes.

The wheel goes back.
How is it with the child?
How is it with the world?
Born, born, we know how it goes.

Never look at the child.
Give it to bloody ground.
By this dream we are bound.
Born, born, we know how it goes.

Riding between these hills,
Woman and man alone
Enter the battle-line.
Born, born, we know how it goes.

They childless disappear
Among the fighting men.
Two thousand years until they come again.
Born, born, we know how it goes.

WHO IN ONE LIFETIME

Who in one lifetime sees all causes lost,
Herself dismayed and helpless, cities down,
Love made monotonous fear and the sad-faced
Inexorable armies and the falling plane,
Has sickness, sickness.   Introspective and whole,
She knows how several madnesses are born,
Seeing the integrated never fighting well,
The flesh too vulnerable, the eyes tear-torn.

She finds a pre-surrender on all sides:
Treaty before the war, ritual impatience turn
The camps of ambush to chambers of imagery.
She holds belief in the world, she stays and hides
Life in her own defeat, stands, though her whole world burn,
A childless goddess of fertility.

June 1941

LEG IN A PLASTER CAST

When at last he was well enough to take the sun
He leaned on the nearest railing and summed up his sins,
Criminal weaknesses, deeds done and undone.
He felt he was healing.   He guessed he was sane.

The convalescent gleam upon his skin,
With his supported leg and an unknown

Recovery approaching let him black out pain.
The world promised recovery from his veins.

People said "Sin"; in the park everyone
Mentioned one miracle: "We must all be reborn."
Across an accidental past the horns
Blasted through stone and barriers of sense

And the sound of a plaster cast knocking on stone.
He recognized the sound of fearful airmen
Returning, forerunners, and he could not run.
He saw they were not flying home alone.

He stood in a down-torn town of men and women
Whose wasted days poured on their heads as rain,
As sin, as fire—too lame, too late to turn,
For there, the air, everywhere full of planes.

BUBBLE OF AIR

The bubbles in the blood sprang free,
crying from roots, from Darwin's beard.
The angel of the century
stood on the night and would be heard;
turned to my dream of tears and sang:
Woman, American, and Jew,
three guardians watch over you,
three lions of heritage
resist the evil of your age:
life, freedom, and memory.
And all the dreams cried from the camps
and all the steel of torture rang.
The angel of the century
stood on the night and cried the great
notes Give Create and Fight—
while war
runs through your veins, while life
a bubble of air stands in your throat,
answer the silence of the weak:
Speak!

SEA MERCY

The sea dances its morning
On my enlightened bones,
Stones of the lip-warm land
Clap my awakening.
The land is partly lost,
The sea is all water,
Half horror and half blue
Shaking its appetites
Among my senses.
History has commanded
All the rivers—
A ship entered the bay
And the sky sailed in.
The twentieth century
Stares from the high air—
The skin of the land
Is shallow and very green
But the sea   the sea
Is still, the deep scene
Contains the unbroken
Tides of man.
Horror is appetite,
Hell is lonely,
War's a breath.
Wake us   you black
You white   you water.
The scream of the gull:
Land's too shallow
Life's a breath
Sea mercy.
Worms be my carnival
Who cries there is no death?

LONG PAST MONCADA

Nothing was less than it seemed, my darling:
The danger was greater, the love was greater, the suffering
       Grows daily great—

And the fear we saw gathering into that Spanish valley
Is rank in all countries, a garden of growing death;
Your death, my darling, the threat to our lifetime
                    And to all we love.

Whether you fell at Huesca during the lack of guns,
Or later, at Barcelona, as the city fell,
                    You reach my days;
Among the heckling of clocks, the incessant failures,
I know how you recognized our war, and ran
To it as a runner to his eager wedding
                    Or our immediate love.

If I indeed killed you, my darling, if my cable killed
Arriving the afternoon the city fell,
                    No further guilt
Could more irrevocably drive my days
Through the disordered battles and the cities down
In a clash of metal on murder, a stampede of
                    Hunger and death.

Other loves, other children, other gifts, as you said,
"Of the revolution," arrive—but, darling, where
                    You entered, life
Entered my hours, whether you lie fallen
Among those sunlight fields, or by miracle somewhere stand,
Your words of war and love, death and another promise
                    Survive as a lifetime sound.

CHAPULTEPEC PARK / I

The calling and the melody all night long
And then in the first stillness, morning
Leaning over the dark, over the night-park
Combing her blue hair.
After the guitars, after the tide of bells,
Surge, calls, and furious song,
Very softly the trees emerge,
A tree of light beside a tree of darkness.
And in the silent park
A girl opens her eyes and combs her hair.
Freshness of blue wavers among the lakes;
Two people wake, look at the calm forest,

Turn an iron wheelbarrow on its back
And, fanning a little fire under it,
Cook their tortillas.
Morning leans down; morning lifts out of the stone
The angry archaic statue of a god
Watching from live rock.
The Palace whitens, and all the standing fountains.
Snow is shining on the far volcanoes,
We walk smiling down the Philosopher's Footpath.
A young horse runs into the sunlight.

CHAPULTEPEC PARK / II

The city of the heart
Is like this city.   Its names commemorate
Beliefs and lovers, books and the body's forms.
I walk among these avenues whose great
Names speak of places and saints, revolts and flowers.

I walk through the night city; walking hear a cry
Calling, "Slaves demand promises, we need no promises,
We are free; we promise ourselves a living world."
Shadows after the lamps, bruise-color and bronze
On the pure walls of midnight. Dark, my brothers,
Where your dark faces watch against a stubborn sky.

Mystical passion, fury, the taste of the world.
The calling of the world, and everything man fears:
Poetry, poetry, bravery, poverty, war.
And if we weep, it is ourselves we weep,
Not our belief.   But in these streets we see
The cheapest tourists, the twisted cross parade.

The city of the heart knows creeping fire
That beats its towers into storms of flame.
Cynics of power come with their shout of blame,
We wake among the dreams; grace has its ways:
Fire and gleam of blood on stone will fade
Into the moment of proof, blood of our days.

Dawn comes to the city and the spirit's city,
Laughs in the heart like a child, and midday flies
Over the dogs with their sharp and primitive faces
Coursing gay and masterless to the zoo.

The live heart laughs and courses and is free,
For the city contains poverty, bravery, war,
But most, a deepened hope, sunlight and memory.

A GAME OF BALL

On a ground beaten gold by running and
Over the Aztec crest of the sky and
Past the white religious faces of the
Bulls and far beyond, the ball goes flying.

Sun and moon and all the stars of the moon
Are dancing across our eyes like the flight of armies
And the loser dies.   Dark player and bright
Play for the twinned stiff god of life and death.
They die and become the law by which they fight.

Walls grow out of this light, branches out of the stone,
And fire running from the farthest winds
Pours broken flame on these fantastic sands
Where, sunlit, stands the goddess of earth and death,
A frightful peasant with work-hardened hands.

But over the field flash all the colors of summer,
The battle flickers in play, a game like sacrifice.
The sun rides over, the moon and all her stars.
Whatever is ready to eat us, we have found
This place where the gods play out the game of the sky
And bandy life and death across a summer ground.

GOLD LEAF

A shadowy arch calling the clouds of the sun
To enter, enter.   Enter.   But they run.

Their seeking whiteness refuses the false, the thief.
This shadow is rich twilight of gold leaf.

A mask of gold beaten upon the stone
Is a live cheek painted on martyr bone.

If you go through the gold you find a hand
Delicate as foam and at the wrist

Foam and the scarlet cloth of a sick priest.
Until he coughs you will not understand.

You must go deeper to find the pure dark way,
The many crying "Sangre!" "Sangre!" "Sangre!"

Deeper than death the faithful blood will flow
Singing "Mexico!" "Mexico!" "Mexico!"

A serpent in the passionate garden says
"This," looking at men and saying "this, this."

Pain and the desperate music of the poor.
The true darkness.   A naked human door.

Out of this darkness music of the crowd,
Bells raise their circles of truth and find the cloud.

ALL SOULS

The day of life and death offers its flowers:
Branches of flame toward a midnight lake of stars,
And the harsh sunny smell of weeds at noon.
In the clear season, we sit upon the graves
(Northern red leaf, frost-witches and toy ghost):
Here are the crystal skull and flowering bone.

The cloak of blood down the shoulder of the bull.

Whirl of mirrors and light about the blade
And the bullring turning groaning to the sun.—
We are all sitting on graves, drinking together,
Each grave a family gay on the hot grass,
Its bottle, its loaf of bread in a basket,
And a few peaches too perfect ever to wither.

And the river of light down the shoulder of the hill.

The drink of flowers and fire in the sun,
The child in pink holding her sugar skull—
This appetite raving on death's high holiday:
Love of the dead, fierce love of the alive.
We eat the feast of our mortality,
Drink fiery joy, and death sinks down with day.

O in the burning day of life and death
The strong drink running down the shoulder of the grave!

EVENING PLAZA, SAN MIGUEL

No one will ever understand that evening
Who has not lain the night with a changeable lover,
Changeable as that last evening.

No one who has not ever seen that color
Change and travel the hills, the irrelevant bells
Ringing the changes,

And seen the green enter the evening sky,
Reluctant yellow come and the cathedral
Unfold in rose—

And stood under that rose of stone, remembering rose
Spattered in feasts of rockets, interrupted
By the black downdrawn line

Of the down-turning wheel of carnival—will ever know
The evening color filtered through cinnamon
And how the birds came down

Through the bars of yellow and the bars of green
Into the brandy dusk and the leaves of night,
A touch, a shadow of touch, when breasts

Lift their little branches, and showers and flares of fire
Rise in the blood, in spite of the word of war,
In spite of evening coming down like a lover,

Like the birds falling among the trees, like music
As the trees close, and the cathedral closes.
No one will know who in a stranger land

Has never stood while night came down
In shadows of roses, a cloud of tree-drawn birds,
And said, "I must go home."

BEAST IN VIEW

Configurations of time and singing
    Bring me to a dark harbor where
    The chase is drawn to a beginning.
    And all the myths are gathered there.

I know the trees as fountains and the stars'
    Far fires fountains and your love
    A vivid fountain, and the bars
    Broken about me let me move

Among the fountains.   At last seeing
    I came here by obscure preparing,
    In vigils and encounters being
    Both running hunter and fierce prey waring.

I hunted and became the followed,
    Through many lives fleeing the last me,
    And changing fought down a far road
    Through time to myself as I will be.

Chaos prepared me, and I find the track,
    Through life and darkness seek my myth—
    Move toward it, hunting grow more like,
    Draw near, and know it through our path.
    Know only that we run one path.

Letter to the Front

LETTER TO THE FRONT

I

Women and poets see the truth arrive.
Then it is acted out,
The lives are lost, and all the newsboys shout.

Horror of cities follows, and the maze
Of compromise and grief.
The feeble cry Defeat be my belief.

All the strong agonized men
Wear the hard clothes of war,
Try to remember what they are fighting for.

But in dark weeping helpless moments of peace
Women and poets believe and resist forever:
The blind inventor finds the underground river.

II

Even during war, moments of delicate peace
Arrive; ceaseless the water ripples, love
Speaks through the river in its human voices.
Through every power to affirm and heal
The unknown world suggests the air and golden
Familiar flowers, and the brief glitter of waves,
And dreams, and leads me always to the real.
Even among these calendars of fire.

Sings: There is much to fear, but not our power.
The stars turn over us; let us not fear the many.
All mortal intricacies tremble upon this flower.
Let us not fear the hidden.   Or each other.
We are alive in an hour whose burning face
Looks into our death, death of our dear wish.
And time that will be eating away our flesh
Gives us this moment when blue settles on rose
And evening suddenly seems limitless silver.
The cold wind streaming over the cold hill-grasses
Remembers and remembers.   Mountains lift into night.
And I am remembering the face of peace.

I have seen a ship lying upon the water
Rise like a great bird, like a lifted promise.

III

They called us to a change of heart
But it was not enough.
Not half enough, not half enough
For all their bargaining and their art.

After the change of heart there comes
The savage waste of battlefield;
The flame of that wild battlefield
Rushes in fire through our rooms.

The heart that comes to know its war
When gambling powers try for place

Must live to wrestle for a place
For every burning human care:

To know a war begins the day
Ideas of peace are bargained for,
Surrender and death are bargained for—
Peace and belief must fight their way.

Begin the day we change and so
Open the spirit to the world.
Wars of the spirit in the world
Makes us continually know
We fight continually to grow.

IV / Sestina

Coming to Spain on the first day of the fighting,
Flame in the mountains, and the exotic soldiers,
I gave up ideas of strangeness, but now, keeping
All I profoundly hoped for, I saw fearing
Travellers and the unprepared and the fast-changing
Foothills.   The train stopped in a silver country.

Coast-water lit the valleys of this country—
All mysteries stood human in the fighting.
We came from far.   We wondered, Were they changing,
Our mild companions, turning into soldiers?
But the cowards were persistent in their fearing,
Each of us narrowed to one wish he was keeping.

There was no change of heart here; we were keeping
Our deepest wish, meeting with hope this country.
The enemies among us went on fearing
The frontier was too far behind.   The fighting
Was clear to us all at last.   The belted soldiers
Vanished into white hills that dark was changing.

The train stood naked in flowery midnight changing
All complex marvellous hope to war, and keeping
Among us only the main wish, and the soldiers.
We loved each other, believed in the war; this country
Meant to us the arrival of the fighting
At home; we began to know what we were fearing.

As continents broke apart, we saw our fearing
Reflect our nations' fears; we acted as changing
Cities at home would act, with one wish, fighting
This threat or falling under it; we were keeping
The knowledge of fiery promises; this country
Struck at our lives, struck deeper than its soldiers.

Those who among us were sure became our soldiers.
The dreams of peace resolved our subtle fearing.
This was the first day of war in a strange country.
Free Catalonia offered that day our changing
Age's hope and resistance, held in its keeping
The war this age must win in love and fighting.

This first day of fighting showed us all men as soldiers.
It offered one wish for keeping.   Hope.   Deep fearing.
Our changing spirits awake in the soul's country.

V

Much later, I lie in a white seaport night
Of gongs and mystery and bewildered mist
Giving me a strange harbor in these white
Scenes, white rivers, my white dreams of peace.
And a ship lifted up on a sign of freedom.
Peace sharp and immediate as our winter stars.
A blue sailor with a cargo of guitars.

I saw a white ship rise as peace was made
In Spain, the first peace the world would not keep.
The ship pulled away from the harbor where Columbus
Standing on his black pillar sees new worlds;
And suddenly all the people at all the rails
Lifted their hands in a gesture of belief
That climbs among my dreams like a bird flying.
Until the world is lifted by one bird flying
An instant drawing to itself the world.

VI

Home thoughts from home; we read you every day,
Soldiers of distances.   You wish most to be here.
In the strange lands of war, I woke and thought of home.
Remembering how war came, I wake and think of you,
In the city of water and stone where I was born,

My home of complex light.   What we were fighting for,
In the beginning, in Spain, was not to be defined.
More human than abstract, more direction than end.
Terror arrived intact, lit with the tragic fire
Of hope before its time, tore us from lover and friend.
We came to the violent act with all that we had learned.

But now we are that home you dream across a war.
You fight; and we must go in poetry and hope
Moving into the future that no one can escape.
Peace will in time arrive, but war defined our years.
We are like that young saint at the spring who bent
Her face over dry earth the vision told her flowed,
Miring herself.   She knew it was water.   But for
Herself, it was filth.   Later, for all to come
Following her faith, miraculous crystal ran.

O saint, O poet, O wounded of these wars
To find life flowing from the heart of man.
We hold belief.   You fight and are maimed and mad.
We believe, though all you want be bed with one
Whose mouth is bread and wine, whose flesh is home.

VII

To be a Jew in the twentieth century
Is to be offered a gift.   If you refuse,
Wishing to be invisible, you choose
Death of the spirit, the stone insanity.
Accepting, take full life.   Full agonies:
Your evening deep in labyrinthine blood
Of those who resist, fail, and resist; and God
Reduced to a hostage among hostages.

The gift is torment.   Not alone the still
Torture, isolation; or torture of the flesh.
That may come also.   But the accepting wish,
The whole and fertile spirit as guarantee
For every human freedom, suffering to be free,
Daring to live for the impossible.

VIII

Evening, bringing me out of the government building,
Spills her blue air, her great Atlantic clouds

Over my hair, reminds me of my land.
My back to high stone and that man's golden bands
Who said of our time which has only its freedom,
"I will not ever say 'for a free world,'
'A better world' or whatever it is;
A man fights to win a war,
To hang on to what is his—"
Consider this man in the clothes of a commander.
Remember that his field is bottled fizz.

O the blue air and the nightsound of heartbeats—
Planes or poems or dreams direct as prayer.
The belief in the world, and we can stand with them,
Whoever clearly fights the order of despair.
In spite of the fascist, Malicioso King,
Contractor, business man and publisher,
Who will hire a man to hire another man
To hire someone to murder the man of strong belief.
Look at him at the Radio City bar;
Remember that he functions best as thief.

O the clouds and the towers are not enough to hide
The little sneer at freedom, the whisper that art died.
Here is the man who changed his name, the man who dyed his
    hair;
One praises only his own birth; one only his own whore.
Unable to create or fight or commit suicide,
Will make a job of weakness, be the impotent editor,
The sad and pathic bull always wishing he were
The bullfighter.   But we remember the changes that he made,
Screaming "Betrayed!" He forever betrays.   He alone is
    betrayed.

They are all here in this divided time:
Dies the inquisitor against the truth,
Wheeler, Nye, Pegler, Hearst, each with his crews,
McCormick, the Representatives whose crime
Is against history, the state, and love.
I hold their dead skulls in my hand; this death
Worked against labor, women, Jews,
Reds, Negroes.   But our freedom lives
To fight the war the world must win.
The fevers of confusion's touch
Leap to confusion in the land.

We shall grow and fight again.
The sickness of our divided state
Calls to the anger and the great
Imaginative gifts of man.
The enemy does his rigid work.
We live fighting in that dark.
Let all the living fight in proof
They start the world this war must win.

IX

Among all the waste there are the intense stories
And tellers of stories.   One saw a peasant die.
One guarded a soldier through disease.   And one
Saw all the women look at each other in hope.
And came back, saying, "All things must be known."

They come home to the rat-faced investigator
Who sneers and asks, "Who is your favorite poet?"
Voices of scissors and grinders asking their questions:
"How did you ever happen to be against fascism?"
And they remember the general's white hair,
The food-administrator, alone and full of tears.

They come home to the powder-plant at twilight,
The girls emerging like discolored shadows.
But this is a land where there is time, and time;
This is the country where there is time for thinking.
"Is he a 'fellow-traveler'?—   No.   —Are you sure?   —No."
The fear.   Voices of clawhammers and spikes clinking.

If they bomb the cities, they must offer the choice.
Taking away the sons, they must create a reason.
The cities and women cry in a frightful voice,
"I care not who makes the laws, let me make the sons."
But look at their eyes, like drinking animals'
Full of assurance and flowing with reward.
The seeds of answering are in their voice.
The spirit lives, against the time's disease.
You little children, come down out of your mothers
And tell us about peace.

I hear the singing of the lives of women,
The clear mystery, the offering and pride.

But here also the orange lights of a bar, and an
Old biddy singing inside:

Rain and tomorrow more
They say there will be rain
They lean together and tell
The sorrow of the loin.

Telling each other, saying
"But can you understand?"
They recount separate sorrows.
Throat. Forehead. Hand.

On the bars and walls of buildings
They passed when they were young
They vomit out their pain,
The sorrow of the lung.

Who would suspect it of women?
They have not any rest.
Sad dreams of the belly, of the lip,
Of the deep warm breast.

All sorrows have their place in flesh,
All flesh will with its sorrow die—
All but the patch of sunlight over,
Over the sorrowful sunlit eye.

X

Surely it is time for the true grace of women
Emerging, in their lives' colors, from the rooms, from the
    harvests,
From the delicate prisons, to speak their promises.
The spirit's dreaming delight and the fluid senses'
Involvement in the world.   Surely the day's beginning
In midnight, in time of war, flickers upon the wind.

O on the wasted midnight of our pain
Remember the wasted ones, lost as surely as soldiers
Surrendered to the barbarians, gone down under centuries
Of the starved spirit, in desperate mortal midnight
With the pure throats and cries of blessing, the clearest
Fountains of mercy and continual love.

These years know separation.   O the future shining
In far countries or suddenly at home in a look, in a season,
In music freeing a new myth among the male
Steep landscapes, the familiar cliffs, trees, towers
That stand and assert the earth, saying: "Come here, come to me.
Here are your children."   Not as traditional man
But love's great insight—"your children and your song."

Coming close to the source of belief, these have created
Resistance, the flowering fire of memory,
Given the bread and the dance and the breathing midnight.
Nothing has been begun.   No peace, no word of marvellous
Possible hillsides, the warm lips of the living
Who fought for the spirit's grace among despair,
Beginning with signs of belief, offered in time of war,
As I now send you, for a beginning, praise.

The Soul and Body of
John Brown

THE SOUL AND BODY OF JOHN BROWN

Multitudes, multitudes in the valley of decision!
JOEL III : 14

His life is in the body of the living.
When they hanged him the first time, his image leaped
into the blackened air.   His grave was the floating faces
of the crowd, and he refusing them release
rose open-eyed in autumn, a fanatic
beacon of fierceness leaping to meet them there,
match the white prophets of the storm,
the streaming meteors of the war.

   Dreaming Ezekiel, threaten me alive!

   Voices: Why don't you rip up that guitar?
   Or must we listen to those blistering strings?

The trial of heroes follows their execution.   The striding
wind of nations with new rain, new lightning,

destroyed in magnificent noon shining straight down
the fiery pines.   Brown wanted freedom.   Could not himself be free
until more grace reached a corroded world.   Our guilt his own.
Under the hooded century drops the trap—
There in October's fruition-fire three
tall images of him, Brown as he stood on the ground,
Brown as he stood on sudden air, Brown
standing to our fatal topmost hills
faded through dying altitudes, and low
through faces living under the dregs of the air,
deprived childhood and thwarted youth and change:
     fantastic sweetness gone to rags
     and incorruptible anger blurred by age.

Compel the steps of lovers, watch them lie silvery
attractive in naked embrace over the brilliant gorge,
and open them to love: enlarge their welcome
to sharp-faced countrysides, vicious familiar windows
whose lopped-off worlds say *I am promise,* holding
stopgap slogans of a thin season's offering,
false initials, blind address, dummy name—
enemies who reply in smiles; mild slavers; moderate whores.
There is another gorge to remember, where soldiers give
terrible answers of lechery after death.
Brown said at last, with a living look,
"I designed to have done the same thing
again on a larger scale."   Brown sees his tree
grow in the land to leap these mountains.
Not mountains, but men and women sleeping.

       O my scene! my mother!
       America who offers many births.

Over the tier of barriers, compel the connected steps
past the attacks of sympathy, past black capitals,
to arrive with horizon sharpness, marching
in quick embrace toward people
faltering among hills among the symptoms of ice,
small lights of the shifting winter, the rapid snow-blue stars.
This must be done by armies.   Nothing is free.
Brown refuses to speak direct again,
    "If I tell them the truth,
      they will say I speak in symbols."

White landscapes emphasize his nakedness
reflected in counties of naked who shiver at fires,
their backs to the hands that unroll worlds around them.
They go down the valleys.   They shamble in the streets,
Blind to the sun-storming image in their eyes.
They dread the surface of their victim life,
lying helpless and savage in shade parks,
     asking the towers only what beggars dare:
     food, fire, water, and air.

Spring: the great hieroglyph : the mighty, whose first hour
collects the winter invalids, whose cloudless
pastures train swarms of mutable apple-trees
to blond delusions of light, the touch of whiter
more memorable breasts each evening, the resistant
male shoulders riding under sold terrible eyes.
The soldier-face persists, the victorious head
asks, kissing those breasts, more miracles—
Untarnished hair!   Set them free!   "Without the snap of a gun—"
More failures—but the season is a garden after sickness;
     Then the song begins,
     "The clearing of the sky
     brings fulness to heroes—
     Call Death out of the city
     and ring the summer in."

Whether they sleep alone.   Whether they understand darkness
of mine or tunnel or store.   Whether they lay branches
with skill to entice their visions out of fire.
Whether she lie awake, whether he walk in guilt
down padded corridors, leaving no fingerprints.
Whether he weaken searching for power in papers,
or shut out every fantasy but the fragile eyelid to
     commemorate delight . . .
     They believe in their dreams.

They more and more, secretly, tell their dreams.
They listen oftener for certain words, look deeper
in faces for features of one remembered image.
They almost forget the face.   They cannot miss the look.
It waits until faces have gathered darkness,
and country guitars a wide and subtle music.

It rouses love.   It has mastered its origin:
   Death was its method.   It will surpass its
   furious birth when it is known again.

   Dreaming Ezekiel, threaten me alive!

Greengrown with sun on it.   All the living summer.
They tell their dreams on the cool hill reclining
after a twilight daytime painting machines on the sky,
the spite of tractors and the toothless cannon.
Slaves under factories deal out identical
gestures of reaching—cathedral-color-rose
resumes the bricks as the brick walls lean
away from the windows, blank in bellwavering air,
a slave's mechanical cat's-claw reaping sky.
The cities of horror are down.   These are called born,
and Hungry Hill is a farm again.

      I know your face, deepdrowned
      prophet, and seablown eyes.

Darkflowing peoples.   A tall tree, prophet, fallen,
your arms in their flesh laid on the mountains, all
your branches in the scattered valleys down.
Your boughs lie broken in channels of the land,
dim anniversaries written on many clouds.
There is no partial help.   Lost in the face of a child,
lost in the factory repetitions, lost
on the steel plateaus, in a ghost distorted.
Calling More Life.   In all the harm calling.
Pointing disaster of death and lifting up the bone,
heroic drug and the intoxication gone.

      I see your mouth calling
      before the words arrive.

Buzz of guitars repeat it in streamy
summernoon song, the whitelight of the meaning
changed to demand.   More life, challenging
this hatred, this Hallelloo—risk it upon yourselves.
Free all the dangers of promise, clear the image
of freedom for the body of the world.
After the tree is fallen and has become the land,
when the hand in the earth declined rises and touches and
after the walls go down and all the faces turn,

the diamond shoals of eyes demanding life
deep in the prophet eyes, a wish to be again
threatened alive, in agonies of decision
part of our nation of our fanatic sun.

Elegies
Six to Nine

SIXTH ELEGY. RIVER ELEGY

In burning summer I saw a season of betrayal,
the world fell away, and wasteful climbing green
covered the breaking of bodies, covered our hearts.
Unreal in the burning, many-motioned life
lay like a sea, but fevers found my grief.
I turned in that year to retrieve the stainless river,
the lost, the flowing line of escaped music.

Year of judgment!   Century of betrayal!
They built their cities on the banks of war
and all their cities are down, the Floating Man
swims in the smoke of their sky, the Double Woman
smiles up through the water with her distorted mouth.
I stand over reflection as the world darkens in
destruction of countries, all souls downward set,
life narrowing to one color of a choked river
and hell on both its banks.   My city, my city!
They never built cities.   Cities are for the living.
They built for the half-dead and the half-alive.
Their history is a half-history.   And we go down.
They built their villages whose lame towers fell
where error was overgrown until the long
tentacular ruin touches all fields.   My love!
Did I in that country build you villages?
Great joy my love, even there, until they fell
and green betrayal climbed over the wall.

Defeat and raging and a burning river.
Half-faced, half-sexed, the living dead arrive
passing, a lip, a breast, half of a hand.

Gaudy sadistic streets, dishonest avenues
where every face has bargained for its eyes.
And they come down to the river, driven down.
And all the faces fly out of my city.
The rich streets full of empty coats parading
and one adolescent protesting violin,
the slums full of their flayed and faceless bodies,
they shiver, they are working to buy their skin.
They are lost.   They come down to look for life in a river,
plunge, turn and plunge, they cannot change their life,
swimming, their head is in another world.

World without form.   Chaos beaten and beaten,
raging and suffering and hoping to take shape.
I saw your summer.   I saw your river flow.
I being wasted everywhere saw waste.
Hell's entropy at work and torment general,
friend against most-known friend, love fighting off love.
They asked for an end to emptiness; their sick throats filled
    with foam,
prayed to be solved, and rose to deal betrayal.
And I falling through hell passed many friends, and love,
and a haunted woman warned me as I fell.
Downward through currents, the horrors with little hands.

The chaos, the web of the heart, this bleeding knot;
raises me swimming now, one moment in the air
and light is on my face, the fans over the river
of wind, of goodness.   Lie gasping on this shore,
there is nothing in the world but an honest word
which the severed-away may speak before we die.

Let me tell you what I have held to all along:
when I said that I loved you, when I crossed the frontier,
when I learned the obscurities of a frightened child,
when I shut the door, and felt the sprouting tears,
when I saw the river, when I learned resurrection,
the joy of your hands in a pain that called More Life.
Let me tell you what I have meant all along:
meaning of poetry and personal love,
a world of peace and freedom, man's need recognized,
and all the agonies that will begin that world.

Betrayed, we are betrayed.   The set of the great faces
mean it, the following eyes.   They are the flayed men,

their strength is at the center, love and the time's disease
lie at their skin.   The kiss in the flaring garden
when all the trees closed in.   The knotted terrible lips.
The black blood risen and the animal rage.
The last fierce accident, whose back-thrown drowning head
among the escaping sound of water hears
slow insane music groping for a theme.

My love, reach me again.   The smell of the sea,
wind-flower, sea-flower, the fallen gull-feather.
Clear water and order and an end to dreams:
ether-dreams, surrounded beasts, the aftertoll of fear,
the world reduced to a rising line of water,
the patient deserted by the analyst.
To keep the knowledge that holds my race alive:
spiritual grace of the material word.

I walked under the sky, and the high clouds
hollowed in ribs arched over their living heart:
the world, the corporeal world that will not die.
No, world's no heart—here is yourself walking
in a cage of clouds looking up wanting one face
over you and that look to fill the sky.
Carrying counter-agony into the world,
dream-singing, river-madness, the tragic fugal love
of a theme balancing another theme.

Disorder of suffering, a flight of details, a world
with no shadows at noontime and never at night a light.
Suddenly the flame-blue of a drunken sky
and it is the change, the reds and metals of autumn.
But I curse autumn, for I do not change,
I love, I love, and we are far from peace,
and the great river moves unbearably;
actual gestures of giving, and I may not give.
Water will hold my shadows, the kiss of darkness,
maternal death's tender and delicate promises
seethe at the lips, release and the full sleep.

Even now the bright corporeal hand
might come to redeem the long moment of dying.
Even now if I could rest my life,
my forehead on those knees and the arriving shadows
in rising quiet as the long night arrives.
Terror, war, terror, black blood and wasted love.

The most terrible country, in the heads of men.
This is the war imagination made;
it must be strong enough to make a peace.
My peace is strong enough if it will come
flowing, the color of eyes.   When the world burns away
nothing is left can ever be betrayed.

All broken promises, adulterate release—
cast in the river Death, charred surface of waste,
a downward soulset, never the old heaven
held for a moment as breath held underwater;
but we must rise into a breathing world.
And this dark bellowing century, on its knees—?
If all this must go down, it must.
And all this brilliance go to dust?
Only the meanings can remain alive.
When the cemeteries are military objectives
and love's a downward drawing at the heart
and every letter bears the stamp of death.

There is no solution.   There is no happiness.
Only the range must be taken, a way be found to use
the inmost frenzy and the outer doom.
They are here, they run their riot in the clouds,
fly in our blood and over all our mountains,
corrupt all waters, poison the pride of theme.

Years of judgment!   Century screaming for
the flowing, the life, the intellectual leap
of waters over a world grown old and wild,
a broken crying for seasonal change until
O God my love in time the waste become
the sure magnificent music of the defeated heart.

Summer 1940

SEVENTH ELEGY. DREAM-SINGING ELEGY

Darkness, giving us dream's black unity.
Images in procession start to flow
among the river-currents down the years of judgment
and past the cities to another world.

There are flat places.   After the waterfall
arched like the torso of love, after the voices

singing behind the waterfall, after the water
lying like a lover on the heart,
there is defeat.

And moving through our spirit in the night
memories of these places.
Not ritual, not nostalgia, but our cries,
the axe at the heart, continual rebirth,
the crying of our raw desire,
young.   O many-memoried America!

In defeat there are no prophets and no magicians,
only the look in the loved and tortured eyes
when every fantasy restores, and day denies.
The act of war debased to the act of treason
in an age of treason.   We were strong at the first.
We resisted.   We did not plan enough.   We killed.
But the enemy came like thunder in the wood,
a storm over the treetops like a horse's head
reared to a great galloping, and war
trampled us down.   We lost our young men in the
     fighting,
we lost our homeland, our crops went under the frost,
our children under the hunger.   Now we stand
around this fire, our black hills far behind,
black water far before us, a glitter of time on the sea,
glitter of fire on our faces, the still faces—
stillness waiting for dreams
and only the shadows moving,
shadows and revelations.

In the spring of the year, this new fighting broke out.
No, when the fields were blond.   No, the leaves crimson.
When the old fighting was over, we knew what we were
seeing as if for a first time our dark hills masked with
     green,
our blond fields with the trees flame-shaped and black
in burning darkness on the unconsumed.
Seeing for a first time the body of our love,
our wish and our love for each other.
Then word came from a runner, a stranger:
"They are dancing to bring the dead back, in the
     mountains."

We danced at an autumn fire, we danced the old hate and
  change,
the coming again of our leaders.   But they did not come.
Our singers lifted their arms, and a singer cried,
"You must sing like me and believe, or be turned to rock!"

The winter dawned, but the dead did not come back.
News came on the frost, "The dead are on the march!"
We danced in prison to a winter music,
many we loved began to dream of the dead.
They made no promises, we never dreamed a threat.
And the dreams spread.

But there were no armies, and the dead were dead,
there was only ourselves, the strong and symbol self
dreaming among defeat, our torture and our flesh.
We made the most private image and religion,
stripped to the last resistance of the wish,
remembering the fighting and the lava beds,
the ground that opened, the red wounds opening,
remembering the triumph in the night,
the big triumph and the little triumph—
wide singing and the battle-flash—
assassination and whisper.

In the summer, dreaming was common to all of us,
the drumbeat hope, the bursting heart of wish,
music to bind us as the visions streamed
and midnight brightened to belief.
In the morning we told our dreams.
They all were the same dream.

Dreamers wake in the night and sing their songs.
In the flame-brilliant midnight, promises
arrive, singing to each of us with tongues of flame:
"We are hopes, you should have hoped us,
We are dreams, you should have dreamed us."
Calling our name.

When we began to fight, we sang hatred and death.
The new songs say, "Soon all people on earth
will live together."   We resist and bless
and we begin to travel from defeat.
Now, as you sing your dream, you ask the dancers,
in the night, in the still night, in the night,

"Do you believe what I say?"
And all the dancers answer "Yes."

To the farthest west, the sea and the striped country
and deep in the camps among the wounded cities
half-world over, the waking dreams of night
outrange the horrors.   Past fierce and tossing skies
the rare desires shine in constellation.
I hear your cries, you little voices of children
swaying wild, nightlost, in black fields calling.
I hear you as the seething dreams arrive
over the sea and past the flaming mountains.
Now the great human dream as great as birth or death,
only that we are not given to remember birth,
only that we are not given to hand down death,
this we hand down and remember.

Brothers in dream, naked-standing friend
rising over the night, crying aloud,
beaten and beaten and rising from defeat,
crying as we cry: We are the world together.
Here is the place in hope, on time's hillside,
where hope, in one's image, wavers for the last time
and moves out of one's body up the slope.
That place in love, where one's self, as the body of love,
moves out of the old lifetime towards the beloved.
Singing.

Who looks at the many colors of the world
knowing the peace of the spaces and the eyes of love,
who resists beyond suffering, travels beyond dream,
knowing the promise of the night-flowering worlds
sees in a clear day love and child and brother
living, resisting, and the world one world
dreaming together.

EIGHTH ELEGY. CHILDREN'S ELEGY

Yes, I have seen their eyes.   In peaceful gardens
the dark flowers now are always children's eyes,
full-colored, haunted as evening under fires
showered from the sky of a burning country.

Shallow-featured children under trees
look up among green shadows of the leaves.
The angel, flaming, gives — into his hands
all is given and he does not change.
The child changes and takes.
All is given. He makes and changes.
The angel stands.

A flame over the tree. Night calling in the cloud.
And shadow among winds. Where does the darkness lie?
It comes out of the person, says the child.
A shadow tied and alive, trying to be.

In the tremendous child-world, everything is high,
active and fiery, sun-cats run through the walls,
the tree blows overhead like a green joy,
and cloudy leopards go hunting in the sky.

The shadow in us sings, "Stand out of the light!"
But I live, I live, I travel in the sun.

———————

On burning voyages of war they go.
Like starving ghosts they stumble after nuns.
Children of heroes, Defeat the dark companion.
But if they are told they are happy, they will know.

Who kills the father burns up the children's tears.
Some suffering blazes beyond all human touch,
some sounds of suffering cry, far out of reach.
These children brings to us their mother's fears.

Singing, "O make us strong O let us go—"
The new world comes among the old one's harms,
old world carrying new world in her arms.
But if you say they are free, then they will know.

War means to me, sings a small skeleton,
only the separation,
mother no good and gone,
taken away in lines of fire and foam.
The end of war
will bring me, bring me home.

The children of the defeated, sparrow-poor and starved,
create, create, must make their world again.
Dead games and false salutes must be their grace.
One wish must move us, flicker from our lives
to the marred face.

My child, my victim, my wish this moment come!
But the martyr-face cries to us fiercely
"I search to learn the way out of childhood;
I need to fight.   I wish, I wish for home."

This is what they say, who were broken off from love:
However long we were loved, it was not long enough.

We were afraid of the broad big policeman,
of lions and tigers, the dark hall and the moon.

After our father went, nothing was ever the same,
when mother did not come back, we made up a war game.

My cat was sitting in the doorway when the planes
went over, and my cat saw mother cry;
furry tears, fire fell, wall went down;
did my cat see mother die?

Mother is gone away, my cat sits here coughing.
I cough and sit.   I am nobody's nothing.

However long they loved us, it was not long enough.
For we have to be strong, to know what they did, and then
our people are saved in time, our houses built again.

You will not know, you have a sister and brother;
my doll is not my child, my doll is my mother.

However strong we are, it is not strong enough.
I want to grow up.   To come back to love.

I see it pass before me in parade,
my entire life as a procession of images.
The toy, the golden kernel, the glass lamp.

The present she gave me, the first page I read,
the little animal, the shadowless tall angel.
The angel stands.   The child changes and takes.
He makes a world, stands up among the cousins,
cries to the family, "Ladies and gentlemen—
The world is falling *down!*"   After the smooth hair
darkens, and summer lengthens the smooth cheek,
and the diffuse gestures are no longer weak,
he begins to be the new one, to have what happened,
to do what must be done.

O, when the clouds and the blue horse of childhood
melt away and the golden weapons,
and we remember the first public day's
drums and parades and the first angel
standing in the garden, his dark lips
and silver blood, how he stood,
giving, for all he was was given.

I begin to have what happened to me.

O, when the music of carousels and stars
is known, and the music of the scene
makes a clear meeting, greeting and claim of gods,
we see through the hanging curtain of the year
they change each other with one change of love!
see, in one breath, in a look!
See, in pure midnight a flare of broken color
clears to a constellation.
Peace is asleep, war's lost.   It is love.
I wanted to die.   The masked and the alone
seemed the whole world, and all the gods at war,
and all the people dead and depraved.   Today
the constellation and the music!   Love.

You who seeking yourself arrive at these lines,
look once, and you see the world,
look twice and you see your self.

And all the children moving in their change.

To have what has happened, the pattern and the shock;
and all of them walk out of their childhood,
give to you one blue look.

And all the children bowing in their game,
saying Farewell, Goodbye; Goodbye, Farewell.

NINTH ELEGY. THE ANTAGONISTS

Pieces of animals, pieces of all my friends
prepare assassinations while I sleep.
They shape my being, a gallery of lives
fighting within me, and all unreconciled.
Before them move my waking dreams, and ways
of the spirit, and simple action.   Among these
I can be well and holy.   Torn by them I am wild,
smile, and revenge myself upon my friends
and find myself among my enemies.
But all these forms of incompleteness pass
out of their broken power to a place
where dream and dream meet and resolve in grace.

The closing of this conflict is the end
of the initiation.   I have known the cliff
and known the cliff-dream of the faces drowned.
Stood in the high sun, a dark girl looking down,
seeing the colors of water swaying beneath me, dense
in the flood-summer, various as my love
and like my hope enchanted.   Drawn to blue
chance and horizons, and back as sea-grasses move
drawn landward slowly by incoming tides—
and then the final cancelling and choice,
not tilted as flowers under wind, but deep
blessing of root and heart, underwater swung,
wrenched, swayed, and given fully to the sea.
Heaven not of rest, but of intensity.

The forms of incompleteness in our land
pass from the eastern and western mountains where
the seas meet the dark islands, where the light
glitters white series on the snowlands, pours its wine
of lenient evening to the center.   Green
on shadows of Indiana, level yellow miles . . .
The prairie emblems and the slopes of the sky
and desert stars enlarging in the frost
redeem us like our love and will not die.
All origins are here, and in this range

the changing spirit can make itself again,
continually love, continually change.

Our of the myth the mother leaned;
From out the mother shines the child;
Man rises, in the mass contained;
And from this growth creation grows.
The fire through all the spiral flows:
Create the creative, many-born!
And use your love, unreconciled!

―――――――――――

In wheels, in whirlwind, in a storm of power
alive again and over every land
the thunderbird with lightnings at his wrists.
Eclipses uncloud and show us miracle,
gleaming, our ancestors, all antagonists:
Slave and Conquistador, dead hand-to-hand,
scented fastidious Tory with his whore,
distinguished rebel and woman at the plow.
The fiery embryo umbilical
always to failure, and form developing
American out of conflict.

                              Fierce dissenting ghosts,
the second Adams' fever and eagle voice
and Jackson's muscular democratic sense.
Sprung in one birth John Brown, a mad old man
whose blood in a single broken gesture freed
many beliefs; and Lincoln's agony
condemning and confirming.   O, they cry,
the oppositions cry, O fight for me!
Fight, you are bound to freedom, and be free!
When Hawthorne saw the fabulous gift, he tore
flesh from his guilt, and found more guilt; the bells
rang barter of the self, but Melville drowned.
The doubled phantoms bring to our terrible
chaos the order of a meeting-place
where the exchange is made, the agonies
lie down at last together face to face.

In the black night of blood, the forms begin
to glitter alive, fathers of constellations,
the shining and the music moving on.

We are bound by the deepest feuds to unity.
To make the connections and be born again,
create the creative, that will love the world.

Not glistening Indies, not continents, but the world
opening now, and the greatness of our age
that makes its own antagonists of the wish.
We want to find and will spend our lives in finding:
the landfall of our broken voyages
is still our America of contradictions.
Ancestors of that dream lie coupled in our flesh,
pieces of animals, pieces of all our friends
meet in us and we live.   We do not die.

Magical keen Magellan sought a rose
among the compass and legendary winds.
Green sequels rocked his eyes in water; he
hung with the scorpion sun on noon's glass wall,
stared down, down into the future as he sailed.
Fanatic travels, recurrent mysteries.
Those who want the far shore spend their lives on the ocean.
The hand of God flowers in coasts for these.

Those who want only home spend their lives in the sky.
Flying over tonight, while thirteen searchlights join
high incandescent asters on black air.
The blinding center fastens on a plane
floating and white, glare-white; he wanting land
and intimate fertile hours, hangs there.   Sails
great scends of danger, or wades through crazy sand.

Those who most long for peace now pour their lives on war.
Our conflicts carry creation and its guilt,
these years' great arms are full of death and flowers.
A world is to be fought for, sung, and built:
Love must imagine the world.
                              The wish of love
moving upon the body of love describes
closing of conflict, repeats the sacred ways
in which the spirit dances and survives.

To that far meeting-place call home the enemies—
they keep their oppositions, for the strong

ironic joy of old intensities
still carries virile music.

                    O, the young
will come up
              after us
                    and make the dream,
the real world of our myth.
                          But now, the song
they will discover is a shadowy theme—

Today we are bound, for freedom binds us—we
live out the conflict of our time, until
Love, finding all the antagonists in the dance,
moved by its moods and given to its grace,
resolves the doom
                    and the deliverance.

(1948)

THE GREEN WAVE

Let poems and bodies love and be given to air,
Earth having us real in her seasons, our fire and savor;
And, reader, love well, imagine forward, for
All of the testaments are in your favor.

WATER NIGHT

The sky behind the farthest shore
Is darker than I go to sleep.

Blackness of water, the crater at the core,
The many blacknesses begin to gleam.

Rivers of darkness bind me to this land
While overhead the moon goes far to shine,

And now nothing nobody is my own.
The motion of streams glitters before my eyes:

Sources and entrances, they lie no more,
Now darkly keep, now flow now bright

Until all wandering end, a hand
Shine, and the leadings homeward of delight

Seem to begin my deepest sleep
To make a lake of dream.

EYES OF NIGHT-TIME

On the roads at night I saw the glitter of eyes:
my dark around me let shine one ray;   that black
allowed their eyes   :   spangles in the cat's, air in the moth's
    eye shine,
mosaic of the fly, ruby-eyed beetle, the eyes that never weep,
the horned toad sitting and its tear of blood,
fighters and prisoners in the forest, people
aware in this almost total dark, with the difference,
the one broad fact of light.

Eyes on the road at night, sides of a road like rhyme;
the floor of the illumined shadow sea
and shallows with their assembling flash and show
of sight, root, holdfast, eyes of the brittle stars.
And your eyes in the shadowy red room,
scent of the forest entering, various time
calling and the light of wood along the ceiling
and over us birds calling and their circuit eyes.
And in our bodies the eyes of the dead and the living
giving us gifts at hand, the glitter of all their eyes.

THIS PLACE IN THE WAYS

Having come to this place
I set out once again
on the dark and marvelous way
from where I began:
belief in the love of the world,
woman, spirit, and man.

Having failed in all things
I enter a new age
seeing the old ways as toys,
the houses of a stage
painted and long forgot;
and I find love and rage.

Rage for the world as it is
but for what it may be
more love now than last year
and always less self-pity
since I know in a clearer light
the strength of the mystery.

And at this place in the ways
I wait for song.
My poem-hand still, on the paper,
all night long.
Poems in throat and hand, asleep,
and my storm beating strong!

SONG, FROM
"MR. AMAZEEN ON THE RIVER"

Over the water, where I lie alive,
   Grass burns green where the buried are,
   Tall stone is standing   "And the sea
   Gave up its dead."   The wave, the living star,
   Evening and house at river-mouth shine.

The hour of voices on the water and oars
   Speaking of blue, speaking of time.
   His colors, colors of deepness will arrive,
   Island-sleep, keel-sleep, cloud-controlling evening.
   They say to me at last "I am your home."

CLOUDS, AIRS, CARRIED ME AWAY

Clouds, airs, carried me away,
but here we stand
and newborn we begin.
Having seen all the people of the play,
the lights, the map in the hand,
we know there will be wars
all acted out, and know not who may win.

Deep now in your great eyes, and in my gross
flesh — heavy as ever, woman of mud—
shine sunset, sunrise and the advancing stars.
But past all loss
and all forbidding a thing is understood.

Orpheus in hell remembered rivers
and a music rose
full of all human voices;
all words you wish are in that living sound.
And even torn to pieces
one piece sang
Come all ye torn and wounded here
together
and one sang to its brother
remembering.
One piece in tatters sang among its blood:
man is a weapon, woman's a trap;
and so is the hand with the map, my dear,
so is the hand with the colored map.
And I to myself the tightest trap.

Now all is young again:
in a wet night among the household music,
the new time,
by miracle my traps are sprung.
I wished you all your good again
and all your good is here with you,
smiling, various, and true,
your living friends, as live as we.

I believed because I saw not;
now I see,
with love become

so haunted by a living face
that all the dead rise up and stare;
and the dumb time, the year that was
passes away.   Memory is reborn,
form and forgiveness shine.
So in this brilliant dark, dark of the year,
shining is born.
We know what we do,
and turn, and act in hope.
Now the wounds of time
have healed and are grown.
They are not wounds, they are mine,
they are healed into mouths.
They speak past wrongs.   I am born;
you bring shining, and births.
Here are the stories they tell you,
here are their songs.

SALAMANDER

Red leaf.   And beside it, a red leaf alive
flickers, the eyes set wide in the leaf head,
small broad chest, a little taper of flame for tail
moving a little among the leaves like fear.

Flickering red in the wet week of rain
while a bird falls safely through his mile of air.

HIS HEAD IS FULL OF FACES

for Bernard Perlin

Now he has become one who upon that coast
landed by night and found the starving army
Fed on their cheese and wine.   In those ravines
hidden by orphaned furious children lay
while cries and wounds and hour past hour of war
flamed past the broken pillars of that sky.

He saw the enemy.   His head is full of faces—
the living, the brave, a pure blazing alone
to fight a domination to the end.
And now he sees the rigid terrible friend

inert, peopled by armies, winning.   Now
he has become one given his life by those
fighting in Greece forever under a star
and now he knows how many wars there are.

MRS. WALPURGA

In wet green midspring, midnight and the wind
floodladen and ground-wet, and the immense dry moon.
Mrs. Walpurga under neon saw
the fluid airs stream over fluid evening,
ground, memory, give way and rivers run
into her sticky obsessive kiss of branches,
kiss of a real and visionary mouth,
the moon, the mountain, the round breast's sleepless eye.

Shapes of her fantasy in music from the bars,
swarming like juke-box lights the avenues;
no longer parked in the forest, from these cars,
these velvet rooms and wooden tourist camps,
sheetless under the naked white of the moon.
Wet gaze of eye, plum-color shadow and young
streams of these mouths, the streaming surface of earth
flowing alive with water, the egg and its becoming.

Coming in silence.   The shapes of every dread
seducing the isolated will.   They do not care.
They are not tortured, not tired, not alone.
They break to an arm, a leg, half of a mouth,
kissing disintegrate, flow whole, couple again;
she is changed along, she is a stream in a stream.

These are her endless years, woman and child, in dream
molded and wet, a bowl growing on a wheel,
not mud, not bowl, not clay, but this *becoming,*
winter and split of darkness, years of wish.
To want these couples, want these coupling pairs,
emblems of many parents, of the bed,
of love divided by dream, love with his dead wife,
love with her husband dead, love with his living love.

Mrs. Walpurga cries out : "It is not true!"
The light shifts, flowing away.   "It was never like——"
She stops, but nothing stops.   It moves.   It moves.

And not like anything.   And it is true.
The shapes disfigure.   Here is the feature man,
not whole, he is detail, he gleams and goes.
Here is the woman all cloth, black velvet face,
black, head to ground, close black fit to the skin,
slashed at the mouth and eyes, slashed at the breasts,
slashed at the triangle, showing rose everywhere.

Nights are disturbed, here is a crying river
running through years, here is the flight among
all the Objects of Love.   This wish, this gesture
irresisted, immortal seduction!   The young sea
streams over the land of dream, and there
the mountain like a mist-flower, the dark upright peak.
And over the sheet-flood Mrs. Walpurga
in whitened cycles of her changing moon.

The silence and the music change;   this song
rises and sharps, and never quite can scream—
but this is laughter harsher than nakedness
can take — in the shady shady grove the leaves
move over, the men and women move and part,
the river braids and unfolds in mingling song;
and here is the rain of summer from the moon,
relenting, wet, and giving life at last,
and Mrs. Walpurga and we may wake.

A CERTAIN MUSIC

Never to hear, I know in myself complete
that naked integrated music;   now
it has become me, now it is nerve, song, gut,
and my gross hand writes only through Mozart;   see
even in withholding what you have brought to me.

Renewed, foolish, reconciled to myself, I walk
this winter-country, I fly over its still-flock'd clouds,
always in my isolated flesh I take
that theme's light certainty of absolute purpose
to make quick spirit when spirit most might break.

Naked you walked through my body and I turned
to you with this far music you now withhold.
O my destroyed hope!   Though I never again

hear developing heaven, the growing grave-bearing earth,
my poem, my promise, my love, my sleep after love;
my hours, listening, along that music move,
and have been saved and hardly know the cold.

THE MOTIVE OF ALL OF IT

The motive of all of it was loneliness,
All the panic encounters and despair
Were bred in fear of the lost night, apart,
Outlined by pain, alone.   Promiscuous
As mercy.   Fear-led and led again to fear
At evening toward the cave where part fire, part
Pity lived in that voluptuousness
To end one and begin another loneliness.

This is the most intolerable motive :   this
Must be given back to life again,
Made superhuman, made human, out of pain
Turned to the personal, the pure release:
The rings of Plato and Homer's golden chain
Or Lenin with his cry of Dare We Win.

GREEN LIMITS

My limits crowd around me
like years, like those I loved
whose narrow hope could never
carry themselves.

My limits stand beside me
like those two widowed aunts
who from an empty beach
tore me into the wave.

Green over my low head
the surf threw itself down
tall as my aunts whose hands
locked me past help.

The sand was far behind
and rushing underfoot
water and fear and childhood,
surf of love.

Green limits walled me, water
stood higher than I saw—
glass walls, fall back!   let me
dive and be saved.

My limits stand inside me
forever like that wave
on which I ride at last
over and under me.

THE CHILDREN'S ORCHARD

In the full sun.   In the fruitfall season.
Against my knees the earth and the bucket, and the soft blue
    prunes
echoing red   echoing purple   echoing in the silver bucket
sun, and over the flames of earth the sun flies down.

Over my head the little trees tremble alive in their black
    branches
and bare-ribbed boys golden and shouting stoop here to gather
    the blue,
the wild-red, the dark.   Colors of ripeness in the fruitfall
    season.
I will remember the last light on the lowest branch.

Will see these trees as they were in spring, wild black rooted in
    light,
root-deep in noon, the piercing yellow noon of mustard-
    blossom.
Sun breathing on us the scent of heat, richness of air where my
    hands know
blue, full summer, strong sun.   I tell you harvest.

CHRISTMAS EVE

The secret child walks down the street
of the year's winter black and white,
while evening flames, blue-green and high—
the smooth face turns in the snow-smooth street
to lights, star-bubbles, the dark tree,
the giant star in the sacred sky.

Children behind their windows sing
a cradle, a birth, the pilgrim kings,
praising the still and wild.
They praise the face, the quickening,
the various joy, the wound!   They sing
a new prophetic child.

Out of the street, out of the spire,
a slow voice, radio or king,
begins above the mystery.
Tells pain and sweetness, pain and fire.
The bells begin to cast their rings
of celebration down the sky.

The secret child walks down the street
of needle-dark December smells.
She walks with wonder everywhere.
Who is that Child?   Where is that sweet
face of the songs and silver bells,
the broad red saint, the angelhair?

The voice tells ragged ships that sailed
to find that birth and piercèd hand,
a little child among the Jews.
"But I," she says, "I am a child
of Jews—"   Says, "This is Christianland
and things are otherwise.

"People, beasts, and a winter rose,
procession and thorn, the suffering
that had to be, the needed loss
led to this flame among the snows.
Three agents brought about this thing:
the Father, the Jews, the blessèd cross.

"And one of these is ours and overhead;
and one is God;   and one is still outside."
Sure of the birth then, the people all went to sleep.
But the child was awake, and grieved for the time ahead,
awake all night, watching the land and the sky.
Did the child weep?   No the child did not weep.

CRAYON HOUSE

Two or three lines across;   the black ones, down,
into the ground where grass sparkles and shines;
but the foundation is the green and the shine.
Windows are drawn in.   Overhead the sun
surrounded by his crown, continually given.
It is a real place, door, floor, and windows.

I float past it.   I look in at the little children.
I climb up the straight and planted path, alone.
In the city today grown, walking on stone,
a suddenness of doors, windows, bread and rolls.

Roads are in all I know :   weapon and refugee,
color of thunder calling   Leave this room,
Get out of this house.   Even then, joy began,
went seeking through the green world, wild and no longer wild,
always beginning again.   Steady giving and green decision,
and the beginning was real.   The drawing of a child.

A CHARM FOR CANTINFLAS

After the lights and after the rumba and after the bourbon
                     and after the beer
and after the drums and after the samba and after the
                     ice cream and not long after
failure, loss, despair, and loss and despair
There was the laughter and there was Cantinflas at last
                     and his polka
doing the bumps with a hot guitar
turning unique.   Slow.   Slow.   Deprecating
               shoulder up.
               Hand up.
               All the fingers tall.
Panache and rags and triumph and smile—
beggar of light in ridiculous sunlight.

All things human clumsy and fair
as graceful as loving as stupid as true.

And on this floor
the dancers, in this square the little trees,
and on this stage always the clown of our living

gives us our sunlight and our incantation
as sun does, laughing, shining, reciting dawn, noon, and down,
making all delight and healing all ills
like faraway words on jars, the labels in Protopapas' window:
marshmallow, myrtle, peppermint, pumpkin, sesame, sesame,
   squills.

TRADITIONAL TUNE

After the revolution came the Fuehrer;
And after the resurrection, the Christian Era.
Not yet simple and not yet free.

Just after the Exodus, in the divided sea
The chariots drowned, and then the tempering
By forty sandy years of misery.

And after the King of the Jews came Godfrey King;
Kneedeep in blood the children wandering,
Holy Holy Holy hear the children sing.

Now mouthdeep nosedeep the fires reach our eye.
Teach us from torment to fly and not to fly.
Not yet safe, not ready to die.

Illumination and night cast on the eyes of those
Believing and fighting, playing the Worldly Fool,
Fool of Thy Word, who feel the century

Rule, under whose deep wave explosion waits;
We know the dead power of Thy Allied States.
Not yet simple and not yet free.

Sailing, remembering the rock and the child,
Sailing remember the sand, the city, the wild
Holy songs.   Deaths!   Pillar of cloud and sun,

Remember us and remember them and all
Not safe, not free sailing again upon
The sacred dangerous harbor, Jerusalem.

FOGHORN IN HORROR

I know that behind these walls is the city, over these rooftops
   is the sun.

But I see black clothes only and white clothes with the fog
    running in
and all their shadows.
Every minute the sound of the harbor
intruding on horror with a bellow of horror:
blu-a!   blu-aa!   Ao. . . .

I try to write to you, but here too I meet failure.
It has a face like mine.
Silence and in me and over the water
only the bellowing,
Niobe howling for her life and her children.
Did you think this sorrow of women was a graceful thing?
Horrible Niobe down on her knees:
Blu-a!   Blu-aa!   Ao. . . .

Thirty years, and my full strength, and all I touch has failed.
I sit and see
the black clothes on the line are beautiful, the sky drifting
    away.
The white clothes of the fog beyond me, beautiful, and the
    shadows.
Blu-aa!   Blu-aa!   AO.

SUMMER, THE SACRAMENTO

To this bridge the pale river and flickers away in images of blue.
And is gone.   While behind me the stone mountains
stand brown with blue lights;   at my right shoulder standing
Shasta, in summer standing, blue with her white lights
near a twilight summer moon, whiter than snow
where the light of evening changes among these legends.

Under me islands lie green, planted with green feathers,
green growing, shadowy grown, gathering streams of the
    green trees.
A hundred streams full of shadows and your upland source
pulled past sun-islands, green in this light as grace,
risen from your sun-mountains where your voices go
returning to water and music is your face.

Flows to the flower-haunted sea, naming and singing, under
    my eyes

274

coursing, the day of the world.   And the time of my spirit
   streams
before me, slow autumn colors, the cars of a long train;
earth-red, earth-orange, leaf, rust, twilight of earth
stream past the evening river and over into the dark of north,
stream slow like wishes continuing toward those snows.

SPEECH OF THE MOTHER,
FROM "THE MIDDLE OF THE AIR"

Act I, Sc. 4.   She is lit, standing high, with the lit line of
                  Anne's sleeping body at her knee.   Darkness
                  around. Her soliloquy will indicate the passage
                  of a year.

A year passes behind me.   Shadows grow larger.   Time
dissolves to a moment.   I look to my children.   They
change.   A smile, a brush of the lips against my heart;   things
brighten and vanish into a kind of joy, a kind of light.
Chaos began us, war in my own time, war in my children's time,
irrevocable accusation!   I have heard the music of the sounds
   of peace:
music of rivers, of street-corners, of our South,
blues, harvest-songs;   and in the faces of lovers
seen all our challenge shining as a sign
                  to shape the future in love and birth.
Women standing in their houses set around with order —
the bread, the doorways and tables of everyday living
through all the walls have heard the shouts of fighting,
                  planes in the air,
and a shrill cry of women tortured under time,
each one carrying loss like conception   :   a lover gone,
or a son, or her brothers disappeared.   One saying,
   "Spain! Spain!"
One desolate for her unborn children.   One standing alone
outside of lighted windows, or black against raving fires
                  of this year and next year.
Chaos began us, a people skillful in war, young in love,
and in peace unbegun.   A people various as life
whose strength is in our many voices and our hope
of a future of many, each singing his own song.
For we know this struggle   :   more than forces in conflict,
we know it as always the rising changing shadow of a dream.

A woman moving in my own house among my daughters,
I remember their hands when they were little, and smoothing
their shining hair.   They change.   And one will have her child.
                The year passes.   Around me chaos grows.
    And darkly
our time renews itself.   And equilibrium, the healer, the
    young one,
the beginning of new life, poises itself on war.   And life
moves in its sharpened color into another year.
As I grow old, I face the strange seasons, I rejoice in the
    young,
and I say, in suffering, in joy, among the marvelous changes,
                among the accusations, all things glow.

THEN I SAW WHAT THE CALLING WAS

All the voices of the wood called "Muriel!"
but it was soon solved;   it was nothing, it was not for me.
The words were a little like Mortal and More and Endure
and a word like Real, a sound like Health or Hell.
Then I saw what the calling was :   it was the road I traveled,
    the clear
time and these colors of orchards, gold behind gold and the full
shadow behind each tree and behind each slope.   Not to me
the calling, but to anyone, and at last I saw :   where
the road lay through sunlight and many voices and the marvel
orchards, not for me, not for me, not for me.
I came into my clear being;   uncalled, alive, and sure.
Nothing was speaking to me, but I offered and all was well.

And then I arrived at the powerful green hill.

Easter Eve
1945

EASTER EVE 1945

Wary of time O it seizes the soul tonight
I wait for the great morning of the west
confessing with every breath mortality.
Moon of this wild sky struggles to stay whole
and on the water silvers the ships of war.
I go alone in the black-yellow light
all night waiting for day, while everywhere the sure
death of light, the leaf's sure return to the root
is repeated in million, death of all man to share.
Whatever world I know shines ritual death,
wide under this moon they stand gathering fire,
fighting with flame, stand fighting in their graves.
All shining with life as the leaf, as the wing shines,
the stone deep in the mountain, the drop in the green wave.
Lit by their energies, secretly, all things shine.
Nothing can black that glow of life;   although
          each part go crumbling down
          itself shall rise up whole.

Now I say there are new meanings;   now I name
death our black honor and feast of possibility
to celebrate casting of life on life.   This earth-long day
between blood and resurrection where we wait
remembering sun, seed, fire;   remembering
that fierce Judaean Innocent who risked
every immortal meaning on one life.
Given to our year as sun and spirit are,
as seed we are blessed only in needing freedom.
Now I say that the peace the spirit needs is peace,
not lack of war, but fierce continual flame.
For all men   :   effort is freedom, effort's peace,
it fights.   And along these truths the soul goes home,
          flies in its blazing to a place
          more safe and round than Paradise.

Night of the soul, our dreams in the arms of dreams
dissolving into eyes that look upon us.
Dreams the sources of action, the meeting and the end,
a resting-place among the flight of things.

And love which contains all human spirit, all wish,
the eyes and hands, sex, mouth, hair, the whole woman —
fierce peace I say at last, and the sense of the world.
In the time of conviction of mortality
whatever survive, I remember what I am. —
The nets of this night are on fire with sun and moon
pouring both lights into the open tomb.
Whatever arise, it comes in the shape of peace,
fierce peace which is love, in which move all the stars,
and the breathing of universes, filling, falling away,
and death on earth cast into the human dream.
      What fire survive forever
      myself is for my time.

Private Life of the Sphinx

PRIVATE LIFE OF THE SPHINX
for Ella Winter

I

Simply because of a question, my life is implicated:
my flesh and answer fly between chaos and their need.
On the rock I asked the shaky king
one foolish question to make him look at himself—
He looked.   Beheld himself and kingdoms.   Took.
My claws and smile transferred into his myth.

Babble of demand, and answers building the brilliant cities
the standing battlefields and the fields of the fallen down.

Now in this city in the Lounge of Time,
I tell you it was a legend founded on fire,
founded on what we are.   Simply because I asked one
   question,
"What is this, What?"   so that the answer must be "Man."
Because of that they bring their riddles and rhyme
to my door if I houseless run throughout the world,
torse of a woman and quarters of a lion.

278

II

Open war with its images of love and death—
man, an explosion walking through the night in
rich and intolerable loneliness.
Cathedrals writhing gold against their clouds
and a child asking the fiery pure questions.
The monkey-dark, a month of smoky violets,
delicate repose of my reality among
dreams, and the angel of the resurrection,
a mouth overhead, the sky planted with stars.

My questions are my body.   And among this glowing, this sure,
this fact, this mooncolored breast, I make memorial.

III

My body is set against disorder.   Risen among enigmas,
time and the question carry a rose of form,
sing a life-song.   Strangler and bitch, they said,
but they mistook the meaning of my name:
I am the root who embraces and the source.
I sing.   I sing.

In these cities, all suffer from their weaknesses—
they lack some gut, they are ill, they have womb-envy,
run howling from the question and the act.
They bring me their need for answers in their hands and
    eyes.
To embody truth, the Irish old man said.

I remember in Calabria a peasant
broad, smiling, and sly, with a bird throbbing and small
behind his back, in his hands;   and he asked his question.
Is it alive? and he smiled at me.   Then I knew
if I said Yes, he would twist the sparrow's neck.
The fool of time!   I gave him my only answer,
that answer of time:
Fool, I said, you know it depends on you
whether it live or die.

IV

I answer!   I fly reborn from deep escape!
Listen to their cries, the selfsame crying throats,
crying the selfsame need.

Here is my self.   I touch you, life reaches me.
You touch me, I am able to give my gifts.
All the acts flow together, a form being made.
I know a garden beyond questioning—
can almost see night-flowering white mallows,
can almost tell you below the sound of water,
white lilac like a voluptuous light
shining at full on our two faces.—
It goes ahead of our hope.   It is the secret that moves
with the speed of life,
secrets of night and   the street
secrets of milk and dinner and daylight,
enigmas of gardens, the kitchen and the bed,
the riddle and sacrament in the knot of wood,
in the wine, in the water and root the coil of life.

They ask for answers, they starving eat their shadows.
The beginning is always here.   Its green demand.

V

They think I answer and strangle.   They are wrong.
I set my life among the questioning.
The peasant, the wars, the wounded powerful king.
The shining of questions which cannot be concealed
lies in that mirror.   The little child to the mother
of the father's unspoken death, said   :   "You have told me
    yourself."
Even alone, away from daily life, the fire
and monster crown of the legend over me
reaches their eyes   —   children, friendship of lions,
the sense of the world at last broken through to man
in all fury, all sacred open mystery,
is in my question.
                    The stranger, the foreign and strong,
the child and king, wide village eyes of the farm,
the demand loud, or choking in surf-foam,
density of flowers, the faces of all love,
the core of our hope;   stronger than kill,
stronger almost than question, almost than song.

Elegy in Joy

TENTH ELEGY. ELEGY IN JOY

Now green, now burning, I make a way for peace.
After the green and long beyond my lake,
among those fields of people, on these illuminated
hills, gold, burnt gold, spilled gold and shadowed blue,
the light of enormous flame, the flowing light of the sea,
where all the lights and nights are reconciled.
The sea at last, where all the waters lead.
And all the wars to this peace.

For the sea does not lie like the death you imagine;
this sea is the real sea, here it is.
This is the living.   This peace is the face of the world,
a fierce angel who in one lifetime lives
fighting a lifetime, dying as we all die,
becoming forever, the continual god.

Years of our time, this heart!   The binding of the alone,
bells of all loneliness, binding our lands and our music,
branches full of motion each opening its own flower,
lands of all song, each speaking in his own voice.
Praise in every grace
among the old same war.

Years of betrayal, million death breeding its weaknesses
and hope, buried more deep more black than dream.
Every elegy is the present   :   freedom eating our hearts,
death and explosion, and the world unbegun.
Now burning and unbegun, I sing earth with its war,
and God the future, and the wish of man.

Though you die, your war lives   :   the years fought it,
fusing a dead world straight.

The living will be giving you your meanings,
widening to love because of the love of man.
All the wounds crying
I feare, and hope   :   I burne, and frese like yse . . .
saying to the beloved
For your sake I love cities,

on your love I love the many,
saying to the people,
for your sake I love the world.
The old wounds crying
I find no peace, and all my warres are done.

  Out of our life the living eyes
  See peace in our own image made,
  Able to give only what we can give:
  Bearing two days like midnight. "Live,"
  The moment offers; the night requires
  Promise effort love and praise.

Now there are no maps and no magicians.
No prophets but the young prophet, the sense of the world.
The gift of our time, the world to be discovered.
All the continents giving off their several lights,
the one sea, and the air. And all things glow.

Move as this sea moves, as water, as force.
Peace shines from its life, its war can become
at any moment the fierce shining of peace,
and all the life-night long many voices are saying
The name of all things is Glowing.

A beginning, a moment of rest that imagines.
And again I go wandering far and alone,
I rise at night, I start up in the silence—
lovely and silver-black the night remembers.
In the cities of America I make my peace;
among the bombs and commands,
the sound that war makes
NO NO
We see their weeping and their lifetime dreams.

All this, they say to us, because of you.
Much to begin. Now be your green, your burning,
bear also our joy, come to our meeting-place
and in the triumph of the reconceived
lie down at last together face to face.

———————

We tell beginnings : for the flesh and answer,
for the look, the lake in the eye that knows,
for the despair that flows down in widest rivers,

cloud of home;   and also the green tree of grace,
all in the leaf, in the love that gives us ourselves.

The word of nourishment passes through the women,
soldiers and orchards rooted in constellations,
white towers, eyes of children:
saying in time of war What shall we feed?
I cannot say the end.

Nourish beginnings, let us nourish beginnings.
Not all things are blest, but the
seeds of all things are blest.
The blessing is in the seed.

This moment, this seed, this wave of the sea, this look, this
    instant of love.
Years over wars and an imagining of peace.   Or the
    expiation journey
toward peace which is many wishes flaming together,
fierce pure life, the many-living home.
Love that gives us ourselves, in the world known to all
new techniques for the healing of a wound,
and the unknown world.   One life, or the faring stars.

Nine Poems

NINE POEMS
for the unborn child

I

The childless years alone without a home
Flashed daily with the world's glimpse, happiness.
Always behind was the dark screen of loss
Hardly moving, like heavy hardly-moving cloud.
"Give me myself," or "Take me," I said aloud;
There was little to give, and always less to take.
Except the promise, except the promise darkness
Makes, night and daylight, miracle to come.

Flying over, I suddenly saw the traces
Of man : where man is, you may read the wind
In shadow and smoke, know how the wind is gone
And know the way of man;   in the fall of the plane
Into its levels, encounter the ancient spaces:
The fall to life, the cliff and strait of bone.

II

They came to me and said, "There is a child."
Fountains of images broke through my land.
My swords, my fountains spouted past my eyes
And in my flesh at last I saw.   Returned
To when we drove in the high forest, and earth
Turned to glass in the sunset where the wild
Trees struck their roots as deep and visible
As their high branches, the double planted world.

"There is no father," they came and said to me.
—I have known fatherless children, the searching, walk
The world, look at all faces for their father's life.
Their choice is death or the world.   And they do choose.
Earn their brave set of bone, the seeking marvelous look
Of those who lose and use and know their lives.

III

There is a place.   There is a miracle.
I know the nightmare, the black and bone piano,
The statues in the kitchen, a house dissolving in air.
I know the lilac-turreted cathedral
Taking its roots from willows that changed before my eyes
When all became real, real as the sound of bells.
We earthly are aware of transformation;
Miraculously, life, from the old despair.

The wave of smooth water approaches on the sea-
Surface, a live wave individual
Linking, massing its color.   Moving, is struck by wind,
Ribbed, steepened, until the slope and ridge begin;
Comes nearer, brightens.   Now curls, its vanishing
Hollows darken and disappear;   now high above
Me, the scroll, froth, foam of the overfall.
284

IV

Now the ideas all change to animals
Loping and gay, now all the images
Transform to leaves, now all these screens of leaves
Are flowing into rivers, I am in love
With rivers, these changing waters carry voices,
Carry all children;   carry all delight.
The water-soothed winds move warm above these waves.
The child changes and moves among these waves.

The waves are changing, they tremble from waves of waters
To other essentials — they become waves of light
And wander through my sleep and through my waking,
And through my hands and over my lips and over
Me;   brilliant and transformed and clear,
The pure light.   Now I am light and nothing more.

V

Eating sleep, eating sunlight, eating meat,
Lying in the sun to stare
At deliverance, the rapid cloud,
Gull-wing opposing sun-bright wind,
I see the born who dare
Walk on green, walk against blue,
Move in the nightlong flare
Of love on darkness, traveling
Among the rings of light to simple light,
From nowhere to nowhere.
And in my body feel the seasons grow.
Who is it in the dim room?   Who is there?

VI

Death's threat!   Today I have known laughter
As if for the first time;   have seen into your eyes,
Death, past the still gaze, and found two I love.
One chose you gladly with a laugh advancing,
His hands full of guns, on the enemy in Spain.
The other living with the choice of life
Turning each day of living to the living day.
The strength, the grossness, spirit and gall of choice.

They came to me and said, "If you must choose,
Is it yourself or the child?"   Laughter I learned
In that moment, laughter and choice of life.
I saw an immense ship trembling on the water
Lift by a gesture of hands.   I saw a child.   I saw
A red room, the eyes, the hands, the hands and eyes.

VII

You will enter the world where death by fear and explosion
Is waited;   longed for by many;   by all dreamed.
You will enter the world where various poverty
Makes thin the imagination and the bone.
You will enter the world where birth is walled about,
Where years are walled journeys, death a walled-in act.
You will enter the world which eats itself
Naming faith, reason, naming love, truth, fact.

You in your dark lake moving darkly now
Will leave a house that time makes, times to come
Enter the present, where all the deaths and all
The old betrayals have come home again.
World where again Judas, the little child,
May grow and choose.   You will enter the world.

VIII

Child who within me gives me dreams and sleep,
Your sleep, your dreams;   you hold me in your flesh
Including me where nothing has included
Until I said   :   I will include, will wish
And in my belly be a birth, will keep
All delicacy, all delight unclouded.

Dreams of an unborn child move through my dreams,
The sun is not alone in making fire and wave
Find meeting-place, for flesh and future meet,
The seal in the green wave like you in me,
Child.   My blood at night full of your dreams,
Sleep coming by day as strong as sun on me,
Coming with sun-dreams where leaves and rivers meet,
And I at last alive sunlight and wave.

IX

Rider of dream, the body as an image
Alone in crisis.   I have seen the wind,
Its tall cloud standing on a pillar of air,
The toe of the whirlwind turning on the ground.
Have known in myself hollow bodiless shade,
The shadow falling from the tree to the ground,
Have lost and lost and now at last am found
For a moment of sleep and waking, striking root.

Praise that the homeless may in their bodies be
A house that time makes, where the future moves
In his dark lake.   Praise that the cities of men,
The fields of men, may at all moments choose.
Lose, use, and live.   And at this daylight, praise
To the grace of the world and time that I may hope
To live, to write, to see my human child.

SELECTED POEMS

NIGHT FEEDING

Deeper than sleep but not so deep as death
I lay there sleeping and my magic head
remembered and forgot.   On first cry I
remembered and forgot and did believe.
I knew love and I knew evil:
woke to the burning song and the tree burning blind,
despair of our days and the calm milk-giver who
knows sleep, knows growth, the sex of fire and grass,
and the black snake with gold bones.

Black sleeps, gold burns;   on second cry I woke
fully and gave to feed and fed on feeding.
Gold seed, green pain, my wizards in the earth
walked through the house, black in the morning dark.
Shadows grew in my veins, my bright belief,
my head of dreams deeper than night and sleep.
Voices of all black animals crying to drink,
cries of all birth arise, simple as we,
found in the leaves, in clouds and dark, in dream,
deep as this hour, ready again to sleep.

ORPHEUS

I

The mountaintop stands in silence a minute after the murder.
   The women are furies racing down the slope;   far down,
   copper and black of hair, the white heel running, escaped line
   of skirt and foot,
among the leaves and needles of these witness trees.   Overhead,
   clouds, lions and towers of the sky.
Darkness masses among the treetops;   dense shapes bulk among
   treetops over the murdered ground, stain of light glancing on
   the jointed branches.
Light of water, blaze of the comet-tailed stars.
The scene is the mountain, just after the murder, with a dry
   concentrated moon
rocking back and forth between the crowns of trees, back and
   forth, until over this black crown,
attacking the sharp black and the secrecy, moon comes to rest.

And the exhausted
women are streaming down the paths at the foot of the mountain,
  now fleeing,
now halted by the sleep that follows murder.
From this moment, the darkness fills the walls of rivers,
and the walls of houses and in the villages
the walls, the olive groves, remembrances and pillars
of dark. Murder. Scattered and done.
Down in his blood on a holy mountaintop.
All the voices are done;   very deep, they rest, they are alone.
Only the breath around the earth moves, in a slow rested rhythm,
  as the moon
comes to rest over that treepoint swaying like the breast
of an escaping woman.   Down
from the moon one cloud falls and it passes, sails upon
this place in the forest where the god is slain.
These golden breasts have troubled heaven.
But they are breasts of tears;   their act is done;   and down,
here on wet ground, scattered, the flowing man.
Scattered, there lit, in black and golden blood   :
his hand, a foot, a flat breast, phallus, a foot,
shoulder and sloping back and lyre and murdered head.

Hacked, stopped, he bleeds with the long dayblood's life.
Has bled until the moon cleared range and rose, female and male,
shining on treetops and water and on the pieces of a man.

Very quiet, the trees awake.   And find their voices.   But
the clouds are first, they have begun their song
over these air-cut, over these river-cut mountains—
Lost!   they build the sound of Lost!   the dark level clouds
voice under voice arranged in white arpeggios
on the high air, the statement of the sky
rides across, very high, very clear,
singing Lost; lost man.
And the river falls among the plunging forests,
the heartshaped waterfall goes down like the fall of man
seeking, and crying one word, earth's water speaking of harvest.
But moon says No   :   in finished night the great moon overrides,
promising new moons only, saying I know no harvests—
My harvest, declares in whiteness, are the tides to come.
These words are called in a silence
over the scattered man.
The clouds move, the river moves,

the great moon slowly moves; even more slowly now,
the first finger of the right hand.

The right hand stirred in the small grass and said
"Do more; for this is how it is," and died again.

II

Scattered.   The fool of things.   For here is Orpheus,
without his origin :   the body, mother of self,
the earliest self, the mother of permanence.
He is sensation and matter, all forms and no form.
He is the pieces of Orpheus and he is chaos.

All myths are within the body when it is most whole,
all positions being referred to flesh in unity,
slow changes of form, the child and growing man
as friends have seen him, altered by absences and years.
Scatterings cannot discern changes of quality:
This scattered on the mountain is no man
but body as circus.

Sideshow of parts, the freaks of Orpheus.

The wounds :   Touch me! Love me! Speak to me!
The hand risen to reap, standing upon its wrist
and singing, "I will do," among its dreams.
The hunter eye in the forest, going mad.
The waste and shed of song that ritual made,
and the wandering, loss of forms, the darkened light,
as the eye said:

I looked at night, to rainbow-crested moon,
as to round-crested sun I looked at day.
Stare that fertilizes the threshold of square Hell,
stare pacing the forest, staring the death away.

Give everything.   Ask not beyond the daily light.
I shine, am reflected in all that is and will be,
names, surfaces, the void where light is born.
There was something I saw.   Something not to be seen.
But I cannot remember; and I cannot see.

The wounds :   Touch me! Speak to me! Love me!
In darklit death, the strong pyramid heart

knows something of the source, the maze of blood
the deeper fountains and dance of certain colors.
Something was founded at the base of the heart,
it cannot find it now, but the blood's pilgrimage
carries its relics and the sacred banners
far from this mountaintop to the beating valves of the sea.
It cannot clench.
                    There was song, and the tomb of song,
there was love, but it all escapes.   What love?   For whom?

The wounds   :   Speak to me!
The arm that living held the lyre
understands touch me, the thrill of string on hand
saying to fingers   Who am I?
Father of songs,
when all the doors are open,
beyond the clasp of power,
the mastery of undiscovered music,
what laying on of grace?
Healing of the valleys of sacrifice
and five rivers finally trembling down
to open sea.
I almost remember another body,
I almost, another face.

The wounds   :   Love me!
Something turned back, something looked Hellward round.
Not this hard heelbone, something that lived and ran.
The muscles of the thigh are the rapids of a stream,
the knee a monument stone among fast waters,
light flowing under the skin, the current hardnesses,
channels where, secret, the awareness streamed.
                                        No!

That was not how it was!
                        They will say I turned to a face.
That was forbidden.   There was a moment of turning,
but not to a face.   This leg did turn,
there was a turn, and then there was a journey,
and after many dances and wanderings.
Yes;   but there was a face.

Who will speak to the wounds?   Who will have grace,
who will touch this broken, who will dare being whole
to offer healing?   Who broken enough to know
that the gift is the only real, who will heal these wounds?

Rolled like a stone in a riverbed
The stone exposed in the dry riverbed
This head of dreams, horizon of this murder,
rolled on the mountaintop.   The man who is all head,
this is, in the circus.   Arches of music, arches of the brain,
furrows and harvests plowed by song.   Whom song
could never capture.   This it was alive
led Jason past the sirens, this
in Egypt and in Hell had heard of Heaven
and reading Moses found the breath of life,
looked up and listening felt the breath of death
at the left ear, finding then every life
among the men of mud and the men of sunlight
the women turned to light in the eyes of this head.
The head;   the song;   and the way to transcend.
The song and chance.   The way beyond the wound.
Rolled, like the music of an old ballad,
a song of heroes, a stone, a hope, a star over head.

The head turns into a cloud and the cloud rises
unwounded, the cloud assumes the shapes of plants,
a giant plant.   Rolls to the great anvil storm-cloud,
creates the storm.   This is the head of dream.

Only there is a wound that cries all night.
We have not yet come through.   It cries Speak, it cries Turn.

Majesty, lifted omen.   The power to make.
The burning ship that sails to the burning sun
a sun half sky half water wholly flame,
the burning ship half wood half water all fire.
There is no riddle but all is mystery.
There is only life.   To live is to create.
Father of song, in the seed and vaults of the sea,
the wall of light and pillars of desire,
the dark.   The dark.   But I will know again,
I will know more and again,
woman and man.

And turn and arise and give these wounds their song.
They have no song and no music.   They are wounds.
And the air-tree, the air-heart
cannot propose old death-breath any song.
Fountain of air, I see you offering,
this air is a bird among the scenes of the body,
a golden plover, a blackheart plover.
Here is his body and the trees of life,
the red tree, the ivory, the tree of nerves,
powerless to bear another song.
Chopped like the chopped gold of fields harvested,
air falling through many seductive shapes,
cascades of air.
The shadow falling from the tree to the ground.

Let the wounds change.   Let them not cry aloud.

Blood-clothed structure, bone of body's being,
there is no sin here, all the giant emotions
were uncorrupted, but there is no sign.
The bones and the skein of flowing, the many-chaining
blood and the chain of dreams and chain of silver nerves
cannot remember.   They cannot imagine.   No space
is here, no chance nor geometry,
any more than this mountain has its space or chance.
The mountain looks down the road.   It sees the last of the
    women
escaped and alone, running away the road.
It sees one woman in a million shapes,
procession of women down the road of time.
They have changed into weapons;   now they need be whole.
And the pieces of the body cannot be.
They do not even know they need be whole.
Only the wounds in their endless crying.
Now they know.

Touch me!   Love me!   Speak to me!
One effort and one risk.
The hand is risen.   It braces itself, it flattens,
and the third finger touches the lyre.   Wounds of hand.
But it finds thick gold of frame, grasps the frame
with its old fingering of bone and gold.
Now there is blood, a train of blood on grass

as hand swings high and with a sowing gesture
throws the lyre upward.   The lyre is going up:
the old lyre of Orpheus, four strings of song
of the dawn of all things, daystar, daymoon, and man,
hurtles up, whistling through black air.
Tingles in moon-air.   Reaches the other stars.
And these four strings now sing:
Eurydice.

III

Standing in silence on the mountaintop, the trees incline before
   the breath of fire.
Very slowly, the sounds awake.   Breathing that is the
   consciousness, the lifting
and the resting of life, and surf-sounds of many flames.
Flame in its flowing streams about these pieces
and under the sides of clouds and chars the branches.
It does not touch the flesh.   Now the flesh moves,
the hacked foot and the hand and the head,
buttocks and heart, phallus and breast, compose.
Now the body is formed;   and the blood of Orpheus,
spilled, soaked, and deep under the wet ground,
rises in fountains playing into the wounds.
Now the body is whole; but it is covered with murder.
A mist of blood and fire shines over the body,
shining upon the mountain, a rose of form.
And now the wounds losing self-pity change,
they are mouths, they are the many mouths of music.
And now they disappear.   He is made whole.
The mist dissolves into the body of song.

A lake of fire lowers, tendrils level to source,
over the mountaintop many young streams.
Standing newborn and naked, Orpheus.
He has died the death of the god.

His gifts are to be made, in a newfound voice,
his body his voice.   His truth has turned into life.
   — When I looked back in that night, I looked beyond love
      at hell.
   All the poets and powers will recognize.
   I thought the kings of Hell would recognize.
   I misjudged evil.   —
                  He has opened the door of pain.

It is a door and a window and a lens
opening on another land;   pain standing wide
and the world crystallized in broken rains.

Nightmares of scatterings are past, the disc of music and day
makes dawn and the streams make seed of towering fern.
The green night rising in flower,
helmet-flower, nebula-flower, lilacs in their turrets of air,
and stain of morningside bright on the low sky under
new constellations of anatomy.
Ripple of grape, trembling star in the vine of water,
the night-goer rises in color before a parade of clouds.
Now he remembers the real;   remembers love.
His life is simpler than the sum of its parts.
The arrangement is the life.   It is the song.

His death is the birth of the god.
He sings the coming things, he sings arrivals,
the blood reversing from the soaked ground, warmth
passing over the lands where now barren resists,
fertile and wet invite, all in their way receive.
And all the weapons meld into his song.
The weapons, the wounds, the women his murderers.
He sings the leaves of the trees, the music of immense forests,
the young arriving, the leaf of time and their selves
their crying for their needs and their successes,
developing through these to make their gifts.   In flower.
All who through crises of the body pass
to the human life and the music of the source.

Are there songs rising from the broken sources?
The mountain   the bright cloud   and the cities risen.
The faceless and the unborn in their transfigured song.
The god a god because there are birth and death
approaching each other in their blood and fragments,
the death and birth at last identified.
He has died the birth of the god.
The animal and song beneath the skin,
seeking an exit, baited with food and wounds;
no, not an exit.   What are they seeking?

Cyclic dependence   the god and the miracle
needing each other,   and all the wounds are mouths,
weapon to song transfigured.

Song of the air between us, of the voiceless alone,
the cloud diffusing over the island country
pulled down in the shape of a plant, shape of a brain,
collected into the ground and will of man.
Song of the dam destroyed   over the widening river
in a triumph of hope;   song of the flute in the kitchen,
a little bright water boiling on the stove.
Song.   The frozen man, his axe in the sequoia;
blueberries, toyon berries, black galleries of coal,
ferocious gestures of work and the bed of the poor.
The unmade music of the power to rise,
the young and unborn, the throat and hand of song.
The body risen past its other life.

Among the acts and the memories he remembers—
he brings together and he binds—
among the firewind and the cloud chamber,
he is aware, he knows the nature of power,
the nature of music and the nature of love.
Knowing the enemies, those who, deprived at the root,
flourish in thorny action, having lost the power
to act essentially, they fall into the sin
of all the powerless.   They commit their acts of evil
in order to repent, repent and forgive, murder and begin again.

To have gone through.
To live and begin again.
The body alive and offering,
whole, up and alive,
and to all men, man and woman,
and to all the unborn,
the mouth shall sing
music past wounding
and the song begin:

Song

Voices and days, the exile of our music
and the dividing airs are gathered home.
The hour of light and birth at last appears
among the alone, in prisons of scattering.
Seeming of promise, the shining of new stars,
the stars of the real over the body of love.
The cloud, the mountain, and the cities risen.

Solving the wars of the dead, and offering dream
making and morning.   Days and voices, sing
creation not yet come.

(1962)

FROM

WATERLILY
FIRE

THE SPEAKING TREE

for Robert Payne

Great Alexander sailing was from his true course turned
By a young wind from a cloud in Asia moving
Like a most recognizable most silvery woman;
Tall Alexander to the island came.
The small breeze blew behind his turning head.
He walked the foam of ripples into this scene.

The trunk of the speaking tree looks like a tree-trunk
Until you look again.   Then people and animals
Are ripening on the branches;   the broad leaves
Are leaves;   pale horses, sharp fine foxes
Blossom;   the red rabbit falls
Ready and running.   The trunk coils, turns,
Snakes, fishes.   Now the ripe people fall and run,
Three of them in their shore-dance, flames that stand
Where reeds are creatures and the foam is flame.

Stiff Alexander stands.   He cannot turn.
But he is free to turn :   this is the speaking tree,
It calls your name.   It tells us what we mean.

TO ENTER THAT RHYTHM
WHERE THE SELF IS LOST

To enter that rhythm where the self is lost,
where breathing : heartbeat : and the subtle music
of their relation make our dance, and hasten
us to the moment when all things become
magic, another possibility.
That blind moment, midnight, when all sight
begins, and the dance itself is all our breath,
and we ourselves the moment of life and death.
Blinded;   but given now another saving,
the self as vision, at all times perceiving,
all arts all senses being languages,
delivered of will, being transformed in truth —
for life's sake surrendering moment and images,
writing the poem;   in love making;   bringing to birth.

FOR A MEXICAN PAINTER

Carlos, your art is embryos,
These eyes are shaping in the dark;
There is a fate map in this red
Line and that bright red line,
The earliest map of all.

These eyes are shaping in the dark
Toward the requirement of light
And all will grow as they have grown;
Even transplanted will perform
Selfwise, themselves, this one, that one.

Deep in the hieratic blood
Toward sleep toward dream the process goes,
Toward waking move the sex, the heart,
The self as woman man and rose.
Carlos, your art is embryos.

A SONG OF ANOTHER TRIBE

Guilt   said the bony man
Do you feel guilt
At your desires?
No   I said   my guilt comes when
My desires find no way.
Country of sand and claws;
I wait for my rescuer.
No one will venture there.

Out of long silences
Come I to wordless song
O let my singing bring me
To that place
Where live waters
Rise and go.
There may the living arrive,
Go and return.
Find me, and I find,
And go finding.
A beating sound, I hear
A sound of riding.

Speed after silence
And at last music,
Words of another tribe:

My riding is on swift mares,
My love is by the green water-springs;
For a short moment I will sit there,
I will look upon her wandering face,
I will put an end to the black delay.

SONG

A voice flew out of the river as morning flew
    out of the body of night, a voice sending
    out from the night of the sleeping
Morning : a voice in its own voice, naked, made
    of the whole body and the whole life
But without anything
Breath
Breath of the fire love
Smoke of the poems voices

WATERLILY FIRE

for Richard Griffith

I / The Burning

Girl grown woman   fire   mother of fire
I go to the stone street turning to fire.   Voices
Go screaming   Fire   to the green glass wall.
And there where my youth flies blazing into fire
The   dance   of sane and insane images, noon
Of seasons and days.   Noontime of my one hour.

Saw down the bright noon street the crooked faces
Among the tall daylight in the city of change.
The scene has walls   stone   glass   all my gone life
One wall a web through which the moment walks
And I am open, and the opened hour
The world as water-garden   lying behind it.
In a city of stone, necessity of fountains,
Forced water fallen on glass, men with their axes.

An arm of flame reaches from water-green glass,
Behind the wall I know waterlilies
Drinking their light, transforming light and our eyes
Skythrown under water, clouds under those flowers,
Walls standing on all things stand in a city noon
Who will not believe a waterlily fire.
Whatever can happen in a city of stone,
Whatever can come to a wall can come to this wall.

I walk in the river of crisis toward the real,
I pass guards, finding the center of my fear
And you, Dick, endlessly my friend during storm.

The arm of flame striking through the wall of form.

II / The Island

Born of this river and this rock island, I relate
The changes : I born when the whirling snow
Rained past the general's grave and the amiable child
White past the windows of the house of Gyp the Blood.
General, gangster, child.   I know in myself the island.

I was the island without bridges, the child down whose blazing
Eye the men of plumes and bone raced their canoes and fire
Among the building of my young childhood, houses;
I was those changes, the live darknesses
Of wood, the pale grain of a grove in the fields
Over the river fronting red cliffs across —
And always surrounding her the river, birdcries, the wild
Father building his sand, the mother in panic her parks —
Bridges were thrown across, the girl arose
From sleeping streams of change in the change city.
The violent forgetting, the naked sides of darkness.
Fountain of a city in growth, an island of light and water.
Snow striking up past the graves, the yellow cry of spring.

Whatever can come to a city can come to this city.
Under the tall compulsion
                              of the past
I see the city
                change like a man changing
I love this man
                    with my lifelong body of love

I know you
              among your changes
                            wherever I go
Hearing the sounds of building
                            the syllables of wrecking
A young girl watching
                            the man throwing red hot rivets
Coals in a bucket of change
How can you love a city that will not stay?
I love you
              like a man of life in change.

Leaves like yesterday shed, the yellow of green spring
Like today accepted and become one's self
I go, I am a city with bridges and tunnels,
Rock, cloud, ships, voices.   To the man where the river met
The tracks, now buried deep along the Drive
Where blossoms like sex pink, dense pink, rose, pink, red.

Towers falling.   A dream of towers.
Necessity of fountains.   And my poor,
Stirring among our dreams,
Poor of my own spirit, and tribes, hope of towers
And lives, looking out through my eyes.
The city the growing body of our hate and love,
The root of the soul, and war in its black doorways.
A male sustained cry interrupting nightmare.
Male flower heading upstream.

Among a city of light, the stone that grows.
Stigma of dead stone, inert water, the tattered
Monuments rivetted against flesh.
Blue noon where the wall made big agonized men
Stand like sailors pinned howling on their lines, and I
See stopped in time a crime behind green glass,
Lilies of all my life on fire.
Flash faith in a city building its fantasies.

I walk past the guards into my city of change.

III / Journey Changes

Many of us   Each in his own life waiting
Waiting to move   Beginning to move   Walking

And early on the road of the hill of the world
Come to my landscapes emerging on the grass

The stages of the theatre of the journey

I see the time of willingness between plays
Waiting and walking and the play of the body
Silver body with its bosses and places
One by one touched awakened into into

Touched and turned one by one into   flame

The theatre of the advancing goddess   Blossoming
Smiles as she stands intensely being in stillness
Slowness in her blue dress advancing standing I go
And far across a field over the jewel grass

The play of the family stroke by stroke acted out

Gestures of deep acknowledging on the journey stages
Of the playings the play of the goddess and the god
A supple god of searching and reaching
Who weaves his strength   Who dances her more alive

The theatre of all animals, my snakes, my great horses

Always the journey   long   patient   many haltings
Many waitings for choice and again easy breathing
When the decision to go on is made
Along the long slopes of choice and again the world

The play of poetry approaching in its solving

Solvings of relations in poems and silences
For we were born to express   born for a journey
Caves, theatres, the companioned solitary way
And then I came to the place of mournful labor

A turn in the road and the long sight from the cliff

Over the scene of the land dug away to nothing and many
Seen to a stripped horizon carrying barrows of earth
A hod of earth taken and emptied and thrown away
Repeated farther than sight.   The voice saying slowly

But it is hell.   I heard my own voice in the words
Or it could be a foundation   And after the words
My chance came.   To enter.   The theatres of the world.
308

IV | *Fragile*

I think of the image brought into my room
Of the sage and the thin young man who flickers and asks.
He is asking about the moment when the Buddha
Offers the lotus, a flower held out as declaration.
"Isn't that fragile?" he asks.　　The sage answers:
"I speak to you.　　You speak to me.　　Is that fragile?"

V | *The Long Body*

This journey is exploring us. Where the child stood
An island in a river of crisis, now
The bridges bind us in symbol, the sea
Is a bond, the sky reaches into our bodies.
We pray : we dive into each other's eyes.

Whatever can come to a woman can come to me.

This is the long body : into life from the beginning,
Big-headed infant unfolding into child, who stretches and finds
And then flowing the young one going tall, sunward,
And now full-grown, held, tense, setting feet to the ground,
Going as we go in the changes of the body,
As it is changes, in the long strip of our many
Shapes, as we range shifting through time.
The long body : a procession of images.

This moment in a city, in its dream of war.
　　　　　　　　We chose to be,
Becoming the only ones under the trees

　　　　　　　　　　　　　when the harsh sound
Of the machine sirens spoke. There were these two men,
And the bearded one, the boys, the Negro mother feeding
Her baby. And threats, the ambulances with open doors.
Now silence. Everyone else within the walls. We sang.
　　　　　　　We are the living island,
We the flesh of this island, being lived,
Whoever knows us is part of us today.

Whatever can happen to anyone can happen to me.

Fire striking its word among us, waterlilies
Reaching from darkness upward to a sun
Of rebirth, the implacable.　　And in our myth
The Changing Woman who is still and who offers.

Eyes drinking light, transforming light, this day
That struggles with itself, brings itself to birth.
In ways of being, through silence, sources of light
Arriving behind my eye, a dialogue of light.

And everything a witness of the buried life.
This moment flowing across the sun, this force
Of flowers and voices body in body through space.
The city of endless cycles of the sun.

I speak to you   You speak to me

(1957)

FROM

ONE LIFE

The poems in ONE LIFE are interspersed among the narrative in prose and pieces of documentary evidence, statistics, quotations used as savage humor, headlines.

The book is cut like a film.

Paul is a real boy; his young life is a pilot-image of the conflicts in Wendell Willkie's life, the center of this book

Young

"DOWN FROM CHICAGO BRYAN CAME"

Down from Chicago Bryan came,
His voice was marvelous, silver and free,
He visited the Willkie home;
He said T.R. is all our shame.
Your father has a passion for freedom, Wendell.

When we turn in on ourselves our face.
We are American.   We thrive
Our currency needs a double base,
We are for silver, and we are silver,
Said Mr. Bryan.

The struggle, I heard Mr. Carlisle say,
Finds the holders of idle capital
Here, and those who produce and pay
Here—and where will the party fight?

The party must answer, as each man may.
Don't you agree, Herman?

Don't you agree that there are two ideas
Of government : Make rich the well-to-do,
And their prosperity will rain on you.
The Democrats' idea, however, is
Make strong the base, make the masses prosperous,
Their wealth will sprout and flower for all of us.
Oh, let him do it, Herman.   He's only—what?—four?

They tell us the cities want to stick to gold.
The cities rest on our prairies.   If they burn
And we are all that's left, those stones will rise again.
My throat does tickle.   I think I'm catching cold.
If only my throat holds out for the whole campaign!
Could I trouble you for a hot compress, Herman,
Or perhaps a gargle?

Your father is saying It is hard
To keep the people on their guard
Or to make them take the longer view.

313

All you are saying may be true, but
What about imperialism?

Our thoughts cannot be stopped by seas.
Oh, no, said Bryan.
But these are sins and contraries,
The founders hated such as these.
And the Louisiana Purchase? said your father.

That wasn't imperialism, Bryan said.
Of course not, said your father.
But if McKinley's ugly head
Looks out from Washington, I dread
The future poor, the future dead,
And Teddy Roosevelt,
Said Mr. Bryan.

Rang and rang, rang in the small boy's head.

And a girl singing in the symbol air, crossing of gold, a
    polished staff of music,
Intent as Wales, enormous violet. Then the edge lit cloud
Balanced the steeple for a moment, while the high ritornel
Sang slender in her throat, Light of light, God of God,
Sang all the lamps of sorrow, sang figurations of the swirling
        Captives, their rare release.
Sorrow has repetition, sang, but joy, but joy
        Has continuity.

The fleeting furnace moon raising his white powers
Will shiver alive tonight before that ritual face;
Love with her graces and ways, open as peonies,
Running with all the animals of heaven
        In grass of green
Eternal orchards, until the soul of the boy says to the singer,
        Gwyneth, you are my song.
Fifteen years to drift to the shore of this ocean,
Finding the wet and patterned sand, pillars and floor of fire.
All in the mercy of earth, the enlarging flower
That conquers death and sin, that sheds on the village
Of brick, fire, glass, tin and invented money
        Incense and hungry bells.
Ringing and hungering where the enormous ransomed boy

Now rings and hungers
In starved and golden air.

But in these years, what is free, what is strong?
People, strength.   He had heard this always,
The mud of our towns turning into stone cities,
The fire of our wealth, space of our own time
Flowing beyond our eyes.   Now he can see the older
Faces rising : authors of our belief, image-faces of active
Sources like lines his father called in the morning,
The music of difference, all alive.
The founders of law and this people, who set in diversity
The base of our living.
Actual diversity of days and sources, smiling in disagreement,
    strengthened by one another,
Until the idea of diversity becomes our strength, sacred to us.
The range broadening, the potential becoming a way and a song.
Many have fought this reality.   We know the wounds,
On the body of work and of heroes, and in all of us.   Wounds
    of our green belief;
Many have seen in the growing of their lives that dwarfing
    wound, the starving out of their chances by the rigid, who
    have no hope but the static, the dead fact and size,
Not the strength that we laugh in beginning, the pleasure moving
    toward unknown making; but hard control, clanging of doors
    closing like burial, the signals of wreck—
Deforming the children in the galleries of coal, deforming the
    woman in her pride of home, deforming us in our dream and
    in bed and as we look in one another's faces,
Seeing the terrible still poem.
Into this time
Vision sails.   In the midland, thinking of ocean,
Among constraint, brooding on our long hope,
That hope in distinctness rides, full of our powers.
Riding in light
Into the movement of our bodies, into our words,
In all we love.

When the young man reaches his full height, sharpened on the
    arguments of his strong house, mixed in the opposites of all he
    knows, tall in the heat, and waiting to speak.

Has moved finally to the front of the stage, has felt for the first time all the eyes.

They are waiting for him to declare his entire form. Faces composed in a habit of boredom.

They come from these fields, split by these towns run central through them as they sleep; they walked these streets of smoke, they drove these heavy horses to the barn, slept with the same women, were lost too in these swamps of black and ancient green.

Deep in these graveyard nights found girls throwing defies of their bodies to death on the grave-grass and on the porches and behind the brickyards and under the knotted trees.

Judges of all hope work out the same whisky, the same riverbanks and barrooms, bury in themselves the same bodies and the same images, are burned in the memory of the color of fire

When they hear the doors strike shut behind them, the gongs of time like closed-down metal mills,

And they know now they are called to breathe in air of the same belief, the warm deep native earth and air, already surrendered and done to death,

To cut their time with an edge of new-cut finding.

The young man takes his wavering breath. He is naming himself in the tribe ceremony.

Prepared for speech among many wakings in the lights of his lifetime, he speaks to these faces.

Under and before him, faces of judges,
Discovering provocation.

His legs feel very long to him and the ideas feel holy.

It comes to him now that the courts are sworn to these old ideas, green stalks of being, that the courts are all of choice.

The choice of growth is of the closing and opening of doors.

Doors of our rock, yes, clanging of mountains,

Through which our grandfathers drove their seed. Mountains, and seas of exile and of choice,

By whose unforeseen stars we made landfall, our coast being always choice

In another freedom. Though we may land here there is no other landing, to choose our meaning we must make it new.

He knows the animals of boyhood and the west.

Freedom to him is a constant and a bond.

Close to our wildness, be fierce and be safe,

316

Be fast and be feeding,
Be strong according to our own kind.

They rule out of our justice and our despair
The strength of our strength.   The meanings turn, resolve
Into the play of our night, our flowering.
Not that the day of truth is given the lie,
But cut down long before.   And with ourselves cut down.

Domination of smoke.   The portraits are official,
Say Lie, say Complexity is weakness.
We want our many-rooted heart.   Flesh of our penetration
Allowing the empire of noon and midnight.
The rich, black-fielded life of the center, forests
Of corn and desires.   These fields go deep
While madness and silence stifle the grass.

A woman is running down the moonlight highway
Of buried Indiana, underground.
Whatever slave : factory or teaching woman
She joins our buried life, the floods of secrecy
Told at the riverbank Don't flow, don't flow.

They are passing a law against the life of the river,
The bodies of our truth are in bed tonight.
Horizon of rumor in the Tenderloin, under red light,
Parade of clouds as far as the Barbary Coast,
In the back rooms, in pilot-houses, past thick reeds whistling,
Through swamps silvered with marvelous adolescents,
The girl of Eden admitting all her life.
Singing on the moonridden cry of loons.

Will they stifle the grass and the young lying together,
The Lincoln stories, the twisting and lilacs of New England?
The swarming lives from the Carolinas calling
Truth and the mockingbird, the big river or the sea?
The eyes of the child and the children's zodiac?
Lack, rape, and silence.   A summer evening, will you,
Of burning crosses, of instruments of torture
Who pretend not to recognize each other?
Sitting on the corner of Main and Jackson, the half-lit
Limping fortuneteller of all our fortunes.
In this one the generative secrets burn,

And he is all of us, bound in our same false secrets,
Lies concerning the communion of man and man,
Deep lies of brokenness between woman and man,
All torn apart by the mask of men.

WILLKIE—STOPLESS FALLING THROUGH AIR

For the first time today
I see for the first time
Throwing myself away
Into the flood of chance.

Falling, meet the dark flame
Over America,
There is a lie in the curse
Of the fall of man.

I know the shaking doom
With doom the only sure.
Earth rushing up at my eyes
With the speed of fear.

Possibility.
My fingers do their work.
Fallen into a trap,
I hang and drink the black

Drink of shock, I swing
From lack of frame to frame,
And toward myself I swing
Slowly becoming man

Among all things, a knot
Of possibility,
A man among meanings
Swinging down the sky.

Now I remember love
I remember time
I do not deny surrender
Nor the womb.

Begun again, I praise
The fall for being sure,
May I fall whole and perceiving
On the arisen shore.

If you look at your succession of desires,
A running flame, a parade of leaders
Chosen for representing true your need,
Or your parade of dreams, the lifetime theater
Telling you everything sacred is remembered,
The lie and the counter-lie are lost in truth;
If you see your life as a procession of images
You will know you have not forgotten a single meaning.
We have known all of this all along.

To find a way to proceed from the revelation.

They have threatened us with the penalties of division—
What became of the war, the sea of immense soldiery
Sent over in endless liquid fields of sunset?
Did it melt to a handful of lies?
No.   The war did not melt away.
Where did your childhood go, and the sword of the garden?
You will see them today.

Questionnaire.   Write on two sides of the paper only.
Do you believe in your body?   Answer yes or no.
Do you acknowledge your soul?   You know they are separate:
How long have you known?

When you say Peace, do you think War?   Two seconds.
When they say Female, do you think Male? Two seconds.
When they say Good, do you think Evil?   Two seconds
We have given you, always the opposites.   Submit.

You have felt stillness, guilt, and the death-wish,
Haven't you?   When?   How often?   How recently?
You know what is meant by these, don't you know, don't you
Know how they were reached and how they were chosen?
The smile is vicious, since the verdict is.

Time and the rose of form have rung your name.
Under the laws of growth, the immortal law,
You may choose in your own voice, and every day.
You need not ever accept their ideas of guilt,
You need not accept their ideas of innocence.

One voice will say in the sounds of penalties
War and No-War, Good and No-Good, Male and No-Male,

319

And what are growth and form and the human wish?
I will tell you a story.

These are the people who will not stay discovered.
Sunrise over horizons of new eyes, the twilight arch
Allowing spurs of cloud-informed evening, prows of
Cumulus heading west
To the cloudmakers, fathers of clouds and rivers.

This is a man discovering revelation.
America revealed that will not stay discovered.
Continually found.   Related to all finding.
Look at the man, he can be recognized.
Look at yourself.   We are his record.

A time of finks and nobles,
With a field office as bond between client and operatives,
The correspondents and crooked men at work in the plants,
And a force of professional spies sent from place to place.
The back-room boys are always on hand, for shadowing, guard
    work or the simpler forms : eavesdropping, dictaphone work,
    hanging around.
When the strikes come the offensive arm, the nobles,
Can round up a slugging gang from the street-corners
And, most efficiently, bring in strikebreakers.
The national officers handle the big accounts : General Motors
    or Bethlehem Steel.

GRAND CENTRAL STATION

All the way to the city a crying in the air.
He walks the ramp into this shell of sound,
Acres of goodbye and the noise of the ocean
Of the waste of power.
                              Smell of the rock and metal;
Steel-pale and blue, the names of the calling
Fly up to the ceiling, the names of cities and stars
To justify distance.   And the cries of parting.
Just listen to that, says the outsider in triumph.
Listen to all that noise!
Wheels and galleries of the control of tears.
Goodbye, honey, goodbye.   Goodbye.

Tunnels and wheels of language, an inordinate mouth
Shouting into a skin of echo.   Poison, intoxication
Of immense foregrounds, the deeper bells of the past
Losing themselves in boasts and breakers, each man carrying
Sound like a name, like clothing, a proof assumed.
A man saying Hello walks up the ramp.   His wife.   His son.
Hell, mother, says Willkie.   We'll take this town!

Tree of Rivers

"ALL THE WAY THROUGH THE FOREST"

All the way through the forest, a sound of birdsong,
The lightning-bird singing through the wilderness.
I see him flying before the invented speed.   Body of shadow,
    wings of light,
In the leaf forest and the needle forest.   Clusters of song flying
Past the thickets unbroken, and glimpses of river
And the dual-noted thrush, two or three times.

Just after the steaming rains, when each leaf stands up clear,
Individual on the branch, when the tree has made its relation
With the slope of hillside and the strike of starlight, bearing each
    storm of its lifetime in its body, and standing
In the relation to the rest of the forest—just after the form-giving
    storms and the rains of growth
A car full of men drives into this country.   One man gets out,
    slams the car door,
Saying, "I want to walk.   Wait for me up the road."
His smile suddenly brutal, "I want to see it before it sees me."

After the road, the woods are axless and pathless; the great
    mists
Hang over the sycamores, darkening and thickening in the
    stillness
Above the black-green, into the green.   The man's walking
Bends the small pliant branches.   One note of the car horn
Gives him direction : he keeps his shoulder to it, and goes
    with his arm braced

Pushing through the forest.   Deep grass and moss bed
Cover the rock, cover the ledge, cover the fallen tree.
Far ahead, the distant green of spring shining on dogwood
   where the light falls through,
The ribs, the braces of trees.   Along these arches
He sees the bear turning away from him, browner than
   branches.
Everything glitters.   The full drop hangs
On the hard bud.
Underfoot, moss springs down, leaving water.
The drop trembles.
He goes invading.
Bright the drop falls.
His face hardens with his inward glare.
Goes plunging through the forest.
Spruce, firs.   The oxalis ground, the fern of the woods,
In delicate tolerance, the patience balancing,
Bending and recording.
                              Now the sawbriars
Catch him, and his breath hisses caught.
Before his foot.   The snakehead prodding the air,
Erect and advanced from the thick coil,
Silent, not calling on his rattles.   Touching and touching
The space between them.
He stares at the snake.   It glitters and glistens before him.
The guardian; and a darkness winds his face.
The forest stands as free behind as it stands before him; but a
   limit
Has been marked, a threshold indicated in the coil.
He waits.   He knows that if at the end of the long waiting,
Unendurable waiting, if then he can go ahead, he will come into
   a further country.
A leaf comes down, a hand in the air
Rocking down, and the snake withdraws his head,
In an arch over a coil assumes his next shape,
Looks once at the man, a flat unlit stare
Before he pours himself away.
A little moving water is left where he was,
Moving silver like the model of a river
Before it exhales upward into the branches.
The man walks over the earth where it was.
He pushes further into wilderness
With a stirring in himself of sadness,

Of past fear and of recognition.
A word has been spoken in a language
For which he has been homesick.
This is a language which he cannot remember,
All he knows is that he knows the word.
The word of the snake.

Deep grass and moss bed
A murmur of wells.
Before him, a cleft of rock
Holding water moving and curving.
Strung from rock to rock across his path
He sees his way crossed by a spider web.
Spiderspan wider than spears met to guard
The gates of the forest.
It shivers in the light, a faint breeze
Sways it like fantasies of bridges in India.

The man knows this is the final obstacle.
The bull of dream lowers his head now, he shuts his bull-blue
    eyes,
Now he is running and he jumps the water,
Tearing the web.
It is torn, it sticks to his fingers and his hair;
He has cleared in one jump the forest; he is standing
On a shoulder of rock above a hidden farm.

The man is dropping down, dropping down
To a green yard and growing grass
And a woman with a water-pail
Standing in the doorway.
This is a young woman, big-breasted, slender-waisted,
Sets her pail on the floor, smoothes her straw-bright hair,
Waits for his nearing.

Morning, he greets her. Morning, she answers. You came
down from the overhang. That's a knotty way. There's the path
just beside you. She looks at his thorn-caught legs. He smiles; for
anyone else he would feel a fool. He has only a city answer: It's
been years since I walked through anything but streets or parks.
I wanted to see them building from this side.

—Streets and parks are far from home
Can you hear the river from here?

The sound of building in the air?
—All I hear is rushing of water, very near.

—Down in the gully, come and see,
April water doing ruin.
We've had some ruin here.
You've got honey in your hair, Mister.

He puts his hand up to his head and touches
The sticky places.   The web adheres.
I came through a spider-web, he says and laughs—

They look through each other's eyes.
—I'll take you across, she says.   Just let me look,
I'll make sure the baby's asleep.

She takes the bucket in.   When she comes out,
She narrows her eyes against daylight.
The sky gray, developing purple.   That's storm, she says.
Yes, he's asleep.   I can go down there now.
You a government man?

—Not on your life.   I'm with the company.
You know the wires strung along the valley?
That company.   Do you have light in the house?
—They haven't brought light in, she said.   We're going to,
    though.   We're going where it is.   The dam's moving us
    out.
He tries to say he is sorry.   They are walking past the yard,
    through the stand of hickories, then along the road.
There's no loss, she says.   It's hard for the old ones.   They
    think of the doors and the steps, they think of the graves
As if they were children.   I'm ready to go today.
My child's a baby; he's one; I'm alone with him.
His dad went to West Virginia to build a tunnel
When everything here had been bad for a long time.
Built the tunnel.   It gave him crystal in his breathing,
His chest turned to crystal, they say, before he died.
I'd like to move to the outskirts of town.
They'll move me, they say, and the boy, near a school.
They tell me I can learn.   A trade, something like that.

I'm sorry about your husband, he says.   And you don't hate to
    leave?
I should think having them tell you what to do—

How can I say it to you?   She turns on him.   Her eyes going
    dark.
The boy was born just after they broke the news.
I didn't know how I'd get through.   The birth
Was so much leaving and putting away myself and starting
    again.
Another birthing seems easy and right.
When the man talks about The Valley, he tells me
What I have thought and kept secret, telling it open and plain.

They have come to the rushing of the creek, foaming tawny
    and white.
Endless and potent along the road, violent and turning
The rocks downhill, dragging the whips along.
—It looks higher than the road over there, said the woman.
—You had a bad time of it last year, he said.
—Twisted the door off, spilled mud ankle deep in.
But down in the cove they had real trouble, where the houses
    float by.
And their cattle drown.   The chickens are swept away
Afterward.   There was fever, too.   The creek's just as high now
And they do say the rains are still to come.—
The sky dark, the clouds very fast.
—Next year! she says.   The wind blows it away.
Next year it'll be built.   There! she says, pointing down.

Down past the treefall slopes, the bend of the river.
Past the darkened branches, below the darkened sky,
The treefall slope, thick forest down to a wild river
Choked purple, raging upon the curve, pale in the rapids,
Insane noises driven by storm.
                                        Over them
A stroke of lightning is laid across the river
Stopping the rush, the rapids, the windflowing leaves.
Law blazing across the river.

The moment is stopped.   Then blindness, lifting of blindness.
They see the smoke-forest.   Command of thunder.
Streaking of light, Moses across the river.
Inexorable light.   A wall of law.
—Where the lightning struck.   They mean to build there,
The woman is saying.   They talk about a highway
That will reach the dam, somewhere along here—look,
On this tree.   Over her head, a slash of blue color

Painted on bark.   That's the surveyor's mark.
They think to build where we are now.—

The forest leaves whistle in a forerunner breeze.
Now the rain, says Willkie.
I must get back to the highway.

Not leaves, not lightning, not that greatness of rivers.
The woman who sees herself in her lifetime, moving,
The man at work who uses the valleys
And still sustains the valleys.
The water-spiral turns the fire
That breaks upon the miles of air,
Leaps through the furnaces of change
To make and make. From those steel pools
The healing of earth is given a man.
He rides his pastures to the sun,
The great sun pours hot power down
To feed the feeding mouths, to bind
Earth to earth and man to man,
Until earth stores the waters up
To course the water-spiral new,
Whirlpool and embryo.

A tree of rivers flowing through our lives;
These lives moving through their starvation and greatness,
Masked away from each other, masked in lack.
Each woman seen as a river through whom lifetime
Gives, and feeds.   Each man seen giving and feeding.
Under all the images, under all growth and form.   The energy
    of each, which is relation,
A flare of linked fire which is the need to grow,
The human wish for meaning.
                                        Roots of diversity
Each being witness to itself, entering to relate,
Bearing the flood, the food, the becoming of power,
Which is our eyes and our lives
Related, in bonds of flow.

The power of war leads to a plan of lives
Involving rivers.   The many-stated million

Human concerns.　This touches, this gives life
To all its forms.　Now clothe our force,
Make it as flexible as a man venturing
To fend for himself in his own enterprise.

Now in the unity of all vision, unity of the land, the forests
　　and water,
See nature, the nation, as a web of lives
On the earth together, full of their potencies.
The total unity, reached past images,
Reaching past the naming of religions.
We reach to create.　That is our central meaning,
Suggestion of art and altar in all our passwords,
For the meaning of "mirror of nature," the meaning of "image
　　of God"
Is a simple fiery meaning : man is to create.
Making, singing, bring the potential to day.

SLOW DIALOGUE BETWEEN PAIN AND ROOSEVELT

　　　　Warm in the pool the wasted man
　　　　Among his mutilations swam.
　　　　Lay in the sun of his despair
　　　　While time ran around the year.
　　　　　　　Legs of his wounded days
　　　　Refused, refused.　He turned to pain,
　　　　The arrogant and dwindled man
　　　　Saying, Do not surrender me.
　　　　Though frightful time outrun my praise.

PAIN:　　　I remember the player's thighs,
　　　　The skill and locking of the knees,
　　　　The ruthless muscles of the wise.
　　　　Time running frightful in sunrise
　　　　Outrunning you, outrunning light,
　　　　Races through the dream of night.
　　　　Torment lays forfeit all your dream.

THE SELF:　The core of my arrogance
　　　　Has been transmuted, but your fires
　　　　I cannot yet meet with praise.
　　　　When the boy's muscles are my dream
　　　　And the man's withered legs my day

All I am and all I seem
Will find the way, will find the way.

PAIN: I am the thread, I am the bait,
I am the pride of your despair.

THE SELF: There are legs I shall outrun.
Speed of this resurrection
Will find me in the spectral dance
Before the real, before the real.
Somewhere my next life waits and sees
Time and the heart of man at race.
The wish can heal, the wish can heal.
There is such freedom in this place.
Warmth of the many-minded free,
Outblazing personal liberty.

The cause racing, and the root
To be found.   A young man wrote
All of this long ago.
We believe ourselves by slow
Turnings of the living heart.
Pain of that growth will give us start.
To stand so braced will be my pride.
I have been born and I have died;
Pain sends me on my wandering,
Warns me of enemies about:
We Refuse is their war shout.
Pain sets my hand a growing root upon,
The weapon of the wounded king.

In the warm pool the wasted man
Swam laughing in the sun.

———————

Gullies as deep as halls held these surveyors,
Their bobs and blueprints. But men have drowned in the eaten
Land, the river ate them too.   You know the river
Cannot be looked at unless you see the forest,
The forest will not speak until you call the people.
Look at these people's lives and you will see it clear.

After explosions filling these valleys, clear
Outlander voices ring across the sky, and people
Prepare to move the dead from the graves, the river

Is coming over the bottomland and forest,
A little fightin creek would have eaten
The porch, the chickencoop, all but the surveyors.

The spools of cable, the pylons like surveyors
Walk, signal to the lives of all these people.
Their lives are real and face the tree of the forest,
And face the tree of time and the tree of the river
Singing a secret of growing and not being eaten
Until they are given as food.   And the valley stands clear.

Now that the river has changed, my dear,
And summer has changed and the winter weather,
I cannot foretell three days together,
I cannot foretell two days, my dear.
In the hills or in the town
The landmarks are all gone and down,
The signs are new and strange, my dear,
The signs are new and strange
And how shall I foretell, my dear?
What one thing do you need to hear?
What shall I say will come?   —Change.

The tarpaper shack and the red rose bush.
Smoking crystal of the hill.
The brush of the shorelines, fever in its sting.
Don't tell me the water's still risin!
Go down to the rail gate, see where the rundown is.

There is a cloud on this house and the smoking crystal
Holds waters that will drench the oil lamp out.
One flashflood left me only my coffeepot.
That's nature's way, my walnut Granther said.

The dragons of burning ran along the mountain
A scar lighting the overflow; the forest
Pulls back from the highway, in mortal insult.
Spring bringing floodwaters.   Now the Negroes come
Over the runoff sloping, ankle-deep, with their blues
And watermelon smiles.   They know the suffering flood,
They are dark and they sing.   They know potential joy,
Flames, lightning, and the gully-buried man;
All the sky-stars and all the leaves on the tree.

Joy white and absolute, potential joy.
Ice and snow melting in the spring. Amen.

Who shall bar with his arms the heavy rains?
Had me a man, the man pleased me. Amen.

From kinsee to caintsee it's been rainin here,
I never longed west of the Mississippi. Amen.

Downpours standin up to the bankgrass,
I've been a good wife. I want the snowfed Trinity. Amen.

Water spread over a lake to the windowsill
The tin cans silver, my kitchen window plants. Amen.

My brooms, my yard goods, the honeysuckle vines,
And three left shoes go washing past the bank. Amen.

Drowning of a deal table and eighteen head of cattle.
The whole section's under water and me singin Amen.
    I do sing Amen.

But next life, next life, or maybe next year, Lord,
Lay lightning across your river and your poor woman's Amen.
    Amen, Amen.
    I do sing Amen.

They dug up the grave, while a banjo and two guitars
Were quiet. Hush your music, Sourwood Mountain,
We'll dance the Bird Cage again tonight.

Move the peacock quilt, pack up your favorite kettle,
There's extra homespun and the kerosene stove.
You will never forget the time the floor moved.

Frail pillars of reason held you with a creek gone crazy,
At five-thirty we heard the millrace and running stone.
The stars are nearly out and the legless shadows

Are men who have come to help hurt that my river done.

PORTRAIT OF A MAN, WITH
A BACKGROUND OF HOLDINGS

Standing against the gorge, he sees the slides of light.
Where lightning lay, they are building.   The surfaces are lit.
The dam that is almost finished stands in seamless night
Declaring its form with a clear speaking.
The man leans on his railing.   He thinks : I will listen.
Bulbs of violent light swing on their own wires,
Lines of the downstream face flow down the slope of dream.
Spillway of loyalties shining, the gate of fire.

He forgets the police on a hot summer night long past
Later finding the wound between his shoulder blades;
He thinks of the women opened before him, flowers of
    summer,
The first cry of his son at which all waterfalls
Waited like streams of wine bitter in Spain.
Riches of breathing, fantastic poverty.
The running of stones in this riverbed.

Corngreen and fields of thirst, he thinks.   I know a woman
The river of whose mouth, whose sea of flowers
I saw in the hot fields of the past, at night.
Over all images a lightning stroke of law
Has been laid across, white structure on the river
To stop my profit's streams, to make a tree
Celebrating the years of growth and form.

The pacemaker image.   A pulse and pattern of light.
The mirror image of my waste, in the ferocious cities
Whose roaring and giant fibres find my exultation
Outward in the shout, while what I stare at is
The dam I tried to murder for years; or sail
In a boat the color of violins among
A school of condoms floating in the Sound.
Beyond naming, waste!   The legs of the withered man.
My summons from the great web and the woman
In glimpses accepted, for long forgot.   I think
I am wheat dormant in the seedman's hand.

ARE YOU BORN? / I

A man riding on the meaning of rivers
Sang to me from the cloud of the world:
Are you born?   Are you born?
My name is gone into the burning heart
That knows the change deep in the form of things.
—I saw from the treeline all our cities shine.
A woman riding on the moon of ocean
Sang to me through the cloud of the world:
Are you born?   Are you born?
The form of growing in leaf and crystal flows,
And in the eyes and rivers of the land.
—From the rock of our sky, I came to recognize.

A voice riding on the morning of air
Sang to me from the cloud of the world:
Are you born?   Are you born?
Bring all the singing home;
There is a word of lightning in the grass.
—I stood alive in the young cloud.

ARE YOU BORN? / II

A child riding the stormy mane of noon
Sang to me past the cloud of the world:
Are you born?   Are you born?
The form of this hope is the law of all things,
Our foaming sun is the toy of that force.
Touch us alive, developing light!   Today,
Revealed over the mountains, every living eyes.

Child of the possible, who rides the hour
Of dream and process, lit by every fire.
Glittering blood of song, a man who changed
And hardly changed, only flickered, letting pass
A glint of time, showers of human meanings
Flashing upon us all : his story and his song.
The song of a child; the song of the cloud of the world,
Born, born, born.   Cloud became real,
                                    and change,
The starry form of love.

A STORY

There is a child. He comes from far. By boats and trains, cities that move, houses that sail away. He comes from the country of war to a field at peace. Day lilies, yellow daisies, Queen Anne's lace. A barrel, a box of sand. He is four years old; he looks up into Miss Lorence's eyes. Many children, playing.

CHILD:	Look, look!
MISS LORENCE:	Yes, I'm looking.
CHILD:	I'm way up in the sky!
2ND CHILD:	Moo, moo. I don't like you.
CHILD:	I do magic.
2ND CHILD:	What magic?
CHILD:	Want to see?
	I do magic very well.
	Step there. Put one foot there.
	Now I need the latter.
	Hold it! (To the young woman)
	What's your name?
MISS LORENCE:	Miss Lorence. What's yours?
CHILD:	Paul.
MISS LORENCE:	Paul is slight, Paul is small,
	Paul wants to feel, he wants to smell,
	He wants to taste, to see, hear. Everything.
	He is slight, his eyes blaze blue,
	White-skinned, cocky, knobby, as
	Fragile as a closed-down spring.
PAUL:	Where is father?
MISS LORENCE:	Far. Your mother does not know.
	It is the war. It is the war.
PAUL:	Who is Hitler?
	What is sound?
	How does it feel to die?
	What does a worm think? Miss Lorence?
	How long does it take to grow up?
	Miss Lorence—I will talk to you.
	The little house I like, the kitten I like.
	It went to a little wood, to a little Paul,
	When it came to Paul it cried.
	In a basket, like Paul the baby, in far land,
	To Paul's father. The father of Paul

Kissed the kitty and cried.
Unhappy was he.   Why is he?
Because I have no kitty, because the father
Of Paul is in a far country.
Not in this town is he,
Not in this house,
Not in the room or the bedroom.
Far away, far away.   When will he come to us,
When will we be happy, seeing him company?
Not for long, for long, for long.
Cry we, for it is a long time, and far away.

ANOTHER DAY

MISS LORENCE: The child among his powers gathering
His words, his rich articulate joys and fears.
They are our fears, our joys, the questions of
all.
His creations are real.   His agonies
Are curiously related to the trouble of the
people of the world.

PAUL: There was a boy once, lived in a little house.
A big man came, started eating and eating.
He got to the boy, boy said, Dog, dog save
me.
Dog jumped the ocean and saved the little boy.
Then they lived together.
The giant was discouraged.
After a while he saw his mother.   Yawn I.
A man came and ate up the little pig.
How discouraging!   How sad!
*Dis*couraged little pig.
I am tired.   Rest I will.

ANOTHER DAY

PAUL: And then the cow did write.
His mother said sleep, sleep,
The other cows are outside,
You have been bad,
More than the black cow,

More than the white;
Go to sleep.
You are a baby cow.
Your father is in the creek.
I had no home and I cried
Master, master!
I want some water or I will be sad.

ANOTHER DAY

PAUL:	I will now sing a song for you, Miss Lorence. Will you write it down?
MISS LORENCE:	Yes. I'd like to.
PAUL:	No. I cannot sing today. My songs are tired. They are unhappy.
MISS LORENCE:	I can write down your unhappy song.
PAUL:	No. You sing me a song.
MISS LORENCE:	Shall I sing Sacramento? Buckeye Jim?
PAUL:	No, no. You must not sing those songs. Sing your new song. About me. Sing about that grownup downstairs Who lives in a tree.
MISS LORENCE:	Who lives in a tree?
PAUL:	The man with the grass in his lovely hair. The wild, happy man, with the bears, and the large scamper.
MISS LORENCE:	The words are masks, the words are a stream; they mask his open fears. The apprehensions stand there.
PAUL:	I don't want to rest. Once upon a time there was a Miss Lorence, who was going away, away, away, away. Don't go away to leave me. Sit on my bed not to leave me. A skylark am I, wildly I walk, walk, walk, walk. Mittens here in my bed. There. I hit you, but I love you. When you die you stop. Don't really worry, dear you.

I do not really die.   Do not believe anything I
    tell you,
Or unless you really see.
Sometimes I joke.
This is school.   Not sky, not home, but
    school, school, school.
What is my shadow?   It is me,
But not a mirror.

ANOTHER DAY

PAUL: You sit there because I like to look at you.
                I would like to live with you.
                Why don't you come live with me?
                This little fish went in the water,
                But there came a boat and smack,
                Killed at once.
                That is the end of my story.
                Which is a love story, Miss Lorence.
                What do you know about love, Miss Lorence?
                Once upon a time there was a big, big, big man.
                A zero man.
                I dreamed about the school and people.
                Miss Lorence was a snowman.
                I dreamed about me, sleeping in a box
                Because I had no house.
                And we cried.
                I dreamed about a hundred miles on a boat.
                And the boat went on swimming in my head.
                Wicked witch.   Pony.   Zero.   Clay.
                All my head is gone.
                Shot off by a gun.
                Your head will be gone too
                If the men, the men, the *men* shoot you.
                It will be too bad when your head is shot off.
                You are a dear little baby.
                Once there was a man called Jew
                And he was chased and he was shot
                And he ran but he was shot
                Wee Willie Winkie.
                —Antonia, you are a zero.

Have you ever "rapping at a window, tapping
   at a lock," Miss Lorence?
I am a quiet little boy because I must be quiet.
Come sit beside me, Miss Lorence.

They talk to each other, and he holds her hand. The small,
knotty boy, with a young woman bending over him, curved and
evocative, giving him his rest and his stories as November
deepens.

PAUL: Miss Lorence, you are a tree with leaves on,
         A strong stone, a brook.   Look,
         Water running in brooks, in brooks, in brooks,
         Which are purple and white streams,
         Screens, screams and cries and loud noises.
         Oh, what a singer am I.
         Little songs and cries.

         I want to want to want to get up.

         But I will sing a loo a loo a loo.
         The old man named Loo
         And he went to an eye
         And he lived in the eye.
         What a lot he could see.
         Once upon a time
         There was an end of my story.
         I do not like the black sky.

His gay words, words of delight. But the real fears, the
questions, the real real emerging. Father, Hitler, war, shooting,
Jews, death, safety.

PAUL: What do you write?
         Write me a song.
         What about?   The fish I do not know.
         —The man had little streams.
         And a bright pain.
         It was bright when he pushed
         With a noise and a bar.
         A tooth.   With a hole.
         There can be holes in the ground,

Can there be holes
In the white sky?
The sky is a tree.   It spreads.
Does it hurt the ground to have holes?
Why, the sky was *white*.

PAUL: Do you know Hitler?   Does he like you?
                  I know him.
MISS LORENCE: Do you?
PAUL: He doesn't like me.   He shoots people.
MISS LORENCE: Why doesn't he?
PAUL: Because—I don't know.
                  I lived away over the river.
MISS LORENCE: In Germany?
PAUL: I lived in a million houses.
                  My father is in Krieger land.
                  Not this land, not this America,
                  But a Krieger land.
                  That is a land of guns.
                  That is a shooting land.
                  I remember the dogs in the park.
                  Far away.   I remember.
                  That park we saw the dogs.
                  When we went home again
                  We stepped the leaves apart.
                  I want to get up.

ANOTHER DAY

PAUL: Miss Lorence, we are new to each other,
                  Because I have not been to you for long, for
                      long, for long.
                  You are a dear little tree.
                  Sit by me close.
                  I am a little horse who is going to sing.
                  Such a lot of songs I have to sing,
                  For I have not been to you for so long.
                  Did you ever have a red pain
                  In your throat?   Mine was, it was mine.
                  Now I am here I can sing to you
                  A little song all for you.
                  You make me happy.

Shall I say it in German, in French?
No. I will not.
I will just say it to you in talk.
It is a little song about me.
I am happy with you, happy like happy
At birthday candles
And little gold shoes
That Jesus wears.
Little gold shoes.

———

Yes, a nice child. Isn't he a nice child?

ANOTHER DAY

PAUL: You can't come with us.
We have business to do.
We have to go over to Germany
But we'll be back in a minute.
We have to go to Hitler's land
To shoot him.
But you are a lady so you can stay home.
Men take care of ladies.

MISS LORENCE: Who are you going to shoot?

PAUL: Hitler of course, the bad wolf.
If you are in trouble with Hitler you'd better
    not come on the ferryboat.
If you are don't come here with us,
You'll make more trouble than we have.
Are you a Jew?
It's being Jews that makes the trouble.
It makes people worry.
Are you Jew?

MISS LORENCE: No.

PAUL: That is why you are not worried.   That is
    why you are happy.

———

His father is lost and away. Paul never asks for help or
sympathy. He is detached and proud. Now, around New Year's
Day, he stops being Paul. The brittle four-year-old turns into
something else: the farthest he can imagine, the oldest he can

339

travel. He announces to everyone that he is Timmy Torin, he is
nine and can do anything. He is his own hero. And his father is
lost.

PAUL: My name is Timmy Torin.
             I can do more things when I'm bigger.
             You like me big don't you?
             If somebody was lost I could find them
             Any time my mommy tells me or you tell me.
             I'm a very big boy.
             I'm not afraid.
             You know about Jesus, little Lorence?
             Some day I will tell you all about Jesus.
             My father is dead, he is an angel.
             When you are blind you cannot see but black.
             When you are blind, it is like you are nothing
             And are dead.   How is that?
             Somebody says, When you are dead you are
                 stopped.
             And other people say
             You go to the sky and watch and sing.

             Miss Lorence, I am tired.
             You can have one of my blocks.

The sea has opened, the limit of his dream
Has split; now lights announce him to the day.
He is born; and asleep, awake, and soon the warm
Taste of the second world calls him to understand
Power drawn on the tides of sweetness in.
His strength allowing change, letting him choose and grow
Again, and the curve of the world is breast, the breathing land
With his own breathing tells of peace and form.

Not now, but much later, does the world fall away.
This is myself, says the child.   My self, we all did say.
There is my mother, whose pleasure, whose deep need
It was to feed me singing, or recoil.
And then the fable, the terrible forgetting.
A cold distortion twisting past the leaves.
Was there a Garden?   Was there a Tree of Sin?
What was my exile but from memory?

340

Refusal, flowering, was the only tree.
It grew until the truth was almost lost.
Cast, the obliterate spirit sang its loss.
Dream and the sea open.
All things find their change.
        The child remembers : the child is the tree;
The tides, the leaves, the city, the true relation.
The world was the mother, the world; it was always the world
Pure, fierce, all moving and all reconciled.

A structure is rising. It takes on shape, it takes on meaning
Where there was formless waste.   Go down the valley,
Eye of creation, sings the voice of the girl
Through cloverfield.   Green water is the spring of the year,
Jade green in summer; autumn bright blue, for winter
    waterblack.
The wall's detail, discrimination of blue
Standing above the wall, where developing water
Coils, sheathes, transforms itself turning, into light.
Fusing of images and further change.
Fire and music, interchangeable.
Fusing of flow, dividing and further blue.

There is control here, for all things in relation
Find their offerings and give.   A tendency toward life.
The man at peace with his life and its flashing,
A climax forest at peace with its fields.
When the storms come, there is something in us
That has always been ready to greet the storm.
An impulse running through a valley of process
Quickens the blossoming, whose orange on evening
The fiery action of men and women emerges.
And daughter-stars, daughter-forests of our range
Dance with the central prince the dance of reign.
We know the light incarnate, we have seen
At last that the flashing is our old light, and flesh.

Under stones, under leaves, under links of purpose,
Appetite up so tall, the power is given
Along the hillsides of risk, the spiral dances
Within its own symmetry.   But women, but men, but women
And men in the dances and risks of birth
In which love and the spirit are reborn.

This also from lightning given and growing power.
Lightning which is the word.   The gift and power.   Love.

In the last hour of night, a zebra racing dawn,
Black-and-white hour that feeds the night and the light,
Feeding the strong infants; when the well is open;
When all the birds of day begin to sing.
He turning in sleep finds through a journey of dream
One woman in whom all the rivers of his storm
Cluster and fill, as words, as woman.   Finds
The running of stones in a riverbed
Troubling hillsides with their leaves
Over black branches.   Swinging-to of mountains
No heavier than sails riding to rendezvous.
Dense in our blood, abstract as the idea of God.
As smoky misereres, as the birthcry.
The big few clusters, the body of a man.
The clusters of her body.   Sleep of gardens,
Sleep of rain, always distant and present
As your own deprived childhood.   No.   Not deprived.
Yes.   For it never saw it was deprived.
But there was the unknown, the great dream of the poor
And of all men; your childhood found that friend.
Was it the faceless, the man in the purple graveyard?
No.   Hidden.   And kind.   In endless offering.
And now in early sleep, a ripple uncovering
The roots of the diverse, the city of love.

A note in music.   His sleep going long and along.

Fields where we slept
Lie underwater now
Clay meadows of nightmare
Beneath the shallow wave.

A tremor of speech
On all lips and all mirrors;
Pink sweater and tornado
Act out the spiral dawn.

South lies evocative
On one fine Negro mouth.

342

Play of silver in streams
Half lake under.

High on the unplowed red
And waterweeds respond,
Where Sheriff Fever
Ordered me to trial.

Where once hatred and fear
Touched me the branch of death,
I may float waves of making
Hung above my lost field.

Remember they say and Incarnatus Est,
The fire-tailed waves, never forget the eyes
Of the distorted jailers or their kindness
Even while they were torturing Mr. Crystal.

Psalms awake and asleep, remember the manmade
Lake where those barren treecrowns rode.
Where air of curses hung, keel of my calm
Rides our created tide.

He turns through the lucid stars of a lit city
In sleep.   He is walking past the snake and the spiderthread.
"And they do say the rain's to come."

The flood-woman ankle-deep, staring upon his eyes
In a dream of rivers, water whirls here like the sound
Of voices, of swans.   The faring.   Below him turns
A house swimming, a broken-legged table and three chairs.
Past him in all that filth, a message in a bottle,
Too far to reach, and four stiff-legged chickens.

Ocean of our refusal, pouring its waste
Over the mind of man.
A choice between evils.
These evils are of us, that we did not respond:
Poverty, hunger, war.

The flood and the woman staring upon his eyes.
This flowing away is the lives of all I love.
Are you saying this is not water but lives?
Of course it is water.   Fool!   Of course it is lives.

He breaks as the river knots about their knees:
I thought I could bring life to such a pitch
That you and I and all things might be seen
With our own fire burning.   Something like Eden.
She is water to the thighs.   Relinquishing daylight, cries,
Where four rivers meet!
I like Eden our parents alive and corruptless,
Our parents thirteen years old, each one his own,
Slenderer than time, meeting in their first powers
And making us again.
Now her voice twirls past domes and nebulas,
The tilted courtroom sailing by as columns.
All stars, all cities variable.
And sondes and angels, swimming
Flood at his throat.
He knows something is safe.   The whirlpool,
He says, the embryo.
Before him floating and grave
The face of a child within the water-spiral.
A thin boy carrying a growing shoot.
Image of the continual self he shines
The edgewise spiral of all the hourlines.
Because you do require, the child is saying.
These are the bonds among things; they are the spirit
When you do recognize.
Even when all the voices are denied.

He starts awake in the city.   Orion believing
And erect stretches the sky of night.
That's all very well, thinks, seeing the clock; but I
Am practical : I can forget.   And sleep.

The tree of rivers seen and forgotten,
With all its lightnings laid over it, the white law.
Strokes of the spirit on the flowing spirit
Seen, forgotten, and seen, until the source.
But the source, simple and various
As possibility, the nest of light,
Is open; what do you forget who have forgotten?
At home or hunting, forgetting takes your throat.

This dream of rivers responding, as many lives respond:
The cant of a dam and the running of fresh waters
Allow discovery deep in the city of your days
Starting up, before your faces born,
Born and reborn of your perceive,
Of your smile that you recognize
The meanings as they move.

Convention

"THIS IS GOING TO BE ABOUT SMOKE"

This is going to be about smoke.
Blindness, shouting of smoke, the dice pitted with mines and
    tunnels.
Black hills, flights of paper over the lines of glaciers,
Railway stations in the zebra hour of morning
When the only ones awake are the mothers of infants
Staring at dawn, sky of the fountains.
                            Smoke
Of hotels, of women wanting to be raped, of the plush sofas
That long only to float into empty houses.
Smoke of concessions, the crystal chandeliers
Whose teardrops ring and say, Choose between evils,
You live in the world, you must learn to choose between evils.
Two gray colors of smoke waiting to be chosen.
Will nobody tell them? They do not seem to know.
I will. My brothers of smoke, my brothers,
You do not have to choose between evils.

———————

This is what lit the hunters of smoke and the paths of the forest.
    The tracking and the advantage of the steaming quarry,
This is what the pillars of fluted thought, the image vibrating
    through all the dances to the unknown where the leap is,
This is what the event and the battle-rags, the women secret in
    their suffering, the long rages of the pioneers, the glory standing
    over a final valley,

This is what they led to in their charts of vision : the sweat of
   bargaining and the smoky gold eagles,
The indirect lighting and the gamblers' despair.
Shifting landscapes of a Convention Hall.
This is a bazaar where there are nothing but drugstores
Each one has a single drug tested only on mandrills.
This is a dry arroyo expecting the avalanche,
Thirty-seven men offering foolproof ways of survival.
They trade their partisans.   That is their method of choice.
When they say survival, they do not mean living under the
   avalanche.
They do not recognize the existence of the avalanche.
They mean how to set up shop in the arroyo,
And show a profit after the first six months.

In a summer forest, when the profuse season
Let fall as burning flowers the burning flowers.
The cities of Europe fall as people chopped down and dying.
The skies see hairy fire.   The children see
Their mothers opening as nobody had told them
People can open.   News sometimes comes of Father.
Then no longer.   What horror the children see
Will not be acted out upon the world
For fifty years, or a hundred, as horror bursting
Or anti-horror working in their children.
A neat correctly dressed man with a picnic smile
Is drawing his feet up under him in a dance
In the summer forest.   He makes a little stamping
Pulling his knees up, a shiny little dance
Called Hitler Jigging.   The Forest of Compiègne.
The beds and chimneys and toys and linen and wood
Of many houses are not interested in this dance
And in China they have been fighting for a long time
Dragging thousands of miles the idea of man.

What were his dreams during these nights? Unknown.

Ice-gate over the land, a shock of closure.
Across the country now, a many-worked crying
That masks a silence.   The rising water and the entrapped air.

346

These are ice-crises in the history of ice,
And nothing is known of the life of ice in earthquake.
But all of this is about applause,
All of this is the fullness of values,
Commitment and refusal, the demand of the root
And the freezing of shallow streams.
When ice first forms
Snowfall and frozen rain may be its friends,
Deep roots recapture
Sleep of the heavy rain, the water rains,
Much of the gathering is underground.
These forces are not delicate, they are subtle,
They are like quicksand, not a material,
But a condition.
They are not forces, they are men and women.
The crest gates waiting,
The wheeled gates sealed.

Campaign

"SUN ON THE FACES"

Sun on the faces.   On the knotted rocks.
Sun on the iron.   Sun on the dust of the roads.
The ravel of cloud, the silver chalkings of track
Lying westward through the dappled pass
South of the city where the mist flowed in.

Distance and the crowd.
The train goes dark-green westward
Over the free, light-gray crystals of rock.
Early morning the moment of thin air
4 a.m. and the cattle lying down
And all the cattle get up from their knees.
Early morning, the chill before the sun
And eleven men standing at a railroad crossing
The arm of the signal swinging Stop red Look red Listen.

Stop.   People standing, looking separate in the morning air.
The little river over speckled stones
Passing the section crew.   They wave.   They wave.
The iceman and the gandy dancers,
And three blasts on the whistle for a penny.

In the smoke cities, sitting on the fences,
They shine in their leather, but they make no sign.
They hear the speaking in a pause of worlds
Roaring, in the haze roaring, in the stench
Of the slaughter of animals he roars. They make no sign.
In their stained aprons they listen, standing; they turn
Back to the cool immense bloodyards.
                                    His voice
Diminishing down the raspit avenues.   Promises
Individual Man, but vaguely, and the vague cities
Promised, and downward through industrial
Illinois, vaguely, and
                        through the blaze of town
Downstate, glowing, the summer leaves, the faces
Lit by September and inlit by the deep
Summer-end need for spiritual change.
                                The hoarse raven
Croaks in his throat, Rock Island, the swaying
Train carries these panicky friends, advisers of symptoms,
Sending their telegrams.

The man sits in the rocking bedroom, claws
Hooked in his throat : anger and rage, pain
And refusal of pain.   All right.   Finally, Let him in.
But I don't need him.

From the throat he can rally strength.   Remembering
Words to light home of track with the light of concentrated
Meaning and love past stupid pain.
But these are the towns listening : Galesburg, Joliet,
Peoria glowing, the ramshackle uniform and painted
Houses waiting : Missouri.   He had puddled steel outside
    Chicago,
Where the huge fires roar, opening night, smoking
Pink smoke, yellow smoke, white, on the ochre

Air over Gary.   Here, in broad dayland,
Had lain on the freights among the metal noises
Hiss of sand, relief of steam, and a bell wagging
Where now the faces ring unanswerable
And the limitless ragged sunset
Serves only a man on the grass
Exhausted, in overalls, not hearing,
Or not caring if he hears.

There is a knotless line westward, past terraces
High on the roads, the black form of a car
Traveling under.   Here, the clear glittering throat
The long pull of track that seals the black
Of quick sleep among the counting, among the hammering
Until the machine, blades whirling, dances the dance
Of Steel, and the machine chips and tightens and screams
A man saying, "A good steel rail will last."
A man saying, "He will need more than parades."

How was he first aware he would never walk again?
How did he ward off his mother's submissive hope?
How did he master his eyes?   Unlock his knees?
Did he know the danger for his back and arms?
Did he suspect he might never have his hands?
And his hope?   And his will?   And his wife?
And the night visitations when the mutilated
Processions filled the world and his room of dream?
Water did this, the pool told him;
He panted, he swam : Water will get me out again!

Voice did this, Willkie heard the memory,
Voice, get me out again!

Street corner to corner he will talk all day,
Feasting on talk at midnight to the last
Listening man. In Willkie, the child's food
Made breath, the bread made word, where love
Is the word.
                    Doctor Barnard hearing
The rasping impossible voice under the beating light,

Rocking among the train : My God, I can't make him stop.
He goes right on night and day.
                                        Words traveling
Straight on the land.   A train traveling, white
Plume over her back, over the rusty spurs
Never seen varnish; the network of glitter over
The network of track.
                                        Down into Oklahoma,
Stretched beside overgrown dry creosote
Over the track, broomcorn, and again
The crowds at the tail platform,
Willkie talking : You mothers, you fathers . . .

The track cuts west.   Slant roof, sun-catcher,
Outhouse, and barbed wire, the scrub growing up hill,
And a man in overalls walking the eleventh furrow.
The hard eyes of bigots.   The hard eyes of the poor.
Full moon at Skelly Stadium, the crowd
Roaring through Tulsa, the screams of wild turkeys,
The underground black sounds of strength, Negroes and oil,
In a growing city.   After the tents and clapboards,
The spinning of chance, the spinning dance of derricks
On the horizon through the pecan grove,
Across the broomcorn, across the tumbleweed,
Past the false-fronted clapboard, the pipeline, and this crowd,
Deep-throated, hard-riding, impoverished as by war,
Eaten away by dust the eroder, water,
Poverty the eroder and the eroder oil.
Waiting for fullness under the open moon.

I saw the footpath beside the telegraph poles
Waver among the knotted weeds,
Straighten.   A child here
In faded clothes among the faded words:
The sheetflood washed me clean.
My hilltop when I ran alone
Is put to pasture, ridge the contour round,
How shall I be, how shall I be found?
Furrows hold ice, furrows hold snow,
Plow the slope that I name home.
Dust my mother overturned,
Sand and dust and wind have come,

To burn my days, until I go
To find the garden of the wind,
The pleasant garden of the world,
Where the sheetflood lost its force
Wrapped all its water in a bud,
Where bud and seed and fledgling bird,
Where the child will tell his word,
Where all the streams are from.

I used to press tools in the Texas oil fields.
We produce 60% of the oil of the world.
    (Let the streetlamps burn all night!)

Amarillo in the morning heat
Away from the boom-town, infancy,
Used to be made of buffalo-hide,
Ain't made of buffalo-hide no more.
Little boys of the Panhandle
Used to pitch pennies at the yellow houses
Used to gather buffalo-bones.
Ship away the buffalo-bones.
Barbed wire was invented here:
Sing me a boardwalk in an old ghost town,
Gun play near the courthouse : Now vote me in,
I'll give a lot each for every vote,
Turn the LX into Amarillo,
Hot in the morning.

Down the Staked Plains the color winds
Rising through mirage.   The still
Elusive colors graze these hills,
Drink at these caves, go hunting in this sky.
The colors feed; or go hunting; or they hear.
Pause of colors before change.
A stranger, from the East, and talking fast,
Looks at a unique man,
The man from Tucumcari
Knows cattle and tourists.   He stares at the candidate.
The great pure Apache watches from his eyes,
Ferocious dawns do climb the Walls of Bronze.
Two from Gallup remember the strike.
A carpenter from Conchas Dam,
A handful of people from Mimbres Valley,

Alamogordo, the Oscura Mountains,
A few curiosities down from Taos
Listen to Willkie. Spit. Shake hands.

Out of the throats of volcanoes : rocks : volcanoes forgotten :
    a word craggy and pinnacled:
Shiprock : the shape of a cry issuing : as people, as rock:
Among the rivers in a dry country : invasion of dunes, the white
    sand in the wash : from the cave waters
Given, erect crystals : pinnacles in the flows : a cap of lava over
    the rock:
Cliffs vermilion and undermined : retreating cliffs
For the rainwash, the sheetflood overthrow
Reaches them : they deploy, in summer thunderstorms
In the shale, in softness, until the softness goes;
The ruined villages of rock, and the people.

There they slept.   They left the train.
Three planes from the plateau airport.
Through the low overcast into the phoenix sun.
Willkie then looking down, burned in his rage,
Hostile and sweating, saw the eaten country
Pinnacles into waves receding, the treeform famine
Of water vanished; the waves minimized to a ripple of terraces.
And all the people invisible.
Came down
To bleachers piled with local cotton and beef,
Hills of oranges, glass honey-hives.

The professionals see the signs in the dice, the signs in the cards
    and clouds,
Over their drinks they curse at the candidate, a renegade enemy
    whose sudden cause
Was rammed down their throats; he is wrecking their only chance.
The Dream of Business is a failing image.
Among the predictions, statistics, in the crowds,
The explosive seeds of defeat.   Their deadliest fears
Run damp in their bones.   More than torches by night,
More than pennons, candy, and speechmaking,
A campaign is slavery, they say,
The tiring slavery : to plan, to counsel, to control.

Above all : to carry out.
Willkie shows courage.   Willkie will shout.
Forthright, alone, he speaks his mind.
But the party needed another kind—
A man who will accept support.
No benefit here of party or plan.
Joe Martin sacrificed himself, wanting a giant to fight a giant.
—He's not a giant!
He draws his crowds.
Dead whales on flatcars draw their crowds.
Nobody votes for a dead whale.

Parades.   Rattle of palm trees.   The silver planes.
Statues : Prometheus and General Otis.
Searchlights demanding.

This is the journey into the people, asking for consent, for
    sanction, for belief.
Concrete parades, stabbings and fortunetelling,
Gin, roughage, the studios on Christmas Eve, spotlit groceries
    and the prayer marathon.
The rose window copied from Rheims, the Aztec temple designed
    by the architect who believes in function.
Great ancient lizards and tar pits, the skeletons of pale fine starlets,
Some Rembrandts, a cafeteria (white tile and potassium broth)
Where you pay what you think the meal was worth.
The Strip, the Bowl, the Derby, the Easter Cross,
The Troc, the Wee Kirk; the neon in the graveyard,
Saying on and off, Father.   On and off.   On and off.
The oil well in the sea.

They pray.   Security against oldness
And death—for the gilding of all things.
Under the lights.   On the porches, rocking, and at the Iowa
    picnic.
Drugged by wanhope, seduction, or the drugs.
Among the filling stations, between the orange trees,
Burst with illusion, listening for the faint
Tympans of rumor.   Fame.   Disaster.   Or the sudden
Wild nimbus that cheats prediction and the grave.
A tower of linked intestines, cemented, climbing

Over the orange faces, digesting the world.
It cannot; it turns to digest itself.

But the incredible fifteen-year-old
Uncorrupt in her moment, standing at Vine.

¶*From the Committee to Aid Migratory Workers:*
    We were accused of contributing to radical causes.
    When you are told a person is sick or in need,
    You don't ask him his religion, nationality or politics . . .

They will be obsessed by the word "security."

¶*When Hollywood gets aroused, it gets* aroused.

¶*This is not a campaign. It's a crusade.*
                                —Willkie at Long Beach

Up past the burnt hills.   Distance and the crowd,
The track, development, the tracks on their light-gray crystal,
The knotless, nodeless line.   Struck into water-light.
No but knotted, cloved, notched, scarred, traveled brightened
    by tears,
Good steel rails and riding them
Development riding on the tracks of law.
North in a ravel of cloud, into
The dappled pass south of the city.
Mist flowing over toward San Francisco
The power towers walking, Spaniards' ghosts,
The silver-white unborn.

A network that emerges.   At the ocean
Two musics tighten, floating gongs, bells inward
From the network to the eyes of a man
Whose pulse burns in his blue eyes when he sees the bridge.

A red bridge fastening this city to the forest,
Telling relationship in a stroke of steel;
Cloud-hung among the mist it speaks the real,

354

In the morning of need asserts the purest
Of our connections : for the opposites
To call direct, to be the word that goes,
Glowing from fires of thought to thought's dense snows,
Growing among the treason and the threats.

Between the summer strung and the young city,
Linking the stonefall to the treefall slope,
Beyond the old namings of body and mind
A red bridge building a new-made identity:
Communion of love opened to cross and find
Self the enemy, this moment and our hope.

Power never dominion.
Some other power.
Some force flaking in light, avalanches of lilies,
Days and the sun renewed in semen, pure
Among the uncorrupted fires, fire's ancestor,
Forgotten; worshipped secretly;
Where the vestigial Lucifer regales
Craters of memory; where leans
Some fleshly girl, the shaped stones of desire
Leaping in color at her human cunt.
They will translate this girl.   She will appear
In textbooks as a sacrificed antelope
Guilt running shiny over the short fur.
Ideas of shame did split that throat.
But none of that is true tonight.
The girl was leaning over the crater, I dreamt it,
The shriveled flowers twisted in her hair,
And jewels budded at her throat.
The girl of choice, remembering the past fires,
Praising the word, the columns in the grove,
Arbor vitae uterinae
Locked by such branches, light in the dense forest,
Praising the world unknown and feeling beat
Among her branches
A human child.
Brambles of sense! and that responding power
Rocking the fullness of time.
Until it shall be, what never was:
River and born and dream.

Canals of music downward serenade
New satin gleams under her haunches;
And, running laterally,
And backwards across ripples,
Passing the lower stairs,
Even above the unforgettable murmur,
The sound of oars.

Body of the splendid, bear me now!
Completed by orbits of unhorsèd comets,
The bronze, paternal stars.

Cave of their messengers,
Thalamic cleft where the divorcèd myth
Begged to be nursed through hysteria that leap year,
Sank at the window—O the famous view!
This side or that side of the balcony
Falling, the graceless sanatorium swan,
Breaking nobody's kneecaps but her own.

Passes the pear orchard near the middle hill
At the wind's moment when all sails are lowered,
A small bird kiares, slope of his flight, the blue
Yielding flutes of his feathers, that small wing
Bounds us above—kiar! Inscribing our horizon.
A high note over our necessity.

———————

A filament carrying morning through the waves,
A nerve singing branches.
Orbits of pear blossom
Recurring while the wars declared themselves;
On the red rails, the train hurling his words
Down all the arteries of tears.

Endure, grandmother of all music,
Crystal in Asia, indelible pinnacles
Color of going to sleep
Above the breastës gold.
Endure, sing : deep night in Abyssinia
Waits for a messenger, heat
Of that ancient waiting
Rising from tongues of lions.
The jagged time, the jagged time of clues,

All broken inheritances riding home
Past columns and ruins, down the edge-lit clouds
Reaching back to the well at home, a twilight girl
Wherefrom new breasts, new sources, feed the dawn.
Singing develop
The sapphire climbing song
Flaring, a woman's eternal jugular cry.
An Ethiopian Jew praising the world,
The flying psalm inviting creation come.

Osiris in his veins praising the world away.

Wine that is poetry—inclare! inclare!
The conqueror of all attractive dragons
Is in that vice and white and steam.

He waited.   He saw the water.
But the recurrent branch
Flew backward on the track in early day,
Warning him against compliance, breaking
In blossom said, Willkie!
You must defy them or be lost!
The foam spinning on water straight beneath
Will tell another myth, and spin and drown.
Far down under the trestle invisible.
His sense of the real leaves him.   Dizzy and blind.
Will go to Washington.

THE YOUNG MEN

The surface shine, the inner steel of track
Carry September ringing to a boy
Miles down and decades past, a maroon sweater
Haunting a plexus of rails.
A spur leading nowhere.
And silos, like ill-launched rockets, hurling tall
Such faulty upright weight five miles downtrack
As feeds the colored cattle, as feeds the governor,
As feeds the party wheelhorse as feeds me.

Ascending ties, a hymn of ladders.   Colder.
I urge my wretched urgings clamber out,
Holding the frozen ironwork.
Coldbitten indecent lavender and white,

357

The naked noses and naked stares recede.
I hear the patching words that ring like coin
Behind the platform, my penny monument.

At a certain moment the railway forfeits metal,
Speed seizes this track, we are going fast.

The calendar's contagions, days, declarations,
Flaunted away on a Hollywood montage.
There must be a darkened third-run movie house
Behind that ice-clad coalyard where they show
Quiet.   A willow.   Some hammock-pampered girl
In a Middle Western college; pipedreams of reassurance
And a low speaking voice.

Waterfalls
Narrow, behind me.

All the American rivers
Controlled into metal systems,
Narrow as rails.

Firing down endless, successful rapids,
The tiny inconspicuous steely rapids
This train, my dragon, a Cherokee canoe
Clipping back birchbark over carbon paper
Pouring the smoke of my statement,
Tobacco that is the barn-hung skins of prophets
Pouring smoke out, that hardens into scars.

Effigy and belief!   The track flattening south,
Splits from before backward, far into silver,
Opening into the small lost villages.
Sidings of young men propped against sycamores,
With eighteen miles between any two of them.
Their hopes are hanging three feet above their eyes;
Their girls away at a dance; all their big powers
Lifted up, and alone.
Lost villages, my frontier; our crest and crown;
My brothers who will never vote for me.
My lost self who will never vote for me.

———————————

Until I stand on the January platform
(Bunting and boards), Connecticut Avenue

That lowcut archway into the histories.
Speaking the inaugurals of these same young men,
Declaring a specific amnesty.
Then, eighteen miles apart, the muscular young
Arrogant fools, the founders of our future
With their ideas of freedom as relation
To human process, will push their shoulderblades
Against their treetrunks
And rear, like a tidal wave upon Peru.

Some fool with space on his left hand and his right
Will stare down-track.
The free, watery, liquid rails
Will seal our fire across the seamless land,
Fusing, fusing.   Fusing
A new age.
The streaming hours of man,
The plant spread to the green sun.

That's what it'll take; not anything like these
Seven long years of Washington afternoons,
Shaking official syllables out of my creases:
Pork-barrel and candy-stick.

———————————

Then I forget.
The star in the nets of heaven
Blazed past my breastbone.
Did I forget that fire?
I forgot.
In my net of growth, my words are unreal to me.

A Coast of Images

"KNOWLEDGE MY NAKEDNESS"

Knowledge my nakedness,
Where is the accurate, the innocent skillful man,
The accurate shining, behind whose forehead lie what young
    dreams?
I am the present, and I know your face.
Mercy must enter grace,
Wisdom this wilderness.
These are thick forest fears whose hidden rivers
Are the past under leaves feeding each taproot of our lives.
The present touches again, again, again, continual music.
The touching by majestic images of common day.
Have you looked at the Bible since you changed your mind?
Certain Mozart applies, recurrences of Beethoven;
All are true.
And now only the new is accurate.

—————————

Leaving New York, I looked back fourteen times:
Once when the bridge was cloven, and the driver
Chose smoothly.   I saw the city emerge; but you
Sleep somewhere, who in my waking never sleep.

The highway leaps.   I look back many times.
Now again, I know the splitting everywhere:
Clouds, roads, words given me from you, this river
Dividing us, locking you back to the dreams of islands,
Locking me now to voyage and to air.

LAT. 10° NORTH, LONG. 45° WEST

Roundabout hours of air, slanting past Massachusetts above the
    slate of rain,
Plane over the hard ocean, construction of rock whose law
Offers its gray erect.   The strength of this bare floor
Appears as ledges where pale moss lies, and the dry ocher
    green
Of moss in these crevices seems to move a little; lichen the
    color of unripe apples

Or the shadow of walking figures, ice-color hands shivering
Above rock-blue and rock-green.   Figures of clouds.
But these quartz fragments and plains we know are sea.
However classic the crystal lattices,
Speed makes them; this storm is over the mind and the
     Atlantic.
Work on the chart; and land where you can land.

Ice from the wings, a rattle against metal. All right, come
     down.
At the Azores, the sea is a flight of stairs,
A flight of leaves as spearsmen over flat courtyards
Whirling, the blown archaic curtains of the world.
Red roads of Horta where nothing has subsided.
Not surf, not history, dissipations of foam,
The whips and winds.
And America asking personal questions.
—All right.   If we're to be held up twenty-four hours.
He will in that case set out to see the island.

He would do as he had done in other states:
Interview the natives.
A party of tourists, leaning on the wind.

Radio silence of aircraft over the dense ocean,
The American silence within our flood of sound.
You know that our speed over the clouds of ocean
Cannot approach the cry of a burning city.
You know that this cry arriving is only our own speed
Screaming its own pleasures and names, in flying.
Among this high air only the rage of speed
Can reach us.   How can one child saying Mother?

How can these bone-cold naked men, standing all day
And then forced to sing and then to dig their graves?
I hear the grating of shovels.   Or is the wind of day?
Or songs from all Europe and Asia in the smoke of Poland?

Here the propeller drifts into a rising high tight
Strong infant's cry in China, under gongs.   Noises of flapping.

And the squeaks and grincing of barbed wire knotted tight.
Slower than steps, the tentative walk on the ghetto pavement.

No bones could go so slow as these slow swollen children.
They cover their eyes. Their mouths. You cannot hear their
    cries.
This is the missile waste, all agony, famine, a child deciding
That life is like this agony that has surrendered its cries.
Sound carrying through sound.
                    Alive, awake, or with all their veins broken,
Waves of their cry to us : Make, for we may not make.

Whatever roams the air is traveling
Over these griefs, these wars and this good.
Whatever cries and flowers, lives and can farther find
Than the threshold of sense; I know the piercing name;
Among all the silence, in pain, the birth-cry came.
Salt of these tears whitens my eyelashes.

Whatever ploughs the land turns into food:
Before my face, flowers, color which is form.
Bravery ploughs the season, turns to birth
Upon the sex-sown people-flowering earth.
A year turns in its crisis.   In its sleep.
Whatever ploughs our dreams is ours to keep.

Whatever ploughs our dreams is ours to give:
The threshold rises and changes.
I give, I perceive;
Here are the gifts of day risen at last;
Blood of desire, the riding of belief
Beyond our fury and our silences.

THE JETTY. DOVER

Whipping the face.   Europe, with all her winds.
Shore-wind of despair and beginnings.   The big guns.
Whose word is the shape of storm.   Who offer choice
Only of death or growth.

Either a man is a visitor in hell
Or his shoulders become a coast of images:
Fireflood twisting the girders and nave of things

To leave the scars and the spire.
Receding, sees the traveler and the hill
Facing each other in a world of meaning.
Everything else carried its own destruction,
And now again is beginning to be born.

The docks and the steel towns and the shadow plants
Reflect our forms of hope; a man's a visitor
Between the whistling crests of storm.
                                        Storm breaks,
And he in conflict remembers Eden, not dream,
Not womb, not garden, but city of God
City being the form of our wishes for each other,
That burn in cities throughout the human night
Tonight, only a few miles apart.
The chain of lifetimes burning locks his life
To the arm of the jetty stretched into the sea.
To the credence of definite objects, doorsills, nails driven in,
The zone of silence, meaning explosion,
Or Liverpool and Auntie Lizzie McHeice,
A bottle of beer and a notable buttonhole.

The bricks and the spillways of fire,
The pilgrim of surfaces knows these appetites
Deep in the split race of his roots of dream.
He lies down here to bury his old self.
It will restore his earth as fire never can,
Nor blood.   There is no other sacrifice
Beyond commitment, where the terms are born,
Where giving is taking, where all feeds on all
In the human process.   When he wakes
He will venture out into the same besieged
City but smell a difference in the singe
And the air's change.   He will be horrified
To hear himself use the phrases of the other country.
He will look for the fine relations even in his own words.
He will recall, even in death, even in dream, even in his
    sharpest-focused joy
The full birth in its wild simplicities.
He was standing on the jetty at Hell's Corner,
Rings of desire for Europe, no, America, no, the limitless spirit
    of the born and unborn
Fall over his head.
And at his back there is nothing but the future.

A GAME OF DARTS AT
THE CHESTERFIELD ARMS

But they are accurate.   That is a target.
He throws the first.   It looks erect
Far from the eye, over the whitebreast girl
Past thirty years of tulip trees.

The second makes a ray
Across stupidity.   Across his own;
Into the edict.   Life goes here and there
Into the land within the land, the deeper secret.

The throwing of secrets, edged and weighted bright.
Directness to the mind; the woman stumbling home
Where there is no home will fall again.   However.
The idiot running under Orion.   However.

The flight of birds escapes from your planting.
Sharp arrows overtake you and go through you
And surpass you and race with your name into daybreak,
And all this is your riddle and your game.

———————

As he stood near the plane, they heard him say:
"I am of purely German descent."
The morning blew his words away.
"My grandparents left Germany in protest."
Prepotent grandfather, your seaports and your sea
"And I, too, claim that right."
I now newborn. Protest prepareth me.
"Tell the German people . . .
"I speak for my countrymen of German ancestry.
"They, too, believe in human rights and Freedom."

———————

Where will you be tonight? Past Lisbon, flying.
And your message, tonight? Scattered on Germany.

A Proving Flight

"WIND ARROW, WIND ROSE"

Wind arrow, wind rose, the wind currents in air,
A spiral staircase down the height of sky.
Chart of the urgencies of sail.
Shrouds tight, salted and glittering,
And the glittering lips of fifty-six sailors
All asleep four hundred years of water
Among the cycles of drift.   Forgetfulness.

To follow the hard sunlight on the northern harbor
Into the glint, choppy waves off the breakwater
Where a wife and son and a few frozen newsmen
Wait after headwinds.

Between the little flags, the son of the public man
Runs to the float, while in the middle distance
The wife of the public man and the photographers
Wait at the windows.

Others wait.   Words wait.   The memory in craters
Among the unanswered fires, fire's ancestor,
Power without dominion, to which I testify
In word waking and dreaming.

Power flaking in light down avalanches
Of all their words and faces, days after sleeplessness
Where one man, fed on sleep and food, loved by women
May voyage and wait far past defeat.

Say it depends on the interpretation.
Want the romantic?   Talk to the passenger.
The classic, profit-taking logic?   The President is with us.
However, if you demand another arrangement
Responsible, uncorrupt—really?   The truth?
Here is the clean-eyed pilot.

   The pilot, speaking: It was a marvelous flight. *Fantastic!* Not
a single coincidence!

Open System

"WHEN HE BEGAN TO WITNESS"

When he began to witness, it was not to a journey,
Nor the questions, nor the answers, nor fiery London.   Whole
For the first time in imagination, man in conflict
May tell, as he enters, that there is an entrance.
Fire never yet felled this man's pillar;
His bed is at home, where he knows it is.
Love weaves him in, love guards the locks, and love
Sends his eyes a bravery of language.
But the eyes of the man are the eyes of witness
He will never acknowledge the old polarities.
Question and answer carry the oppositions,
And success.   And defeat.
                                    Now no one can declare
With any finality, The Day After The War.
He suddenly says, the open ways are sure,
The certain relationships are Offer and Give.
Even to see that fire
Allows me to witness.   Now I begin to name
The name of beginning and making, the first word.

———————————

Rang and rang, rang in a small boy's head.
Going through the same course: the meanings and knowings.

ANOTHER DAY. IN A FIELD OF PEACE
THE CHILD, PLAYING. THE CHILD
PREPARING FOR DAYTIME SLEEP

PAUL: Miss Lorence, until I get to be somebody else—big me—
    I'm Timmy Torin.
    My horse at home is not really a real horse.
    I told you that a time ago.   It is not true.
    I love to tell you things.   Some are real,
    Some are not, just fooling.
    You don't mind?   I wouldn't, except that I'm older than you
        and bigger than you and I can do it.   Big people do.

You know, I certainly do like Ropsie in that little, little skirt
   with her fat legs out.
I'll take care of you, Miss Lorence.
Just tell you things sometimes,
Fooling.

––––––––––––––––

The child wakes in the morning to enter a country
Where the rivers are striped with fire and the tigers
Say their word before they eat you, and the leaves cry out
And the stars are the parts of song.   They are music
And they stand clear in the blue and risen sky.
The tigers eat them and the child eats them.
Do birds eat stars?
They do.   And morning.   And all doorkeepers.

ANOTHER DAY. A GAME OF TOYS.
PAUL, TELLING THE GAME:

One Shall Be the Mother and One Shall Be the Father

The father shall shine. The father shall stand at home. Now
   he shall go to work. Now war. Now the father has to
   wait. Now the horse shall give him a ride. A hahaaaa.

One Shall Be Mad

Now let one be mad.   Which one shall be mad, the father or
   the mother, the mother or the father?
No, the father.
What does he do when he is mad?   What shall he do?
The father is mad and what shall he do?
The father has to hit the mommy.
Then what does the mommy do?
The mommy pushes him off the table.
They have to go up again.   Both of them.
Down they are.   They have to walk.
They have to get up again.
Make believe.

One Shall Be the Baby

The baby is in the mountains, in the tall mountains.
You know the mountains?   I went into my book.

You know my book of mountains.   Ice, snow, far to fall.
I was the person who knows the way.
You must not stay in the mountains all night long.
There is a rope, and a man behind.
The mountains are bad.
They can make you dead in lots of ways.
They are prettier than a little hill, though,
Or a rose.
Very big, very pretty, and you can't understand them.
But the man and I went on and he fell.
He fell and fell because he was tired.
He fell in the holes in the snow, and he fell on the rocks, and he
    would be dead all ways but I held him on the rope and pulled
    him back.   Safe.
I will tell you more, later on.

One Shall Be Paul and One Shall Be Hitler

In the closet is a man, a bad man.
Hitler shoots.   He shoots me if I go there.
Would I shoot?   I don't know how to shoot.
He shoots the whole house down.
Paul comes out now into the flat world.
It rains.   It rains.
Hitler never lies down.   He shoots.
But Paul lies down.   And now Paul is asleep.
What is he dreaming?
He's dreaming that now Hitler isn't Hitler.   No more.
Hitler pushes up his feet like this.
He is the father.   Is he?
He pushes up his feet like the father.

What Shall All Four of Them Be?

Yes, now they are going to sleep.
It's night.   It's night.

A Dream of Night

He's dreaming.   He's dreaming about the day his father says,
    It's morning
And he has a little baby when he woke up.

Here the Game Ends

ANOTHER DAY. THE CHILDREN
ARE ALL EATING

—This dinner is too rich for you, Paul.
—Do not say that is so. Anything like that. We are good and rich.
—Baloney.
—Baloney is not a word, it is a thing. It is a meat.
Words still do tell about things.
The word says what is the thing.
It must be, or how would you know?
Baloney *is* a word, Tom.
—What?
—Oh! . . . You are too little for me.

When I drink milk I put my nose in it, way, and blow, foo, and it makes sprickles, fat.

—Oh, he *is* sweet. I do love him sometimes.
. . . Why must one love one's children?
Why does one love one's children?
Out of a sense of guilt at having given birth to them, I suppose.
We used to say constantly—all my friends in England and I—
Oh, how I hate my children.
Here you people never allow yourselves to say that.
Is it so bad to say? I do not see how people can help hating their children sometimes. It is natural.

(She has such a quaint European way of putting things at times, doesn't she? That remark about hating your children! Of course she's had a hard time but it's too bad she's so bitter.)

PAUL: The father dreams that he was hid in a tree
   And she dreams she is washing the dishes.
   She *is* washing the dishes
   And she dreams that she's playing.   See?
   A dream of houses.
MISS LORENCE: What was the dream that time?
PAUL: I don't know.
MISS LORENCE: About the little baby?
PAUL: That's a long dream.

How can you explain to children? It's not so hard to explain to them that there is a war, but how can you tell them that their father is in prison?

———————

Now he plays with the other children.
The words recede.   He works through bitter things.
But the war did not stop when bitterness stopped.
His father came not.   And the guns went on.

———————

Do you know what I play to be, in bed at night?
I play to be a little baby.   Do you know why?
People take care of little babies.
Of course they don't have as much fun as grownup people cause
    they are so little and can't walk or have knives or eat cake or
    anything, but they do get taken care of.
I used to want to grow up to be big.
That's what I used to play at night in bed.
But I'm going to grow up anyway.
So I don't think about that any more if it's going to be anyway.
I think about if I was a little baby.
I wouldn't have to do things I don't like to do,
Shot by a gun I would be dead
But I wouldn't know why about it,
Because babies are so little little that they don't *know* about
    things.
They are just small and eat and sleep and never have to worry.
So I play I am a baby and do not have to do things for myself
    or worry.

———————

¶Youth shapes its own destiny.
                                                    —*Motto of the Hitler Youth*

———————

Among our new-found powers.

I pulled him back.
Do you know, Miss Lorence, why we were there, in those cold
  dark mountains?   We were running away from a man, from
  Hitler.
He was going to hurt me and to hurt the man worse.
Hitler is a bad thing.   He is the worst thing in the world.
. . . I helped the man.   I did not let him fall.
I helped him with the rope.
Do you know who I was helping?
I was helping Fritzel, my father, to get away from that bad land
  to come here where Mommy and Ropsie and I are, where it
  is safe.
It is safe for a while.
It is more safe than it is in that bad land.
If you say anything or do anything that those people do not like
  they may kill you or hunt you and you do not even know
  why.
They kill you too if you are a Jew, even if you do not do *any*thing.
That is why I was taking my father away from that land.

. . . This is not true, Miss Lorence.
I just pretend.
I would like to do that.
But I was not really in the tall mountains,
I did not really bring my father here.
When I get bigger I must do this.
But I am too little now.
I used to think I could do anything, like this,
Anything I wanted to, but now I am older
And I know:
I am not old enough to do anything.
Children must wait to grow up.
But I wish that I could help my Fritzel
And there are other people who need to be helped.
It takes so long to grow.

—My toes feel like nothing they are so cold. Little sticks of
wood. They'll break off if I knock. What does a stick of wood
feel like, Miss Lorence?

—Well, a live stick, pretty good I guess. Happy. Full of sap.
—What is sap?
—Sap in a tree is like blood in you.
—You know a thing? About the blood in me . . .
Inside me it is all wet and blood and moving,
But outside so dry and careful.
All the time people are asleep or awake
Their inside is there doing things. Did you know that?
Your insides never stops.
The blood is always there and all inside it is moving
And it is blood and it is never stopping.
So funny, all wet inside and all dry outside.
Everybody like that. I am.
Why, Miss Lorence, you are.
I wonder what you look like inside. Did you ever think about it?
   —People look pretty much alike inside. I could show you a
picture, a drawing . . .
   —A picture that would be for you would be for me too?
   —Yes.
   —Then we are alike, you and me are alike?
   —Yes, but so are most people alike.
   —But their outsides is different. You and me don't *look* alike.
   —No, but inside of you is like inside of me, only you are a
little smaller.
   —But I am a boy and you are a girl.
   —Yes, some things are different in boys and girls, but lots of
things are just alike.
   —*Well.* But why don't people look alike outside?
   —Some people look like their mothers, Paul. I do. Or a mother
and father mixed, nose like one, eyes like the other. Or a father.
   —It is very hard for me to think that you have a father and
a mother. Where are they? Are they around here?
   —No, they are both dead.
   —Oh, in the war?
   —No, they just died.
   —Well, you don't need any now. You're all big enough to take
care of yourself. I'll take care of you, Miss Lorence.—But don't
you think it's funny about people's blood being inside their skin?
And your insides.
   —Yes.
   —Are you sure your mother and father were not in the war?
   —No. They really weren't.
   —Did no blood come out?

—No, They just died quietly.

—In the war there is a lot lot of blood, and people hurt and hurt and die . . . It is too bad that there are children dead who can never never get old.

—It would be too bad not to grow up.

—Yes, lots of fun being grownup. You have to do some things you don't like, though, and nobody takes care of you.

—Would you like somebody to take care of you?

—I can do it pretty well. You come live with me. You can sleep in my bed. My mommy will take care of you. Or maybe I could come live with you . . .

But it doesn't matter where you live or what you do, you still have your insides.

He turned cruel. Absorbed in his own cruelty, he drove the children, drove them by will, goading their wills, manipulating everything they began to do. He turned into a dark leader, small and ferocious.

And they were fascinated. They followed. He drove them as if with whips into a dance; and they ran, dancing and hypnotized.

He was full of hatred. He was in torment, hating and defying his grownups, goading his generation to frenzy.

For a while, for a short while, it was full cruelty. Assailed he was, with danger over his life-space. Fretful he was, restless and stern, the artificial boasting king. Loud and unreal to himself, with all his conflict packed for him to carry, and the admiring, the pity of the adults, out of reach.

But at the moment at which the grownups would have stopped it, at the moment when the five-year-olds would have turned on Paul, it was as if he remembered. He was on his journey, he was moving toward his world. The long exchange with Miss Lorence—her cheek bent over him as he lay himself down, her short soft questions, the open feeling of her answers, came back to him like Eden. It had always been there. And his own people, the five-year-olds! He remembered the other life: communication.

He turned back to his own group with his whole life in his act of choice.

ANOTHER DAY.
FOR A MOMENT SLIPPING BACK,
AGAIN THE UNREAL KING

Let's throw it. Let's throw ice at her face . . .
You should throw back!
You should *hurt* me, Miss Lorence, not just stand there and laugh.
Why do you let me hurt you?
You hurt *too*.

She throws the snowball.

He howls, the howling biting; the biting sobbing, the sobbing thrown down in a snowdrift.

MISS LORENCE: Shall I go?

PAUL: I hate you. I hate you.
No, no, you mustn't go.
I need you. Stay here. Why did you hurt me?

MISS LORENCE: But I didn't really. . . . You know . . . And besides
. . . why did you cry?

PAUL: You wanted to hurt me. You threw snow at me.
You were not my friend.

MISS LORENCE: But you asked me to throw snow. You cried when I didn't.

PAUL: I didn't really want you to.

MISS LORENCE: Then why did you ask me to?

PAUL: I wanted to hurt you
So you should hurt me;
But I didn't really want you to.

MISS LORENCE: I'm sorry I hurt you. I didn't want to.
I was just playing your game with you.

PAUL: It was not a game.

MISS LORENCE: You really wanted to hurt me?

PAUL: Yes. But not really.
Often I hate you, but I love you too.
I want to hurt you, but I don't want you to be hurt.
(He takes her hand and clings, for the first time in weeks.
Sighs and gets up.)

PAUL: Well, I guess I could go upstairs now.

He was soft and quiet all that day. School went on. He painted his pictures and modeled in clay. He was very still, but not dependent.

The sky is a tree.   It spreads . . .
I fly on the shiny hills to a bear's house . . .
My clock is magic.
I dreamed about the zero
And about Elizabeth
And about Miss Davison.
I dreamed about the mat . . . the doorbell, the whole, whole,
    whole, whole, whole, Miss Lorence . . . the world, the world.

ANOTHER DAY

Day lilies, yellow daisies, Queen Anne's lace. A barrel, a box of
sand, a bucket of water. There is a child. He looks up into the
young woman's eyes, and away down the path.

Toward him is walking a broad tall man, broader than the
bear, smiling and blue-eyed. Willkie is walking between two girls
in their clear summer colors, on his way up the college hill. He
sees the little knotted boy, and the young woman, dark, in her
dress of the most deep rose, color of inner petals.

He smiles at the girl and the child. They look up at him, their
faces lit from everywhere.

The child goes on playing in the sandbox.

The man stops. Did you want to speak to me? he says, abruptly.

Yes, says the girl. Did you believe what you said in your
speech?

That's right, he says.

Maybe there should be other words for these things, says the
girl, half smiling.

The students watch his face. I'll tell you, he says heavily, I
never have held with those who blame our troubles on words.

But you used to say things that were—slightly different. Didn't
you?

I guess I am—slightly different, by now, he says. But I still like
people to disagree with me.

What a pity, she answers, and her smile opens to him. This
time, I've been agreeing.

I'd like to talk to you more about this, he says. Later?

Perhaps later.

Fine boy, says Willkie. Although, for him, the child is too thin
and pointed, his haircut outlandish, his look not really direct.
Your brother?

He's my friend Paul, says the girl, touching the child's arm. A
gleam passes over the shallow-featured face.

Where do you come from? the child asks Willkie. He speaks
very quickly, with a curious, aggressive charm, like a trace of
accent.

Indiana. And just now England.

Indiana? What country is that?

America. The U.S.A. Right in the middle of it. He recognizes
suddenly: the child's a refugee, of course. But all my people came
from Germany.

Mine too; yes, Miss Lorence? says the child. And through
England, too. Yours . . . why did they come here? he asks the
man.

Partly to come away from there; mostly to live here.

Oh, says the boy. He is finished talking. He looks down at the
sand, and picks up the bucket of water. In a curve of motion, he
pours out the water, brilliant under sunlight, upon the yellow
sand. Willkie looks down. The water is traveling over; the sight
hits him with a shock like pain; as if his heart were turning against
him and attacking.

The sand, with the streams running through it, is striking his
sight with the shape of a tree of rivers. Gullies, branches, the
widened valleys down. Glinting on water. The shadows beside
the grains, in his clear sudden sight. Ground coming up, and his
sight, swinging through the precise air, until he looks down again
at the sand. He sees it as a field under his fall when he fell with
a parachute, a long time ago; he sees it as a bowl of food, a small
boy staring down at the creases of a landscape, hills, juices, and
islands where a small strange child is playing. Waiting before
him, strong and running bright. As a bowl of food; as the earth
seen far-off; as sand in a box; brown branches traced wet in a
strong symbol, where a child plays, pouring out his summer.

STATEMENT BY WILLKIE AFTER
RETURNING FROM ENGLAND

It is not only the present that is at stake.
Somewhere in this confusing world we must find—we must
  build—a future for ourselves.
We must now have courage, bravely to do the things that we
  know ought to be done.
And we must lay the foundations for the world of the children.
That world cannot be a closed system.
It must be an open system.
It must be a world in which we share the responsibilities. They
  are many, but they lead to the great prospect—of peace.

Leaf

"DURING THE JOURNEY THERE COME MOMENTS OF WAKING"

During the journey there come moments of waking
When you will find, growing among your dream,
A sense of light.   The setting constellation
Has gone far under while you fade in, fade out,
On the threshold of the recognizable.

Again, far off your road!   But showers of fire
Burst in your body; now you can remember as
If for the first time the other waking that
Spoke one word to you.   Daybreak.   The
Actual day.

———————————

Child of the root, among your apples and forests,
I see a bird whose gaze and claws are fire
Fasten upon you.   In your shape of becoming,
You and your bird change to a stream of water
Through whom light pours, to the present breaking its banks.
A pride of making, that can destroy its objects.
Looking ahead, to a distant point,
Creation unbegun.

———————————

Not leaves, not lightning, not that greatness of rivers.
The hand and spirit volunteer.
We think to build again, finer nor before.

The water-spiral turns the fire
Broken upon the miles of air,
Leaps through our furnaces of change
To make and make.

The great sun pours his power down.

———————————

¶*Water power is really a form of sun power.*

———————————

A sound of screaming for thirteen centuries.
Look at the clock.   It has never moved.
A sound of weeping for the generations.
Open your eyes.   Monday morning.
In all the cities they are telling fortunes
According to patterns flown by the bombing planes,
And the shape of the Leader's genitals.

Bird-voice in darkness.   Tremor of day moving.
The rocks accept brightness, now we imagine trees,
Across the crystals of time forming, suddenly
Feel the flaw of cold breeze following bird-voices.
The river remade, the invitation of water
Flowing down toward the heart of my beloved.

A small man walks, thin cane, clown's feet of grace,
Imagining in cold air down Charlie Street.

The water-hammer, the history of ice,
The rising water and the entrapped air.
Drift-pinned, drift-bolted, the rage beats at the gates.
The crest gates and the wheeled gates' seals give way.
When the forces pass the limits of the dam,
There is pure overturning.   In height, in fetch,
The waves increase, the floors of galleries
Give way.   The roots of the forest trees open a path,
Open, in bedrock, seams.   Scarring and scouring, now
Flood-flow and future floods begin to shine.

¶*For of the soul the body form doth take;*
   The soul is form and doth the body make.

Here the journey is begun again.

Everything here is real and of our joy.
The rivers are real, they come bringing their colors,
The lives flow through us too in meaning, in form
Which is meaning and motion.   Nothing here is unreal.
The beginning is giving; and the land is wide.

378

Daring of voices and faces, the moment being in flow,
Our selves being now, we and our word alive.

Throw away the code : there is no success or failure,
You will move through success and you will never fail,
For if you take the steps and take the songs
You will be changed in the taking
As if changed by song.
It will sing in your waking,
And in your rest
Breathe with your breathing—
Making, will break and make.
The masks of the beginning and the end
At last have begun to move.   They move away.
The songs of your lifetime sing and say and relate:
You are the beginning, as you are the end.
The song is song, it sings, and it is real.

Journey

"DEEP IN THE CENTURY OF OPPOSITES"

Deep in the century of opposites,
The myth of mission is the tourist's dream.
He will fly over the zebra-colored cliffs,
Carrying letters, he lands within a war.

He is the big enigma and mask of power.
The fluid desert war and the sea—hieroglyphs
Holding him while he swims with General Fever
Are the response and law of Africa.

This is the threshold : Spain and Carthage lie
Over the ocean, but he goes otherwhere.
In meteor noon, each flaming with its star
The shifting and the warring pyramids.

Egypt is saved, the general said again.
He cannot dream the double fantasy

All that the battle has sent us from its fire:
The film whose heroes are war and the enemy
The poem in the soldier's Highland tongue:
*Worse than all Rommel's guns, that my young darling should prove false
and a liar.*

WILLKIE: WORDS FROM RUSSIA

When I flew into Russia I said to my friend
Now I suppose I go into darkness.
I was wrong.

          I have been given every chance;
Every question of mine has been answered.
I have seen in my own way. I have talked with the leaders
And with men and women on the assembly lines, on the farms,
    and on streetcorners.
I have come and gone, and asked questions, as I would at
    home.
No man can understand this people without years of study
But there are facts we must know.
Here I have realized meanings: A *people's war,*
The Russian people, The resolve to destroy fascism.
The Russian people, in the fullest sense.
Long and bitter winter ahead, every third person slaves at
    home,
The farmland gone, the coal-land gone, the clothing nearly
    gone.
No medicines. Five million people killed. Hurt. Gone.
The millions of women and the nine-year-olds
Running the farms and machines.
The Russian people chose victory or death.
They talk of the victory.

As I learn at first hand, I ask myself, What is the most effective
    way we can help win the war by helping these heroic allies?
—A real second front, at the earliest the military leaders . . .
And some may need public prodding.
Next summer may be too late.

It is easy to sit in America in comfort.
They die by the thousands to hold Stalingrad.
If the Russian front is ours and Britain's, as it surely is,
Whoever dies tonight at Stalingrad
Dies for us, at our door.

The soldier is not impressed by the expert's term, "risk,"
We can make, and make a bridge to Stalingrad,
We can help Russia with winter food,
The hungry lions cannot fight.

We can, in this time, do two disparate things:
We can ease the pain and we can raid the cities.
Stop the suffering; a thousand plane raids.

What do you know of America? I asked a little Russian schoolgirl.
—Money, fat men, skyscrapers, lots of ships and airplanes.
And what do you think of America? I asked her father.
He thought a little, then said, A land where democracy
Will at last break down injustice, where many shrewd eyes
Look steadily and with hope into the future;
A land of brilliant techniques and plenty,
And of people who, like us,
Strive to a distant point.

A man in a plane looks at the surface of land.
Down, he stares down; he sees the narrow papers,
His information on China and the book about China;
He sees his legs and his feet; he sees his hands; they are still.
Far down air crumpled, old ranges, the green of the silk route.
You cannot know, you cannot share, this land, the papers say to him
Or the last country or the ones before.   And do you know your
    land?
You on your ignorant journey.   He sees : It is my journey.
He sees that he does not know.   But the voices blow through him.
He sees that he has not spoken.   But the voices are here.
The world not beneath him, however sheer he flies.   The world
Around him and through him always.   O to be home, now.
He stretches, a big man in a plane. Home, he thinks. I am not
    great enough.
I wish I were home.   Before the voices speak,
Any of the voices, he knows.   He surely knows:
The journey is my home.

Into the the air far.   Into the opposites.
Driving through sky into the otherworld,
In a real plane with four real whirls before him

Carrying him into his fantasy.
Now the dance of split and deliverance
Opens in swans before the wings.
Flowers, clouds, a game of paper kings.
And will you kill my dark lord down
Who stares the fiery lady?   Luck
Is not the mirroring, is not the word,
Not the skillful red and black.
The enemy, the enemy.
How fare the wings around the wind,
Spun blade and angle of attack?
How take the ancient mountains of the soul,
And play, the flight forward being flight back?
My drink is airy gold.   The cards I held
Are the same cards my card-hand hold,
While minutes, great miles of Asia, pass.
This jack, this statistical crowd,
Two-colored, while we're flying to the world.
Around the world, we say.   I might have known
There's no way round my life or round the world.
There is only through.

Where all his meanings lead:
Into the fantasy of the opposite.

———————————

It is the sixth year of the war in China.
The children of the first winter help with the babies.
Not even a clash in the north for some time now.
The Long March is legend; Taerchwang's a song;
Splinters of autumn drift over this year.
How can strangers be told?   A soldier stands still,
He wavers on his feet; the army has stood for three years,
Lacking the strength to advance.
The boys who went away to war five years ago
Wrote a letter or two, then died; anyway did not write.
The soldiers waver, are thin in their torn clothes.
But they hold.   The cliff-city holds.
Not the blazing, not the wild turning, not the lonely stand.
There was a silence then; but now the fire has fallen
On the exotic silent cities, in a storm on London.
Not alone, not unknown here, faces endowed with stillness.
"The general's white hair, and the soldier's tears."

———————————

Sounds of night in the country of the opposites.
Music for the first time, on incredible instruments:
The rapids of a river, a woman's kitchen stove,
A village crossroads with its forgotten language;
Clank and chuckle of gambling; one line of a song;
The strings of lost limitless time.   Music.
Voice of a cat you knew before you learned to speak.
Voices of waterfalls, steel whirls, many small flowers,
Voices of a dream of the animals of heaven
        Raised through the hungering
Of some one thin wavering unransomed boy
        In starved and golden air.
A sheer black music, rare-lit joining of waters.
Night-sound in the country of the opposites.

WILLKIE IN THE GULLIVER

When after the screens of the evening of defeat
You try the remote clean air, withdrawal, think of him.
He was like many of us.   He had lost.
He flew to the many, making a crisis of choice
Lead toward the solving of barriers; learning, flying, crossed
Level after level of process, where we come
To ourselves, to the voiceless many who never in time
Choose against life.   We find the direct voice.

Remembering limits, in the days of death,
All the faring that follows our first sight of the face
Of all things beginning again past deepest defeat.
Think now all of us of our loved and great,
Traveling new to make human the bonds of breath
After defeat; for all men; by God's grace.

Down the straits flying, looks at the surfaces.
Down, staring down, he sees the narrow places,
The opposites and the space between opposites.
He sees his legs and his feet; his big hands moving.
A narrow place like the road like the endless channel
Yellowing his shoulders with mortality;
Narrow as the knife of his life and death, a blade of rail along
    which he ran, and they shot at him.
Narrow, a running spark between opposites.

He stretches, a big man in a plane.   He thinks of a woman
Who is a sea of meanings, whose flower of rivers
He knows as a speaking of dreams.   He wants his speaking
Out into darkness like a speaking to one woman.
Forever; whether it be narrow; whether it be his death
—A clenching of the heart, in an instant hidden—
Or whether his life, a spark between opposites.
Striking a firefall in which there flare no fears
Doubled, no poles, for between runs fire.
The journey is his; how can his voice be him?
My voice, my life, he knows; my life, my home.

Dam of Silence

"DREAMING WE WERE AWAKE, WE HEARD THE RIVERS"

Dreaming we were awake, we heard the rivers
And seeing in sleep through the eye's meteor
A forest of light through which all rivers run
We ran, we ran upon the waves of stairs.
We juggled our entrances, losing our inner time,
And thought of the dead, who have entered the universe,
Running and running to the fading door.
The living will be giving us one song.
Congregation of sperm, in related music.
Sing down the legacy : Dominion solving hope!
O my own heart, forgive me, let me live.

Light falling on that filled will drives
The mares of energy, breakneck and black,
Into our days, into our days.
A man's life and the buried life,
Leading and losing.   A leap upon the dark.
They cannot find him now who gave him gifts:
His throat is vulnerable.   His endless body

Now is his strength, it is his penetration:
His appetites, his hope, are his wide images,
They are the world that enters and they are his own self.
Women like images, friends like ideas of man,
Arrive in meanings that are hated and found.
Find him.   He is somehow yourself.   His eyes your eyes.
The myth of your journey, your living traveler,
In the middle of life breathing the sequences
Of revelation; your story and your song.

The Double Death

"TO KEEP THE WEAKNESS SECRET"

To keep the weakness secret. To deny it and break through.
In the dream of chieftains, the corn distinct again in gold-white
tuft-feathers. The roads all paved, stony, savage; the knocking in
the chest resumed.
　　Your father has a passion for freedom
　　Rang and rang in the small boy's head.
I will go to the doorstep of a woman will keep me secret. He
stands, in Rushville, on the threshold of Mary Sleeth's house. I've
known her long, he thinks; she speaks out, she'll keep a secret;
and stares at her out of his cloud.—Take me in and keep me here.
　　—What's the matter, Wendell? Come in.
　　—Thanks. Nothing. At all.
　　—You look as though you need a doctor, Wendell.
　　—Swear to me now.

The man sits in the rocking bedroom, claws
Hooked in his heart: anger denying rage,
Pain and refusal of pain, an image of himself.
Chill, and renewed, the animal, predatory,
Grips a stone statue of a stone hero.

　　—Swear to me you will not call a doctor, Mary.

―――――――――

A woman hiding the exposed hidden man, whisper of green in
    the night, weakness like blood over the green night,
Seed blown by the wind over rock.   Cracks in the rock.
A great flight of clouds.   The cry of meteors falling.
In a rich sunny autumn, this implacable cold.
Mary, Mary, hide me!
Concealing what the man has always concealed
From his own eyes.

Now that the sunburst throws over him its sack of nails,
Torture and a jungle of kings and monkeys,
And pain prepared in darkness so the muscles lock
Flowing away in confusion.   My wounded king,
Father of pain.   He will not think of the man
Finding a newborn son, himself in the pool.
Hide me, he hears his stripped heart wanting said.
Hide me from eyes and voices.

I am the man hidden in incident,
The boy as fluid as the tulip tree,
The angel, his glowing shoulder to the stone,
About to roll away all dead things.
Wounded.   Now hide me, Mary.
I cannot be that man, boy, angel, stone.
There is a hunting animal on my soul.
I refuse the smell of his breath!
You hide me now.   I am not done for yet.

She swears. She turns down the bed and draws the blinds.

In your time, there have been those who spoke clearly
For the moment of lightning.
Were we all brave, but at different times?
Even raped open and split, even anonymous,
They spoke.   They are not forgotten.
But they are.   In late summer; forgot; caught at cross-
    purposes,
Interrupted in an hour of purity,
Their lives careening along in the fierce cities,
Through atrocious poverties and magnificence,
The unforgotten, the early gone forgot.

Late daytime, and nothing left to hide but an eye endowed
With the charred, guilty, gouged by war, the raging splendor;
Despised like you, criminal in intent; sunburnt, in love and
    splendid;
This heart, naked and knocking, going in clouds,
Smoke and a cry of light.
In pain, the voice of pain.   The shadow of your cry.
And never forget : you are magnificent beyond all colors.

Wheels and galleries of the control of tears,
The cries of parting, and the claws of ferocious
Pain with its filth coating the sharpened claw-tips,
Rot of the will in concealment from itself. Distance,
Fear; smell of the city of pain.
                                    His wife.

MARY SLEETH

So going slowly now
A man from his green,
In a hid groaning light;
So ill concealed
The grinding of his pain
Amazes my square house
With its dark rays.

Lights my days now
With betraying,
A man against himself,
His life broken open,
All his refusals
Reflected back again
On his blue eyes.

He always ready
To break down doors
Stood in my doorway
Begging my hiding—
Nothing will keep him now
From his soul and the world,
Least not his own self,
Its hiding and its cries.

When the true things meet us at the place we reach, they are all
    real, all dreams,
Hidden by incident, often, they stand clear, here they are;
The mottled frayed fish in the pool leaps, the magnificence,
Epiphany among the sparks and rags of God.
Before the opening of the world, in our own time,
When the air we feed on gives us magnificence in conflict,
A naked man in this stream may leap, may pour his energy
Into all lives, pouring himself out on the forming light
Where power-crossed creatures soar, trees up and over us,
Our joy, our meaning, our love, even in dream.

              To go   to make   to flow
              To rise   to break   to grow
              To shine and to stand;
              To join and to separate
              To give and to take
              To destroy and to defend
              All beginning in end beginning
              Spirit through world acting
              World without end.

The brilliant, the full-bodied, the real of the world in their powers,
The faces of these people always with their lights, one face, one
    face.
The process being the hero and the song.   And the light in a
    face.   One darklit voice.
One deaf musician with his two hundred amens, his endless
    climbing of life, saying "peace" to the trumpets.
The singing of all the voices, your chance and your choice,
Making your acts
And your imaginings.
Related to finding, whether or not we are found.

HE HAD A QUALITY OF GROWTH

No one ever walking this our only earth, various, very clouded,
    in our forests, in all the valleys of our early dreams,
No one has ever for long seen any thing in full, not live
As any one river or man has run his changes, child
Of the swarms and sowings.   Death nor the woman, seed

Of the born, all growing, going through the grass.
However deep you have looked into the well of the cradle
Or into any dream or open eyed the grave
While the soul, many-leaved and waiting,
Began to assume another exact flower.
Smoke and smell in the wind, a single life!
However true you tell, you never have told.
And even that is not altogether true. It changes, we say, changes,
   for yes,
Indeed we all know this, any, any of us, there are secrets known
   to all.

Was it indeed shown you in a flash of journey, the flicker along
   change?
In the fine shadow between the curve of lips, shadow of days
   lengthening,
In the flicker of meaning revealed by many windows;
In the form of the eye, the form of words, of the word; meaning
   that formed
These marvelous genitals, nameless as God;
Or in the informing light behind his dream, and he was dreaming
   of you.
Did his own self escape him, now to reach us, reaving the edge
   of cloud?

Has a gift then been given, each other giving our lives?

As air is given to the mouth of all?

TIME HINDER NOT ME;
HIS ARMS REACH HERE AND THERE

I WILL NOT CARE FOR TIME. FORBIDDING ME

———————————

Peace the great meaning has not been defined.
When we say peace as a word, war
As a flare of fire leaps across our eyes.
We went to this school.   Think war;
Cancel war, we were taught.
What is left is peace.
No, peace is not left, it is no canceling;
The fierce and human peace is our deep power
Born to us of wish and responsibility.

¶I realize the consequences of that which was done on the desert, at Alamogordo.

The work in the loss of mass.
The work in the lifetimes of the fixed stars.
The work in ideas of unstability:
> divisible and transmutable as matter,
> divisible and transmutable as idea,

The inner passage of lifetimes and of forms.
Relations of stars and of the stages of life.
The half-life of the forms.
The laws of growth and form.

I have tried to show the atom as a source
A source of energy.
I have touched on another question:
Might energy become a source of atoms?
If this relationship is real,
The universe passes along a way of cycles.
A process of matter dissolving in the stars,
Turned into radiation, passing through forms
Again to matter; again, perhaps, to birth.

Lilienthal said : I heard him saying words like these.
Almost like these words:
My convictions are not so much against, as for.
I believe—and I conceive law to rest here, as does religion—
The fundamental truth, the integrity of the individual;
That all we build be designed to promote and protect and
    defend
The integrity and the dignity of the individual.
This the essential meaning of our nation,
As it is essentially the meaning of religion.

Any forms, then, which make men means rather than ends,
Which exalt any institution above the importance of men,
Which rest on an arbitrary power over men,
Are contrary to that conception and my meaning.
That I deeply oppose, and I deeply disbelieve.

Out of this central core of a belief
That all men are the children of God
That their lives come first and are sacred,
A great belief grows in civil liberties,
In their protection; a repugnance to theft
Of these liberties and a human being's good name,
By innuendo or by open lies.
Here is no ethical standard, nor in the state
Which exercises blind powers over the human heart.
Occasionally, all these things are done
In the name of democracy.
They can tear our people apart.

I believe in the capacity of our central belief
To survive its trials provided only we
Practice, in daily life, daily, our truths.
They are affirmative.   That is their hope in this world.
This I deeply believe.

In Praise of Process

"BREAKING THE NETS OF THE WORLD"

Breaking the nets of the world, in glimpses going
Among the mountains of light and the mountains of darkness.
All of his gateways were the opposites.

If you should mourn him now, you will know whom you
    mourn.
Whenever you hate him, and he must be hated,
You will know what you hate.   Whatever in him you love
You will see in yourself who are your brother.
All the legends are for him and against him.
When he saw his life false, founded on oppositions,
In the face of love, in the masks of judges;
When he knew he was strong and heard every summoning;
When he fought, when he drank, when he walked into the
    world;

When he forgot the moment of revelation.
His monsters, his valleys, his waves, his rains of paper,
All spoke to him, and all the masks of power.

Wounded he lay.   And for good reason.
His wounds our wounds.   His masks our milestones.
The guardians of recovery be our guardians,
Exultations of towers sting our healing;
—The leap that fulfills him, the laugh and the forgetting,
Are all your dreams, are all your dreams.

The nets of sleep are broken.   The four colors of daybreak
Shine clear where the wish stands, having body and knowing
These rooted forests are familiar country.
The nets of the opposites and the nets of refusal
Swing at the pliant windows of our birth.
Nets of his emerging all can see.

Fire of making streaming over the lives
Of our fathers' youth gave him, gave us our fire.
Stony constraints, the lips of a judge denying
Found weakness everywhere wishing to be Holdfast,
Repeating rejections and a mimic doom.
The rivers of all grace streamed through his years,
Even among the iron islands, chance;
And in the acting-out, the rivers are changing:
They are a net of snare or a living tree.
For in the breaking of things, continual choice
Is the glimpse of birth, given him, given all of us
Who know in ourselves his fullness and refusals.

Now light says Amen to shadows and takes all things
Into another morning where the moment
Offers necessity at last its flower,
Offers the meanings which are the clues of form.
The man who fought off human meanings finds
All avenues full, a procession of images
Confronting him with the chain of his lifetime dreams.
For all things grow, remade as rivers that time
Turns to resolve hostilities of power.

———————

He is breaking the nets in his wildness for the real.
Rivers, and wrestlings, the theater of time
Disclose his need to grow, which is the bond of man.

The holy linkings acknowledged and the search
Seen with its meanings, and the love of man
Seen with the meanings of the lives we praise.
Identified with our flesh, the living flower
Of consciousness, the soul which is the form,
Giving the human power.

Most human power of the bonds of man!
All things are taken in the net of meaning,
Assuming form.   The form is the light of day,
The net, the need, changing desire, the morning
Of man in our full value whose name is peace.
Peace is the growing form and the cry of Holy
In the city of the world, in the eyes of children.
The light on the rivers and on the poor is peace,
Light that by being requires, from all who see,
Beauty and change and life.   The life of peace,
Peace the necessity of growth, clue of our ways.

Music of growth, the world's magnificence,
Is born, the break of day, child of the world.
      Now in the net of forces
The stars of these migrations being our days
Do take their changes, another constellation.
Although today their broken-crested light
Shines on our blackened poverty of wars.
There is the seed of the gift diversity
Declaring the pride of man, allowing lightnings kneel
On the horizon of difference, shocking the blaze awake.

The central mysteries and dance of initiation,
The language and links of making, and the process
We bless that discovers self and the self of the world
In one law moving and given : the form of the love of
   growth.
By that light, by that infinite rich darkness
Many shinings of truth making aware,
A flare against corruption and forgetting,
Declare and create that the human light of meanings
Let us give us ourselves
Linked, given, and in glimpses going.

(1958)

BODY
OF WAKING

HAYING BEFORE STORM

This sky is unmistakable. Not lurid, not low, not black.
Illuminated and bruise-color, limitless, to the noon
Full of its floods to come. Under it, field, wheels, and
   mountain,
The valley scattered with friends, gathering in
Live-colored harvest, filling their arms; not seeming to hope
Not seeming to dread, doing.
                    I stand where I can see
Holding a small pitcher, coming in toward
The doers and the day.
                 These images are all
Themselves emerging: they face their moment: love or go
   down.
A blade of the strong hay stands like light before me.
The sky is a torment on our eyes, the sky
Will not wait for this golden, it will not wait for form.
There is hardly a moment to stand before the storm.
There is hardly time to lay hand to the great earth.
Or time to tell again what power shines past storm.

PHANERON

Whatever roams the air is traveling
Over these griefs, these wars and this good.
Whatever cries and changes, lives and reaches
Across the threshold of sense; I know the piercing name;
Among my silence, in cold, the birth-cry came.
Salt of these tears whitens my eyelashes.

Whatever plows the body turns to food:
Before my face, flowers, color which is form.
Cries plow the sea and air and turn to birth
Upon the people-sown, people-flowering earth.
A year turns in its crisis. In its sleep.
Whatever plows our dreams is ours to keep.

Whatever plows our dreams is ours to give:
The threshold rises and changes.
I give, I perceive;
Here are the gifts of day risen at last;
Blood of desire, the riding of belief
Beyond our fury and our silences.

Phaneron—anything over the threshold of sense; a perception word first used by Charles S. Peirce.

Stallions go leap, and rimfire knows,
Where there was sleep the ware eye goes,
Out of the rotten climbs the rose.
　I will remember how the music went
　When he sang down my fears.

A murder ballad blown by the moon away,
And all your dreaming could not make him stay.
He wants the blue counties, the way to Africa.
　Lean east lean west, the thousand ocean knows,
　How soon do you come to the center again?

Nightmary, zip me up, the avenue
Is black, I'll start in the dark of the moon—
Flat miles away my love who never knew
　Wakes and leans on the windowsill,
　Wanting the sea-breasts of an unborn girl.

Hills climb, songs climb, and I will find him out,
My child will leap like stallions from my mouth
Before the traveler moon can light my heart.
　There'll be a gun, and there'll be storms of roses,
　All Indiana crystal in my tears.

A BIRTH

Lately having escaped three-kinded death
Not by evasion but by coming through
I celebrate what may be true beginning.
But new begun am most without resource
Stupid and stopped. How do the newborn grow?
I am of them. Freshness has taken our hearts;
Pain strips us to the source, infants of further life
Waiting for childhood as we wait for form.

So came I into the world of all the living
The maimed triumphant middle of my way
Where there is giving needing no forgiving.
Saw now the present that is here to say:
Nothing I wrote is what I must see written,
Nothing I did is what I now need done.—
The smile of darkness on my song and my son.

Lately emerged I have seen unfounded houses,
Have seen spirits not opened, surrounded as by sun,
And have, among limitless consensual faces
Watched all things change, an unbuilt house inherit
Materials of desire, that stone and wood and air.
Lit by a birth, I defend dark beginnings,
Waste that is never waste, most-human giving,
Declared and clear as the mortal body of grace.

Beginnings of truth-in-life, the rooms of wilderness
Where truth feeds and the ramifying heart,
Even mine, praising even the past in its pieces,
My tearflesh beckoner who brought me to this place.

KING'S MOUNTAIN

In all the cities of this year
I have longed for the other city.

In all the rooms of this year
I have entered one red room.

In all the futures I have walked toward
I have seen a future I can hardly name.

But here the road we drive
Turns upon another country.

I have seen white beginnings,
A slow sea without glaze or speed,
Movement of land, a long lying-down dance.

This is fog-country. Milk. Country of time.

I see your tormented color, the steep front of your storm
Break dissipated among limitless profiles.

I see the shapes of waves in the cross-sea
Advance, a fog-surface over the fog-floor.
Seamounts, slow-flowing. Color. Plunge-point of air.

In all the meanings of this year
There will be the ferny meaning.

It rises leaning and green, streams through star-lattices;
After the last cliff, wave-eroded silver,

Forgets the limitations of our love,
These drifts and caves dissolve and pillars of these countries
Long-crested dissolve to the future, a new form.

MOTHER GARDEN'S ROUND

The year was river-throated, with the stare of legend,
Then truth the whirlwind and Mother Garden. Death.
And now these stars, antlers, the masks of speech,
And the one ghost a glove in the middle of the floor.
     Garden my green may grow.

If you were here tonight, my heart would rest,
Would rest on a support, happy thereon.
Something is dancing on leafdrift, dancing across the graves:
A child is watching while the world breaks open.
     Garden my green may grow.

Speed of a red fox running along this street.
Everyone could have seen it, no one is now awake.
Separations all year and the seeking of roots.
It was a lie, Mother Garden, they do not wish for death.
     Garden my green may grow.

They wish only to live again. No more the whirlwind.
One colored pebble now, one look, the singular
Opening of the lips; a leaf happens to speak.
I remember in love you walked to me straight across that
  room.
     Garden my green may grow.

The suffering of your absence flies around me now,
No house can keep out this flying of small birds.
Feathers, bird-feathers, settle upon my waking.
The agonies are open. Faces, dead within them; and on these
  faces
And filling the clefts and on my hands and eyes
The little fresh pain flutters. Whitening the grass,
Snowing through the windows. Drifting over the floor.
Touching my face when, almost, touch means kindness.
My dear dream, Mother Garden. We wish to be born again.
     Death death may my green grow.

RITE

My father groaned; my mother wept.
Among the mountains of the west
A deer lifted her golden throat.

They tore the pieces of the kill
While two dark sisters laughed and sang.—
The hidden lions blare until

The hunters charge and burn them all.
And in the black apartment halls
Of every city in the land

A father groans; a mother weeps;
A girl to puberty has come;
They shriek this, this is the crime

The gathering of the powers in.
At this first sign of her next life
America is stricken dumb.

The sharpening of your rocky knife!
The first blood of a woman shed!
The sacred word: Stand Up You Dead.

Mothers go weep; let fathers groan,
The flag of infinity is shown.
Now you will never be alone.

RINGLING

for Toni

Lattice of his back grows, the dolphin-arching, till
That ripple, that stress, dance on a board on a ball,
Bracing are planted among the unbalanced seas
Rooted in whirlwind, flanks of a man whose torse
Unknots becoming the face of all control
Trembling past his tornadoes, rouse of storm
Walking upon one point of make and build.
Black copper acrobat from Ecuador.

Is followed by the blonde and summer one
Fallen in whiteness upon her smooth trapeze,

Swung to no heavier and softer force
Than Monet's waterlilies in his light suspended
Or floating in our joy, or floating in circus air,
The calm eye at the core of the hurricane.

AFTER THEIR QUARREL

After the quarrel in the house I walked the grasses of the field
Until the hissing of breakers and the hissing on the sand
Lowered, and I could see the seed heads and the sky.

A pod of the milkweed burst; it was speaking to me:
Never mind, never mind. All splits open. There is new inside,
We witness. Downwind, the softened asters let me see

A lengthened sky in its mixed oranges of sunset
Gone east and west, glazing the first bare branches.
The branches said: We know you. I remembered a tiger

The winter I was five not leaping in my dream but fusing
All my wishes to run, with his endless glowing look telling:
I recognize you. Kill them if they deny; or wake them. Now
    wake!

Autumn announcing birds, the flights calling from sunset.
One bird crying: I see you down there, bird! The quick furry
    ground
Moves with me in small animals whispering:
You are like us, too. And the stars.—I my own evidence

That even the half-eaten and accursed can be a season.
Search yourself, said all the field, understand growth.
When lack consents to leave its seed, waste opens, you will see
Even there, the husband of the spring, who knows his time.

TREE

It seemed at the time like a slow road and late afternoon
When I walked past a summery turning and saw that tree in the sun.
That was my first sight of it. It stood blasted open,
Its trunk black with tar on its unsealed destruction.
You could see blue through that window, endless sky in the
    wound

Bright blue past the shining of black harm. And sound
Fresh wood supported branches like judge's arms,
Crutch under branch, crutch where the low hand leaned,
Strong new wood propping that apple-tree's crown.

And the crown? World-full, beneficent, round,
Many-branching; and red, apple-red, full of juices and color-ripe,
The great crown spread on the hollow bark and lived.
Lavish and fertile, stood on her death and thrived.

For three years remembering that apple-tree,
I saw in it the life of life in crisis,
Moving over its seasons, meeting death with fruition.
I have been recognizing all I loved.

Now, after crisis of day and crisis of dream,
That tree is burning and black before my years.
I know it for a tree. Rooted and red it bears.
Apple and branch and seed.
Real, and no need to prove, never a need
For images: of processs, or death, or flame; of love, or
    seeming, or speed.

THE RETURN

An Idea ran about the world
screaming with the pain of the mind
until it met a child
who stopped it with a word.

The Idea leaned over those newborn eyes
and dreamed of the nature of things:
the nature of memory and the nature of love;
and forgave itself and all men.

Quieted in a sea of sleeping
the Idea began its long return—
renewed by the child's sea-colored eyes
remembered the flesh, smiled and said:

I see birds, spring and the birthplace
unknown by the stable stone.
I know light and I know motion
and I remember I am not alone.

The Idea voyaged nearer my breathing, saying
Come balance come
into the love of these faces and forces
find us our equilibrium.

And the child stirred, asking his questions.

The Idea grew more fleshly and spoke:
Beaten down I was
Down I knew very long
Newborn I begin.

And the child went on asking his questions.

The Idea journeying into my body
returned, and I knew the nature of One,
and could forget One, and turn to the child,
and whole could turn to the world again.

Until the pain turns into answers
And all the masters become askers
And all the victims again doers
And all the sources break in light.

The child goes alive, asking his questions.

UNBORN SONG

Rabbits breed, flies breed, said the virgin lady;
But I
Cannot find my fulness where they rise,
My many children, their burning mouths and eyes,
Their bodies that have other fathers made.

The wife gone sterile in her weeping said
Flies breed, rabbits breed;
Faith of our time falls hissing on the sand,
Hard sand, is the hand of man set against hope? My bed
Whispers to me all year my love my hope my land.

Rabbits breed, flies breed, cried the infinite hearts of all the
    unborn,
In shady leafy places, underseas and in dim rooms, in the prodigal
    dark, all things are made again, but here

Among the new dreams and new nightmares, who listens, who
    believes? They give their stone demand
To the born, to the seed and seeking. While change emerges like
    another power from power, no longer the old good and evil,
    but a blessing that fares in the world, among the cities torn
    down
Crying awake, among the clouds who move calling do.
The mouth saying nothing. The air saying live and die.
The womb saying welcome, the sun saying Dare.

THE TWO ILLUMINATIONS

Storm and disorder and the giant emotions,
The seven deadly sins, they scatter all my hope.
To gather them in change I summon up the image
Of all arrangement in equilibrium.
Moments of poise in the middle of madness;
Sharpened as a forest is sharpened by fire,
I mean destroyed.

O abstract jealousy, half angel and half bird,
The bird smashing itself on the lighthouse's flying eye.
Tonight able at last to imagine perfect love—
Out of all murders
                    midnight in desire.

Now in a twilight moment I summon up twilight,
The two illuminations that can tell
Nothing in any second by themselves—
Only the body's knowledge, many fresh mornings,
Newborn experience says this flicker of air
Over the face, this time's quick light is dawn.

I think too of a longhanded mime of form,
A dancer carrying two great eggs, intricacies
Of music and equilibrium: the boy
A Javanese temple-dancer, thin-fingered, dancing
Turret-crowned, in his dark hands balancing
The eggs.

            Come back to me soon. You are my breath and wine.
Did we then wrestle as if we were our angels?
There is peace also,
                    love changing like religion.

Around your image now my prodigal wishes
Gather in, like the eye's color in brightened rooms,
Contract like a cloud of birds about a tree.

F . O . M .

the death of Matthiessen

It was much stronger than they said. Noisier.
Everything in it more colored. Wilder.
More at the center calm.
Everything was more violent than ever they said,
Who tried to guard us from suicide and life.
We in our wars were more than they had told us.
Now that descent figures stand about the horizon,
I have begun to see the living faces,
The storm, the morning, all more than they ever said.
Of the new dead, that friend who died today,
Angel of suicides, gather him in now.
Defend us from doing what he had to do
Who threw himself away.

EXILE OF MUSIC

for Naginski

In the last bus last night that dead musician
Rode, I saw him riding, all his orchestras
Lost past belief and under Egypt plowed
By rusty knives, the noise-machines of grief.

Thunder of the senses died,
Stabbed in their singing by a sleepwalker.
You were the man in whose voices the green leaf
Of form was singing, the bird riding the cloud.

Minotaur underwater in the cedar lake,
Naginski, you are your own exile of music.
There were three roads going through that whole land:
The bird's, the bed's, or suicide.

He meant to drown his self. He drowned his life.
Silence lay down fanatically straight.
I am your exile, he sang from his dead mouth,
From the water-maze reaching out his hand and one green leaf.

ON THE DEATH OF HER MOTHER

A seacoast late at night and a wheel of wind.
All those years, Mother, your arms were full of absence
And all the running of arrows could never not once find
Anything but your panic among all that substance,
Until your wide eyes opened forever. Until it all was true.
The fears were true. In that cold country, winter,
The wordless king, went isolate and cruel,
And he alone real. His armies all that entered.

But here is peacock daybreak; thought-yoked and warm, the
  light,
The cloud-companions and the greenest star.
Starflash on water; the embryo in the foam.
Dives through my body in the waking bright,
Watchmen of birth; I see. You are here, Mother, and you are
Dead, and here is your gift: my life which is my home.

"MAKE AND BE EATEN"

Make and be eaten, the poet says,
Lie in the arms of nightlong fire,
To celebrate the waking, wake.
Burn in the daylong light; and praise
Even the mother unappeased,
Even the fathers of desire.

Blind go the days, but joy will see
Agreements of music; they will wind
The shaking of your dance; no more
Will the ambiguous arm-waves spell
Confusion of the blessing given.

Only and finally declare
Among the purest shapes of grace
The waking of the face of fire,
The body of waking and the skill
To make your body such a shape
That all the eyes of hope shall stare.

That all the cries of fear shall know,
Staring in their bird-pierced song;
Lines of such penetration make

That shall bind our loves at last.
Then from the mountains of the lost,
All the fantasies shall wake,
Strong and real and speaking turn
Wherever flickers your unreal.

And my strong ghosts shall fade and pass
My love start fiery as grass
Wherever burn my fantasies,
Wherever burn my fantasies.

HERO SPEECH

from a play

When the hero of the threshold enters our lives and our houses
The wish that is most human in all of us deepens and feels
    saved; it rises
To another level of desire. Himself the man, himself the
    animal,
Himself the moment makes new the forms, makes our song
    and our prayer.
We look at our lives renewed, we have let go of the fear
That went through the old minutes. Our selves begin to speak:
"There was curse on his house. Or blessing. But there is
    choice."
Say of this flier, "A skill has taken possession of the man."
The young saying Dare, the old Praise air, but keep on land.

When we see the hero, his act seeming accomplished, we wish
    for him the leader's lifetime,
The drums being here, the loudspeakers, sharp trumpets,
    acclaim of sunlight;
The joy of time is the leap forward of a man or a people.
The moment of the leap is ready today.
We look again for the laws of history in the hero's face and his
    lifetime,
But it is not like that—he has his speech of thanks, his dazzled
    smile of sunlight.
Our acceptance is flowering and sheds on his air triumph.
Our delight is the herald of certain public voices
Arriving to tell us as they always tell us
Take the act and postpone the meanings.

In the world of listen and touch, shining and sounding,
Love and the hero,
God give us each his sin to awaken him.

When in our deep delight we take the gifts of the hero
We are glad, we become responsible. And in an age at war,
Dead power, the lying opposites, the great cities fighting in the air,
We think of flying, the flying of all dreams,
The ancient reaching for the chance to return changed.
In deepest power the changing and opening, the seed obeying
    its own law.
When we at last take the moment and meanings
There will be set in motion our most dear wish—
For the wish for escape is only a part of the wish,
The wish for death is not what they say it is.
It is a dancing tribal woman who stands among a room
And says, "Won't somebody come and kill me?" and
    somebody does;
This is in order that she dance the dance of rebirth. Tomorrow.
For the plane is not over power, and the weapons are all
    weapons,
But the seeds of all things are the ways of choice, of the forms
Declaring the energy we breathe and man,
Breaking. Changing. Forever broken and made.

Through our own need
We come again to our own deep,
We go and grow.
The peace of growth may follow; now we see war in loss,
When we imagine peace it is process, is seed.
It will be given its body when we give it.

But here the nearest: this moment, this hero.

THE WATCHERS

for Carson and Reeves

She said to me, He lay there sleeping
Upon my bed cast down
With all the bitterness dissolved at last,
An innocent peace within a sleeping head;
He could not find his infant war, nor turn
To that particular zoo, his family of the dead.

I saw her smile of power against his deep
Heart, his waking heart,
Her enmity, her sexual dread.

He said to me, She slept and dreaming
Brought round her face
Closer to me in silence than in fire,
But smiled, but smiled, entering her dark life
Whose hours I never knew, wherein she smiles.
Wherein she dim descending breathes upon
My daylight and the color of waking goes.
Deep in his face, the wanderer
Bringing the gifts of legend and the wars,
Conspiracy of opposing images.

In the long room of dream I saw them sleep,
Turned to each other, clear,
With an obliterated look—
Love, god of foreheads, touching then
Their bending foreheads while the voice of sleep
Wept and sang and sang again
In a chanting of fountains,
A chattering of watches,
Love, sang my sleep, the wavelight on the stone.
I weep to go beyond this stone and the waterlight,
To kiss their eyelids for the last time and pass
From the delicate confidence of their sly throats,
The conversation of their flesh of dreams.
And though I weep in my dream,
When I wake I will not weep.

A BALLAD THEME

She tells:

Sing I chant I
To music in new morning heard
My need has become a bird
And is flown and is free

My need grew stormy and wild
No love of mine had made a child
No song of mine had made my love
To plant my life

Need grew deep about my heart.
They came then with their steely knives
They said Your song has many lives
Now choose you

They split my life while I did sleep
The joy of chance was in my dream
Loving and remembering
The nature of memory

Of the nature of time was all my dream
The nature of love and of forgetting
I dreamed the series of eternity
While I lay bleeding

The joy of choice I sing
That out my wound did spring
My son and my song
Sing I chant I

Now the child is alive and young
And the child I among my veins
Sings and says with every breath
Sing I chant I

ASLEEP AND AWAKE

Asleep and awake, I wake.
Never having written
What I have to say.
No poem offers of me
My central meaning,
I have danced to my naming
And danced away.

Now I move past my dreams:
They yield processions of
Changing images.
I want to speak the clear
The intricate meeting-place
Of all things with all desires:
Cut down by risk to the root
Where everything is given.
The finding of the child,

The lost voices, songs of all
Who take their meanings.
They are beginning the songs.

Mortal, awake, I sing and say
All is immortal, all
Save personality.
Yes, your passion, yes, the time of a flower.
Move in all your meanings,
Go lit by many fires,
Deep in the secret fires
All speak to all.
The deep life lives and dies
Changes, sings, and sings.
Speak before I sleep,
Before the keepings are given,
I find my time, and speak,
Driven toward love and music,
Music of forms and desires.

OF MONEY. AND THE PAST.

These coins and calendars stood for the moon, strong boys,
And the resinous storerooms of a house in silence.
Too many losses among the possible.
But only when you hear their fearful music:
Nothing at all and then the front door slamming,
The cave of sound at the station after all hope has gone,
Fifteen wire hangers jangling in emptied closets.

When you discover the real, lying under, and still,
Among the silences green morning reopening.
Now your invisible path between the brambles opens
To the hill of oyster-shells under the hills of cloud
And the hard knuckles of a boy poverty-driven
And the moon rising in a smell of vanilla.

Voices of money, voices of your past,
The swinging music in these voices telling:
No, no, you must go. Now. Go from this bay to where
You can bridge backward and forward and move toward form.
From here there is nothing. Nothing for you here.
Somewhere you may find something. But not here.

Do not look here, not now. Not anywhere here.
Nowhere, nowhere, nothing anywhere here.

Beyond these coins and seasons, then look back.
When the black voices turn brilliant and call: Here!

"LONG ENOUGH"

"Long enough. Long enough,"
I heard a woman say—
I am that woman who too long
Under the web lay.
Long enough in the empire
Of his darkened eyes
Bewildered in the greying silver
Light of his fantasies.

I have been lying here too long,
From shadow-begin to shadow-began
Where stretches over me the subtle
Rule of the Floating Man.
A young man and an old-young woman
My dive in the river between
And rise, the children of another country;
That riverbank, that green.

But too long, too long, too long
Is the journey through the ice
And too secret are the entrances
To my stretched hidingplace.
Walk out of the pudorweb
And into a lifetime
Said the woman; and I sleeper began to wake
And to say my own name.

THE LOAN

You told me resurrection in images of roots,
Taking upon your summer my defeats.
Now I take on myself your wound's meaning
Private self-given torment, on my mouth.

The open grave stood in your eyes
Past the colors of our meeting—

413

Stain-moon, accepted curse of a false sun
Your guardians rising at your head.
A mask sang out, swinging away,
The verdicts proven fallacies,
"Lay you sweetly down to bed!"—
But the mask cannot kiss this away, nor wake—
Only you can wake, making go on to make;
Even when all your hope
Is buried dreaming,
The meanings move. Though my words are a loan,
Though your body I love vanish
Evading through our century among
These nightmare judgments of innocence and guilt.

All that I know from you of resurrection
Be passed on as branches, as one leaf.
Even the root of need.
The wound reaches its opposite, shines on my face, a flower
Bright among violence, the passion that is peace.
We have promises to make:
We saw that in each other's eyes.
Not to accept the curse, but wake,
Never to act in formal innocence.
It was not the maze of the time
But possibility we felt
In full gaze as we began to wake.
Not the lock of these years of silence,
We knew lack, we knew withholding, but there was more, the
    body of love said so—
Deep it was buried, but it lay there, in all eyes, in the meaning
    of sex
Waiting for more life, for it was more, and lively,
More a child running in the fields for his joy of running,
A running like creation, beginning now to make
Day and idea, his acts, his dreams, his waking,
His live ideas of innocence.

POURING MILK AWAY

Here, again. A smell of dying in the milk-pale carton,
And nothing then but pour the milk away.
More of the small and killed, the child's, wasted,

Little white arch of the drink and taste of day.
Spoiled, gone and forgotten; thrown away.

Day after day I do what I condemned in countries.
Look, the horror, the waste of food and bone.
You will know why when you have lived alone.

CHILDREN, THE SANDBAR, THAT SUMMER

Sunlight the tall women may never have seen.
Men, perhaps, going headfirst into the breakers,
But certainly the children at the sandbar.
Shallow glints in the wave suspended
We knew at the breaker line, running that shore
At low tide, when it was safe. The grasses whipped
And nothing was what they said: not safety, nor the sea.
And the sand was not what they said, but various,
Lion-grained, beard-grey. And blue. And green.
And each grain casting its shadow down before
Childhood in tide-pools where all things are food.
Behind us the shores emerged and fed on tide.
We fed on summer, the round flowers in our hands
From the snowball bush entered us, and prisoner wings,
And shells in spirals, all food.
                              All keys to unlock
Some world, glinting as strong as noon on the sandbar,
Where men and women give each other children.

BORN IN DECEMBER

for Nancy Marshall

You are like me born at the end of the year;
When in our city day closes blueness comes
We see a beginning in the ritual end.

Never mind: I know it is never what it seems,
That ending: for we are born, we are born there,
There is an entrance we may always find.

They reckon by the wheel of the year. Our birth's before.
From the dark birthday to the young year's first stay
We are the ones who wait and look for ways:

Ways of beginning, ways to be born, ways for
Solvings, turnings, wakings; we are always
A little younger than they think we are.

THE SIXTH NIGHT: WAKING

That first green night of their dreaming, asleep beneath the
  Tree,
God said, "Let meanings move," and there was poetry.

NEVERTHELESS THE MOON

Nevertheless the moon
Heightens the secret
Sleep long withheld
Dry for a rain of dreams—
Flies straight above me
White, hot-hearted,
Among the streaming
Firmament armies.
A monk of flames
Stands shaking in my heart
Where sleep might lie.

Where you all night have lain.
And now hang dreaming,
Faded acute, fade full,
Calling your cloudy fame,
A keen high nightlong cry.
Rises my silent, turning
Heart. Heart where my love
Might lie, try toward my love
Flying, let go all need,
Brighten and burn—
Rain down, raging for life
Light my love's dream tonight.

SPEED, WE SAY

Speed, we say of our time: racing my writing word
The jet now, the whole sky screaming his name, Speed.

But I know rapider, someone hauling horizons in
Beside whom the racing of the suns seems tame.

I know faster than the flashing of suddenly recognized love
Or yellow spring going glimpsing his green fame,
Love after long suffering like inward lightning,
Assumed and lived through where now lovers lie warm,

Wild and at peace among their colors. Speed. And now
One quick-color mouth saying, "Now, love, now;
I have my spirit now, newborn and given,
The live delight;

It now is immediately not only spirit, not only mine, but
    delight the forerunner
Of the depth of joy, most subtle, most rapid.
My two speeds, now, at last
Related, now at last in the same music—
Light running before light."

THE BIRTH OF VENUS

Risen in a
welter of waters.

Not as he saw her
standing upon a frayed and lovely surf
clean-riding the graceful leafy breezes
clean-poised and easy. Not yet.

But born in a
tidal wave of the father's overthrow,
the old rule killed and its mutilated sex.

The testicles of the father-god, father of fathers,
sickled off by his son, the next god Time.
Sickled off. Hurled into the ocean.
In all that blood and foam,
among raving and generation,
of semen and the sea born, the
great goddess rises.

                    However, possibly,
on the long worldward voyage flowing,
horror gone down in birth, the curse, being changed,

417

being used, is translated far at the margin into
our rose and saving image, curling toward a shore
early and April, with certainly shells, certainly blossoms.

And the girl, the wellborn goddess, human love—
young-known, new-knowing, mouth flickering, sure eyes—
rides shoreward, from death to us as we are at this moment, on
the crisp delightful Botticellian wave.

THE PLACE AT ALERT BAY

Standing high on the shoulders of all things, all things.
Creation pole reaching over my teeming island
That plays me at last a fountain of images.
Away from the road, life rising from all of us,
The grove of animals and our souls built in towers.
A music to be resumed in God.

Our branched belief, the power-winged tree.
Tree of meanings where the first mothers pour
Their totems, their images, up among the sun.
We build our gifts: language of process offers
Life above life moving, a ladder of lives
Reaching to time that is resumed in God.

Did the thunderbird gave you yourself? The man mourning?
The cedar forest between the cryings of ravens?
Everfound mother, streaming of dolphins, whale-white moon.
Father of salmon-clouded seas, your face.
Water. Weatherbeaten image of us all.
All forms to be resumed in God.

For here, all energy is form: the dead, the unborn,
All supported on the shoulders of us all,
And all forever reaching from the source of all things.
Pillars of process, the growing of the soul,
Form that is energy from these seas risen,
Identified. Resumed in God.

VOICES OF WAKING

for the eightieth birthday of Frances G. Wickes

Whenever you wake, you will find journeying—
Even in deep night, dreams surrounding your dreams—

The song of waking begun, prepared in silence,
Planted in silence as her life is planted
Among the constellations and the days.

Whenever you wake, you will hear entering
The song of meanings, a melody of green;
The image of a legendary woman
Dancing among her mercies, in essence emerging
Female to leap into the dragon-throning sea.

Voices of nourishing, lifting the newborn up,
Away,—they lift away, newborn to all,
To the nourisher, to self born, to new life.
Voices of waking that journey in our lives
As renaissance and rain of images.

All of the people of the play are here,
In a storm of light; birthday; at any moment.
Full in their powers, and the voice of waking
Sings for beginnings; she sings, wherever waking is.

Wherever the deep moon stands, the song arrives.
Nevertheless the moon goes voyages.

Nevertheless, the journeying is time:
Makes birthdays, makes this birthday a resonance
And the remote boundaries of imagining
Acknowledge the voices, her daily human voice,
Blessing this birthday moment her monument.

Deep in the waking, her life builds in light
The vision of the body of the soul.

DIVINING WATER

We stood around the raw new-planted garden
Parables green and yellow in the ground
The old man with his branch paced the diagonal

The rare Negro girl accepted a forked branch
And paced her line   The corners of an ancient
Dance-figure now we were as we stood watching

Everything was there in the moment there
Random and light in the dance on young grass flaming up
While the old man held his branch and walked toward water

Walked to that moment where the branch dives down
We stood in the moment random funny rare
Everything here and everything contained

In a strong diving a diving of the swan's strong neck
Diving of prayer leaping to find deep under
Reason and rock the cold sweet-driven springs

Everything being here in the moment here
Belief and disbelief the dry light on the grass
And the old man with lit eyes

Calculations of willow, predictions done in peach-branch
Dancing of the young dark over wellwater
The way we guess where lies the buried life

But not for days after the eyes and dance
Did the deep fountain show   Do they divine each other?
The man drove true   the moment was all water

And time the branch drove and the hand of man
It shines awake it glitters on the grass
Now waters divine man we all know what he was

SUITE FOR LORD TIMOTHY DEXTER

I

They face us in sea-noon sun, just as he saw them waiting,
Bolted down, fastened together by their nailhead proverbs.
The sun still pouring all male all female through their blood
And away through the salt marsh and the white salt sand
Sea-blaze over their shoulders, fantasy
A blue invisible mountain up whose side
Laughter and sharp clouds race as he saw them ride
In witness when he as a boy walked down
With morning for a sign.
Smelling of acid, like his trade.
Ready to throw their lifeday down their throats like wine,
Death-rotten proverbs and the jokes all made,
Himself the wine-bottle burning in the sun.

More here than power over proverbs. But that power pours
  here

And the sure sun of story, on top the live gold mast.
What's strong, what's lost? What boy walked salty in the light?
A raging worshipping fantastic man,
Tasting money and words, live-breasted women,
The tanner's boy streaked with truth. In the young States
He saw young morning. Wild he was.
And most
A clap of mockery clean in the sea-brightness,
A legend of this coast.

II | *How to Impress Massachusetts*

A name's a name but
Nothing's the same,
Now King-No-More knows
Lady-No-More;
There may be shame but
He's Mr. Guilt, and
Hell is Mr. War.
The wooden golden eagle
Announces from the rooftree:
Miss Equal, Mr. E.,
Dr. and Mrs. Eden, and
I am Miss Liberty.
But we see Timothy,
No more the colonized,
Look around after labor.
Not a single neighbor
Gives him his due acclaim.
Timothy's surprised:
A harsh laugh, a short knife,
Started his prodigious life.
But he took hold of fate,
Invested in the State, with
Money not worth a damn.
"I," he said, "am what I am,
What's to be done will be done,
The capital will be Washington.
Mr. Hamilton keeps his word,
This country's bond's as sound as me,
Timothy.
What 'dyou say?
'Sound as I'—?

The tanner's boy,
after we become
the United States,
invests in our
currency, which
is generally
regarded as
worthless;

421

Very well; me is I,
I the tree
Flourishing."
Mr. Hamilton truly meant
An almost infinite per cent
Would accrue
Quickly to
The trustful and the nourishing.
The newborn Federal bank has stirred.   becomes rich,
Timothy is a sword.
A sword without blessing,
A sword without fame,
A sword bearing no signal name.
If Newburyport
Will be blind,
Will seem bored,
Never mind.
New Hampshire's kind, and
Calls him "Lord."   and acquires
Apprentice then, on the road   his new
Next day wore his freedom suit,   first name.
Brided widow and won his house,
Ground their proverbs underfoot.
A poor boy made and found
And funding came to his own tune.
"Lord" is the center of that sound,
And all the songs proclaim
He is the bright blue morning rhyme,
A great name rides before his name.
Turn, burn, and overturn!
Among the squarest houses, he
Is more than Timothy,
And more than merry.
Can forever now retort
Very much Newbury-
Port:
The voice of the people and I can't help it,
But all's easy and no bones broken,
All is well, all in Love.
The first Lord of the age has spoken.
Now all the torment Massachusetts bore
Triumphs in a blaze of love.
Love, love, fantasy,

For
Out of shame and poverty,
From oppression, commerce, war,
Rose a new sovereignty:
The states are free and trade is free
And Dexter's Lord Timothy.

III / Three Nights I Dreamed

Sharp clouds and a sea-moon sang to me
Where were you born my young my dear
I said nowhere vary your singing   He makes his
Now where was your mother shaded, they   fortune as
     sang,   a merchant:
Nowhere I answered the ring the rung
Dark bells rang and I was young—
O on the water then, wine on the sea—
Nowhere they cried and they sang to me—
Nowhere my dear my darling,
My dearly darling beware.

Where and nowhere and then the singing changed
Past hills of prophecy the words went ranging,
The colors of the words to images
Went formed. And all I saw was warming-pans,
Three nights of warming-pans until I woke   selling warming-
And a great ship's bare spars sailing my   pans in the
     window,   West Indies,
Up to my tall room window a ship's spars,
And I remembered all the nights and wars,
Sang in my waking of poverty and dream:
My dearly darling beware.

The sun all male and female through me poured,
Awake I bought a cargo all of dream,   where they are
Warming-pans for the South, to all the   snapped up for
     roaring   molasses-ladles;
Nothing, to those who mock at my song.
I have entrusted south my folly cargo,
A full hold coming home now showers gold.
My warming-pans sailed gently to Jamaica—
The lids ripped off, made fine molasses-ladles,
Rum, rum, my darling beware.

Gold I am, lord of the cats of gold,
Mittens and kittens and coals of gold,
Malta, the Baltic, the Caribbee,
And Britain commend their money to me
As I go funding among the dreamers,
Among their golden nightmares ringing
Among their proverbs a wine-gold bell,
Sounding a folly my dear my darling
My dearly darling dream well.

And then, to spite their business saying, cats to Malta; mittens north; and, finally, coals to Newcastle.

IV / *Kings and Contemporaries*

How can I speak to them today? What can I know,
What can I show so that we see ourselves?
Voices of stinted singing in the towns,
Voices of wildness and fear of wilderness.
The rhythm, the root. Gathering in
Sources of music and the wild sea-rose.

Sea-music and the sea building its waters,
The weathervane beast. My song.

Whenever I say what I mean
They mock and call me mad.
They slip my meaning—
When I mock at them, I
always make money—
How can this go on?
Harum scarum, merchant marum,
My house is built, and my wall of pillars,
A noted house to the Isles of Shoals.
My kings, my presidents, stand round:
I speak in images so they may know
My gold spread-eagle on the cupalow.
Dr. Franklin, Mr. Hamilton, John Hancock, Rufus King,
John Jay, two grenadiers.
Four lions, and here the roof runs so,
That a lamb can lie down with one of the
    lions,
And an eagle on the cupalow.

He sets up, around his house, the figures of those he most admires.

One unicorn, one dog, one horse,
And in the Garden Adam and Eve—
I will if I please have Adam and Eve.
424

If no man murders me summer or snow
I'll carry this to its fair concluding
With an eagle on the cupalow.

Three of the apostles, viz.
St. Paul St. Peter and St. John.
Venus, Hiram, and Solomon—
The President's platform and columns
  grow—
I meant marble, but wood it is,
And an eagle on the cupalow.

The Royal Arch,
with lifesize
painted figures
carved by Joseph
Wilson, the
figurehead
sculptor.

George Third, L'Ouverture,
Lord Nelson Baron of the Nile.
Constantinople's Grand Signior,
All heroes, each one in his style—
The Chief Cornplanter with his bow,
His moccasins, arrows, and tomahawk,
And an eagle on the cupalow.

———————

Black rum and silver gin,
Drink for this company.
For the resident poet, Jonathan Plummer,
With a wheelbarrow full of broadsides and haddock—
Malaga wine for Madam Hooper,
Timothy Dexter's fortune-teller;
And for brandy-breasted Lucy, Lucy Lancaster,
Daughter of princes in Africa,
Feathers and majesty—what for her?
Black rum and silver gin
And a coach with cream-color horses.

Filisy, folosy, silver gin,
Stingalum, stangalum, wine for day,
Ram pan, muski dan,
And wine for night on the sound blind sea.
Stingalum, stangalum, buck.

Rum, whalerbone, whackerbone,
Waterfront, turnpike, Merrimack bridge,
Sea-berry, sea-gold, pine-forest edge;
Wire, briar, limber lock,
Timothy's a red red rock
Surrounded by waves of whisky and wine,

Loving waves called Jonathan,
Lucy Lancaster, Madam Hooper,
And a coach with cream-color horses.

V / The Pickle; The Temple

THE PICKLE

I will say what I mean here; in a book;
I wants to make
My Enemies grin
Like a cat over
A hot puddin.

If you can bear the truth
Then I will tell the truth:
Man's the best animal,
And the worst—
All men, I say, are more or
Less the Devil's.
Odds make the difference
And there's a sight of odds.
Some half, some quarters.
Odds make the difference.
I see in all places God, the God
Of nature in all things.
We live and move in God,
We live in God.

From *A Pickle For
the Knowing Ones,*
Timothy Dexter's book.

When great powers ruled,
I was born.
In a snowstorm, the signs
In the seventh house.
Mars came forward
Holding the candle—
Jupiter stood by.
I was to be
One great man.
(I think I am a Quaker
But have so little sense
I can't deceive.)
The bubble is the soul . . .
Man is the giant toad . . .
I have thoughts about clocks

Of his birth
and becoming.

426

Nobody will believe.
Ask me and I will tell.

———————

Now turn the system of knowledge
Into light—
Parents and masters begin, begin schoolmasters
At Cadameys and Collegeys,
Begin ministers,
Leave off, scarecrows in courage,
Brave good apelets—
One thing masters must teach:
Have good manners
To parents and people in streets,
And don't be too nosey.
I recommend a school   A plan for
Of languages,   the young:
Scholars to go to
Far parts to trade—
Go supercargo
To learn navigation
And character.
There will in time take
Many brave men,
Advantage to merchants
And funding to country—
Wise men pos-pos on this.
Goodbye—Timothy Dexter.

———————

I command peace and the
Gratest brotherly love
And Not fade, be linked
Together with that best of troue Love
So as to govern all nasions
On the fass of the gloub
Not to
Tiranize over them   A Congress of Nations;
But to
Put them to order . . .
A Congress of nasions
To be allways in france
All Despouts is
To be there settled

And this way be Dun
This will balless power
And then all was Dun
A Way—there-for I have the Lam
To Lay Dow with the Lion
Now this may be dun
If the powers would
A geray to Lay whats called
Devel to one side

I being a man without learning
Please to give me Light.   His appeal.

The knowing ones complain
Of my book
The first edition
Had no stops
I put in a Nuf here
And they may peper
And solt it as they please

,,,,,,,,,,,,,,,,,,,,,,,,,,,,,,,
,,,,,,,,,,,,,,,,,,,,,,,,,,,,,,,
....
,,,,,,,,,,,,,,,,,,,,,,,,,,,,,,,
...........!!!!!!!!!!!..........
..............!!!!!!!............
................!!!.............
.................!..............
,,,,,,,,,,,,,,,,,,,,,,,,,,,,,,,
.........???????????.........

THE TEMPLE

Then with a touch of the gout, and being
A little sober in the morning
I raised in the garden a Temple of Reason
For my own funeral,
Furnished with pipes and tobacco, a speaking trumpet
And fireworks in the tomb,
A Bible to read, and some good songs.

I sent out invitations.
Now it was time to begin.

It was a fine clear day,
I had fine pallbearers
Lord East Lord West Lord North and Lord South
Lord Megul and Lord Shambow.
The minister made his prayer—
Doctor Strong, he was—
And the flimsy sextons were there
And very much crying.
About 3000 came,
Oh, half the town, I'd say.
The procession wound
Under my window
Across the garden to my
Temple of Reason.
My coffin was long ready,
Painted in my house.
White lead inside
And outside touched with green.
Noble trimmings, eight handles
And an uncommon lock.
Now it was put into the
Temple of Reason.
Out in the kitchen I was
Beating my wife;
The ghostly lady
Had hardly mourned at all.

Very few people
Should attend funerals.
Many catch cold, and we
Want to settle Ohio;
We can't spare these beauties
To die so soon.

He holds his
own funeral,

and watches from
an upper
window.

VI | *The Kind of Woman*

Ghostly in my house
A woman I married—
Ghostly up the stairs,
Like snow in the hall.

429

At midnight in her bed
The ghostly-breasted;
I cannot have her ghost
Walking my palace.
They say she is alive.
I say she will ever be
Mrs. Dexter that was.
The attacks of the ghost
Will not let me sleep.—
Now to save my life.

He is haunted by
his living wife.

I will sell the house,
Horses, the cream-color horses
And the coach.
If not I will let it.
Wait. I can sweep my house
And get all anew
And go out of hell.
I will advertise.

"I must have a
Companon four
good by all."

"A very colding wife
Is poison to me.
I wish to be still
And master of my cash;
And therefore I wish for
One very good housekeeper.
Them that know me know
The kind of woman.
Now I will say
What kind of a person,
From thirty to forty
And a good jade
That will trot pace and gallop—
Not to heave one off
But, rather of the two,
Heave on.—I mean right well.
Now stop, I got off the path;
Now I am honest: I wish for
A middling woman for size,
Sensible honest and comely,
Knowing when to speak
And when to be silent,
With a nose like mine."

A feat of laughter and a coastwise dance
Among the ills of ocean, in pauper light
Imagining truth, at dawn turning from madness
Into the unknown world, up blue invisible
Mountains of fantasy climbing
To the sea.
Where he as a boy walked down, salty, in brightness
Raging and worshipping.
Their faces turn again the nailhead stare
Of proverbs glaring at the intuitive.
My old head has
Worn out three bodies.
Amen. Clean truth.
Pay the whole debt, it will make nations tremble.
Keep up to what we set out to be, honest republicans,
No king, but you won't go it long without being honest;
If dishonest, you must have a king.
Keep Judas out of your councils.
Watch day and night, for mankind is mankind.
Jockey-handed priests, deacons, grunters, whiners—
(And I will show you one more private torture:
Abraham Bishop my son-in-law from whom
I live in hell on earth; pity me, fellow mortals,
A.B. mad with learning, as poor as a snake,
As proud as Lucifer. A.B. is a beast,
A Connecticut bull, short neck, thick curly hair.
When I see my father, the great good man,
Father Thomas Jefferson, he'll shed great tears with grief.)

A sortment, a sortment is good in a shop.

How many nicknames three things have:
Sex and glory and the grave.

Now I suppose I may guess
As it is guessing time:
I guess the world is all one
Very large living creature;
Mankind is the master beast,
As in the sea the whale
Is head fish—master over the
Whole of beasts and fish,

But still we're all one creature.
Man is the masterly beast,
And also the worst of the whole,
Knowing the most and acting the worst
According to what we know.

I think when the candle goes out
Men and women are done at one blow,
We will lie then as dirt of rocks
Until the great gun go—
9,000,000,000 tons
Of the best good powder.
That will shake and bring all the
Bones together,
Then the world will be to an end.
All kinds of music then,
And funding laid aside,
The melody will be very great,—
Now why won't you believe me?

It is as true as apple-seed,
The sea and sea-music.
True as the voices that through me burn—
As true as we died and we are born,
Apple-seed and apple-thorn
Calling root and calling hand,
Saying Amen, mockery, Amen, fantasy,
Sea-music and the sea.

(1968)

THE SPEED
OF DARKNESS

I / Clues

THE POEM AS MASK

Orpheus

When I wrote of the women in their dances and wildness, it
    was a mask,
on their mountain, gold-hunting, singing, in orgy,
it was a mask; when I wrote of the god,
fragmented, exiled from himself, his life, the love gone down
    with song,
it was myself, split open, unable to speak, in exile from myself.

There is no mountain, there is no god, there is memory
of my torn life, myself split open in sleep, the rescued child
beside me among the doctors, and a word
of rescue from the great eyes.

No more masks! No more mythologies!

Now, for the first time, the god lifts his hand,
the fragments join in me with their own music.

WHAT DO I GIVE YOU?

What do I give you?   This memory
I cannot give you.   Force of a memory
I cannot give you : it rings my nerves among.
None of these songs
Are made in their images.
Seeds of all memory
Given me give I you
My own self.   Voice of my days.
Blessing;   the seed and pain,
Green of the praise of growth.
The sacred body of thirst.

THE TRANSGRESS

That summer midnight under her aurora
northern and still we passed the barrier.

Two make a curse, one giving, one accepting.
It takes two to break a curse

transformed at last in each other's eyes.

I sat on the naked bed of space,
all things becoming other than what they seem

in the night-waking, in the revelation
thundering on tabu after the broken

imperative, while the grotesque ancestors fade
with you breathing beside me through our dream:

bed of forbidden things finally known—
art from the symbol struck, living and made.

Branch lifted green from the dead shock of stone.

THE CONJUGATION OF THE PARAMECIUM

This has nothing
to do with
propagating

The species
is continued
as so many are
(among the smaller creatures)
by fission

(and this species
is very small
next in order to
the amoeba, the beginning one)

The paramecium
achieves, then,
immortality
by dividing

But when
the paramecium
desires renewal
strength   another joy

this is what
the paramecium does:

The paramecium
lies down beside
another
paramecium

Slowly   inexplicably
the exchange
takes place
in which
some bits
of the nucleus of each
are exchanged

for some bits
of the nucleus
of the other

This called
the conjugation of the paramecium.

JUNK-HEAP AT MURANO

for Joby West

You told me : they all went in and saw the glass,
The tourists, and I with them, a busload of them, a boatload
Out from Venice. We saw the glass making.
Until I, longing for air—longing for something—walked
    outside
And found my way along the building and around.
Suddenly there the dazzle, all the colors, fireworks and jewels in
    a mound
Flashing from the heap of glass thrown away. Not quite
    perfect. Perhaps a little flawed. Chipped, perhaps.
        Here is one.
And handed me the blue.

I looked into your eyes
Who walked around Murano
And I saw far behind, the face of the child I carried outdoors
    that night.

You were four. You looked up into the great tree netting all of
    night
And saw fire-points in the tree, and asked, "Do birds eat
    stars?"

Behind your eyes the seasons, the times,
assemble; dazzle; are here.

CLUES

How will you catch these clues at the moment of waking
take them, make them yours?   Wake, do you,
and light the lamp of sharpest whitest beam
and write them down in the room of night on white—
night opening and opening white
paper under white light, write what streamed
from you in darkness
into you by dark?

Indian Baptiste saying, We painted our dreams.
We painted our dreams on our faces and bodies.
We took them into us by painting them on ourselves.

    When we saw the water mystery of the lake
after the bad dream, we painted the lines and masks,
when the bear wounded me, I painted for healing.
When we were told in our dreams, in the colors of day
red for earth, black for the opposite, rare green, white.
Yellow. When I dreamed of weeping and dreamed of sorrow
I painted my face with tears, with joy.
Our ghost paintings and our dreams of war.
The whole brow, the streak, the hands and sex, the breast.
The spot of white, one hand black, one hand red.
The morning star appearing over the hill.
We took our dreams into our selves.
We took our dreams into our bodies.

IN OUR TIME

In our period, they say there is free speech.
They say there is no penalty for poets,
There is no penalty for writing poems.
They say this.   This is the penalty.

DOUBLE DIALOGUE:

Homage to Robert Frost

In agony saying : "The last night of his life,
My son and I in the kitchen : At half-past one
He said, 'I have failed as a husband. Now my wife
Is ill again and suffering.' At two
He said, 'I have failed as a farmer, for the sun
Is never there, the rain is never there.'
At three he said, 'I have failed as a poet who
Has never not once found my listener.
There is no sense to my life.' But then he heard me out.
I argued point by point. Seemed to win. Won.
He spoke to me once more when I was done:
'Even in argument, father, I have lost.'
He went and shot himself. Now tell me this one thing:
Should I have let him win then? Was I wrong?"

To answer for the land for love for song
Arguing life for life even at your life's cost.

THE SIX CANONS

(after Binyon)

Seize structure.
Correspond with the real.
Fuse spirit and matter.
Know your own secrets.
Announce your soul in discovery.
Go toward the essence, the impulse of creation,
    where power comes in music from the sex,
    where power comes in music from the spirit,
    where sex and spirit are one self
    passing among
    and acting on all things
    and their relationships,
    moving the constellations of all things.

FORERUNNERS

Forerunners of images.
In morning, on the river-mouth,

I came to my waking
seeing carried in air
seaward, a ship.
Standing on stillness
before the bowsprit
the man of spirit
—lookout aloft, steersman at wheel, silence on water—
and the young graceful man holding the lily iron.
I dream of all harpooning and the sea.

Out of Seville, after Holy Week I heard the
story of the black carriage and a lordly woman.
Her four daughters, their skirts of black foam,
lace seethed about them; drawn by four horses,
reined in, their black threads in the coachman's hands.
Far ahead on invisible wire
a circus horse making his shapes on the air.
Between us forever enlarges Spain and the war.

Far in New Jersey, among split-level houses,
behind the concrete filling-station I found
a yellow building and the flags of prayer.
Two Tibetans in their saffron bowed, priests
of their robes, their banners, their powers.
Little Tibetan children playing stickball
on the black road.
Day conscious and unconscious.
Words on the air.
Before the great
images arrive, riderless horses.
Words on an uproar silent hour.
In our own time.

ORGY

There were three of them that night.
They wanted it to happen in the first woman's room.
The man called her; the phone rang high.
Then she put fresh lipstick on.
Pretty soon he rang the bell.
She dreamed, she dreamed, she dreamed.
She scarcely looked him in the face
But gently took him to his place.

And after that the bell, the bell.
They looked each other in the eyes,
A hot July it was that night,
And he then slow took off his tie,
And she then slow took off her scarf,
The second one took off her scarf,
And he then slow his heavy shoe,
And she then slow took off her shoe,
The other one took off her shoe,
He then took off his other shoe,
The second one, her other shoe,
A hot July it was that night.
And he then slow took off his belt,
And she then slow took off her belt,
The second one took off her belt . . .

THE OVERTHROW OF
ONE O'CLOCK AT NIGHT

is my concern.   That's this moment,
when I lean on my elbows out the windowsill
and feel the city among its time-zones, among its seas,
among its late night news, the pouring in
of everything meeting, wars, dreams, winter night.
Light in snowdrifts causing the young girls
lying awake to fall in love tonight
alone in bed; or the little children
half world over tonight rained on by fire—that's us—
calling on somebody—that's us—to come
and help them.
                        Now I see at the boundary of darkness
extreme of moonlight.
                        Alone.   All my hopes
scattered in people quarter world away
half world away, out of all hearing.
                                      Tell myself:
Trust in experience.   And in the rhythms.
The deep rhythms of your experience.

AMONG GRASS

Lying here among grass, am I dead am I sleeping
amazed among silences   you touch me never

Here deep under, the small white moon
cries like a dime and do I hear?

The sun gone copper or I dissolve
no touch no touch   a tactless land
denies my death my fallen hand
silence runs down the riverbeds

One tall wind walks over my skin

                              breeze, memory
bears to my body (as the world fades)

                                   going in
very late in the world's night to see roses opening
Remember, love, lying among roses.
Did we not lie among roses?

WHAT I SEE

Lie there, in sweat and dream, I do, and "there"
Is here, my bed, on which I dream
You, lying there, on yours, locked, pouring love,
While I tormented here see in my reins
You, perfectly at climax. And the lion strikes.
I want you with whatever obsessions come—
I wanted your obsession to be mine
But if it is that unknown half-suggested strange
Other figure locked in your climax, then
I here, I want you and the other, want your obsession, want
Whatever is locked into you now while I sweat and dream.

BELIEVING IN THOSE INEXORABLE LAWS

Believing in those inexorable laws
After long rebellion and long discipline
I am cut down to the moment in all my flaws
Creeping to the feet of my master the sun
On the sea-beach, tides beaten by the moon woman,
And will not think of you, but lie at my full length
Among the great breakers. I find the clear outwater
Shine crash speaking of truth behind the law.

The many-following waves turn into you.
I see in vision that northern bay : pines, villages,

442

And the flat water suddenly rears up
The high wave races against all edicts, taller,
Finally powerful. Water becomes your mouth,
And all laws all polarities your truth.

SONG : LOVE IN WHOSE RICH HONOR

Love
in whose rich honor
I stand looking from my window
over the starved trees of a dry September
Love
deep and so far forbidden
is bringing me
a gift
to claw at my skin
to break open my eyes
the gift longed for so long
The power
to write
out of the desperate ecstasy at last
death and madness

NIOBE NOW

Niobe
    wild
        with unbelief
            as all
                her ending
                    turns to stone
Not gentle
      weeping
          and souvenirs
              but hammering
                  honking
                      agonies
Forty-nine tragic years
          are done
             and the twentieth century
                    not begun :

All tears,
      all tears,
            all tears.
Water
    from her rock
         is sprung
             and in this water
                 lives a seed
That must endure
       and grow
         and shine
            beasts, gardens
                at last rivers
A man
    to be born
       to start again
          to tear
          a woman
             from his side
And wake
    to start
       the world again.

SONG : THE STAR IN THE NETS OF HEAVEN

The star in the nets of heaven blazed past your breastbone,
Willing to shine among the nets of your growth,
The nets of your love,
The bonds of your dreams.

AIR

Flowers of air
with lilac defining air;
buildings of air
with walls defining air;
this May, people of air
advance along the street;
framed in their bodies, air,
their eyes speaking to me,
air in their mouths made
into live meanings.

GIFT

the child, the poems, the child, the poems, the journeys
    back and forth across our long country
        of opposites,
and through myself, through you, away from you, toward
    you, the dreams of madness and of an
        impossible complete time—
gift be forgiven.

CRIES FROM CHIAPAS

Hunger
      of mountains
            spoke
               from a tiger's throat.
Tiger-tooth peaks.
         The moon.
             A thousand mists
turning.
      Desires of mountains
              like the desires of women,
moon-drawn,
        distant,
          clear black among
               confusions of silver.
Women of Chiapas!
         Dream-borne
            voices of women.
Splinters of mountains,
          broken obsidian,
             silver.
White tigers
        haunting
          your forehead here
              sloped in shadow—
black hungers of women,
           confusion
              turning like tigers

And your voice—

I am
    almost asleep
        almost awake
            in your arms.

THE WAR COMES INTO MY ROOM

Knowing again
      that nothing
          has been spoken
              not now
                  not this night time
the broken singing
        as we move
           or of
             the endless war
                our lives
that above all
       there is not said
          nothing
            of this moment
in the poems
      our love
        in all the songs
           now I will
             live out
               this moment
saying
   it
     in my breath
        to you
          across the air

DELTA POEMS

Among leaf-green
this morning, they
walk near water-blue,
near water-green
of the river-mouths

this boy   this girl
they die with their heads near each other,
their young mouths

―――――――

A sharp glint out among the sea
These are lives coming out of their craft
Men who resemble. . . .
Sound is bursting the sun
Two dead bodies against the leaves
A young man and a girl
Their heads close together
No weapons, only grasses and waves
Lives, grasses

―――――――

Something is flying through the high air over the river-mouth
    country,
Something higher than the look can go,
Higher than herons fly,
Higher than planes is it?
It is nothing now
But now it is sound beyond bigness
Turns into the hugeness : death. A leaf shakes on the sky.

―――――――

Of the children in flames, of the grown man
his face burned to the bones, of the full woman
her body stopped from the nipples down, nursing
the live strong baby at her breast
I do not speak.

I am a woman
in a New York room
late in the twentieth century.

I am crying. I will write no more.―
Young man and girl walking along the sea,
among the leaves.

―――――――

Fresh hot day among the river-mouths,
yellow-green leaves   green rivers running to sea.
A young man and a girl

447

go walking in the delta country
The war has lasted their entire lifetime.
They look at each other with their mouths.
They look at each other with their whole bodies.
A glint as of bright fire, metal over the sea-waters.

A girl has died upon green leaves,
a young man has died against the sky.
A girl is walking printed against green leaves,
A young man walks printed upon the sky.

I remember you. We walked near the harbor.
You a young man believing in the future of summer,
in yellow, in green, in touch, in entering,
in the night-sky, in the gifts of this effort.
He believes in January,
he believes in the pulses beating along his body,
he believes in her young year.

I walk near the rivers.

They are walking again at the edge of waters.
They are killed again near the lives, near the waves.
They are walking, their heads are close together,
their mouths are close as they die.
A girl and a young man walk near the water.

SPIRALS AND FUGUES

Spirals and fugues, the power most like music
Turneth all worlds to meaning
And meaning to matter, all continually,
And sweeps in the sacred motion,
Spirals and fugues its lifetime,
To move my life to yours,
    and all women and men and the children in their light,
The little stone in the middle of the road, its veins and
    patience,
Moving the constellations of all things.

448

ANEMONE

My eyes are closing, my eyes are opening.
You are looking into me with your waking look.

My mouth is closing, my mouth is opening.
You are waiting with your red promises.

My sex is closing, my sex is opening.
You are singing and offering : the way in.

My life is closing, my life is opening.
You are here.

FIGHTING FOR ROSES

After the last freeze, in easy air,
Once the danger is past, we cut them back severely;
Pruning the weakest hardest, pruning for size
Of flower, we deprived will not deprive the sturdy.
The new shoots are preserved, the future bush
Cut down to a couple of young dormant buds.

But the early sun of April does not burn our lives :
Light straight and fiery brings back the enemies.
Claw, jaw, and crawler, all those that devour.
We work with smoke against the robber blights,
With copper against rust; the season fights itself
In deep strong rich loam under swarm attacks.

Head hidden from the wind, the power of form
Rises among these brightnesses, thorned and blowing.
Where they glow on the earth, water-drops tremble on them.
Soon we must cut them back, against damage of storms.
But those days gave us flower budded on flower,
A moment of light achieved, deep in the air of roses.

FOR MY SON

You come from poets, kings, bankrupts, preachers,
    attempted bankrupts, builders of cities, salesmen,
the great rabbis, the kings of Ireland, failed drygoods
    storekeepers, beautiful women of the songs,

great horsemen, tyrannical fathers at the shore of ocean, the
    western mothers looking west beyond from their
        windows,
the families escaping over the sea hurriedly and by night—
the roundtowers of the Celtic violet sunset,
the diseased, the radiant, fliers, men thrown out of town, the
        man bribed by his cousins to stay out of town, teachers,
            the cantor on Friday evening, the lurid newspapers,
strong women gracefully holding relationship, the Jewish girl
        going to parochial school, the boys racing their iceboats
            on the Lakes,
the woman still before the diamond in the velvet window, say-
    ing "Wonder of nature."
Like all men,
you come from singers, the ghettoes, the famines, wars and
        refusal of wars, men who built villages
that grew to our solar cities, students, revolutionists, the
        pouring of buildings, the market newspapers,
a poor tailor in a darkening room,
a wilderness man, the hero of mines, the astronomer, a white-
        faced woman hour on hour teaching piano and her
            crippled wrist,
like all men,
you have not seen your father's face
but he is known to you forever in song, the coast of the skies,
        in dream, wherever you find man play playing his part
            as father, father among our light, among our darkness,
and in your self made whole, whole with yourself and whole
        with others,
the stars your ancestors.

POEM

I lived in the first century of world wars.
Most mornings I would be more or less insane,
The newspapers would arrive with their careless stories,
The news would pour out of various devices
Interrupted by attempts to sell products to the unseen.
I would call my friends on other devices;
They would be more or less mad for similar reasons.
Slowly I would get to pen and paper,
Make my poems for others unseen and unborn.

In the day I would be reminded of those men and women
Brave, setting up signals across vast distances,
Considering a nameless way of living, of almost unimagined
    values.
As the lights darkened, as the lights of night brightened,
We would try to imagine them, try to find each other.
To construct peace, to make love, to reconcile
Waking with sleeping, ourselves with each other,
Ourselves with ourselves. We would try by any means
To reach the limits of ourselves, to reach beyond ourselves,
To let go the means, to wake.

I lived in the first century of these wars.

THE POWER OF SUICIDE

The potflower on the windowsill says to me
In words that are green-edged red leaves :
Flower   flower   flower   flower
Today for the sake of all the dead   Burst into flower.

(1963)

THE SEEMING

for Helen Lynd

Between the illuminations of great mornings
there comes the dailiness of doing and being
and the hand as it makes as it brightens   burnishes
the surfaces   seemings   mirrors of the world

We do not know the springs of these colored and loving
acts   or what triggers birth   what sleep is
but name them as we name bird-wakened morning
having our verbs of the world
to which all action seems
to resolve, being

to go, to grow, to flow, to shine, to sound, to glow,
to give and to take, to bind and to separate,
to injure   and to defend

we do not even   not even know why we wake

but some of us showing the others
a kind of welcoming
bringing a form to morning
as a woman who recognizes
may offer us the moment and the names
turning all shame into a declaration
immediately to be followed by
an act of truth
until all seemings are
                    illumination
we see in a man a theme
a dream taking over
or in this woman going today who has shown us
fear, and form, and storm turned into light
the dailiness of our being and doing
morning and every time the way to naming
and we see more now coming into being

see in her goings as in her arrivings
the opening of a door

SONG FROM PUCK FAIR

Torrent that rushes down
Knocknadober,
Make the channel deeper
Where I ferry home.

Winds go west over
Left-handed Reaper
Mountain that gathered me
Out of my old shame—

Your white beard streaming,
Puck of summertime,
At last gave me
My woman's name.

NOT YET

A time of destruction. Of the most rigid powers in ascendance.
Secret plots against them, open work against them in round
   buildings.
All fail. Any work for fluency, for freedom, fails.

Battles. The wiping out of cities full of people.
Long tracts of devastation.

In one city : a scene of refugees, each allowed to take
a suitcase of bedding, blankets, no more. An old man, a professor.
He has hidden a few books and two small statues in a blanket
and packed his case. He comes in his turn to the examining desk.
He struggles about the lie he needs to tell. He lies, he declares
    nothing.
Even after the lie, the suitcase is thrown over the cliff
where all the statues lie broken, the books, pictures, the records.

Long landscapes of devastation. Color modulated between
sparse rigid monuments. Long orange landscapes
shifting to yellow-orange to show a generation.
Long passage of time to yellow. Only these elite,
their army tread on yellow terrain. Their schools. Their
    children.

A tradition of rigor, hatred and doom is now
—generations after—the only sole tradition.
I am looking at the times and time as at a dream.
As at the recurrent dream of a locked room.
I think of the solution of the sealed room mystery
of the chicken and the egg, in which the chicken
feeds on his cell, grows strong on the sealed room
and finally
                in strength
                        eating his prison
pierces the shell.
                        How can this room change state?
I see its sky, its children. I cannot imagine.

I look at the young faces of the children
in this tradition, far down the colors of the years.
They are still repeating their shut slogans
with "war" substituted for freedom. But their faces glow.
The children are marvelous, singing among the wars.
They have needed the meanings, and their faces show
this : the solution.
                The words have taken on
all their forbidden meanings. The words mean their opposites.
They must, they are needed.

Children's faces, lit, unlit,
the face of a child.

LANDSCAPE WITH WAVE APPROACHING

I

All of the people of the play were there,
swam in the mile-long wave, among cliff-flowers
were pierced, hung and remembered a sunlit year.

II

By day white moths, the nightlong meteors
flying like snow among the flowery trees—
hissing like prophecy above those seas.

III

The city of the past. The past as a city
and all the people in it, your childhood faces,
their dances, their words developing, their hands.

IV

The fertile season ending in a glitter;
blight of the forest, orange, burning the trees away,
the checkered light. Full length on naked sand.

V

All of the people of the play were there,
smiling, telling their truths, coming to crisis.
This water, this water, this water. These rocks, this piercing
   sea.

VI

Flower of time, and a plague of white trilling in sunlight,
the season advancing on the people of the play,
the scars on the mountains and the body of fire.

Carmel, California

SEGRE SONG

Your song where you lie long dead on the shore of a Spanish
   river—

your song moves under the earth and through time, through
   air—
your song I sing to the sun as we move
and to the cities
sing to the mimosa
sing to the moon over my face

BUNK JOHNSON BLOWING

in memory of Leadbelly
and his house on 59th Street

They found him in the fields and called him back to music.
Can't, he said, my teeth are gone.   They bought him teeth.

Bunk Johnson's trumpet on a California
early May evening, calling me to
breath of . . .
up those stairs . . .
calling me to
look into
the face of that
trumpet
experience
and past it
his eyes

Jim and Rita beside me. We drank it. Jim had just come back
from Sacramento the houses made of piano boxes the bar
   without
a sign and the Mexicans drinking we drank the trumpet music
and drank that black park moonlit beneath the willow trees,
Bunk Johnson blowing all night out of that full moon.
Two-towered church. Rita listening to it, all night
music! said, I'm supposed to, despise them.
Tears streaming down her face. Said, don't tell my ancestors.

We three slid down that San Francisco hill.

CANNIBAL BRATUSCHA

Have you heard about Mr. Bratuscha?
He led an orderly life
With a splendid twelve-year-old daughter,

A young and passionate wife —
    Bratuscha, the one they call Cannibal.

Spring evening on Wednesday,
The sky is years ago;
The girl has been missing since Monday,
Why don't the birches blow?
    And where's their daughter?

Nine miles to the next village
Deep in the forested past —
Wheatland, marshland, daisies
And a gold slender ghost.
    It's very difficult to keep them safe.

She hasn't been seen and it's Thursday.
Down by the river, raped?
Under the birches, murdered?
Don't let the fiend escape,
    First, we'll track him down and catch him.

The river glittering in sunlight,
The woods almost black — and she
Was always a darling, the blonde young daughter,
Gone gone vanished away.
    They say Bratuscha is ready to talk.

O God he has told the whole story;
Everything; he has said
That he killed his golden daughter
He ate her, he said it!
    Eaten by the cannibal, Cannibal Bratuscha.

Down at the church her mother
In the confession booth —
She has supported his story,
She has told the priest the truth;
    Horror, and now the villagers gather.

They are ready to lynch Bratuscha,
Pounding at his door —
Over the outcries of the good people
Hear the cannibal roar —
    He will hold out, bar the doorway, fight to the death.

But who is this coming, whose shadow
Runs down the river road?

She is coming, she is running, she is
Alive and abroad —
    She is here, she is well, she was in the next village.

The roaring dreams of her father :
He believed all he confessed —
And the mother was threatened with hellfire
By the village priest
    If she didn't tell everything, back up what Bratuscha said.

This all took place some time ago
Before all villages joined —
When there were separate, uncivilized people,
Only the birds, only the river, only dreams and the wind.
    She had just gone off for a few days, with a friend.

But O God the little Bratuscha girl
What will become of her?
Her mother is guilt suggestion panic
Her father of dreams, a murderer
    And in waking and in fantasy and now and forever.

Who will help her and you and me and all those
Children of the assumption of guilt
And the roaring fantasy of nightmare
The bomb the loathing all dreams spilt
    Upon this moment and the future and all unborn children.

We must go deep go deep in our lives and our dreams —
Remember Cannibal Bratuscha his wife and his young child
And preserve our own ideas of guilt
Of innocence and of the blessed wild
    To live out our own lives to make our own freedom to make
    the world.

WHAT HAVE YOU BROUGHT
HOME FROM THE WARS?

What have you brought
home from the wars, father?
Scars.
We fought far overseas; we knew
the victory must
be at home.

But here I see
only a trial by time
of those
who know.
The public men all shout : Come bomb,
come burn
our hate.
I do not
want it shot;
I want it solved.
This is the word
the dead men said.
They said peace.
I saw in the hot light
of our century
each face killed.

ONE MONTH

for Dorothy Lear

All this time
you were dead and I did not know
I was learning to speak
and speaking to you
and you were not there
I was seeing you
tall, walking the corridor
of that tall shining building
I was learning to walk
and walking to you
and it was not true
you were still living still lying still
it was not true
that you were giving me a rose
telling me stories
pouring a wine-story, there were bubbles in it
all this time
I was remembering untrue
speaking untrue, seeing a lie.

It is true.

SILENCE OF VOLCANOES

I

The mountains and the shadows move away
Under their snows to show an immense scene:
A field of cathedrals. Green domes eye-green,
Domes the color of trumpets. Obliterated rose
And impure copper. Vaults are pale shoulders.
Grass-haired and deformed,
The dome-capped pyramid to the god of the air.
A white dome under these volcanoes.
This is the field that glittered in massacre,
Time is boiling with domes.

II

A woman has been begging for ninety-seven years.
The singing of her words against shadows of gold.
I see her lean her face against this scene.
The domes dissolve. All her unfallen tears.
I remember a room for sale in a picture
Torn as this landscape
Obsessed by a single thing.

III

A hall at the National Pawnshop crowded with unsold bureaus.
In sharp paint at the end of a blind aisle
Red-robed and listening, the saint looks at the Sign.
Books fold him in, strict black-and-white tile
Lead to a sleeping garden where his lion,
The guardian, lies in a silence of volcanoes.
Hung in that air, there pierces his leaning soul
The cheap tin trumpet that is the voice of God.

Mexico

WHAT THEY SAID

: After I am dead, darling,
   my seventeen senses gone,
  I shall love you as you wish,
   no sex, no mouth, but bone —

in the way you long for now,
with my soul alone.

:   When we are neither woman nor man
but bleached to skeleton —
when you have changed, my darling,
and all your senses gone,
it is not me that you will love:
you will love everyone.

A LITTLE STONE IN THE MIDDLE
OF THE ROAD, IN FLORIDA

My son as a child saying
God
is anything, even a little stone in the middle of the road, in
  Florida.
Yesterday
Nancy, my friend, after long illness:
You know what can lift me up, take me right out of despair?
No, what?
Anything.

THE BLUE FLOWER

for Frances C. Wickes
on her ninetieth birthday,
August 28, 1965

Stroke by stroke, in the country of the fragile
stroke by stroke, each act a season
speaking the years of making
this flower
shining over the fears
over the cities
and the camps of death.
Shines from a field
of eighty-seven years,
the young child and the dream.

In my city of stone,
water and light
I saw the blue flower
held still, and flying —
never seen by me
but in your words given;
fragile, mortal
that endures.

By turns flying and still.
"Angkor Vat, a gray stone city
but the flight of kingfishers
all day enlivened it"—
a blue flash given to us, past stone and time.

Blaze of mortality
piercing, tense
the structure of a dream
speaking and fragile,
momentary,
for now
and ever and all ·
your blue flower.

WOMAN AS MARKET

Forgetting and Remembering

What was it? What was it?
Flashing beside me, lightning in daylight at the orange stand?
Along the ranks of eggs, beside the loaves of dark and light?
In a moment of morning, providing:
the moment of the eggplant?
                    the lemons? the fresh eggs?
with their bright curves and curves of shadow?
the reds, the yellows, all the calling boxes.
What did those forms say? What words have I forgotten?
what spoke to me from the day?
God in the cloud? my life in my forgetting?
I have forgotten what it was
that I have been trying to remember

WORD OF MOUTH

I / The Return

Westward from Sète
                as I went long before
along my life
         as I went
             wave by wave—
the long words of the sea
                the orange rooftop tiles
back to the boundary
            where I had been before.

Spain.
            Sex of cactus and of cypresses,
Tile-orange, green;   olive;   black.   The sea.
One man.   Beethoven radio.   War.
Threat of all life.   Within my belief's body.
Within my morning, music.   High colored mountain
along the seacoast
           where the swallows fly.

Prolonged
beyond your cries and your cities.
Along my life and death backward toward that morning
when all things fell open and I went into Spain.

One man.   Sardana music.   This frontier.
Where I now come again.
             I stop.
                I do not pass.

Wave under wave
            like the divisive South
afire in the country of my birth.

A moment of glass.   All down the coast I face
as far as vision, blue, memory of blue.

Seen now.   Why do I not go in?   I stand.
I cannot pass.   History, destroyed music.

Note: The country is the Catalan border of France and Spain. The two times are
July, 1936, the beginning of the war, and the time of my return to the border
in 1963.

I need to go into.
In a dream I have seen
Spain, *sleeping children:*
before me:
as I drive
as I go
(I need to go into
this country
of love and)
wave after wave
they lie
in a deep forest.
As the driving light
touches them
(I need this country
of love and death)
they begin to rouse.
They wake.

II / Word of Mouth

Speeding back from the border.
A rock came spinning up
cast from the wheels of a car.
Crackled the windshield glass.
Glitter before my eyes like a man made of snow
lying over the hood, blind white except for glints
an inch of sight where Languedoc shines through.

You on my one side, you on the other!
What I have is dazzle.   My son; my friend;
tell me this side and tell me that side,
news of the road near Agde.

Word from this side, word from the tree-side—
Spain at our back : agony : before me, glitter,
today
blinding my eyes, blind diamonds, one clear wound.

Something is flying out of the sky behind me.
Turning, stirring of dream, something is speeding,
something is overtaking.

Stirrings in prisons, on beds, the mouths of the young,
resist, dance, love.   It drives through the back of my head,

through my eyes and breasts and mouth.
I know a harvest : mass in the wine country.
A lifetime after, and still alive.

Something out of Spain, into the general light!
I drive blind white, trusting news of this side,
news of that side, all the time the line of the poem:
Amor, pena, desig, somni, dolor.
The grapes have become wine by the hand of man.
Sea risen from the sea, a bearded king.

The seaward cemetery risen from the sea
like a woman rising.
              Amor.
                        Phases of sun.
The wine declared god by the hand of man.
Pena.
              A rumor given me by this side and that side.
We drive in brilliant glitter, in jungle night, in distant war,
in all our cities, in a word, overtaking.
                          Desig.

A cry received, gone past me into all men,
speaking, into all women.
                    A man goes into the sea,
bearded fire and all things rise from this blaze of eyes,
living, it speaks, driving forth from Spain,
                         somni, dolor,
These cliffs, these years.   Do we drive into light?
Driven, live, overtaken?
               Amor, pena, desig.

Note: The line is from a Catalan poem in *Cantilena* by Joseph Sebastien Pons.
   Love, agony, desire, dream, suffering.

ENDLESS

Under the tall black sky you look out of your body
lit by a white flare of the time between us
your body with its touch its weight   smelling of new wood
as on the day the news of battle reached us
falls beside the endless river
flowing to the endless sea
whose waves come to this shore a world away.

Your body of new wood your eyes alive barkbrown of
   treetrunks
the leaves and flowers of trees   stars all caught in crowns of
   trees
your life gone down, broken into endless earth
no longer a world away but under my feet and everywhere
I look down at the one earth under me,
through to you and all the fallen
the broken and their children born and unborn
of the endless war.

II / Games

THE BACKSIDE OF THE ACADEMY

Five brick panels, three small windows, six lions' heads with
   rings in their mouths, five pairs of closed bronze doors—
the shut wall with the words carved across its head
ART REMAINS THE ONE WAY POSSIBLE OF SPEAKING
   TRUTH.—
On this May morning, light swimming in this street, the
   children running,
on the church beside the Academy the lines are flying
of little yellow-and-white plastic flags flapping in the light;
and on the great shut wall, the words are carved across:
WE ARE YOUNG AND WE ARE FRIENDS OF TIME.—
Below that, a light blue asterisk in chalk
and in white chalk, Hector, Joey, Lynn, Rudolfo.
A little up the street, a woman shakes a small dark boy,
she shouts What's wrong with you, ringing that bell!
In the street of rape and singing, poems, small robberies,
carved in an oblong panel of the stone:
CONSCIOUS UTTERANCE OF THOUGHT BY SPEECH
   OR ACTION
TO ANY END IS ART.—
On the lowest reach of the walls are chalked the words: Jack is
   a object,
Walter and Trina, Goo Goo, I love Trina,
and further along Viva Fidel now altered to Muera Fidel.

A deep blue marble is lodged against the curb.
A phone booth on one corner; on the other, the big mesh
   basket for trash.
Beyond them, the little park is always locked. For the two
   soldier brothers.
and past that goes on an eternal football game
which sometimes, as on this day in May, transforms to
   stickball
as, for one day in May,
five pairs of closed bronze doors will open
and the Academy of writers, sculptors, painters, composers,
   their guests and publishers will all roll in and
the wave of organ music come rolling out into
the street where light now blows and papers and little children
   and words, some breezes of Spanish blow and many
         colors of people.
A watch cap lies fallen against a cellophane which used to hold
   pistachio nuts
and here before me, on my street,
five brick panels, three small windows, six lions' heads with
   rings in their mouths, five pairs of closed bronze doors,
light flooding the street I live and write in; and across the river
   the one word FREE against the ferris wheel and the roller
         coaster,
and here, painted upon the stones, Chino, Bobby, Joey, Fat-
   moma, Willy, Holy of God
and also Margaret is a shit and also fuck and shit;
far up, invisible at the side of the building:
WITHOUT VISION THE PEO
and on the other side, the church side,
where shadows of trees and branches, this day in May, are
   printed balanced on the church wall,
in-focus trunks and softened-focus branches
below the roof where the two structures stand,
bell and cross, antenna and weathervane,
I can see past the church the words of an ending line:
IVE BY BREAD ALONE.

MOUNTAIN : ONE FROM BRYANT

Wildflowers withering with the same death.
Grave a slope, threw she long shadows,
Mountains o'erlooking earth, affect and places

High.　　On God that time, the elder worshipper,
Deemed spirit, made here a tribe of offering,
Bear and wolf of skins shaggy, maze of ears
And garlands lay.　　Mother, my dreams, night and
Mockings like friends, pastimes hate I
And business accursed upon me glares;
The life of the sick is sorrow, guilt, and love.
Eye her then, vain in might, simple as heart.
Heaven props earth with columns; mountains raise
Distances, blue in hills, upward swell fields.
Man has ages for soil, mining himself
To paradise.　　The scene murmurs.　　Struggle with winds,
Hear depth dizzy the ear, a thunderbolt of whiteness.
Centuries of growth, darkness of capitals,
Pinnacles and trees shaggy and wild.
North to the drowned!　　and nations separate the world.
Shriek eagle in your torrent solitude.
Glens of secret, down into forest-tops,
Beneath a wide-spread earth; majesty and beauty
Fail.　　Foot mountains.　　Though rocky our ascent,
Face nature in harmony, lovely, and face it!　　wild.

Note: This is a poem of William Cullen Bryant's that is run backward ("What?" said Denise Levertov. "You mean 'Foul Water' instead of 'Waterfowl'?" "Exactly," I said.) The poem is "Monument Mountain," out of which I took key words and phrases and ran the film backward.

THE FLYING RED HORSE

On all the streetcorners the children are standing,
They ask What can it mean?
The grownups answer　　A flying red horse
Signifies gasoline.

The man at the Planetarium,
Pointing beyond the sky,
Is not going to say that Pegasus
Means poetry.

Some of our people feel like death,
And some feel rather worse.
His energy, in this night of lies,
Flies right against the curse.

What's *red?*   What is the *flying horse?*
They swear they do not know,
But just the same, and every night,
All the streetcorners glow.

Even the Pentagon, even the senators,
Even the President sitting on his arse—
Never mind—over all cities
The flying red horse.

III / The Outer Banks

THE OUTER BANKS

I

Horizon of islands shifting
Sea-light flame on my voice
                        burn in me
                                    Light
flows from the water from sands   islands of this horizon
The sea comes toward me across the sea.   The sand
moves over the sand in waves
between the guardians of this landscape
the great commemorative statue on one hand
        —the first flight of man, outside of dream,
                seen as stone wing and stainless steel—
and at the other hand
        banded black-and-white, climbing
the spiral lighthouse.

Note: This country, the Outer Banks of North Carolina, is a strong country of
    imagination: Raleigh's first settlements, in which Thomas Hariot the scientist
    served a year in the New World, were here; the Wright Brothers flew from
    here; Hart Crane's "Hatteras" is set among these sand-bars, these waters.
    Several journeys here, the last one for the sake of the traces of Thomas Hariot
    (toward a biography I was writing) led me to this poem. The *Tiger,* in the last
    part of the poem, is one of the ships sent out by Raleigh. The quotations are
    from Selma, Alabama, in 1965. The truncated wing is a monument to the
    Wright Brothers. The spiral lighthouse is Hatteras light.

II

Flood over ocean,
avalanche on the flat beach. Pouring.
Indians holding branches up, to
placate the tempest,
the one-legged twisting god that is
a standing wind.
Rays are branching from all things:
great serpent, great plume, constellation:
sands from which colors and light pass,
the lives of plants.   Animals.   Men.
A man and a woman reach for each other.

III

Wave of the sea.

IV

Sands have washed, sea has flown over us.
Between the two guardians, spiral, truncated wing,
history and these wild birds
Bird-voiced discoverers : Hariot,   Hart Crane,
the brothers who watched gulls.
"No bird soars in a calm,"   said Wilbur Wright.
Dragon of the winds forms over me.
Your dance, goddesses in your circle
sea-wreath, whirling of the event
behind me on land as deep in our own lives
we begin to know the movement to come.
Sunken, drowned spirals,
hurricane-dance.

V

Shifting of islands on this horizon.
The cycle of changes in the Book of Changes.
Two islands making an open female line.
That powerful long straight bar a male island.
The building of the surf
constructing immensities
between the pale flat Sound
and ocean ever
birds as before earthquake

winds fly from all origins
the length of this wave goes from the great wing
down coast, the barrier beach in all its miles
road of the sun and the moon to
a spiral lighthouse
to the depth turbulence
lifts up its wave like cities
the ocean in the air
spills down the world.

VI

A man is walking toward me across the water.
From far out, the flat waters of the Sound,
he walks pulling his small boat

In the shoal water.
A man who is white and has been fishing.
Walks steadily upon the light of day
Coming closer to me where I stand
looking into the sun and the blaze inner water.
Clear factual surface over which he pulls
a boat over a closing quarter-mile.

VII

Speak to it, says the light.
Speak to it music,
voices of the sea and human throats.
Origins of spirals,
the ballad and original sweet grape
dark on the vines near Hatteras,
tendrils of those vines, whose spiral tower
now rears its light, accompanying
all my voices.

VIII

He walks toward me.   A black man in the sun.
He now is a black man speaking to my heart
crisis of darkness in this century
of moments of this speech.

The boat is slowly nearer drawn, this man.

The zigzag power coming straight, in stones,
    in arcs, metal, crystal, the spiral

in sacred wet
                schematic elements of
cities, music, arrangement
spin these stones of home
                      under the sea
return to the stations of the stars
and the sea, speaking across its lives.

IX

A man who is bones is close to me
drawing a boat of bones
the sun behind him
is another color of fire,
the sea behind me
rears its flame.

A man whose body flames and tapers in flame
twisted tines of remembrance that dissolve
a pitchfork of the land worn thin
flame up and dissolve again
                      draw   small   boat

Nets of the stars at sunset over us.
This draws me home to the home of the wild birds
long-throated birds of this passage.
This is the edge of experience, *grenzen der seele*
where those on the verge of human understanding
the borderline people stand on the shifting islands
among the drowned stars and the tempest.
"Everyman's mind, like the dumbest,
claws at his own furthest limits of knowing the world,"
a man in a locked room said.

Open to the sky
I stand before this boat that looks at me.
The man's flames are arms and legs.
Body, eye, head, stars, sands look at me.

I walk out into the shoal water
and throw my leg over the wall of the boat.

X

At one shock, speechlessness.
I am in the bow, on the short thwart.

He is standing before me amidships, rowing forward
like my old northern sea-captain in his dory.
All things have spun.
The words gone,
I facing sternwards, looking at the gate
between the barrier islands.   As he rows.
Sand islands shifting and the last of land
a pale and open line   horizon
sea.

With whose face did he look at me?
What did I say?   or did I say?
in speechlessness
move to the change.
These strokes provide the music,
and the accused boy on land today saying
What did I say?   or did I say?
The dream on land last night built this the boat of death
but in the suffering of the light
moving across the sea
do we in our moving
move toward life or death

XI

Hurricane, skullface, the sky's size
winds streaming through his teeth
doing the madman's twist

and not a beach not flooded

nevertheless, here
stability of light
my other silence
and at my left hand and at my right hand
no longer wing and lighthouse
no longer the guardians.
They are in me, in my speechless
life of barrier beach.
As it lies open
to the night, out there.

Now seeing my death before me
starting again, among the drowned men,
desperate men, unprotected discoverers,

472

and the man before me
here.
Stroke by stroke drawing us.
Out there? Father of rhythms,
deep wave, mother.
There is no *out there.*
All is open.
Open water. Open I.

XII

The wreck of the *Tiger,* the early pirate, the blood-clam's
      ark, the tern's acute eye, all buried mathematical
            instruments, castaways, pelicans, drowned five-
                 strand pearl necklaces, hopes of livelihood,
                    hopes of grace,
walls of houses, sepia sea-fences, the writhen octopus and those
      tall masts and sails,
marked hulls of ships and last month's plane, dipping his salute
      to the stone wing of dream,
turbulence, Diamond Shoals, the dark young living people:
"Sing one more song and you are under arrest."
"Sing another song."
Women, ships, lost voices.
Whatever has dissolved into our waves.
I a lost voice
moving, calling you
on the edge of the moment that is now the center.
From the open sea.

IV / Lives

AKIBA

The Way Out

The night is covered with signs. The body and face of man,
with signs, and his journeys.   Where the rock is split

Note: These two "Lives" are part of a sequence. Akiba is the Jewish shepherd-
    scholar of the first and second century, identified with the Song of Songs and

and speaks to the water;   the flame speaks to the cloud;
the red splatter, abstraction, on the door
speaks to the angel and the constellations.
The grains of sand on the sea-floor speak at last to the noon.
And the loud hammering of the land behind
speaks ringing up the bones of our thighs, the hoofs,
we hear the hoofs over the seethe of the sea.

All night down the centuries, have heard, music of passage.

Music of one child carried into the desert;
firstborn forbidden by law of the pyramid.
Drawn through the water with the water-drawn people
led by the water-drawn man to the smoke mountain.
The voice of the world speaking, the world covered by signs,
the burning, the loving, the speaking, the opening.
Strong throat of sound from the smoking mountain.
Still flame, the spoken singing of a young child.
The meaning beginning to move, which is the song.

Music of those who have walked out of slavery.

Into that journey where all things speak to all things
refusing to accept the curse, and taking
for signs the signs of all things, the world, the body
which is part of the soul, and speaks to the world,
all creation being created in one image, creation.
This is not the past walking into the future,
the walk is painful, into the present, the dance
not visible as dance until much later.
These dancers are discoverers of God.

We knew we had all crossed over when we heard the song.

Out of a life of building lack on lack:
the slaves refusing slavery, escaping into faith:
an army who came to the ocean: the walkers
who walked through the opposites, from I to opened Thou,

---

with the insurrection against Hadrian's Rome, led in A.D. 132 by Bar Cochba
(Son of the Star). After this lightning war, Jerusalem captured, the Romans
driven out of the south, Rome increased its military machine; by 135, the last
defenses fell, Bar Cochba was killed, Akiba was tortured to death at the
command of his friend, the Roman Rufus, and a harrow was drawn over the
ground where Jerusalem had stood, leaving only a corner of wall. The story
in my mother's family is that we are descended from Akiba—unverifiable, but
a great gift to a child.

city and cleave of the sea. Those at flaming Nauvoo,
the ice on the great river: the escaping Negroes,
swamp and wild city: the shivering children of Paris
and the glass black hearses; those on the Long March:
all those who together are the frontier, forehead of man.

Where the wilderness enters, the world, the song of the world.

Akiba rescued, secretly, in the clothes of death
by his disciples carried from Jerusalem
in blackness journeying to find his journey
to whatever he was loving with his life.
The wilderness journey through which we move
under the whirlwind truth into the new,
the only accurate. A cluster of lights at night:
faces before the pillar of fire. A child watching
while the sea breaks open. This night. The way in.

Barbarian music, a new song.

Acknowledging opened water, possibility:
open like a woman to this meaning.
In a time of building statues of the stars,
valuing certain partial ferocious skills
while past us the chill and immense wilderness
spreads its one-color wings until we know
rock, water, flame, cloud, or the floor of the sea,
the world is a sign, a way of speaking. To find.
What shall we find? Energies, rhythms, journey.

Ways to discover. The song of the way in.

  for The Song of Songs

However the voices rise
They are the shepherd, the king,
The woman; dreams,
Holy desire.

Whether the voices
Be many the dance around
Or body led by one body
Whose bed is green,

I defend the desire
Lightning and poetry

Alone in the dark city
Or breast to breast.

Champion of light I am
The wounded holy light,
The woman in her dreams
And the man answering.

You who answer their dreams
Are the ruler of wine
Emperor of clouds
And the riches of men.

This song
Is the creation
The day of this song
The day of the birth of the world.

Whether a thousand years
Forget this woman, this king,
Whether two thousand years
Forget the shepherd of dreams.

If none remember
Who is lover, who the beloved,
Whether the poet be
Woman or man,

The desire will make
A way through the wilderness
The leopard mountains
And the lips of the sleepers.

Holy way of desire,
King, lion, the mouth of the poet,
The woman who dreams
And the answerer of dreams.

In these delights
Is eternity of seed,
The verge of life,
Body of dreaming.

The Bonds

In the wine country, poverty, they drink no wine—
In the endless night of love he lies, apart from love—
In the landscape of the Word he stares, he has no word.

He hates and hungers for his immense need.

He is young. This is a shepherd who rages at learning,
Having no words. Looks past green grass and sees a woman.
She, Rachel, who is come to recognize.
In the huge wordless shepherd she finds Akiba.

To find the burning Word. To learn to speak.

The body of Rachel says, the marriage says,
The eyes of Rachel say, and water upon rock
Cutting its groove all year says All things learn.
Me learns with his new son whose eyes are wine.

To sing continually, to find the word.

He comes to teaching, greater than the deed
Because it begets the deed, he comes to the stone
Of long ordeal, and suddenly knows the brook
Offering water, the citron fragrance, the light of candles.

All given, and always the giver loses nothing.

In giving, praising, we move beneath clouds of honor,
In giving, in praise, we take gifts that are given,
The spark from one to the other leaping, a bond
Of light, and we come to recognize the rock;

We are the rock acknowledging water, and water
Fire, and woman man, all brought through wilderness;
And Rachel finding in the wordless shepherd
Akiba who can now come to his power and speak:
The need to give having found the need to become:

More than the calf wants to suck, the cow wants to give such.

Akiba Martyr

When his death confronted him, it had the face of his friend
Rufus the Roman general with his claws of pain,
His executioner. This was an old man under iron rakes
Tearing through to the bone. He made no cry.

After the failure of all missions. At ninety, going
To Hadrian in Egypt, the silver-helmed,
Named for a sea. To intercede. Do not build in the rebuilt
  Temple.

Your statue, do not make it a shrine to you.
Antinous smiling. Interpreters. This is an old man, pleading.
Incense of fans. The emperor does not understand.

He accepts his harvest, failures. He accepts faithlessness,
Madness of friends, a failed life; and now the face of storm.

Does the old man during uprising speak for compromise?
In all but the last things. Not in the study itself.
For this religion is a system of knowledge;
Points may be one by one abandoned, but not the study.
Does he preach passion and non-violence?
Yes, and trees, crops, children honestly taught. He says:
Prepare yourselves for suffering.

Now the rule closes in, the last things are forbidden.
There is no real survival without these.
Now it is time for prison and the unknown.
The old man flowers into spiritual fire.

Streaking of agony across the sky.
Torn black. Red racing on blackness. Dawn.
Rufus looks at him over the rakes of death
Asking, "What is it?
Have you magic powers? Or do you feel no pain?"

The old man answers, "No. But there is a commandment
    saying
Thou shalt love the Lord thy God with all thy heart, with all
    thy soul and with all thy might.
I knew that I loved him with all my heart and might.
Now I know that I love him with all my life."

The look of delight of the martyr
Among the colors of pain, at last knowing his own response
Total and unified.
To love God with all the heart, all passion,
Every desire called evil, turned toward unity,
All the opposites, all in the dialogue.
All the dark and light of the heart, of life made whole.

Surpassing the known life, day and ideas.
My hope, my life, my burst of consciousness:
To confirm my life in the time of confrontation.

The old man saying Shema.
The death of Akiba.

478

The Witness

Who is the witness? What voice moves across time,
Speaks for the life and death as witness voice?
Moving tonight on this city, this river, my winter street?

He saw it, the one witness. Tonight the life as legend
Goes building a meeting for me in the veins of night
Adding its scenes and its songs. Here is the man transformed,

The tall shepherd, the law, the false messiah, all;
You who come after me far from tonight finding
These lives that ask you always Who is the witness—

Take from us acts of encounter we at night
Wake to attempt, as signs, seeds of beginning,
Given from darkness and remembering darkness,

Take from our light given to you our meetings.
Time tells us men and women, tells us You
The witness, your moment covered with signs, your self.

Tells us this moment, saying You are the meeting.
You are made of signs, your eyes and your song.
Your dance the dance, the walk into the present.

All this we are and accept, being made of signs, speaking
To you, in time not yet born.
                                    The witness is myself.
                                                            And you,
The signs, the journeys of the night, survive.

KÄTHE KOLLWITZ

I

Held between wars
my lifetime
                    among wars, the big hands of the world of death
my lifetime
listens to yours.

The faces of the sufferers
in the street, in dailiness,
their lives showing
through their bodies

a look as of music
the revolutionary look
that says   I am in the world
to change the world
my lifetime
is to love to endure to suffer the music
to set its portrait
up as a sheet of the world
the most moving the most alive
Easter and bone
and Faust walking among the flowers of the world
and the child alive within the living woman, music of man,
and death holding my lifetime between great hands
the hands of enduring life
that suffers the gifts and madness of full life, on earth, in our
    time,
and through my life, through my eyes, through my arms and
    hands
may give the face of this music in portrait waiting for
the unknown person
held in the two hands, you.

II

Woman as gates, saying :
"The process is after all like music,
like the development of a piece of music.
The fugues come back and

                            again and again
interweave.
A theme may seem to have been put aside,
but it keeps returning—
the same thing modulated,
somewhat changed in form.
Usually richer.
And it is very good that this is so."

A woman pouring her opposites.
"After all there are happy things in life too.
Why do you show only the dark side?"
"I could not answer this. But I know—
in the beginning my impulse to know
the working life

                    had little to do with

pity or sympathy.
                    I simply felt
that the life of the workers was beautiful."

She said, "I am groping in the dark."

She said, "When the door opens, of sensuality,
then you will understand it too. The struggle begins.
Never again to be free of it,
often you will feel it to be your enemy.
Sometimes
you will almost suffocate,
such joy it brings."

Saying of her husband : "My wish
is to die after Karl.
I know no person who can love as he can,
with his whole soul.
Often this love has oppressed me;
I wanted to be free.
But often too it has made me
so terribly happy."

She said : "We rowed over to Carrara at dawn,
climbed up to the marble quarries
and rowed back at night. The drops of water
fell like glittering stars
from our oars."

She said: "As a matter of fact,
I believe
                    that bisexuality
is almost   a necessary factor
in artistic production; at any rate,
the tinge of masculinity within me
helped me
                    in my work."

She said : "The only technique I can still manage.
It's hardly a technique at all, lithography.
In it
          only the essentials count."

A tight-lipped man in a restaurant last night saying to me :
"Kollwitz?   She's too black-and-white."

Held among wars, watching
  all of them
  all these people
  weavers,
  Carmagnole

Looking at
  all of them
  death, the children
  patients in waiting-rooms
  famine
  the street
  the corpse with the baby
  floating, on the dark river

A woman seeing
  the violent, inexorable
  movement of nakedness
  and the confession of No
  the confession of great weakness, war,
  all streaming to one son killed, Peter;
  even the son left living; repeated,
  the father, the mother; the grandson
  another Peter killed in another war; firestorm;
  dark, light, as two hands,
  this pole and that pole as the gates.

What would happen if one woman told the truth about her life?
  The world would split open

IV | Song : The Calling-Up

Rumor, stir of ripeness
rising within this girl
sensual blossoming
of meaning, its light and form.

The birth-cry summoning
out of the male, the father
from the warm woman
a mother in response.

The word of death
calls up the fight with stone

wrestle with grief with time
from the material make
an art harder than bronze.

V / Self-Portrait

Mouth looking directly at you
eyes in their inwardness looking
directly at you
half light   half darkness
woman, strong, German, young artist
flows into
wide sensual mouth meditating
looking right at you
eyes shadowed with brave hand
looking deep at you
flows into
wounded brave mouth
grieving and hooded eyes
alive, German, in her first War
flows into
strength of the worn face
a skein of lines
broods, flows into
mothers among the war graves
bent over death
facing the father
stubborn upon the field
flows into
the marks of her knowing—
Nie Wieder Krieg
repeated in the eyes
flows into
"Seedcorn must not be ground"
and the grooved cheek
lips drawn fine
the down-drawn grief
face of our age
flows into
Pieta, mother and
between her knees
life as her son in death
pouring from the sky of

one more war
flows into
face almost obliterated
hand over the mouth forever
hand over one eye now
the other great eye
closed

V / The Speed of Darkness

THE SPEED OF DARKNESS

I

Whoever despises the clitoris despises the penis
Whoever despises the penis despises the cunt
Whoever despises the cunt despises the life of the child.

Resurrection music,   silence,   and surf.

II

No longer speaking
Listening with the whole body
And with every drop of blood
Overtaken by silence

But this same silence is become speech
With the speed of darkness.

III

Stillness during war, the lake.
The unmoving spruces.
Glints over the water.
Faces, voices.   You are far away.
A tree that trembles.

I am the tree that trembles and trembles.

IV

After the lifting of the mist
after the lift of the heavy rains
the sky stands clear
and the cries of the city risen in day
I remember the buildings are space
walled, to let space be used for living
I mind this room is space
this drinking glass is space
whose boundary of glass
lets me give you drink and space to drink
your hand, my hand being space
containing skies and constellations
your face
carries the reaches of air
I know I am space
my words are air.

V

Between   between
the man : act   exact
woman : in curve   senses in their maze
frail orbits, green tries,   games of stars
shape of the body speaking its evidence

VI

I look across at the real
vulnerable   involved   naked
devoted to the present of all I care for
the world of its history leading to this moment.

VII

Life the announcer.
I assure you
there are many ways to have a child.
I bastard mother
promise you
there are many ways to be born.
They all come forth
in their own grace.

VIII

Ends of the earth join tonight
with blazing stars upon their meeting.

These sons,   these sons
fall burning into Asia.

IX

Time comes into it.
Say it.   Say it.

The universe is made of stories,
not of atoms.

X

Lying
blazing beside me
you rear beautifully and up—
your thinking face—
erotic body reaching
in all its colors and lights—
your erotic face
colored and lit—
not colored body-and-face
but now entire,
colors   lights   the world thinking and reaching.

XI

The river flows past the city.

Water goes down to tomorrow
making its children   I hear their unborn voices
I am working out the vocabulary of my silence.

XII

Big-boned man young and of my dream
Struggles to get the live bird out of his throat.
I am he am I?   Dreaming?
I am the bird am I?   I am the throat?

A bird with a curved beak.
It could slit anything, the throat-bird.

Drawn up slowly.   The curved blades, not large.
Bird emerges   wet   being born
Begins to sing.

XIII

My night awake
staring at the broad rough jewel
the copper roof across the way
thinking of the poet
yet unborn in this dark
who will be the throat of these hours.
No.   Of those hours.
Who will speak these days,
if not I,
if not you?

BREAKING OPEN

I / Searching / Not Searching

WAKING THIS MORNING

Waking this morning,
a violent woman in the violent day
Laughing.
                   Past the line of memory
along the long body of your life
in which move childhood, youth, your lifetime of touch,
eyes, lips, chest, belly, sex, legs, to the waves of the sheet.
I look past the little plant
on the city windowsill
to the tall towers bookshaped, crushed together in greed,
the river flashing flowing corroded,
the intricate harbor and the sea, the wars, the moon, the
    planets, all who people space
in the sun visible invisible.
African violets in the light
breathing, in a breathing universe.   I want strong peace, and
    delight,
the wild good.
I want to make my touch poems:
to find my morning, to find you entire
alive moving among the anti-touch people.

               I say across the waves of the air to you:
today once more
I will try to be non-violent
one more day
this morning, waking the world away
in the violent day.

DESPISALS

In the human cities, never again to
despise the backside of the city, the ghetto,
or build it again as we build the despised
backsides of houses.   Look at your own building.
You are the city.

Among our secrecies, not to despise our Jews
(that is, ourselves) or our darkness, our blacks,
or in our sexuality   wherever it takes us
and we now know we are productive
too productive, too reproductive
for our present invention — never to despise
the homosexual who goes building another

with touch   with touch   (not to despise any touch)
each like himself, like herself each.
You are this.

                                   In the body's ghetto
never to go despising the asshole
nor the useful shit that is our clean clue
to what we need.   Never to despise
the clitoris in her least speech.

Never to despise in myself what I have been taught
to despise.   Nor to despise the other.
Not to despise the *it*.   To make this relation
with the it : to know that I am it.

WHAT DO WE SEE?

When they're decent about women, they're frightful about
   children,
When they're decent about children, they're rotten about
   artists,
When they're decent about artists, they're vicious about
   whores,
          What do we see?   What do we not see?

When they're kind to whores, they're death on communists,
When they respect communists, they're foul to bastards,
When they're human to bastards, they mock at hysterectomy—
          What do we see?   What do we not see?

When they're decent about surgery, they bomb the Vietnamese,
When they're decent to Vietnamese, they're frightful to police,
When they're human to police, they rough up lesbians,
          What do we see?   What do we not see?

When they're decent to old women, they kick homosexuals,
When they're good to homosexuals, they can't stand drug
   people,

492

When they're calm about drug people, they hate all Germans,
 What do we see?   What do we not see?

Cadenza for the reader

When they're decent to Jews, they dread the blacks,
When they know blacks, there's always something   :   roaches
And the future and children and all potential.   Can't stand
 themselves
  Will we never see?   Will we ever know?

LOOKING AT EACH OTHER

Yes, we were looking at each other
Yes, we knew each other very well
Yes, we had made love with each other many times
Yes, we had heard music together
Yes, we had gone to the sea together
Yes, we had cooked and eaten together
Yes, we had laughed often day and night
Yes, we fought violence and knew violence
Yes, we hated the inner and outer oppression
Yes, that day we were looking at each other
Yes, we saw the sunlight pouring down
Yes, the corner of the table was between us
Yes, bread and flowers were on the table
Yes, our eyes saw each other's eyes
Yes, our mouths saw each other's mouth
Yes, our breasts saw each other's breasts
Yes, our bodies entire saw each other
Yes, it was beginning in each
Yes, it threw waves across our lives
Yes, the pulses were becoming very strong
Yes, the beating became very delicate
Yes, the calling   the arousal
Yes, the arriving   the coming
Yes, there it was for both entire
Yes, we were looking at each other

DESDICHADA

I

For that you never acknowledged me, I acknowledge
the spring's yellow detail, the every drop of rain,
the anonymous unacknowledged men and women.

The shine as it glitters in our child's wild eyes,
one o'clock at night.   This river, this city,
the years of the shadow on the delicate skin
of my hand, moving in time.
Disinherited, annulled, finally disacknowledged
and all of my own asking.   I keep that wild dimension
of life and making and the spasm
upon my mouth as I say this word of acknowledge
to you forever.   *Ewig.*   Two o'clock at night.

II

While this my day and my people are a country not yet born
it has become an earth I can
acknowledge.   I must.   I know what the
disacknowledgment does.   Then I do take you,
but far under consciousness, knowing
that under under flows a river wanting
the other : to go open-handed in Asia,
to cleanse the tributaries and the air, to make for making,
to stop selling death and its trash, pour plastic down men's
    throats,
to let this child find, to let men and women find,
knowing the seeds in us all.   They do say Find.
I cannot acknowledge it entire.   But I will.
A beginning, this moment, perhaps, and you.

III

Death flowing down past me, past me, death
marvelous, filthy, gold,
in my spine in my sex upon my broken mouth
and the whole beautiful mouth of the child;
shedding power over me
death
if I acknowledge him.
Leading me
in my own body
at last in the dance.

VOICES

Voices of all our voices, running past an imagined race.
Pouring out of morning light, the pouring mists of Mil
    Cumbres.

Out of the poured cities of our world.
Out of the black voice of one child
Who sleeps in our poverty and is dreaming.

The child perceives and the cycles are fulfilled.

Cities being poured; and war-fire over the poor.
Mist over the peak.
One child in his voices, many voices.
The suffering runs past the end of the racing
Making us run the next race. The child sleeps.
Lovers, makers, this child, enter into our voices.
Speak to the child.   Now something else is waking:
The look of the lover, the rebel and learning look,
The look of the runner just beyond the tape, go into
The child's look at the world.   In all its voices.

August 26, 1968—by invitation for the Olympics. For Otto Boch, who came to
Barcelona July 1936 to run in the Anti-fascist Olympics.

WAITING FOR ICARUS

He said he would be back and we'd drink wine together
He said that everything would be better than before
He said we were on the edge of a new relation
He said he would never again cringe before his father
He said that he was going to invent full-time
He said he loved me that going into me
He said was going into the world and the sky
He said all the buckles were very firm
He said the wax was the best wax
He said Wait for me here on the beach
He said Just don't cry

I remember the gulls and the waves
I remember the islands going dark on the sea
I remember the girls laughing
I remember they said he only wanted to get away from me
I remember mother saying : Inventors are like poets,
                                                    a trashy lot
I remember she told me those who try out inventions are
    worse
I remember she added : Women who love such are the worst
    of all

495

I have been waiting all day, or perhaps longer.
I would have liked to try those wings myself.
It would have been better than this.

IN HER BURNING

The randy old
woman said
Tickle me up
I'll be
dead very soon—
Nothing will
touch me then
but the clouds
of the sky
and the bone-
white light
of the moon
Touch me
before I go
down
among the bones
My dear one
alone
to the night   —
I said
I know I know
But all I know
tonight
Is that the sun
and the moon
they burn
with the one
one light.

In her burning
signing
what does the
white moon say?
The moon says
The sun
is shining.

THE QUESTION

Mother and listener she is, but she does not listen.
I look at her profile as I ask, the sweet blue-grey of eye
going obdurate to my youth as I ask the first grown sexual
question.   She cannot reply.
And from then on even past her death, I cannot fully
have language with my mother, not as daughter
and mother through all the maze and silences
of all the turnings.
Until my own child grows and asks, and until
I discover what appalled my mother long before, discover
who never delivered her, until their double weakness and
    strength in myself
rouse and deliver me from that refusal.
I threw myself down on the pine-needle evening.
Although that old ancient poem never did come to me,
not from you, mother,
although in answer you did only panic, you did only grieve,
and I went silent alone, my cheek to the red pine-needle
earth, and although it has taken me all these years
and sunsets to come to you, past the dying, I know,
I come with my word alive.

RONDEL

Now that I am fifty-six
Come and celebrate with me   —

What happens to song and sex
Now that I am fifty-six?

They dance, but differently,
Death and distance in the mix;
Now that I'm fifty-six
Come and celebrate with me.

MORE CLUES

Mother, because you never spoke to me
I go my life, do I, searching in women's faces
the lost word, a word in the shape of a breast?

Father, because both of you never touched me
do I search for men building space on space?
There was no touch, both my hands bandaged close.

I come from that, but I come far, to touch to word.
Can they reach me now, or inside out in a universe
of touch, of speech is it? somewhere in me, clues?

MYTH

Long afterward, Oedipus, old and blinded, walked the
roads.   He smelled a familiar smell.   It was
the Sphinx.   Oedipus said, "I want to ask one question.
Why didn't I recognize my mother?"   "You gave the
wrong answer," said the Sphinx.   "But that was what
made everything possible," said Oedipus.   "No," she said.
"When I asked, What walks on four legs in the morning,
two at noon, and three in the evening, you answered,
Man.   You didn't say anything about woman."
"When you say Man," said Oedipus, "you include women
too. Everyone knows that."   She said, "That's what
you think."

SEARCHING / NOT SEARCHING

> *Responsibility is to*
> *use the power to respond.*
> *—after* ROBERT DUNCAN

I

What kind of woman goes searching and searching?
Among the furrows of dark April, along the sea-beach,
in the faces of children, in what they could not tell;
in the pages of centuries —
for what man? for what magic?

In corridors under the earth, in castles of the North,
among the blackened miners, among the old
I have gone searching.
The island-woman told me, against the glitter of sun
on the stalks and leaves of a London hospital.
I searched for that Elizabethan man,

the lost discoverer, the servant of time;
and that man forgotten for belief, in Spain,
and among the faces of students, at Coventry,
finding and finding in glimpses. And at home.
Among the dead I too have gone searching,
a blue light in the brain.
Suddenly I come to these living eyes,
I a live woman look up at you this day
I see all the colors in your look.

II / Miriam : The Red Sea

High above shores and times,
I on the shore
forever and ever.
Moses my brother
has crossed over
to milk, honey,
that holy land.
Building Jerusalem.
I sing forever
on the seashore.
I do remember
horseman and horses,
waves of passage
poured into war,
all poured into journey.
My unseen brothers
have gone over;
chariots
deep seas under.
I alone stand here
ankle-deep
and I sing, I sing,
until the lands
sing to each other.

III / For Dolci

Angel of declaring, you opened before us walls,
the lives of children, water as power.
To control the water is to control our days,
to build a dam is to face the enemy.

We will form a new person who will step forward,
he it is, she it is, assumes full life,
fully responsible. We will bring all the children,
they will decide together.

We will ask these children : what is before you?
They will say what they see.
They will say what they don't see.
Once again we breathe in discovery.

A man, a woman,
will discover
we are each other's sources.

IV / Concrete

They are pouring the city:
they tear down the towers,
grind their lives,
laughing tainted, the river
flows down to tomorrow.

They are setting the forms,
pouring the new buildings.
Our days pour down.
I am pouring my poems.

V / Brecht's Galileo

Brecht saying : Galileo talking astronomy
Stripped to the torso, the intellectual life
Pouring from this gross man in his nakedness.

Galileo, his physical contentment
Is having his back rubbed by his student; the boy mauls;
The man sighs and transforms it; intellectual product!

Galileo spins a toy of the earth around
The spinning sun; he looks at the student boy.
Learning is teaching, teaching is learning.
Galileo
Demonstrates how horrible is betrayal,
Particularly on the shore of a new era.

VI | *Reading the* Kieu

There was always a murder within another murder.
Red leaves and rosy threads bind them together.
The hero of Vietnam's epic is a woman
and she has sold herself to save her father.

Odor of massacres spread on the sky.
Loneliness, the windy, dusty world.
The roads crowded with armor and betrayal.
Mirror of the sun and moon, this land,

in which being handed to soldiers is the journey.
Shame, disgrace, change of seas into burnt fields.
Banners, loudspeakers, violation of each day,
everything being unjust. But she does save him,
and we find everything in another way.

VII | *The Floor of Ocean*

Sistine Chapel

Climbing the air, prophet beyond prophet
leaning upon creation backward to the first
creation the great spark of night
breathing sun energy   a gap between finger-tips
across all of space or nothing, infinity.

But beyond this, with this, these
arms raising reaching wavering
as from the floor of ocean
wavering showing swaying like sea-plants
pointing straight up closing the gap between
continual creation and the daily touch.

VIII | *H. F. D.*

From you I learned the dark potential
theatres of the acts of man holding
on a rehearsal stage   people and lights.
You in your red hair ran down the darkened
aisle, making documents and poems
in their people form the play.

Hallie it was from you I learned this:
you told the company in dress-rehearsal

in that ultimate equipped building   what they lacked:
among the lighting, the sight-lines, the acoustics,
the perfect revolving stage, they lacked only one thing
the most important thing.   It would come tonight:
The audience   the response

Hallie I learned from you this summer, this
Hallie I saw you lying all gone to bone
tremor of bone   I stroked the head all sculpture
I held the hands of birds   I spoke to the sealed eyes
the soft live red mouth of a red-headed woman.
I knew Hallie then I could move without answer,
like the veterans for peace, hurling back their medals
and not expecting an answer from the grass.
You taught me this in your dying, for poems and theatre
and love and peace-making that living and my love
are where response and no-response
meet at last, Hallie, in infinity.

IX / The Artist as Social Critic

They have asked me to speak in public
and set me a subject.

I hate anything that begins : the artist as . . .
and as for "social critic"
at the last quarter of the twentieth century
I know what that is:

late at night, among radio music
the voice of my son speaking half-world away
coming clear on the radio into my room
out of blazing Belfast.

Long enough for me to walk around
in that strong voice.

X / The President and the Laser Bomb

He speaks in a big voice through all the air
saying : we have made strength,
we have made a beginning,
we will have lasting peace.

Something shouts on the river.

All night long the acts speak:
the new laser bomb falls impeccably
along the beam of a strict light
finding inevitably a narrow footbridge
in Asia.

XI / Not Searching

What did I miss as I went searching?
What did I not see?
I renounce all this regret.
Now I will make another try.

One step and I am free.

When it happens to us again and again,
sometimes we know it for we are prepared
but to discover, to live at the edge of things,
to fall out of routine into invention
and recognize at the other edge of ocean
a new kind of man   a new kind of woman
walking toward me into the little surf.
This is the next me   and the next child
daybreak in continual creation.
Dayray we see, we say,
we sing what we don't see.

Picasso saying : I don't search, I find!

And in us our need, the traces of the future,
the egg and its becoming.

I come to you searching and searching.

XII / The Question

After this crisis,
nothing being conquered,
the theme is set:

to move with the forces,

how to go on
from the moment that
changed our life,

the moment of revelation,

proceeding from the crisis,
from the dream,
and not from the moment
of sleep before it?

XIII

Searching/not searching.   To make closeness.
For if this communication was the truth,
then it was this communiation itself
which was the value to be supported.

And for this communication to endure,
men and women must move freely.   And to make
this communication renew itself always
we must renew justice.
And to make this communication
lasting, we must live to eliminate
violence and the lie.

Yes, we set the communication
we have achieved
against the world of murder.

Searching/not searching.

after Camus, 1946

XIV

What did I see? What did I not see?
The river flowing past my window.
The night-lit city. My white pointed light.
Pieces of a world away
within my room.

Unseen and seen, the bodies within my life.
Voices under the leaves of Asia,
and America, in sex, in possibility.
We are trying to make, to let our closeness be made,
not torn apart tonight by our dead skills.

The shadow of my hand.
The shadow of the pen.
Morning of the day we reach or do not reach.
In our bodies, we find each other.
On our mouths, inner greet,
in our eyes.

A SIMPLE EXPERIMENT

When a magnet is
struck by a hammer
the magnetism spills out of
the iron.

The molecules
are jarred,
they are a mob going
in all directions

The magnet is
shockéd back
it is no magnet but
simple iron.

There is no more
of its former
kind of accord
or force.

But if you take
another magnet
and stroke the iron
with this,

it can be
remagnetized
if you stroke it
and stroke it,

stroke it
stroke it,
the molecules
can be given
their tending grace

by a strong magnet
stroking stroking
always in the same direction,
of course.

ALONG HISTORY

Along history, forever
    some woman dancing,
    making shapes on the air;
    forever a man
    riding a good horse,
    sitting the dark horse well,
    his penis erect with
        fantasy

BOYS OF THESE MEN FULL SPEED

for Jane Cooper

Boys of these men
    full speed across free,
    my father's boyhood eyes.
    Sail-skating with friends
    bright on Wisconsin ice
    those years away.

Sails strung across their backs
    boys racing toward
    fierce bitter middle-age
    in the great glitter of
    corrupted cities.
    Father, your dark mouth
    speaking its rancor.

Alive not yet, the girl
    I would become
    stares at that ice
    stippled with skaters,
    a story you tell.

Boys of those men
    call across winter
    where I stand and shake,
    woman of that girl.

ALL THE LITTLE ANIMALS

"You are not pregnant," said the man
with the probe and the white white coat;
"Yes she is," said all the little animals.

Then the great gynecologist examined. "You are not now, and
   I doubt that you ever have been," he said with authority.
"Test me again." He looked at his nurse and shrugged.
"Yes she is," said all the little animals, and laid down their
   lives for my son and me.

Twenty-one years later, my son a grown man and far away at
   the other ocean,
I hear them : "Yes you are," say all the little animals.
I see them, they move in great jumping procession through my
   waking hours,
those frogs and rabbits look at me with their round eyes, they
   kick powerfully with their strong hind legs,
they lay down their lives in silence,
all the rabbits saying Yes, all the frogs saying Yes,
in the face of all men and all institutions,
all the doctors, all the parents, all the worldly friends, all the
   psychiatrists, all the abortionists, alll the lawyers.
The little animals whom I bless and praise and thank forever,
they are part of my living,
go leap through my waking and my sleep, go leap through my
   life and my birth-giving and my death,
go leap through my dreams,
and my son's life
and whatever streams from him.

TWO YEARS

Two years of my sister's bitter illness;
the wind whips the river of her last spring.
I have burned the beans again.

IRIS

I

Middle of May, when the iris blows,
blue below blue, the bearded patriarch-
face on the green flute body of a boy
Poseidon   torso of Eros
blue
sky below sea

day over daybreak violet behind twilight
the May iris
midnight on midday

II

Something is over and under this deep blue.
Over and under this movement, *etwas*
before and after, *alguna cosa*
blue before blue
is it
       perhaps
              death?
That may be the wrong word.

The iris stands in the light.

III

Death is here, death is guarded by swords.
No. By shapes of swords
flicker of green leaves
under all the speaking and crying
shadowing the words the eyes   here they all die
racing withering   blue evening
my sister death the iris
stands clear in light.

IV

In the water-cave
ferocious needles of teeth
the green morays
in blue water   rays
a maleficence   ribbon of green   the flat look of
eyes staring   fatal mouth staring
the rippling potent force
curving into any hole
death finding his way.

V

Depth of petals, May iris
transparent   infinitely deep they are
petal-thin   with light behind them

and you, death,
and you
behind them
blue under blue.
What I cannot say
in adequate music
something being born
transparency   blue of
light standing on light
this stalk of
(among mortal petals-and-leaves)
light

II / Orange and Grape

BALLAD OF ORANGE AND GRAPE

After you finish your work
after you do your day
after you're read your reading
after you've written your say   —
you go down the street to the hot dog stand,
one block down and across the way.
On a blistering afternoon in East Harlem in the twentieth
    century.

Most of the windows are boarded up,
the rats run out of a sack   —
sticking out of the crummy garage
one shiny long Cadillac;
at the glass door of the drug-addiction center,
a man who'd like to break your back.
But here's a brown woman with a little girl dressed in rose and
    pink, too.

Frankfurters frankfurters sizzle on the steel
where the hot-dog-man leans   —
nothing else on the counter

but the usual two machines,
the grape one, empty, and the orange one, empty,
I face him in between.
A black boy comes along, looks at the hot dogs, goes on
  walking.

I watch the man as he stands and pours
in the familiar shape
bright purple in the one marked ORANGE
orange in the one marked GRAPE,
the grape drink in the machine marked ORANGE
and orange drink in the GRAPE.
Just the one word large and clear, unmistakable, on each
  machine.

I ask him : How can we go on reading
and make sense out of what we read? —
How can they write and believe what they're writing,
the young ones across the street,
while you go on pouring grape into ORANGE
and orange into the one marked GRAPE —?
(How are we going to believe what we read and we write and
  we hear and we say and we do?)

He looks at the two machines and he smiles
and he shrugs and smiles and pours again.
It could be violence and nonviolence
it could be white and black   women and men
it could be war and peace or any
binary system, love and hate, enemy, friend.
Yes and no, be and not-be, what we do and what we don't do.

On a corner in East Harlem
garbage, reading, a deep smile, rape,
forgetfulness, a hot street of murder,
misery, withered hope,
a man keeps pouring grape into ORANGE
and orange into the one marked GRAPE,
pouring orange into GRAPE and grape into ORANGE forever.

ROCK FLOW, RIVER MIX

       Flickering
       in the buildings

they dance now
hip   face   and knee
dances I hunted for
when at nineteen
I stood at the river
here, the Hudson
hunting for Africa   —
something rumored
caught, poured in shadow and light
face of ecstasy
on film
swivel neck, eternal smile
suffer the night
water flows down
to
today
black theatre, road dusted with light
streaking down over our heads
setting before us, around us
sound track
image track

MARTIN LUTHER KING, MALCOLM X

Bleeding of the mountains
the noon bleeding
he is shot through the voice
all things being broken

The moon returning in her blood
looks down   grows white
loses color
and blazes

. . . and the near star gone   —

voices of cities
drumming in the moon

bleeding of my right hand
my black voice bleeding

LOOKING

Battles whose names I do not know
Weapons whose wish they dare not teach
Wars whose need they will not show
Tear us tear us each from each,
O my dear
Great sun and daily touch.
Fallen beside a river in Europe,
Burned to grey ash in Africa,
Lain down in the California jail,
O my dear,
Great sun and daily touch.

Flaming in Asia today.

I saw you stare out over Canada
As I stare over the Hudson River.

DON BATY, THE DRAFT RESISTER

I Muriel stood at the altar-table
The young man Don Baty stood with us
I Muriel fell away in me
in dread but in a welcoming
I am Don Baty then I said
before the blue-coated police
ever entered and took him.

I am Don Baty, say we all
we eat our bread, we drink our wine.
Our heritance has come, we know,
your arrest is mine. Yes.
Beethoven saying Amen Amen Amen Amen Amen
and all a singing, earth and eyes,
strong and weaponless.

There is a pounding at the door;
now we bring our lives entire.
I am Don Baty. My dear, my dear,
in a kind of welcoming,
here we meet, here we bring
ourselves. They pound on the wall of time.
The newborn are with us singing.

WELCOME FROM WAR

The woman to the man :
What is that on your hands?
It is also on my hands.

What is that in your eyes?
You see it in my eyes, do you?

Is your sex intact? Is mine?
Can it be about life now?

You went out to war.
War came over our house.

Our bed is not the same.
We will set about beginnings.

I kiss your hands, I kiss your eyes,
I kiss your sex.

I will kiss, I will bless
all the beginnings.

FACING SENTENCING

Children remembering sadness grieve, they grieve.
But sadness is not so terrible.   Children
Grown old speak of fear saying, we are to
Fear only this fear itself.   But fear is not to be so feared.
Numbness is.   To stand before my judge
Not knowing what I mean : to walk up
To him, my judge, and back to nobody
For the courtroom is almost empty, the world
Is almost silent, and suppose we did not know
This power to fall into each other's eyes
And say We love; and say We know each other
And say among silence We will help stop this war.

SECRETS OF AMERICAN CIVILIZATION

for Staughton Lynd

Jefferson spoke of freedom but he held slaves.
Were ten of them his sons by black women?

Did he sell them? or was his land their graves?
Do we asking our questions become more human?

Are our lives the parable which, living,
We all have, we all know, we all can move?
Then they said : The earth belongs to the living,
We refuse allegiance, we resign office, and we love.

They are writing at their desks, the thinking fathers,
They do not recognize their live sons' faces;
Slave and slaveholder they are chained together
And one is ancestor and one is child.
Escape the birthplace; walk into the world
Refusing to be either slave or slaveholder.

WHEREVER

Wherever
we walk
we will make

Wherever
we protest
we will go planting

Make poems
seed grass
feed a child growing
build a house
Whatever we stand against
We will stand feeding and seeding

Wherever
I walk
I will make

BRINGING

Bringing their life   these young
bringing their life   rise from their wakings
bringing their life   come to a place
where they make their gifts

The grapes of life of death   of transformation
round they hang at hand   desires   like peace
or seed of revolutions that make all things new
and must be lived out, washed in rivers, and themselves made
   new
and bringing their life   the young   they reach
in their griefs   their mistakes   their discovering
bringing their life   they touch   they take
bringing their life   they come to a place

It is raining fire   they are bringing their life
their sex speaks for them   their ideas all speak
their acts arrive   bringing their life entire
They resist a system of wars and rewards
They offer their open faces   they offer their bodies
They offer their hands   bringing their life entire
They offer their life   they are their own gifts
Make life   resist   resist   make life
Bringing their life entire   they come to this moment
Bringing their life entire   they come to this place

A LOUIS SONNET

For Louis Untermeyer,
his eightieth birthday

The jokes, the feuds, the puns, the punishments,
This traditional man being brave, going in grace,
Finding the structure of lives more than perfected line;
The forms of poetry are his time and space.
He's quirky, he rhymes like daily life; light wine
Is all his flavor, till fierce reverence
Turns delicatessen into delicatesse —
The man who anthologizes experience.

He is anthologized; like a wave of the sea
He is here, he is there, he changes;   impossibly,
He is blue surface, green suspended, the dark deep notes.
A stain of brilliance spreading upward floats
In luminous air; we are luminous, he makes us be
The jokes of Job and Heine's anecdotes.

AFTER MELVILLE

for Bett and Walter Bezanson

I

The sea-coast looks at the sea, and the cities pour.
The sea pours embassies of music : murder-sonata, birth-
      sonata,
the seashore celebrates the deep ocean.

Ocean dreaming all day all night of mountains
lifts a forehead to the wakes of stars;
one star dives into a still circle : birth, known to all.

A shore of the sea, one man as the shore of the sea;
one young man lying out over configurations of water
never two wave-patterns the same, never two same dreamings.

He writes these actualities, these dreamings,
transformed into themselves, his acts, his islands,
his animals ourselves within his full man's hand.

Bitter contempt and bitter poverty,
Judaean desert of our life, being locked
in white in black, a lock of essences.

Not graves not ocean but ourselves tonight
swing in his knowledge, his living and its wake,
travelling in the sea that goes pouring, dreaming
where we flash in our lifetime wave, these breathing shallows
of a shore that looks at the deep land, this island
that looks forever at the sea; deep sexual sea
that breathes one man at the shoreline of emergence.
He is the sea we carry to our star.

II

They come into our lives, Melville and Whitman who
ran contradictions of cities and the one-sparing sea
held in the long male arms   —   Identify.

They enter our evenings speaking—Melville and Crane
taking the wars of our parentage, silence and smoke,
tearing the live man open till we wake.

Emily Dickinson, Melville in our breathing,
isolate among powers, telling us the sea
and the slow dance of the absence of the sea.

Hawthorne whose forehead knew the revelation—
how can we receive the vision at noonday?
Move with the revelation?   Move away?

More violent than Melville   diving the sea deeper
no man has ever gone.   He swims our world
violence and dream safe only in full danger.

Revealing us, who are his afterlife.

III

A woman looks at the sea.
    Woman in whose waiting is held ocean
    faces the other sea where his life drowns and is saved,
    recurrent singing, the reborn wave.

A man looking into the sea.
    He sails, he swims among the opposites,
    diving, making a life among many unknowns,
    he takes for his knowledge the future wake of stars.

The sea looking and not looking.
    Among the old enemies, a transparent lake.
    Wars of the sea and land, wars of air;   space;
    against the corroded wars and sources of wars, a lake of
      being born.

A man and a woman look into each other.
    One man giving us forever the grapes of the sea.
    Gives us marriage; gives us suicide and birth; he drowns
    for the sake of our look into each other's body and life.
    Allowing the great life : sex, time, the feeding powers.
    He is part of our look into each other's face.

THE WRITER

for Isaac Bashevis Singer

His tears fell from his veins
They spoke for six million
From his veins all their blood.

He told his stories.
But noone spoke this language
Noone knew this music.

His music went into all people
Not knowing this language.
It ran through their bodies
And they began to take his words
Everyone the tears
Everyone the veins
But everyone said
Noone spoke this language.

GRADUS AD PARNASSUM

Oh I know
If I'd practised the piano
I'd never be so low
As I now am

Where's Sylvia Beerman?
Married, rich and cool
In New Rochelle
She was nobody's fool,

She didn't write in verse
She hardly wrote at all
She rose she didn't fall
She never gave a damn

But got up early
To practise Gradus
Ad Parnassum — she
Feels fine. I know.

FROM A PLAY : PUBLISHER'S SONG

I lie in the bath and I contemplate the toilet-paper:
Scottissue, 1000 sheets —
    What a lot of pissin and shittin,
    What a lot of pissin and shittin,
Enough for the poems of Shelley and Keats —
All the poems of Shelley and Keats.

IN THE NIGHT THE SOUND WOKE US

In the night the sound woke us.
We went up to the deck.
Brightness of brightness in the black night.
The ship standing still, her hold wide open.
Light shining orange on the lumber
her cargo, fresh strong-smelling wood.
A tall elder sailor standing at the winches,
his arms still, down; not seeming to move,
his hands hidden behind
black leather balcony.
The silver-hair tall sailor, stern and serene his face
turning from side to side.
The winches fell and rose with the newborn wood.
Orange and blazing in the lights it rose.
Vancouver straits, a northern midnight.
Delivered from death I stood awake
seeing it brought to the cool shining air.
O death, skillful, at night, in the bright light
bringing to birth.

Over my head
I see it in the air.

IN THE UNDERWORLD

I go a road
among the upturned
faces in their colors
to the great arch
of a theatre stage

I the high queen
starting in the air
far above my head
royal of the crown
I the tower
go through the wide arch
proscenium queen

The arch shuts down like December
very small all about me
the entrance to this country

Many whispers in the quick dark
Fingers in swarms, breath is busy,
they have reached above my head
and taken off my crown
I go and I go
I have been searching
since the light of all mornings

I remember only a pale brightness
and no more.   What do I remember?
I no longer

They have reached to my jewels
green in this cave, that one, iceberg the blue,
whirled into diamond
in the deep dark taken.

I move into thicker dark,
moss, earth-smell, wet coal.
Their hands are on my stiff robe.
I walk out of my robe.

At my surfaces
they unfasten my dress of softness.
Naked the naked wind
of the underworld.

Rankness at my breasts,
over my flank
giggle and stink
They have taken little knives
my skin lifts off
I go in pain-colored black
trying to find

I walk into their asking
Where is he
they sing on one note
Your lord memory

He your delight
I cannot hear their music
it scrapes along my muscles
they make my flesh go
among the gusts and whispers
they take off my eyes
my lips no more
the delicate fierce places
of identity
everywhere
taken

I, despoiled and clacking
walk, a chain of bones
into the boneyard dark.
One by one.
Something
reaches for my bones.

———————

Something walks here
a little breath in hell
without its ghost.
A breath after nothing.
Gone.
Nothing turns the place
where perceiving was
from side to side.
There is no place.   It has dissolved.
The lowest point, back there, has slid away.

———————

—   What are you working on?
—   Istar in the underworld.
—   Baby, you *are* in trouble.

———————

What calls her?
The body of a woman alive
but at the point of death,
the very old body lying there riddled with life,
gone, gasping at pain,
fighting for words
fighting for breath.

One clear breast looks up out of this gone body
young, the white clear light of this breast
speaks across distance

Remember is
come back.
Remember is
Who is here?
I am here.

At the pit of the underworld
something flickers in her
without anything

Now I remember love
who has set my being on me,
who permits me move
into all being,
who puts on me perceiving
and my bones
in a live chain
and my flesh that perceives
and acts
and my acknowledging skin
my underdress, my dress
and my robe
the jewels of the world
I touch and find
    —I know him and I know
       the breast speaking
       out of a gone woman
       across distances

And my crown a tower.

A voice saying : She went in a queen,
                 she died and came out,
                 goddess.

All our faces in their colors
    staring at the
    arch of this world.

The breast smiles : Do not
    think you are invulnerable!
The breast smiles : Do not
    think you are immortal!

AFTERWARDS

We are the antlers of that white animal
That great white animal
Asleep under the sea
He forgets and dreams so deep he does not
Know his whiteness in the sea-black
Among the plants of night.
His antlers have legs and arms.   Our heads
together being joined
Journey tonight, dreamed in his ocean.

Where we lie afterwards, smoke of our dreams
Goes coiling up, a plant in the dark room.
You were a young boy, you sang in the Polish woods
Limping away away.   I in this city, held
In a dream of children.   Some mythic animal
Rises now, flies up, white from the sea-floor.
In all our death, the glow behind his eyes
Speaks under all knowing : our lives burn.

FLYING TO HANOI

I thought I was going to the poets, but I am going to the
    children.
I thought I was going to the children, but I am going to the
    women.
I thought I was going to the women, but I am going to the
    fighters.
I thought I was going to the fighters, but I am going to the
    men and women who are inventing peace.
I thought I was going to the inventors of peace, but I am going
    to the poets.
My life is flying to your life.

IT IS THERE

Yes, it is there, the city full of music,
Flute music, sounds of children, voices of poets,
The unknown bird in his long call.   The bells of peace.
Essential peace, it sounds across the water
In the long parks where the lovers are walking,
Along the lake with its island and pagoda,
And a boy learning to fish.   His father threads the line.
Essential peace, it sounds and it stills.   Cockcrow.
It is there, the human place.

On what does it depend, this music, the children's games?
A long tradition of rest? Meditation? What peace is so profound
That it can reach all habitants, all children,
The eyes at worship, the shattered in hospitals?
All voyagers?
                    Meditation, yes; but within a tension
Of long resistance to all invasion, all seduction of hate.
Generations of holding to resistance; and within this resistance
Fluid change that can respond, that can show the children
A long future of finding, of responsibility; change within
Change and tension of sharing consciousness
Village to city, city to village, person to person entire
With unchanging cockcrow and unchanging endurance
Under the
            skies of war.

THE RUNNING OF THE GRUNION

for Denise Levertov
and Mitchell Goodman

I

Launching themselves
beating silver
on that precise
moment of tide & moon.

Exact in act
outer limit
stranded on high sand.

With an arched back he
digs their bed
she under him
releases he
fertilizes and
with back arched
covers (sand)
the gleam spawn.

On the lit beach
the hunt begins:
silver buckets.
People run down
for the huge catch.
Pulsing on sand
countless silver.
Highest wave
stretches
among the hunt.
A few of the fish
are washed to sea.

The spawn enclosed
in high sand
rhythms of hot & cool;
a full moon later
the wave foams over;
young grunion
wash to ocean.

Eleven later,
mature, silver,
they return.

People with pails.

II

Sand nailed down
by beating silver
nailed
by live nails

Sand is not crucified
only people
only animals

III

These creatures
cruciform.
To make life.

In the act of life
murder
people with pails

IV

Silver
on silver
birth
and
murder

Not birth
conception

V

Seawave
moon
seasand
at the moment of life
They throw themselves
million silver
upon making

Whether or not
people with pails

SACRED LAKE

some flushed-earth-color pueblo
holding the long-light sunset
shadows go into this ground
the mountain lifting the lake
in an orante gesture
like the men
in their white shirt-sleeves
in the basement of the Planetarium

the mailman the policeman the highschool-teacher
these winter evenings   making their own telescopes
they hold them up to test them the only way
against a ray of light in a gesture of offering.

This long wide gorge and mesa make the gesture
holding each man up against sunset light
and holding Blue Lake up.

III / Breaking Open

BREAKING OPEN

I come into the room   The room stands waiting
river   books   flowers   you are far away
black river   a language just forgotten
traveling blaze of light   dreams of endurance
racing into this moment   outstretched faces
and you are far away
                    The stars cross over
fire-flood   extremes of singing
filth and corrupted promises   my river
A white triangle of need
                    my reflected face
laced with a black triangle   of need

Naked among the silent of my own time
and Zig Zag Zag that last letter
    of a secret or forgotten alphabet
    shaped like our own last letter but it means
Something in our experience you do not know
When will it open open opening
River-watching all night
                    will the river
swing open we are Asia and New York
Bombs, roaches, mutilation   River-watching

Looking out at the river
the city-flow seen as river
the flow seen as a flow of possibility
and I too to that sea.

———————

Summer repetitive. The machine screaming
Beating outside, on the corrupted
Waterfront.
On my good days it appears digging
And building,
On others, its monstrous word
Says on one note Gone, killed, laid waste.

The whole thing   —   waterfront, war, city,
      sons, daughters, me   —
Must be re-imagined.
Sun on the orange-red roof.

———————

Walking into the elevator at Westbeth
Yelling in the empty stainless-steel
Room like the room of this tormented year.
Like the year
The metal nor absorbs nor reflects
My yelling.
My pulled face looks at me
From the steel walls.

———————

And then we go to Washington as if it were
Jerusalem;
and then we present our petition, clearly,
rightfully;
and then some of us walk away;
and then do others of us stay;
and some of us lie gravely down
on that cool mosaic floor,
the Senate.
Washington! Your bombs rain down!
I mourn, I lie down, I grieve.

———————

Written on the plane:
528

The conviction that what is meant by the unconscious is the same as what is meant by history. The collective unconscious is the living history brought to the present in consciousness, waking or sleeping. The personal "unconscious" is the personal history. This is an identity.

We will now explore further ways of reaching our lives, the new world. My own life, yours; this earth, this moon, this system, the "space" we share, which is consciousness.

Turbulence of air now. A pause of nine minutes.

Written on the plane. After turbulence:

The movement of life : to live more fully in the present. This movement includes the work of bringing this history to "light" and understanding. The "unconscious" of the race, and its traces in art and in social structure and "inventions" — these are our inheritance. In facing history, we look at each other, and in facing our entire personal life, we look at each other.

I want to break open. On the plane, a white cloud seen through rainbow. The rainbow is, optically, on the glass of the window.

The jury said Guilty, Guilty, Guilty,
Guilty, Guilty.　　　Each closed face.
I see myself in the river-window.　　　River
Slow going to its sea.
And old, crushed, perverse, waiting,
In loss, in dread, dead tree.

Columbus

Inner greet.　　　Greenberg said it,
Even the tallest man needs inner greet.
This is the great word
brought back, in swinging seas.　　　The new world.

End of summer.
Dark-red butterflies on the river
Dark-orange butterflies in the city.
The young men still going to war

Or away from war, to the prisons, to other countries.
To the high cold mountains, to the source of the river, I too go,
Deeper into this room.

———————

A dream remembered only in other dreams.
The voice saying:
All you dreaded as a child
Came to pass in storms of light;
All you dreaded as a girl
Falls and falls in avalanche —
Dread and the dream of love will make
All that time and men may build,
All that women dance and make.
They become you.   Your own face
Dances through the night and day,
Leading your body into this
Body-led dance, its mysteries.
Answer me.   Dance my dance.

———————

River-watching from the big Westbeth windows:
Powerful miles of Hudson, an east-blowing wind
All the way to Asia.
No.   Lost in our breath,
Sobbing, lost, alone.   The river darkens.
Black flow, bronze lights, white lights.
Something must answer that light, that dark.
Love,
The door opens, you walk in.

———————

The old man said, "The introversion of war
Is the main task of our time."
Now it makes its poem, when the sky stops killing.
I try to turn my acts inward and deeper.
Almost a poem.   If it splash outside,
All right.
My teacher says, "Go deeper."
The day when the salmon-colored flowers
Open.
I will essay.   Go deeper.

Make my poem.

Going to prison. The clang of the steel door.
It is my choice. But the steel door does clang.
The introversion of this act
Past its seeming, past all thought of effect,
Until it is something like
Writing a poem in my silent room.

In prison, the thick air,
still, loaded, heat on heat.
Around your throat
for the doors are locks,
the windows are locked doors,
the hot smell locked around us,
the machine shouting at us,
trying to sell us meat and carpets.
In prison, the prisoners,
all of us, all the objects,
chairs, cots, mops, tables.
Only the young cat.
He does not know he is locked in.

In prison, the prisoners.
One black girl, 19 years.
She has killed her child
and she grieves, she grieves.
She crosses to my bed.
"What do *Free* mean?"
I look at her.
"You don't understand English."
"Yes, I understand English."
"What do *Free* mean?"

In prison a
brown paper bag
I put it beside my cot.
All my things.
Comb, notebook, underwear,

letterpaper, toothbrush, book.
I am rich —
they have given me another toothbrush.
The guard saying:
"You'll find people share here."

———————————

Photos, more precise than any face can be.
    The broken static moment, life never by
    any eye seen.

———————————

My contradictions set me tasks, errands.

This I know:
What I reap, that shall I sow.

———————————

How we live:
I look into my face in the square glass.
Under it, a bright flow of cold water.
At once, a strong arrangement of presences:
I am holding a small glass
under the little flow
at Fern Spring, among the western forest.
A cool flaw among the silence.
The taste of the waterfall.

———————————

Some rare battered she-poet, old girl in the Village
racketing home past low buildings some freezing night,
come face to face with that broad roiling river.
Nothing buried in her but is lit and transformed.

Burning the Dreams

on a spring morning of young wood, green wood
it will not burn, but the dreams burn.
My hands have ashes on them.
They fear it
and so they destroy the nearest things.

Death and the Dancer

Running from death
throwing his teeth at the ghost
dipping into his belly, staving off death with a throw
tearing his brains out, throwing them at Death
death-baby is being born
scythe clock and banner come
trumpet of bone   and drum made of something   —
the callous-handed goddess
her kiss is resurrection

Rational Man

The marker at Auschwitz
The scientists torturing male genitals
The learned scientists, they torture female genitals
The 3-year-old girl, what she did to her kitten
The collar made of leather for drowning a man in his chair
The scatter-bomb with the nails that drive into the brain
The thread through the young man's splendid penis
The babies in flames.   The thrust
Infected reptile dead in the live wombs of girls
We did not know we were insane.
We do not know we are insane.
We say to them : you are insane
Anything you can imagine
        on punishable drugs, or calm and young
        with a fever of 105, or on your knees,
        with the world of Hanoi bombed
        with the legless boy in Bach Mai
        with the sons of man torn by man
Rational man has done.

Mercy, Lord.   On every living life.

———

In tall whirlpools of mirrors
Unshapen body and face
middle of the depth
of a night that will not turn
the unshapen all night
trying for form

———

I do and I do.
Life and this under-war.
Deep under protest, make.
For we are makers more.

but touching teaching going
the young and the old
they reach they break they are moving
to make the world

---

something about desire
something about murder
something about my death
something about madness

something about light
something of breaking open
sing me to sleep and morning
my dreams are all a waking

In the night
wandering room to room of this world
I move by touch
and then something says
let the city pour
the sleep of the beloved
Let the night pour down
all its meanings
Let the images pour
the light is dreaming

The Hostages

When I stand with these three
My new brothers my new sister
These who bind themselves offering
Hostages to go at a word, hostages
to go deeper here among our own cities
When I look into your faces
Karl, Martin, Andrea.

When I look into your faces
Offered men and women, I can speak,

And I speak openly on the church steps,
At the peace center saying : We affirm
Our closeness forever with the eyes in Asia,
Those who resist the forces we resist.
One more hostage comes forward, his eyes: Joe,
With Karl, Martin, Andrea, me.

And now alone in the river-watching room,
Allen, your voice comes, the deep prophetic word.
And we are one more, Joe, Andrea, Karl, Martin,
Allen, me.　　The hostages.　　Reaching.　　Beginning.

That I looked at them with my living eyes.
That they looked at me with their living eyes.
That we embraced.
That we began to learn each other's language.

It is something like the breaking open of my youth
but unlike too, leading not only to consummation
of the bed and of the edge of the sea.
Although that, surely, also.

But this music is
itself
needing only other selving
It is defeated but a way is open:
transformation

Then came I entire to this moment
process and light
　　　to discover the country of our waking
breaking open

THE GATES

For Jacob & Kang & the future

One

ST. ROACH

For that I never knew you, I only learned to dread you,
for that I never touched you, they told me you are filth,
they showed me by every action to despise your kind;
for that I saw my people making war on you,
I could not tell you apart, one from another,
for that in childhood I lived in places clear of you,
for that all the people I knew met you by
crushing you, stamping you to death, they poured boiling
     water on you, they flushed you down,
for that I could not tell one from another
only that you were dark, fast on your feet, and slender.
     Not like me.
For that I did not know your poems
And that I do not know any of your sayings
And that I cannot speak or read your language
And that I do not sing your songs
And that I do not teach our children
          to eat your food
          or know your poems
          or sing your songs
But that we say you are filthing our food
But that we know you not at all.

Yesterday I looked at one of you for the first time.
You were lighter than the others in color, that was
     neither good nor bad.
I was really looking for the first time.
You seemed troubled and witty.

Today I touched one of you for the first time.
You were startled, you ran, you fled away
Fast as a dancer, light, strange and lovely to the touch.
I reach, I touch, I begin to know you.

DREAM-DRUMMING

I braced the drum to my arm, a flat drum, and began to play.
He heard me and she heard me. I had never seen this drum
     before.

As I played, weakness went through me; weakness left me.
   I held my arms high, the drum and the soft-headed long
      stick
I drummed past my tiredness vibrating weakness, past it into
   music,
As in ragas past exhaustion into the country of all music.

Held my arms high, became that vibration, drummed the
   sacrifice of my belly.
He heard me, she heard me,
I turned into the infinity figure, reaching down into the earth
   of music with my legs at last,
Reaching up from the two circles, my pelvic sea,
     mountains and air of breast, with my arms up into music
At last turned into music, drumming on that possessed
   vibration,
Drumming my dream.

DOUBLE ODE

for Bill & Alison

I

Wine and oil gleaming within their heads,
I poured it into the hollow of their bodies
but they did not speak.   The light glittered.
Lit from underneath they were.   Water
pouring over her face, it
made the lips move and the eyes move, she
spoke:
Break open.
He did not speak.
A still lake shining in his head,
until I knew that the sun and the moon
stood in me with one light.

II

They began to breathe and glitter.   Morning
overflowed, gifts poured from their sex
upon my throat and my breast.
They knew.   They laughed.   In their tremendous games
night revolved and shook my bed.   I

540

woke in a cold morning.
Your presences
allow me to begin to make myself
carried on your shoulders, swayed in your arms.
Something is flashing among the colors.   I
move without being allowed.   I
move with the blessing of the sky and the sea.

III

Tonight I will try again for the music of truth
since this one and that one of mine are met with death.
It is a blind lottery, a cheap military trumpet
with all these great roots black under the earth
while a muscle-legged man
stamps in his red and gold
rough wine, creatures in nets, swords through their spines
and all their cantillation in our thought.

Glitter and pedestal under my female powers
a woman singing horses, blind cities of concrete, moon
comes to moonrise as a dark daughter.
I am the poet of the night of women
and my two parents are the sun and the moon,
a strong father of that black double likeness,
a bell kicking out of the bell-tower,
and a mother who shines and shines his light.

Who is the double ghost whose head is smoke?
Her thighs hold the wild infant, a trampled country
and I will fly in, in all my fears.
Those two have terrified me, but I live,
their silvery line of music gave me girlhood
and fierce male prowess and a woman's grave
eternal double music male and female,
inevitable blue, repeated evening
of the two.   Of the two.

IV

But these two figures are not the statues east and west
at my long window on the river they are mother and father
but not my actual parents only their memory.
Not memory but something builded in my cells

Father with your feet cut off
mother cut down to death
cut down my sister in the selfsame way
and my abandoned husband a madman of the sun
and you dark outlaw the other one when do we speak
The song flies out of all of you the song
starts in my body, the song
it is in my mouth, the song
it is on my teeth, the song
it is pouring the song
wine and lightning
the rivers coming to confluence
in me entire.

V

But that was years ago.   My child is grown.
His wife and he in exile, that is, home,
longing for home, and I home, that is exile, the much-loved
    country
like the country called parents, much-loved that was, and exile.
His wife and he turning toward the thought
of their own child, conceive we say, a child.
Now rise in me the old dealings : father, mother,
not years ago, but in my last-night dream,
waking this morning, the two Mexican figures
black stone with their stone hollows I fill with water,
fill with wine, with oil, poems and lightning.
Black in morning dark, the sky going blue,
the river going blue.

Moving toward new form I am—
carry again
all the old gifts and wars.

VI

Black parental mysteries
groan and mingle in the night.
Something will be born of this.

Pay attention to what they tell you to forget
pay attention to what they tell you to forget
pay attention to what they tell you to forget

Farewell the madness of the guardians
the river, the window, they are the guardians,
there is no guardian, it is all built into me.

Do I move toward form, do I use all my fears?

PAINTERS

In the cave with a long-ago flare
a woman stands, her arm up. Red twig, black twig, brown
   twig.
A wall of leaping darkness over her.
The men are out hunting in the early light
But here in this flicker, one or two men, painting
and a woman among them.
Great living animals grow on the stone walls,
their pelts, their eyes, their sex, their hearts,
and the cave-painters touch them with life, red, brown, black,
a woman among them, painting.

RUNE

     The word in the bread feeds me,
     The word in the moon leads me,
     The word in the seed breeds me,
     The word in the child needs me.

     The word in the sand builds me,
     The word in the fruit fills me,
     The word in the body mills me,
     The word in the war kills me.

     The word in the man takes me,
     The word in the storm shakes me,
     The word in the work makes me,
     The word in the woman rakes me,
     The word in the word wakes me.

HOW WE DID IT

We all traveled into that big room,
some from very far away
we smiled at some we knew

we did not as we talked agree
our hearts went fast thinking of morning
when we would walk along the path.
We spoke.   Late night.   We disagreed.
We knew we would climb the Senate steps.
We knew we would present our claim
we would demand : be strong now : end the war.
How would we do it?   What would we ask?
"We will be warned," one said. "They will warn us and take us."
"We can speak and walk away."
"We can lie down as if in mourning."
"We can lie down as a way of speech,
speaking of all the dead in Asia."
Then Eqbal said, "We are not at this moment
a revolutionary group, we are
a group of dissenters.   Let some, then,
walk away, let some stand until they want to leave,
let some lie down and let some be arrested.   Some of us.
Let each do what he feels at that moment
tomorrow."   Eqbal's dark face.
The doctor spoke, of friendships made in jail.
We looked into each other's eyes
and went all to our rooms, to sleep,
waiting for morning.

ISLANDS

O for God's sake
they are connected
underneath

They look at each other
across the glittering sea
some keep a low profile

Some are cliffs
The bathers think
islands are separate like them

BLUE SPRUCE

Of all green trees, I love a nevergreen
blue among dark blue, these almost black

needles guarded the door there was, years
before the white guardians over Sète
. . . that's Sea France at the Sea Cemetery
near Spain where Valéry . . .
those short square Mediterranean
man and woman
couple at the black-cut shadow door
within the immense marine
glare of noon,
and on the beach
leaning from one strong hip
a bearded Poseidon
looking along the surface of the sea
father and husband there he stands
and an invisible woman him beside
blue-eyed   blue-haired   blue-shadowed
under the sun and the moon
they blaze upon us
and we   waiting   waiting
swim to the source
very blue   evening now deepening
needles of light   ever new
a tree of light   and a tree of darkness
blue spruce

ARTIFACT

When this hand is gone to earth,
this writing hand and the paper beneath it,
long gone, and the words on the paper forgotten,
and the breath that slowly curls around earth with
                    its old spoken words
gone into lives unborn and they too gone to earth—
and their memory, memory of any of these gone,
and all who remembered them absorbed in air and dirt,
words, earth, breeze over the oceans, all these now other,
there may as in the past be something left,
some artifact.   This pen.   Will it tell my?   Will it tell our?
This thing made in bright metal by thousands unknown to me,
will it arrive with that unnameable wish to speak a music,
offering something out of all I moved among?
singing for others unknown a long-gone moment in old time
   sung?

                                                    The pen—
will some broken pieces be assembled by women, by guessing
    men
(or future mutations, beings unnamed by us)—
can these dry pieces join?   Again go bright?   Speak to you
    then?

MS. LOT

Well, if he treats me like a young girl still,
That father of mine, and here's my sister
And we're still traveling into the hills—
But everyone on the road knows he offered us
To the Strangers when all they wanted was men,
And the cloud of smoke still over the twin cities
And mother a salt lick the animals come to—
Who's going to want me now?
Mother did not even know
She was not to turn around and look.
God spoke to Lot, my father.
She was hard of hearing.   He knew that.
I don't believe he told her, anyway.
What kind of father is that, or husband?
He offered us to those men.   They didn't want women.
Mother always used to say:
Some normal man will come along and need you.

BOYS IN THE BRANCHES

Blue in the green trees, what are they climbing?
And girls bringing water, what are they watering
With their buckets spilling the wet dark on dry ground?

And up the hill the concrete-mixers rolling
Owned by my father when I was the same youth
As these who are my students, boys in the branches,
Young women in the young trees.

The last few drops from the faucet, carried
To the tan crumbling earth.
The earth belongs to the authorities
Of this college, and the authorities
Have turned the water off, have they?

Ask the owners of colleges, who is in the trees?
Ask the owners of concrete-mixers, who is holding
This acre of city land against the concrete?
We know where the water is.

Blue green students in the branches
Defending the tree.   The trees begin to shudder.
The concrete-mixers roll over exposed roots.

But isn't all this a romantic delusion?
You love the pouring of the city, don't you?
You need the buildings, don't you?
Sift the seeds.   We need to sift the seeds.

We know where the water is.
They have turned the water off.
You don't want buildings not to be built, do you?
The blueprint lies on the flat-top desk.

The building now is two years built,
Most of the boys went off to war,
I don't teach there any more.

Here we go, swimming to civilization,
We who stand and water and sift the seeds,
My students saying their word, it flies behind what I hear in
    the air:
"Time is God's blood," Warren said.   Avra wrote:
"Forgive me, Mother.   I am alive."

SONG : LYING IN DAYLIGHT

Lying in daylight, in the strong
light of all our fantasies,
now touch speaking to touch, touch sees—
night and light, the darkness-stare,
your long look that pierces where
light never came till now—
moving is what we do,
moving we are, searching,
going high and underground,
rain behind rain pouring down,
river under river going
silence on silence
sound under sound.

THE LOST ROMANS

Where are they, not those young men, not those
                young women
Who walked among the bullet-headed Romans with their
                roads, their symmetry, their iron rule—
We know the dust and bones they are gone to, those
                young Romans
Who stood against the bitter imperial, their young
                green life with its poems—
Where are the poems made music against the purple
Setting their own purple up for a living sign,
Bright fire of some forgotten future against empire,
Their poems in the beautiful Roman tongue
Sex-songs, love-poems, freedom-songs?
Not only the young, but the old and in chains,
The slaves in their singing, the fierce northern
                gentle blond rhythms,
The Judean cantillations, lullabies of Carthage,
Gaul with her cries, all the young Roman rebels,
Where are their songs?   Who will unlock them,
Who will find them for us, in some undiscovered
                painted cave
For we need you, sisters, far brothers, poems
                of our lost Rome.

CANAL

Sea-shouldering Ithaca
staring past sunset
after the islands
darkening   closing
The narrow night.   We
came in from Ithaca
into the inland
narrow water
trying to keep awake
while the ship went forward
but sleep came down
shouldering
down like Ithaca.
Night smites, light smites
and again light

in a narrow place
of old whiteness.
We are in
the narrowest place
moving in still
through an ash-white canal
a whitened plant
grappled to this wall
deep-cut, Judean slaves
cut the narrowest place
the ship fares into,
light smites again
the olive-plant in the crevice
captained through light.

FOR KAY BOYLE

What is the skill of this waking?   Heard the singing
of that man rambling up Frederick Street in music
and his repeated ecstasy, in a long shaken line.

After many and many a February storm, cyclamen
and many a curtain of rain, the tearing of all curtains
and, as you said, making love and facing the police

in one afternoon.   A few bright colors in permanent ink:
black sea, light like streetlight green, blue sees in you
the sun and the moon that stand as your guardians.

And the young bearded rebels and students tearing it all away,
all of it, down to the truth that barefaced naked act of
light, streamings of the courage of the sources,
the sun and the moon that stand at your ears.

RESURRECTION OF THE
RIGHT SIDE

When the half-body dies its frightful death
forked pain, infection of snakes, lightning, pull down the
   voice. Waking
and I begin to climb the mountain on my mouth,
word by stammer, walk stammered, the lurching deck of earth.
Left-right with none of my own rhythms.

the long-established sex and poetry.

I go running in sleep,
but waking stumble down corridors of self, all rhythms gone.

The broken movement of love   sex out of rhythm
one halted name   in a shattered language
ruin of French-blue lights behind the eyes
slowly the left hand extends a hundred feet
and the right hand follows follows
but still the power of sight is very weak
but I go rolling this ball of life, it rolls
and I follow it whole up the slowly-brightening slope

A whisper attempts me, I whisper without stammer
I walk the long hall to the time of a metronome
set by a child's gun-target   left-right
the power of eyesight is very slowly arriving
         in this late impossible daybreak
         all the blue flowers open

THE WARDS

St. George's Hospital,
Hyde Park Corner

Lying in the moment, she climbs white snows;
At the foot of the bed the chart relates.
Here a man burns in fever; he is here, he is there,
Five thousand years ago in the cave country.
In this bed, I go wandering in Macao,
I run all night the black alleys.   Time runs
Over the edge and all exists in all.   We hold
All human history, all geography,
I cannot remember the word for what I need.
Our explorations, all at the precipice,
The night-table, a landscape of zebras,
Transistor constellations.   All this music,
I heard it forming before I was born.   I come
In this way, to the place.

Our selves lit clear,
This moment giving me necessity
Gives us ourselves and we risk everything,
Walking into our life.

THE SUN-ARTIST

for Bob Miller

I

The opening of the doors.   Dark.
The opening of the large doors.
Out of the daylight and the scent of trees
and that lake where generations of swans
no longer move among children.   In a poisoned time.
But the bright-headed children move.
Dark, high, the beams of a huge building
exposed in the high dark air.
I see brightness with a shock of joy.

II

Past the darkness a lashing of color.
Not color, strands of light.
Not light but pure deep color beyond color,
like the pure fierce light I once knew, before
a minute of blindness.   These colors are deeper;
the entire range in its millions,
twisting and brilliant traveling.

III

I stand in the strong sun before a bank of prisms.
On the screen in front of me, tangled colors of light,
                              twined, intertwined.
A sensitive web of light changing, for the sun moves, the air
  moves.
The perceiver moves.
                    I dance my slow dance.

IV

The deepest blue, green, not the streams of the sea,
the clear yellow of yellows, not California, more,
not Mediterranean, not the Judean steeps.   Red beyond
                    blood over flame,
more even than visionary America.   All light.
A man braced on the sun, where the sun enters
through the roof, where the sun-follower,

a man-made motor with a gentle motion
just counters the movement of the earth, holds this scene
in front of us on the man-made screen.
Light traveling, meets, leaps and becomes art.

V

Colors move on a screen.   The doors open again.
They run in, the California children.
They run past the colors and the colors change.
The laughter of running.   They cry out, bird-voices,
ninety-seven children, Wow!   Wow!   How come?

VI

Another day.   I stand before the screen,
Alone I move, selecting out my green,
choose out the red with my arm, I let the orange stand,
a web of yellow, the blue stays and shines.
I am part of the color, I am part of the sun.

VII

You have made an art in which the sun is standing.
It changes, goes dark, goes grey.   The sun appears.
You have led me through eleven states of being.
You have invited us all.   Allow the sunlight,
dance your dance.

VIII

Another day.   No sun.   The fog is down,
Doing its slow dance into the city,
It enters the Gate and my waking.
There will be no colors but the range of white.
Before the screen,   I wait.

IX

Night.   What do you know about the light?

X

Waiting.   A good deal like real life.
Waiting before the sea for the fish to run

Waiting before the paper for the poem
Waiting for a man's life to be, to be.

XI

Break of light!   Sun in his colors,
streaming into our lives.
This artist dreams of the sun, the sun, the children of the sun.

XII

Frail it is and can be intercepted.
Fragile, like ourselves.   Mirrors and prisms, they
                    can be broken.
Children shattered by anything.
Strong, pouring strong, wild as the power of the great sun.
Not art, but light.   In distance, in smiting winter,
the artist speaks : No art.
This is not art.
What is *an artist?*   I bear the song of the sun.

POEM   WHITE   PAGE
WHITE   PAGE   POEM

Poem   white page   white page   poem
something is streaming out of a body in waves
something is beginning from the fingertips
they are starting to declare for my whole life
all the despair and the making music
something like wave after wave
that breaks on a beach
something like bringing the entire life
to this moment
the small waves bringing themselves to white paper
something like light stands up and is alive

FABLE

for Herbert Kohl

Yes it was the prince's kiss.
But the way was prepared for the prince.
It had to be.

When the attendants carrying the woman
—dead they thought her lying on the litter—
stumbled over the root of a tree
the bit of deathly apple in her throat
jolted free.

Not strangled, not poisoned!
She
can come alive.

It was an "accident" they hardly noticed.

The threshold here comes when they stumble.
The jolt.   And better if we notice,
However, their noticing is not
Essential to the story.

A miracle has even deeper roots,
Something like error, some profound defeat.
Stumbled-over, the startle, the arousal,
Something never perceived till now, the taproot.

NERUDA, THE WINE

We are the seas through whom the great fish passed
And passes.   He died in a moment of general dying.
Something was reborn.   What was it, Pablo?
Something is being reborn : poems, death, ourselves,
The link deep in our peoples, the dead link in our dead
     regimes,
The last of our encounters transformed from the first
Long ago in Xavier's house, where you lay sick,
Speaking of poems, the sheet pushed away
Growth of beard pressing up, fierce grass, as you spoke.
And that last moment in the hall of students,
Speaking at last of Spain, that core of all our lives,
The long defeat that brings us what we know.
Meaning, poems, lifelong in loss and presence passing forever.
I spilled the wine at the table
And you, Pablo, dipped your finger in it and marked my
     forehead.
Words, blood, rivers, cities, days.   I go, a woman signed by
     you—
The poems of the wine.

BEFORE DANGER

There were poems all over Broadway that morning.
Blowing across traffic.   Against the legs.
Held for a moment on the backs of hands.
Drifts of poems in doorways.
The crowd was a river to the highest tower
all the way down that avenue.
Snow on that river, torn paper
of their faces.

Late at night, in a dark-blue sleep,
the paper stopped blowing.
Lightning struck at me from behind my eyes.

SONG : REMEMBERING MOVIES

remembering movies   love
remembering songs
remembering the scenes and flashes of your life
given to me as we lay dreaming
giving dreams
in the sharp flashes of light
raining from the scenes of your life
the faithless stories, adventures, discovery
sexuality opening range after range
and the sharp music driven forever into my life
I sing the movies of your life
the sequences cut in rhythms of collision
rhythms of linkage, love,
I sing the songs

WORK, FOR THE DAY IS COMING

It is the poem, yes
that it exist   that it grow in reach
that it grow into lives not yet born not yet speaking.
That its sounds move with the grace of meaning
the liquid sharing, the abrupt clash of lives.
That its suggestions climb to
        descend to   the fire of finding
            the last breath of the poem
                and further.

For that I move through states of being,
the struggle to wake, the frightful morning,
the flash of ecstasy among our mutilations,
the recognizing light shining and all night long
am invited led whipped dragged through states of being
toward the
        inviting you through states of being
                    poem.

RECOVERING

Dream of the world
speaking to me.

The dream of the dead
acted out in me.

The fathers shouting
across their blue gulf.

A storm in each word,
an incomplete universe.

Lightning in brain,
slow-time recovery.

In the light of October
things emerge clear.

The force of looking
returns to my eyes.

Darkness arrives
splitting the mind open.

Something again
is beginning to be born.

A dance is
dancing me.

I wake in the dark.

PARALLEL INVENTION

We in our season like progress and inventions.
The inventor is really the invention.
But who made the inventions?   To what uses
Were they put, by whom, and for what purposes?

You made an innovation and then
did you give it to me without writing it down?
Did you give it to her, too?
Did I develop it and give it to him,
or to her, or to them?

Did you quicken communication,
Did you central-control?   And war?   And the soul?

Let's not talk about communication
any more.

Did we deepen our integration ties
did we subsequently grow—
in strength?   in complexity?

Or did we think of doing the same things
at the same time and do them to each other?

And then out of our lovemaking
emergence of priests and kings,
out of our smiles and twists
full-time craft specialists,
out of our mouths and asses
division into social classes,
art and architecture and writing
from meditation and delighting
from our terrors and our pities
"of course," you say, "the growth of cities."

But parallels do not imply
identities—there is no iron law;
we are richly variable
levels of heaven and levels of hell;
ripples of change out from the center
of me, of you, of love the inventor.

After reading an essay by Robert McC. Adams in *Civilization*—found in the
Women's Detention Center, Washington—D.C.D.C.

POEM

Green going through the jungle of those years
I see the brilliant bodies of the invaders
And the birds cry in the high trees, the sky
Flashes above me in bright crevices; time is,
And I go on and the birds fly blurred
And I pass, my eyes seeing through corpses of dead cells
Glassy, a world hardening with my hardening eyes
My look is through the corpses of all the living
Men and women who stood with me and died before
But my young look still blazes from my changing
Eyes and the jungle asserts fiery green
Even though the trees are the trees of home
And we look out of eyes filled with dead cells
See through these hours, faces of what we are.

NOT TO BE PRINTED,
NOT TO BE SAID,
NOT TO BE THOUGHT

I'd rather be Muriel
than be dead and be Ariel.

BACK TOOTH

My large back tooth, without a mate for years,
at last has been given one.   The dentist ground her down
a bit.   She had been growing wild, nothing to meet her, keep
    her sane.
Now she fits the new one, they work together, sleep together,
she is a little diminished but functioning, all night all day.

DESTRUCTION OF GRIEF

Today I asked Aileen
at the Film Library to help me find
those girl twins of the long-gone summer.
Aileen, who were they?
I was seven, the lion circus
was pitched in the field of sand and swordgrass

near the ocean, behind the Tackapoosha Garage.
The ancient land of the Waramaug Indians.
Now there's a summer hotel.
The first day of that circus dazzles me forever.
I stayed.   That evening
the police came looking for me.
Easy to find, behind
the bales of hay, with Caesar's tamer,
the clowns, and the girl twins.
My father and mother forgave me, for they loved
circuses, opera, carnivals, New York, popular songs.
All day that summer, all July and August,
I stayed behind the tents with the twin girls,
with Caesar the lion my friend,
with the lion-tamer.
Do you know their names, Aileen?
The girls went into the early movies.
Late August, Caesar mauled the man's right hand.
I want to remember the names of those twins.
You could see he would not ever keep his hand.
Smell of the ocean, straw,
lordly animal rankness, gunpowder.
"Yes, they destroyed Caesar," I was told that night.
Those twins became movie stars.
Those of us who were there that summer—
Joey killed himself, I saw Tommy
just before the war; is Henry around?
Helene is in real estate—and the twins—
can you tell me their names, Aileen?

TRINITY CHURCHYARD

for my mother & her ancestor, Akiba

Wherever I walked I went green among young growing
Along the same song, Mother, even along this grass
Where, Mother, tombstones stand each in its pail of shade
In Trinity yard where you at lunchtime came
As a young workingwoman, Mother, bunches of your days,
    grapes
Pressing your life into mine, Mother,
And I never cared for these tombs and graves
But they are your book-keeper hours.

You said to me summers later, deep in your shiniest car
As a different woman, Mother, and I your poem-making
 daughter—
"Each evening after I worked all day for the lock-people
"I wished under a green sky on the young evening star—
"What did I wish for?" What did you wish for, Mother?
"I wished for a man, of course, anywhere in my world,
"And there was Trinity graveyard and the tall New York
 steeples."

Wherever I go, Mother, I stay away from graves
But they turn everywhere in the turning world; now,
Mother Rachel's, on the road from Jerusalem.
And mine is somewhere turning unprepared
In the earth or among the whirling air.
My workingwoman mother is saying to me, Girl—
Years before her rich needy unreal years—
Whatever work you do, always make sure
You can go walking, not like me, shut in your hours.

Mother I walk, going even here in green Galilee
Where our ancestor, Akiba, resisted Rome,
Singing forever for the Song of Songs
Even in torture knowing.   Mother, I walk, this blue,
The Sea, Mother, this hillside, to his great white stone.
And again here in New York later I come alone
To you, Mother, I walk, making our poems.

BURNISHING, OAKLAND

Near the waterfront
mouth of a wide shed   open
many-shining bronze flat
ship-propellors hanging in air
propellors lying blunt on ground
The vast sound and shine
screaming its word

One man masked
holding a heavy weight
on the end of a weighted boom
counterbalanced
I see him draw

his burnisher
along the bronze
high scream of burnishing
a path of brightness

Outside, the prowl cars
Oakland police
cruising past
behind them the trailing
Panther cars
to witness to
any encounter

Statement of light
I see as we drive past
act of light
among sleeping houses
in our need
the dark people

Behind my head
the shoulders of hills
and the dark houses.
Here the shine, the singing cry
near the extreme
of the range of knowing
one masked man
working alone
burnishing

THE IRIS-EATERS

for John Cage

It was like everything else, like everything—
nothing at all like what they say it is.
The petals of iris were slightly cinnamon,
a smooth beard in the mouth
transforming to strong drink,
light violet turning purple in the throat
and flashed and went deep red
burning and burning.
Well, no, more an extreme warmth,
but we thought of burning,

we thought of poisons,
we thought of the closing of the throat
forever, of dying, of the end of song.
We were doing it, you understand,
for the first time.
You were the only one of us who knew
and you saved us, John,
with music, with a

           complex

                smile.

SLOW DEATH OF THE DRAGON

The sickness poured through the roads,
The vineyards shook.
A clot formed on the wild river.
The streets and squares were full of crevices.
Poison ran on the church-towers.
The olive trees!
He shook for thirty years,
Held his buttocks tense while his varnished officers
Broke thighs, broke fingers.
A man dies.
The genitals of the South are broken.
Venom pours
Into his provinces of pain.

The surgeons come.
Are there children left alive
Among his bones?   The drugs of choice are used,
Sleep-poison, torture-dream-drink, elixir of silence,
Rousing of memory : the inquisition.
Purgation of the future. "Cut off this lobe," they said.
"The heart is rejecting the present."   On the roads
The dead of the resistance tried to stand
Again, they tried to stand again.
But they were dead.

The surgeons are cutting out his words.
Too late; all the children are silent.
On the central plateau, snow is falling.
Incisions split the open country.   On the coast of pain,
All craft becalmed.   The surgeons are singing.

No, of course the dragon is not dead.
A branch of a tree is dead.
A generation is dead.
Most of the living are silent.
Prepare the ink on the rollers;
This has been a long time coming.
The posters carry one word:
Today!

Send the word underground, where water flows,
Clear, pure, black.
Is it beyond taint?
No, it is not beyond taint.
Certain women and men look at us out of their eyes.
Do they begin to speak
They have been speaking all along.
We can tell by their eyes,
Although their mouths are broken.
Now they are healing their mouths;
They have been speaking during all this dead lifetime.
Has the dragon died?
Something is beginning to be born,
But the seeds of the dragon are also growing in the fresh
    wombs of girls.
O love.   Make the song start.

Summer 1936—Winter 1975

MENDINGS

for Alfred Marshak

You made healing as you wanted us to make bread and poems.
In your abrasive life of gifts,
In the little ravine telling the life of the future
When your science would be given to all,
A broken smile.
In the sun, speaking of the joining of nerve-endings,
Make the wounds part of the well body.
Make a healed life.
You shouted, waving your hand with the last phalange
Of the little finger missing, you whole man,
"Make it well!   Make things accessible!"
He is a pollinating man.   We are his seedlings.

Marshak, I was your broken nerve-endings,
You made your man-made bridges over the broken nerves.
What did you do?   Inspect potatoes, wait for passports, do
   your research,
While the State Department lady was saying, "Let him swim,"
While the chief who had the power to allow your uses
To move, a proper use of plastic, a bridge across broken nerves
Stopped you there (and asked me to marry him).
Saying to you, Marshak, full of creation as the time
Went deeper into war, and you to death:
"The war will be over before your work is ready."

THEN

When I am dead, even then,
I will still love you, I will wait in these poems,
When I am dead, even then
I am still listening to you.
I will still be making poems for you
out of silence;
silence will be falling into that silence,
it is building music.

Two

THE GATES

Scaffolding.   *A poet is in solitary; the expectation is that he will be
tried and summarily executed on a certain day in autumn. He has been
on this cycle before : condemned to death, the sentence changed to life
imprisonment, and then a pardon from his President during a time of
many arrests and executions, a time of terror. The poet has written his
stinging work—like that of Burns or Brecht—and it has got under the
skin of the highest officials. He is Kim Chi Ha.*

   *An American woman is sent to make an appeal for the poet's life.
She speaks to Cabinet ministers, the Cardinal, university people, writers,
the poet's family and his infant son. She stands in the mud and rain at*

*the prison gates—also the gates of perception, the gates of the body. She
is before the house of the poet. He is in solitary.*

I

Waiting to leave all day I hear the words;
That poet in prison, that poet newly-died
whose words we wear, reading, all of us.   I and my son.

All day we read the words:
friends, lovers, daughters, grandson,
and all night the distant loves
and I who had never seen him am drawn to him

Through acts, through poems,
through our closenesses—
whatever links us in our variousness;
across worlds, love and poems and justices
wishing to be born.

II

Walking the world to find the poet of these cries.
But this walking is flying the streets of all the air.

Walking the world, through the people at airports,
this city of hills, this island ocean fire-blue and now this city.

Walking this world is driving the roads of houses
endless tiles   houses, fast streams, now this child's house.

Walking under the sharp mountains through the sharp city
circled in time by rulers, their grip; the marvelous
hard-gripped people silent among their rulers, looking at me.

III / New Friends

The new friend comes into my hotel room
smiling.   He does a curious thing.
He walks around the room, touching
all the pictures hanging on the wall.
One picture does not move.

A new friend assures me   :   Foreigners are safe,
You speak for writers, you are safe, he says.
There will be no car

driving up behind you, there will be
no accident, he says.   I know these accidents.
Nothing will follow you, he says.
O the Mafia at home, I know, Black Hand
of childhood, the death of Tresca whom I mourn,
the building of New York.   Many I know.
This morning I go early to see the Cardinal.
When I return, the new friend is waiting.   His face
wax-candle-pool-color, he saying
"I thought you were kidnapped."

A missionary comes to visit me.
Looks into my eyes.   Says,
"Turn on the music so we can talk."

IV

The Cabinet minister speaks of liberation.
"Do you know how the Communists use this word?"
We all use the word.   Liberation.

No, but look—these are his diaries,
says the Cabinet minister.
These were found in the house of the poet.
Look, Liberation, Liberation, he is speaking in praise.

He says, this poet, It is not wrong
to take from the rich and give to the poor.

Yes.   He says it in prose speech, he says it in his plays,
he says it in his poems that bind me to him,
that bind his people and mine in these new ways
for the first time past strangeness and despisal.

It also means that you broke into his house and stole his
    papers.

V

Among the days,
among the nights of the poet in solitary,
a strong infant is just beginning to run.
I go up the stepping-stones
to where the young wife of the poet
stands holding the infant in her arms.

She weeps, she weeps.
But the poet's son looks at me
and the wife's mother looks at me with a keen look
across her grief.   Lights in the house, books making every wall
a wall of speech.
                        The clasp of the woman's hand
around my wrist, a keen band
more steel than the words
Save his life.

I feel that clasp on my bones.

A strong infant is beginning to run.

VI / The Church of Galilee

As we climb to the church of Galilee
Three harsh men on the corner.
As we go to the worship-meeting of the dismissed,
three state police on the street.
As we all join at the place of the dispossessed,
three dark men asking their rote questions.
As we go ahead to stand with our new friends
that will be our friends our lifetime.
Introduced as dismissed from this faculty, this college,
this faculty, this university.
'Dismissed' is now an honorary degree.
The harsh police are everywhere,
they have hunted this fellowship away before
and they are everywhere, at the street-corner,
listening to all hymns,
standing before all doors,
hearing over all wires.
We go up to Galilee.
Let them listen to the dispossessed
and to all women and men who stand firm and sing
wanting a shared and honest lifetime.
Let them listen to Galilee.

VII / The Dream of Galilee

That night, a flute
across the dark, the sound
opening times to me, a time

567

when I stood on the green hillside
before the great white stone.
Grave of my ancestor
Akiba at rest over Kinneret.
The holy poem, he said to me,
the Song of Songs always;
and know what I know, to love
your belief with all your life,
and resist the Romans, as I did,
even to the torture and beyond.
Over Kinneret, with all of them,
Jesus, all the Judeans,
that other Galilee
in dream across war I see.

VIII / Mother as Pitchfork

Woman seen as a slender instrument,
woman at vigil in the prison-yard,
woman seen as the fine tines of a pitchfork
that works hard, that is worn down, rusted down
to a fine sculpture standing in a yard
where her son's body is confined.
Woman as fine tines blazing against sunset,
wavering lines against yellow brightness
where her fine body becomes transparent in bravery,
where she will live and die as the tines of a pitchfork
that stands to us as her son's voice does stand
across the world speaking

The rumor comes that if this son is killed
this mother will kill herself

But she is here, she lives,
the slender tines of this pitchfork standing in flames of light.

IX

You grief woman   you gave me a scarlet coverlet
thick-sown with all the flowers
and all the while your poet sleeps in stone

Grief woman, the waves of this coverlet,
roses of Asia,
they flicker soft and bright over my sleep

all night while the poet waits in solitary

All you vigil women, I start up in the night,
fling back this cover of red;
in long despair we work   write   speak   pray   call to others
Free our night   free our lives   free our poet

X

Air fills with fear and the kinds of fear:

The fear of the child among the tyrannical
unanswerable men and women, they dominate day and night.

Fear of the young lover in the huge rejection
ambush of sex and of imagination;
fear that the world will not allow your work.

Fear of the overarching wars and poverties,
the terrible exiles,
all bound by corruption until at last!   we speak!

And those at home in jail who protest the frightful war
and the beginning : The woman-guard says to me, Spread your
    cheeks,
the search begins and I begin to know.

And also at home the nameless multitude
of fears : fear in childbirth for the living child,
fear for the child deformed and love, fear
among the surgeries that can cure her, fear
for the child's father, and for oneself, fear.
Fear of the cunt and cock in their terrible powers
and here a world away fear of the jailers' tortures
for we invent our fear and act it out
in ripping, in burning, in blood, in the terrible scream
and in tearing away every mouth that screams.

Giant fears : massacres, the butchered that across the fields of
    the world
lie screaming, and their screams are heard as silence.
O love, knowing your love across a world of fear,
I lie in a strange country, in pale yellow, swamp-green, woods
and a night of music while a poet lies in solitary
somewhere in a concrete cell. Glare-lit, I hear,
without books, without pen and paper.

Does he draw a pencil out of his throat,
out of his veins, out of his sex?
There are cells all around him, emptied.
He can signal on these walls till he runs mad.
He is signalling to me across the night.

He is signalling.   Many of us speak,
we do teach each other, we do act through our fears.

Where is the world that will touch life to this prison?

We run through the night.   We are given his gifts.

XI

Long ago, soon after my son's birth
—this scene comes in arousal with the sight of a strong child
just beginning to run—
when all life seemed prisoned off, because the father's other son
born three weeks before my child
had opened the world
that other son and his father closed the world—
in my fierce loneliness and fine well-being
torn apart but with my amazing child
I celebrated and grieved.
And before that baby
had ever started to begin to run
then Mary said,
smiling and looking out of her Irish eyes,
"Never mind, Muriel.
Life will come will come again
knocking and coughing and farting at your door."

XII

For that I cannot name the names,
my child's own father, the flashing, the horseman,
the son of the poet—
for that he never told me another child was started,
to come to birth three weeks before my own.
Tragic timing that sets the hands of time.
O wind from our own coast, turning
around the turning world.

Wind from the continents, this other child,
child of this moment and this moment's poet.

Again I am struck nameless, unable to name,
and the axe-blows fall heavy heavy and sharp
and the moon strikes his white light down over the continents
on this strong infant and the heroic friends
silent in this terrifying moment under all moonlight,
all sunlight turning in all our unfree lands.
Name them, name them all, light of our own time.

XIII

Crucified child—is he crucified?   he is tortured,
kept away from his father, spiked on time,
crucified we say, cut off from the man
they want to kill—
he runs toward me in Asia, crying.
Flash gives me my own son strong and those years ago
cut off from his own father and running toward me
holding a strong flower.

Child of this moment, you are your father's child
wherever your father is prisoned, by what tyrannies
or jailed as my child's father
by his own fantasies—
child of the age running among the world,
standing among us who carry our own time.

XIV

So I became very dark very large
a silent woman this time given to speech
a woman of the river   of that song
and on the beach of the world in storm given
in long lightning seeing the rhyming of those scenes
that make our lives.
Anne Sexton the poet saying
ten days ago to that receptive friend,
the friend of the hand-held camera:
"Muriel is serene."
Am I that in their sight?
Word comes today of Anne's
of Anne's long-approaching
of Anne's over-riding over-falling
suicide.   Speak for   sing for   pray for
everyone in solitary
every living life.

XV

All day the rain
all day waiting within the prison gate
before another prison gate
The house of the poet
He is in there somewhere
among the muscular wardens
I have arrived at the house of the poet
in the mud in the interior music of all poems
and the grey rain of the world
whose gates do not open.
I stand, and for this religion and that religion
do not eat but remember all the things I know
and a strong infant beginning to run.
Nothing is happening.   Mud, silence, rain.

Near the end of the day
with the rain and the knowledge pulling at my legs
a movement behind me makes me move aside.
A bus full of people turns in the mud, drives to the gate.
The gate that never opens
opens at last.   Beyond it, slender
Chinese-red posts of the inner gates.
The gate of the house of the poet.

The bus is crowded, a rush-hour bus that waits.
Nobody moves.

"Who are these people?" I say.
How can these gates open?

My new friend has run up beside me.
He has been standing guard in the far corner.
"They are prisoners," he says, "brought here from trial.
Don't you see?   They are all tied together."

Fool that I am!   I had not seen the ropes,
down at their wrists in the crowded rush-hour bus.

The gates are open.   The prisoners go in.
The house of the poet who stays in solitary,
not allowed reading   not allowed writing
not allowed   his woman   his friends   his unknown friends
and the strong infant beginning to run.

We go down the prison hill.   On our right, sheds
full of people all leaning forward, blown on some ferry.
"They are the families of the prisoners.   Some can visit.
They are waiting for their numbers to be called."

How shall we venture home?
How shall we tell each other of the poet?
How can we meet the judgment on the poet,
or his execution?   How shall we free him?
How shall we speak to the infant beginning to run?
All those beginning to run?

INDEX OF TITLES AND FIRST LINES